RADIANT
BLACK

URL radiant.black

"F(r)iction #18: Legacy" cover art used by permission of Brink Literacy Project. Artwork by Jessica Fong. Art Directors Dani Hedlund & Helen Maimaris.

IMAGE COMICS, INC. • **Todd McFarlane**: President • **Jim Valentino**: Vice President • **Marc Silvestri**: Chief Executive Officer • **Erik Larsen**: Chief Financial Officer • **Robert Kirkman**: Chief Operating Officer • **Eric Stephenson**: Publisher / Chief Creative Officer • **Nicole Lapalme**: Controller • **Leanna Caunter**: Accounting Analyst • **Sue Korpela**: Accounting & HR Manager • **Marla Eizik**: Talent Liaison • **Jeff Boison**: Director of Sales & Publishing Planning • **Dirk Wood**: Director of International Sales & Licensing • **Alex Cox**: Director of Direct Market Sales • **Chloe Ramos**: Book Market & Library Sales Manager • **Emilio Bautista**: Digital Sales Coordinator • **Jon Schlaffman**: Specialty Sales Coordinator • **Kat Salazar**: Director of PR & Marketing • **Drew Fitzgerald**: Marketing Content Associate • **Heather Doornink**: Production Director • **Drew Gill**: Art Director • **Hilary DiLoreto**: Print Manager • **Tricia Ramos**: Traffic Manager • **Melissa Gifford**: Content Manager • **Erika Schnatz**: Senior Production Artist • **Ryan Brewer**: Production Artist • **Deanna Phelps**: Production Artist • IMAGECOMICS.COM

RADIANT BLACK

VOLUME	OO1
TITLE	(Not So) Secret Origin

CREATED BY		
WRITER	Kyle Higgins	
ARTIST	Marcelo Costa	
CO-WRITER	Cherish Chen	(CHAPTER 06)
GUEST ARTISTS	Eduardo Ferigato	(CHAPTER 05)
	Darko Lafuente	(CHAPTER 06)
GUEST COLORISTS	Natália Marques	(CHAPTER 05)
	Miquel Muerto	(CHAPTER 06)
COLOR ASSISTANT	Rod Fernandes	(CHAPTER 04)
LETTERER	Becca Carey	
SERIES LOGO	Rich Bloom	
EDITOR & DESIGNER	Michael Busuttil	
PRODUCTION ARTIST	Deanna Phelps	

BLACK MARKET NARRATIVE

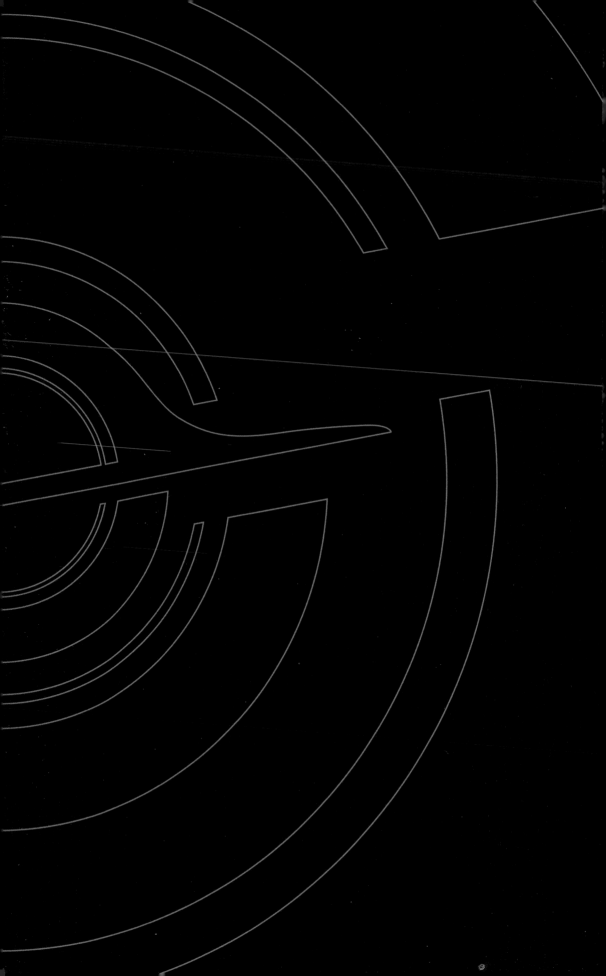

CHAPTER ONE

TITLE   (Not So) Secret Origin

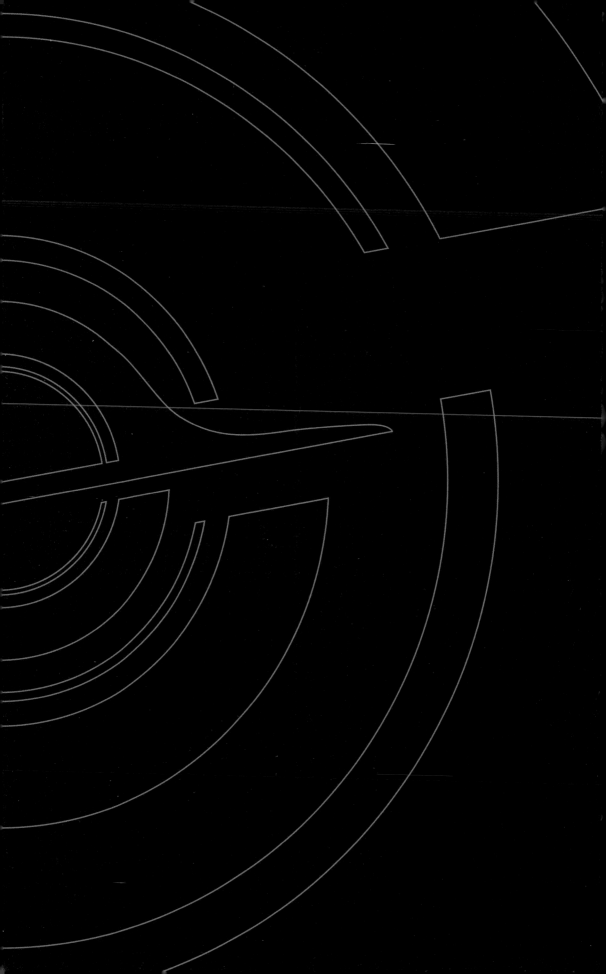

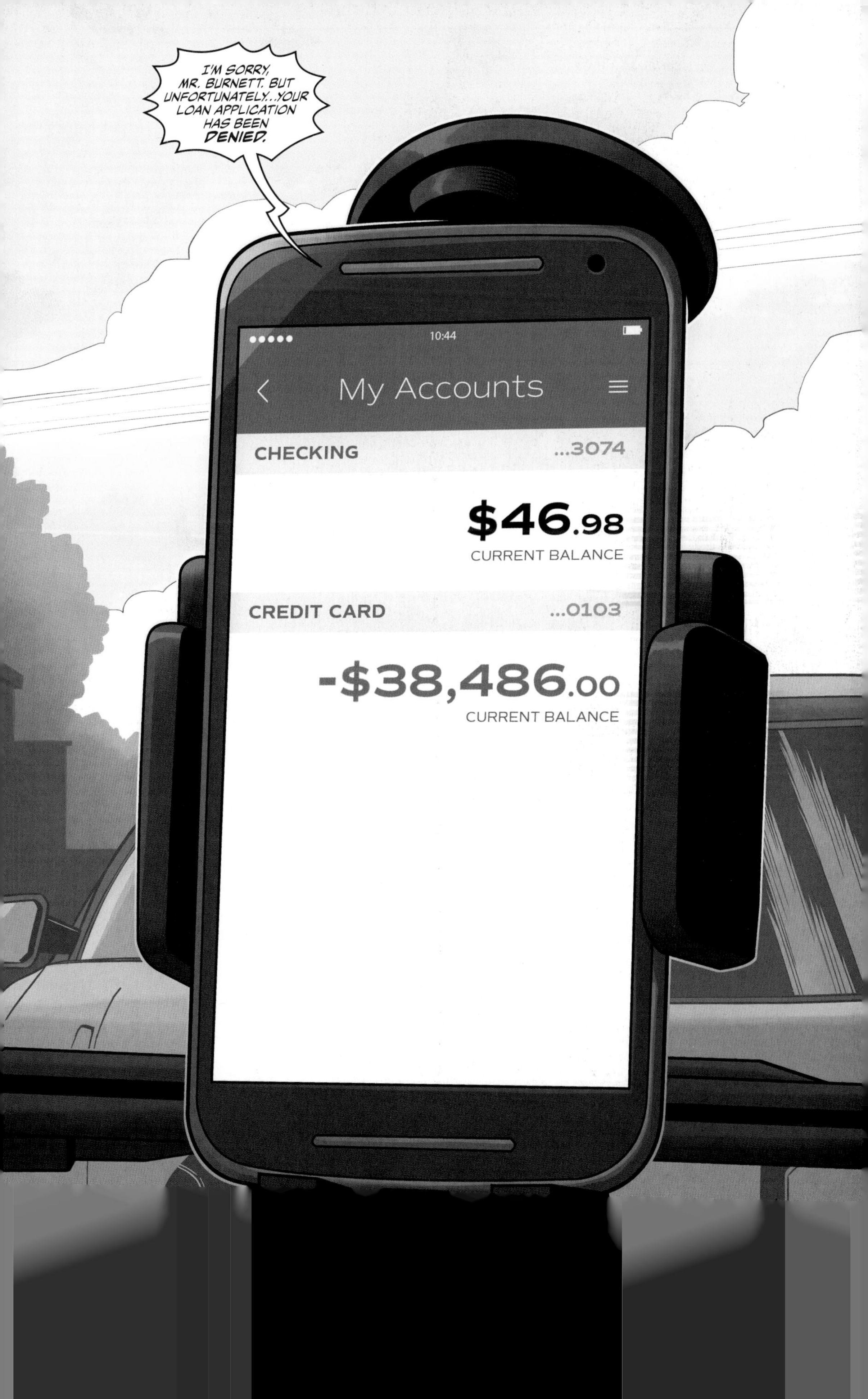
I'M SORRY, MR. BURNETT. BUT UNFORTUNATELY...YOUR LOAN APPLICATION HAS BEEN DENIED.
10:44
My Accounts
CHECKING
...3074
$46.98
CURRENT BALANCE
CREDIT CARD
...0103
-$38,486.00
CURRENT BALANCE

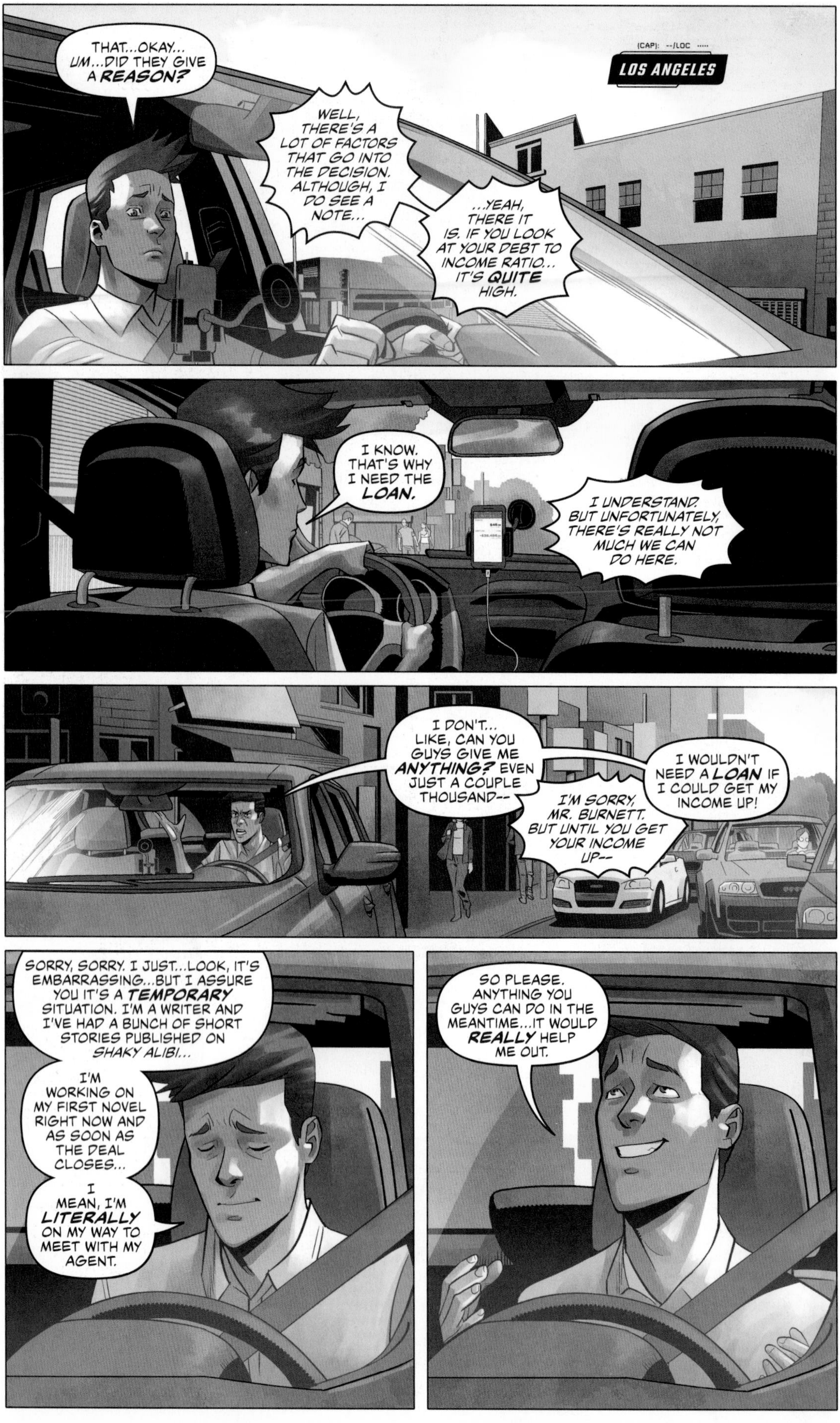
(CAP): --/LOC
LOS ANGELES
THAT...OKAY... UM...DID THEY GIVE A REASON?
WELL, THERE'S A LOT OF FACTORS THAT GO INTO THE DECISION. ALTHOUGH, I DO SEE A NOTE...
...YEAH, THERE IT IS. IF YOU LOOK AT YOUR DEBT TO INCOME RATIO... IT'S QUITE HIGH.
I KNOW. THAT'S WHY I NEED THE LOAN.
I UNDERSTAND. BUT UNFORTUNATELY, THERE'S REALLY NOT MUCH WE CAN DO HERE.
I DON'T... LIKE, CAN YOU GUYS GIVE ME ANYTHING? EVEN JUST A COUPLE THOUSAND--
I'M SORRY, MR. BURNETT. BUT UNTIL YOU GET YOUR INCOME UP--
I WOULDN'T NEED A LOAN IF I COULD GET MY INCOME UP!
SORRY, SORRY. I JUST...LOOK, IT'S EMBARRASSING...BUT I ASSURE YOU IT'S A TEMPORARY SITUATION. I'M A WRITER AND I'VE HAD A BUNCH OF SHORT STORIES PUBLISHED ON SHAKY ALIBI...
I'M WORKING ON MY FIRST NOVEL RIGHT NOW AND AS SOON AS THE DEAL CLOSES...
I MEAN, I'M LITERALLY ON MY WAY TO MEET WITH MY AGENT.
SO PLEASE. ANYTHING YOU GUYS CAN DO IN THE MEANTIME...IT WOULD REALLY HELP ME OUT.

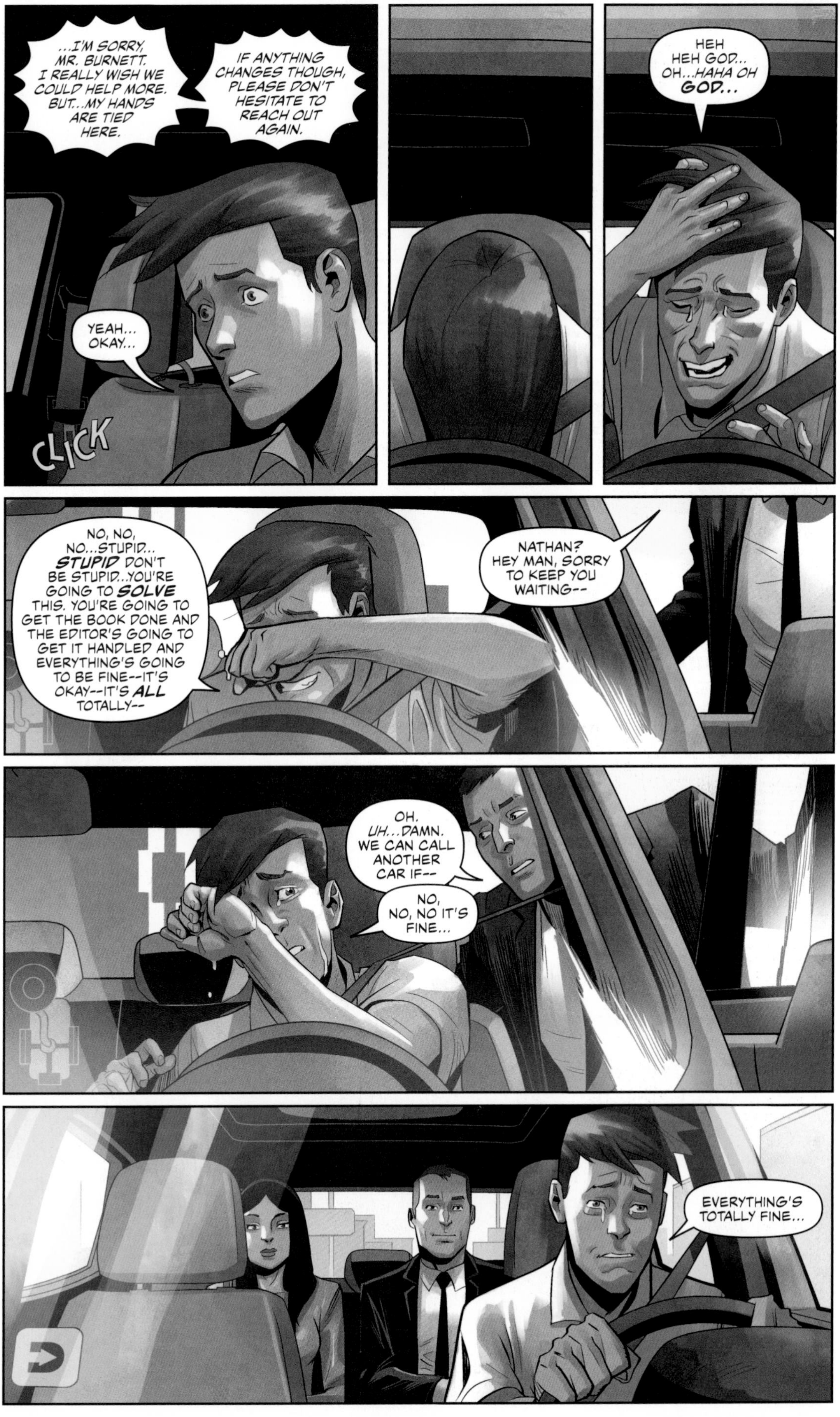
...I'M SORRY, MR. BURNETT. I REALLY WISH WE COULD HELP MORE. BUT...MY HANDS ARE TIED HERE.
IF ANYTHING CHANGES THOUGH, PLEASE DON'T HESITATE TO REACH OUT AGAIN.
YEAH... OKAY...
CLICK
HEH HEH GOD... OH...HAHA OH GOD...
NO, NO, NO...STUPID... STUPID DON'T BE STUPID...YOU'RE GOING TO SOLVE THIS. YOU'RE GOING TO GET THE BOOK DONE AND THE EDITOR'S GOING TO GET IT HANDLED AND EVERYTHING'S GOING TO BE FINE--IT'S OKAY--IT'S ALL TOTALLY--
NATHAN? HEY MAN, SORRY TO KEEP YOU WAITING--
OH. UH...DAMN. WE CAN CALL ANOTHER CAR IF--
NO, NO, NO IT'S FINE...
EVERYTHING'S TOTALLY FINE...

{RAD}: --/TITLE ...

  USR: N/BURNETT ..
  PAS: ******** ...

   ID: 001 ....
  TTL: "NOT_SO_SEC-
        RET_ORIGIN"

{RAD}: --/LOGO ....

RADI

BL

{RAD}: --/TITLE ...

    -: PROTOCOL_CL-
        OSE ....

IANT

LACK

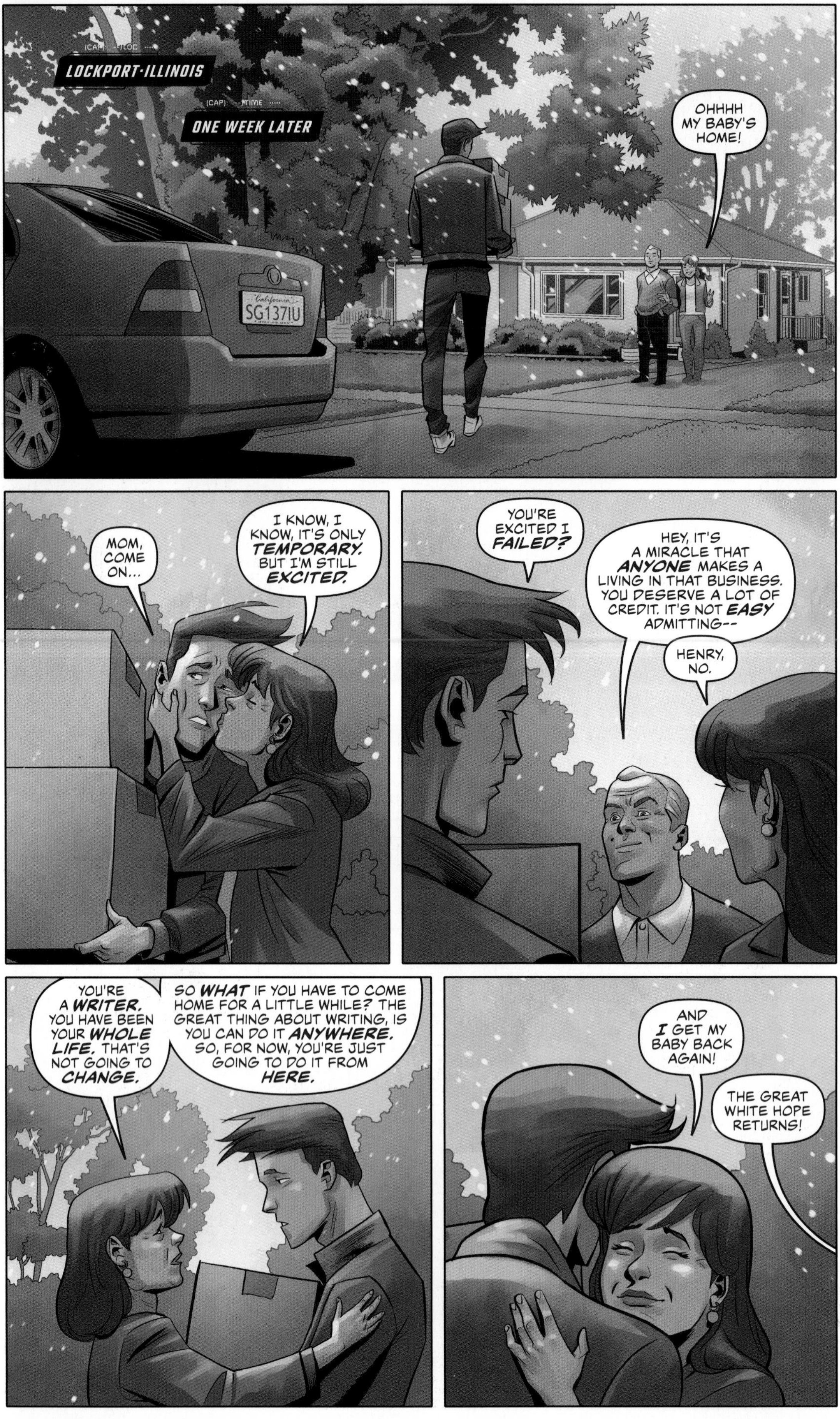
LOCKPORT·ILLINOIS
ONE WEEK LATER
SG137IU
OHHHH MY BABY'S HOME!
MOM, COME ON...
I KNOW, I KNOW, IT'S ONLY TEMPORARY. BUT I'M STILL EXCITED.
YOU'RE EXCITED I FAILED?
HEY, IT'S A MIRACLE THAT ANYONE MAKES A LIVING IN THAT BUSINESS. YOU DESERVE A LOT OF CREDIT. IT'S NOT EASY ADMITTING--
HENRY, NO.
YOU'RE A WRITER. YOU HAVE BEEN YOUR WHOLE LIFE. THAT'S NOT GOING TO CHANGE.
SO WHAT IF YOU HAVE TO COME HOME FOR A LITTLE WHILE? THE GREAT THING ABOUT WRITING, IS YOU CAN DO IT ANYWHERE. SO, FOR NOW, YOU'RE JUST GOING TO DO IT FROM HERE.
AND I GET MY BABY BACK AGAIN!
THE GREAT WHITE HOPE RETURNS!

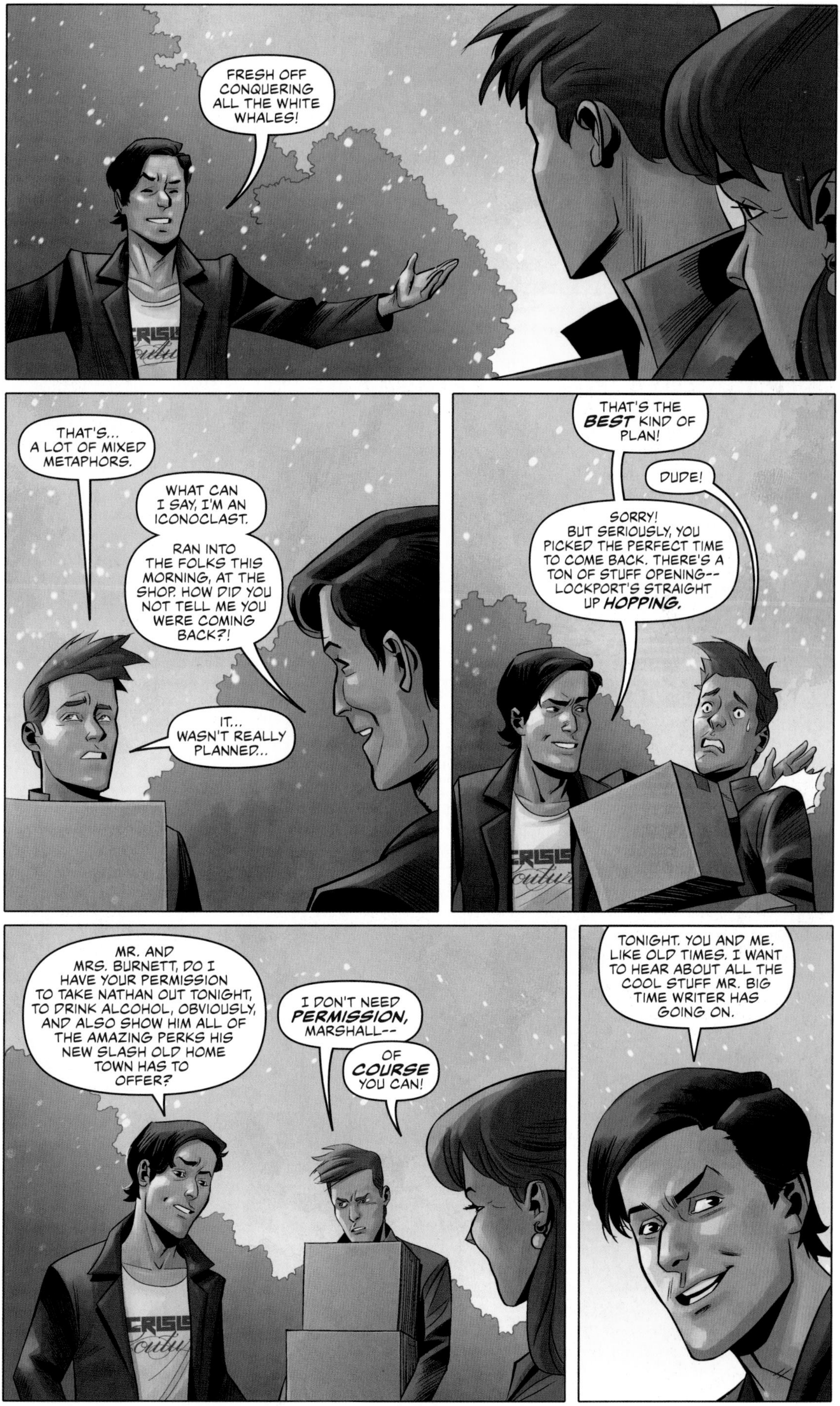
FRESH OFF CONQUERING ALL THE WHITE WHALES!
THAT'S... A LOT OF MIXED METAPHORS.
WHAT CAN I SAY, I'M AN ICONOCLAST.
RAN INTO THE FOLKS THIS MORNING, AT THE SHOP. HOW DID YOU NOT TELL ME YOU WERE COMING BACK?!
IT... WASN'T REALLY PLANNED...
THAT'S THE BEST KIND OF PLAN!
DUDE!
SORRY! BUT SERIOUSLY, YOU PICKED THE PERFECT TIME TO COME BACK. THERE'S A TON OF STUFF OPENING-- LOCKPORT'S STRAIGHT UP HOPPING.
MR. AND MRS. BURNETT, DO I HAVE YOUR PERMISSION TO TAKE NATHAN OUT TONIGHT, TO DRINK ALCOHOL, OBVIOUSLY, AND ALSO SHOW HIM ALL OF THE AMAZING PERKS HIS NEW SLASH OLD HOME TOWN HAS TO OFFER?
I DON'T NEED PERMISSION, MARSHALL--
OF COURSE YOU CAN!
TONIGHT. YOU AND ME. LIKE OLD TIMES. I WANT TO HEAR ABOUT ALL THE COOL STUFF MR. BIG TIME WRITER HAS GOING ON.

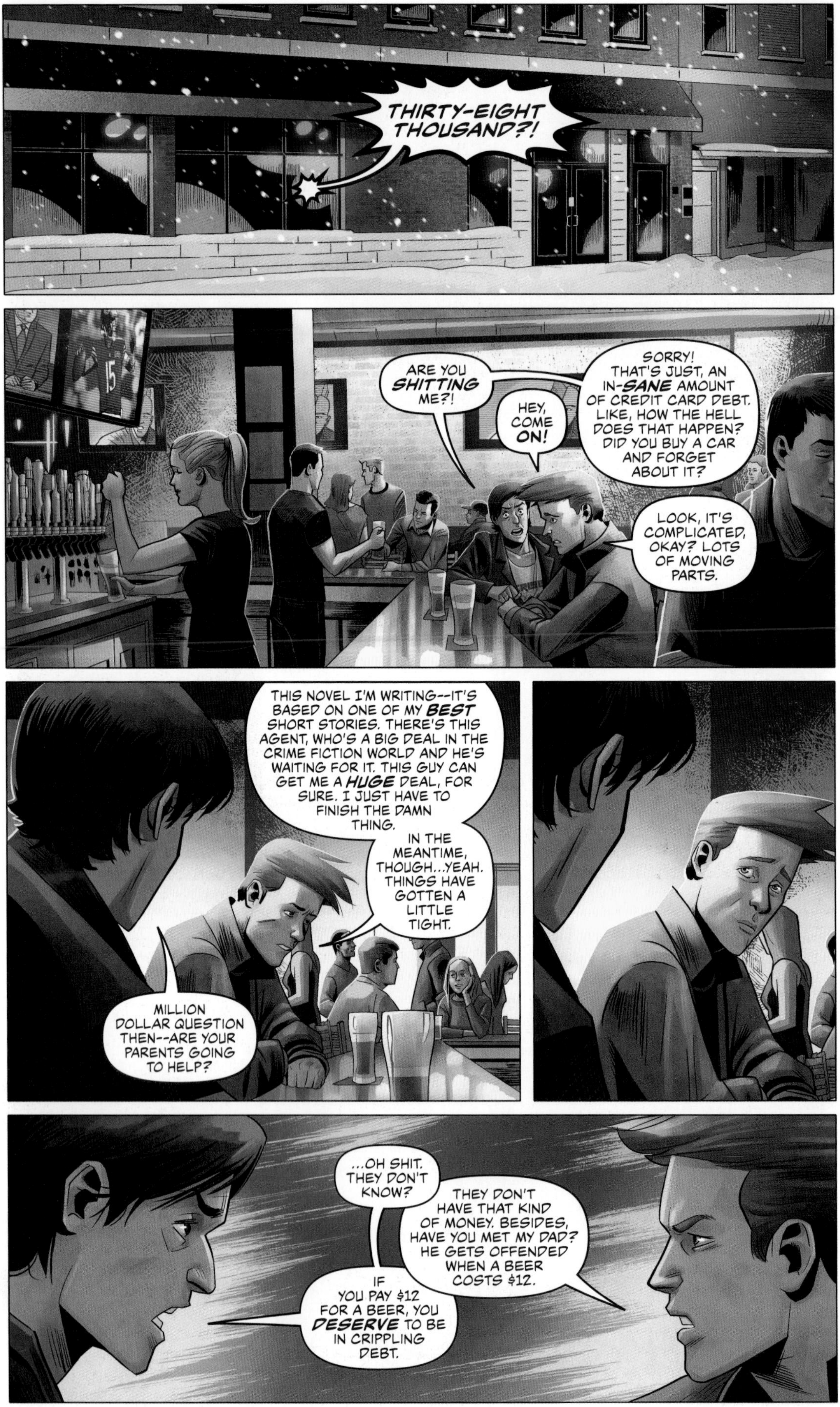
THIRTY-EIGHT THOUSAND?!
ARE YOU SHITTING ME?!
SORRY! THAT'S JUST, AN IN-SANE AMOUNT OF CREDIT CARD DEBT. LIKE, HOW THE HELL DOES THAT HAPPEN? DID YOU BUY A CAR AND FORGET ABOUT IT?
HEY, COME ON!
LOOK, IT'S COMPLICATED, OKAY? LOTS OF MOVING PARTS.
THIS NOVEL I'M WRITING--IT'S BASED ON ONE OF MY BEST SHORT STORIES. THERE'S THIS AGENT, WHO'S A BIG DEAL IN THE CRIME FICTION WORLD AND HE'S WAITING FOR IT. THIS GUY CAN GET ME A HUGE DEAL, FOR SURE. I JUST HAVE TO FINISH THE DAMN THING.
IN THE MEANTIME, THOUGH...YEAH. THINGS HAVE GOTTEN A LITTLE TIGHT.
MILLION DOLLAR QUESTION THEN--ARE YOUR PARENTS GOING TO HELP?
...OH SHIT. THEY DON'T KNOW?
THEY DON'T HAVE THAT KIND OF MONEY. BESIDES, HAVE YOU MET MY DAD? HE GETS OFFENDED WHEN A BEER COSTS $12.
IF YOU PAY $12 FOR A BEER, YOU DESERVE TO BE IN CRIPPLING DEBT.

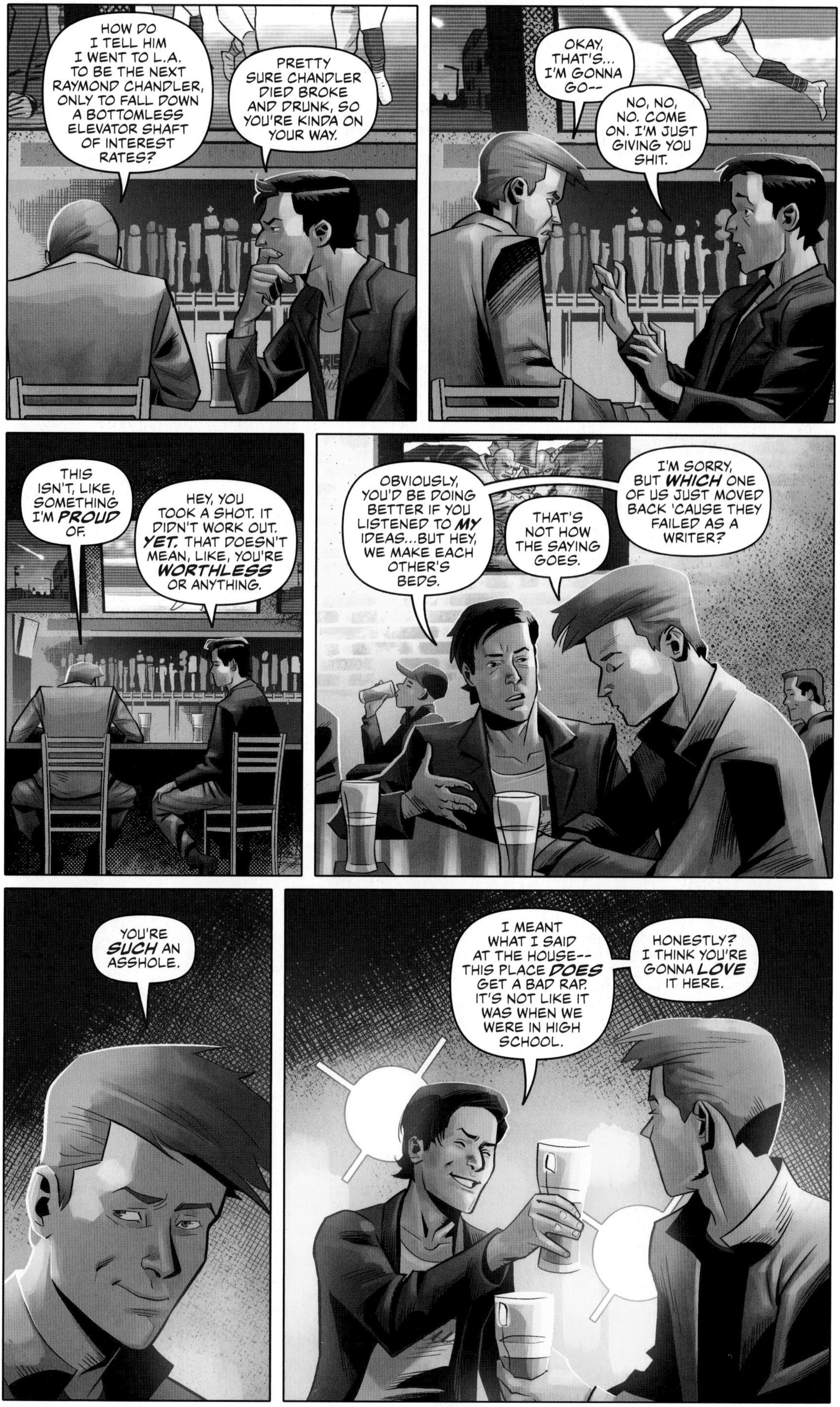
HOW DO I TELL HIM I WENT TO L.A. TO BE THE NEXT RAYMOND CHANDLER, ONLY TO FALL DOWN A BOTTOMLESS ELEVATOR SHAFT OF INTEREST RATES?
PRETTY SURE CHANDLER DIED BROKE AND DRUNK, SO YOU'RE KINDA ON YOUR WAY.
OKAY, THAT'S... I'M GONNA GO--
NO, NO, NO. COME ON. I'M JUST GIVING YOU SHIT.
THIS ISN'T, LIKE, SOMETHING I'M PROUD OF.
HEY, YOU TOOK A SHOT. IT DIDN'T WORK OUT. YET. THAT DOESN'T MEAN, LIKE, YOU'RE WORTHLESS OR ANYTHING.
OBVIOUSLY, YOU'D BE DOING BETTER IF YOU LISTENED TO MY IDEAS...BUT HEY, WE MAKE EACH OTHER'S BEDS.
THAT'S NOT HOW THE SAYING GOES.
I'M SORRY, BUT WHICH ONE OF US JUST MOVED BACK 'CAUSE THEY FAILED AS A WRITER?
YOU'RE SUCH AN ASSHOLE.
I MEANT WHAT I SAID AT THE HOUSE-- THIS PLACE DOES GET A BAD RAP. IT'S NOT LIKE IT WAS WHEN WE WERE IN HIGH SCHOOL.
HONESTLY? I THINK YOU'RE GONNA LOVE IT HERE.

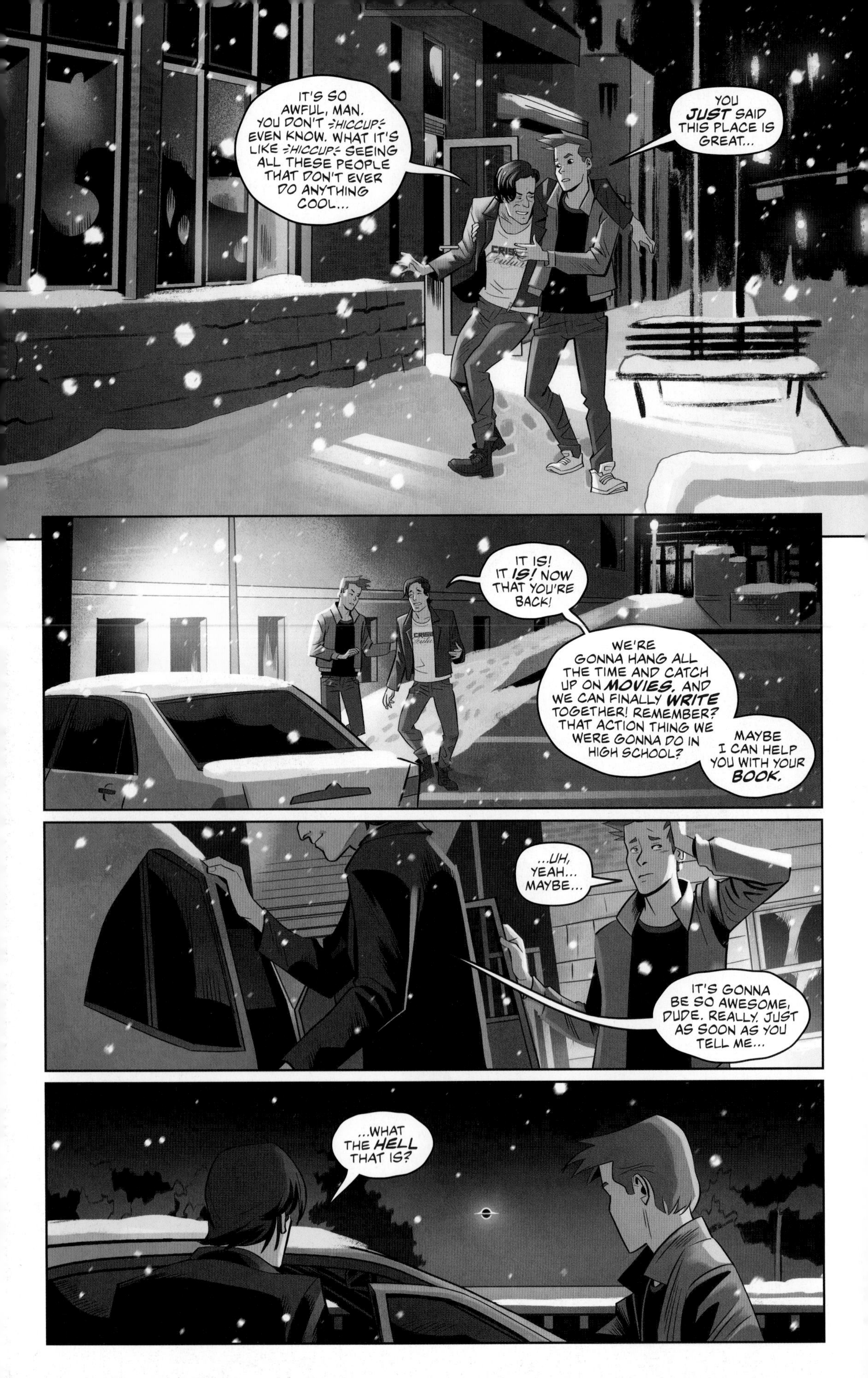
IT'S SO AWFUL, MAN. YOU DON'T *HICCUP* EVEN KNOW. WHAT IT'S LIKE *HICCUP* SEEING ALL THESE PEOPLE THAT DON'T EVER DO ANYTHING COOL...
YOU JUST SAID THIS PLACE IS GREAT...
IT IS! IT IS! NOW THAT YOU'RE BACK!
WE'RE GONNA HANG ALL THE TIME AND CATCH UP ON MOVIES. AND WE CAN FINALLY WRITE TOGETHER! REMEMBER? THAT ACTION THING WE WERE GONNA DO IN HIGH SCHOOL?
MAYBE I CAN HELP YOU WITH YOUR BOOK.
...UH, YEAH... MAYBE...
IT'S GONNA BE SO AWESOME, DUDE. REALLY. JUST AS SOON AS YOU TELL ME...
...WHAT THE HELL THAT IS?

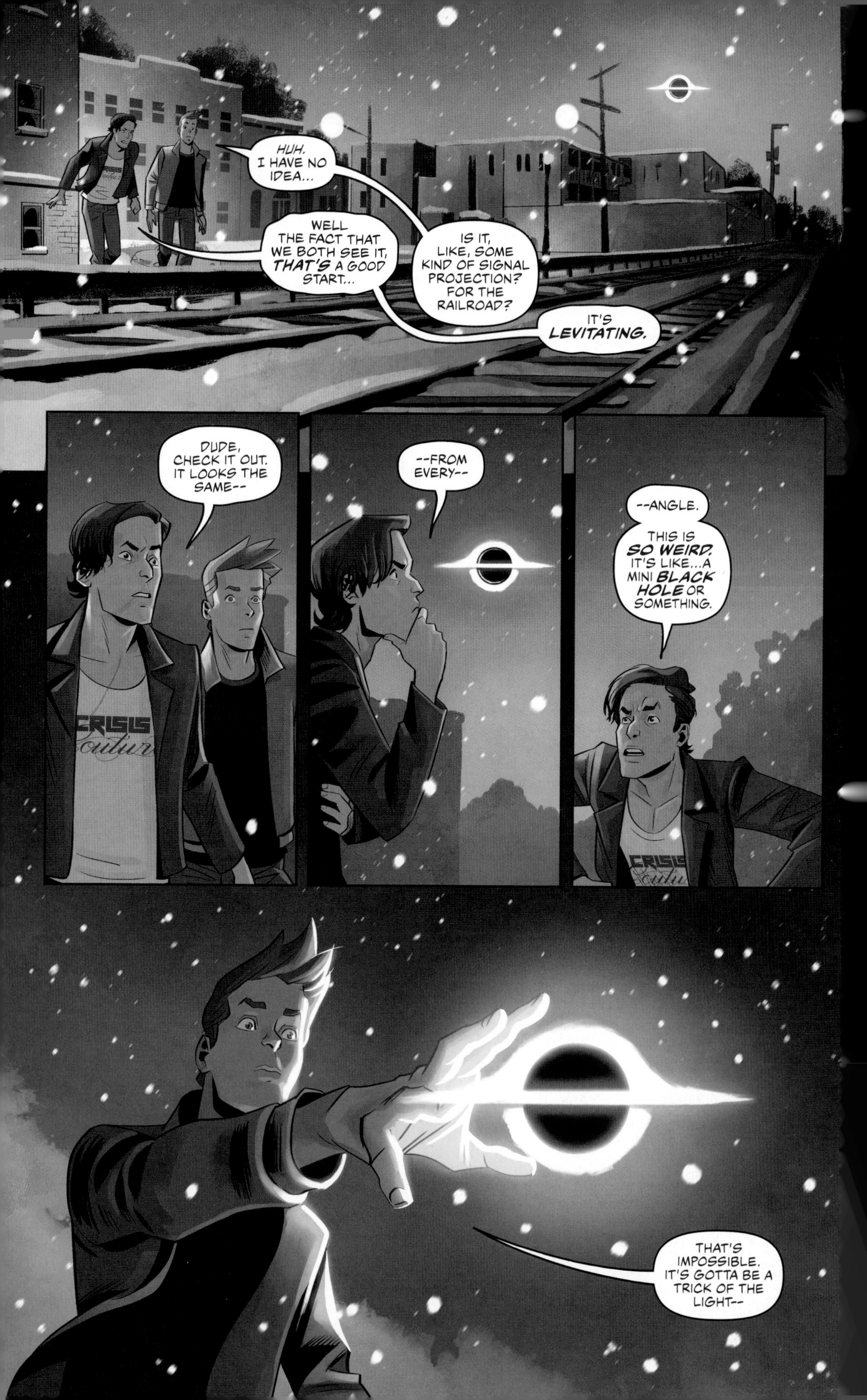
HUH. I HAVE NO IDEA...
WELL THE FACT THAT WE BOTH SEE IT, THAT'S A GOOD START...
IS IT, LIKE, SOME KIND OF SIGNAL PROJECTION? FOR THE RAILROAD?
IT'S LEVITATING.
DUDE, CHECK IT OUT. IT LOOKS THE SAME--
--FROM EVERY--
--ANGLE.
THIS IS SO WEIRD. IT'S LIKE...A MINI BLACK HOLE OR SOMETHING.
THAT'S IMPOSSIBLE. IT'S GOTTA BE A TRICK OF THE LIGHT--

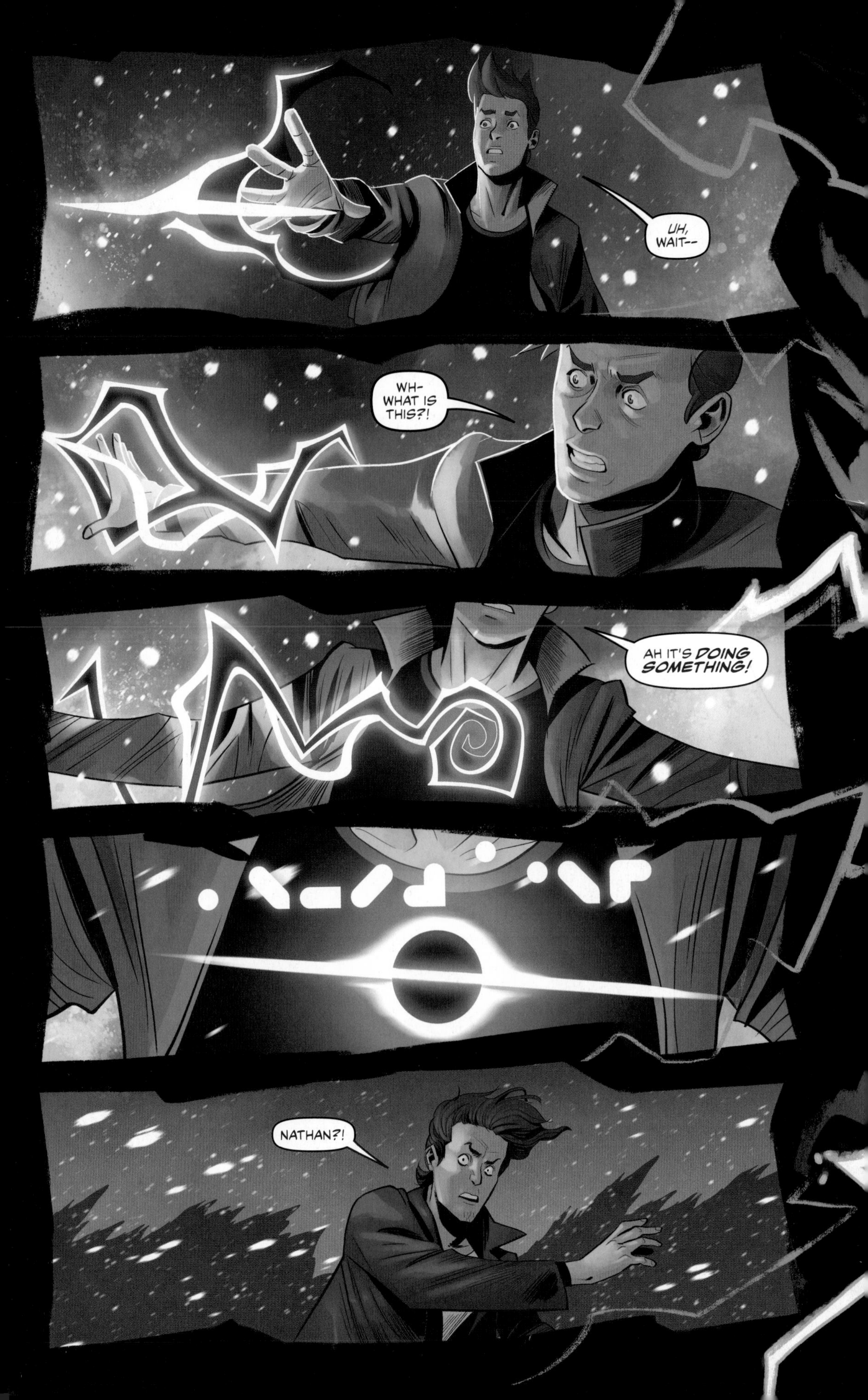
UH, WAIT--
WH- WHAT IS THIS?!
AH IT'S DOING SOMETHING!
NATHAN?!

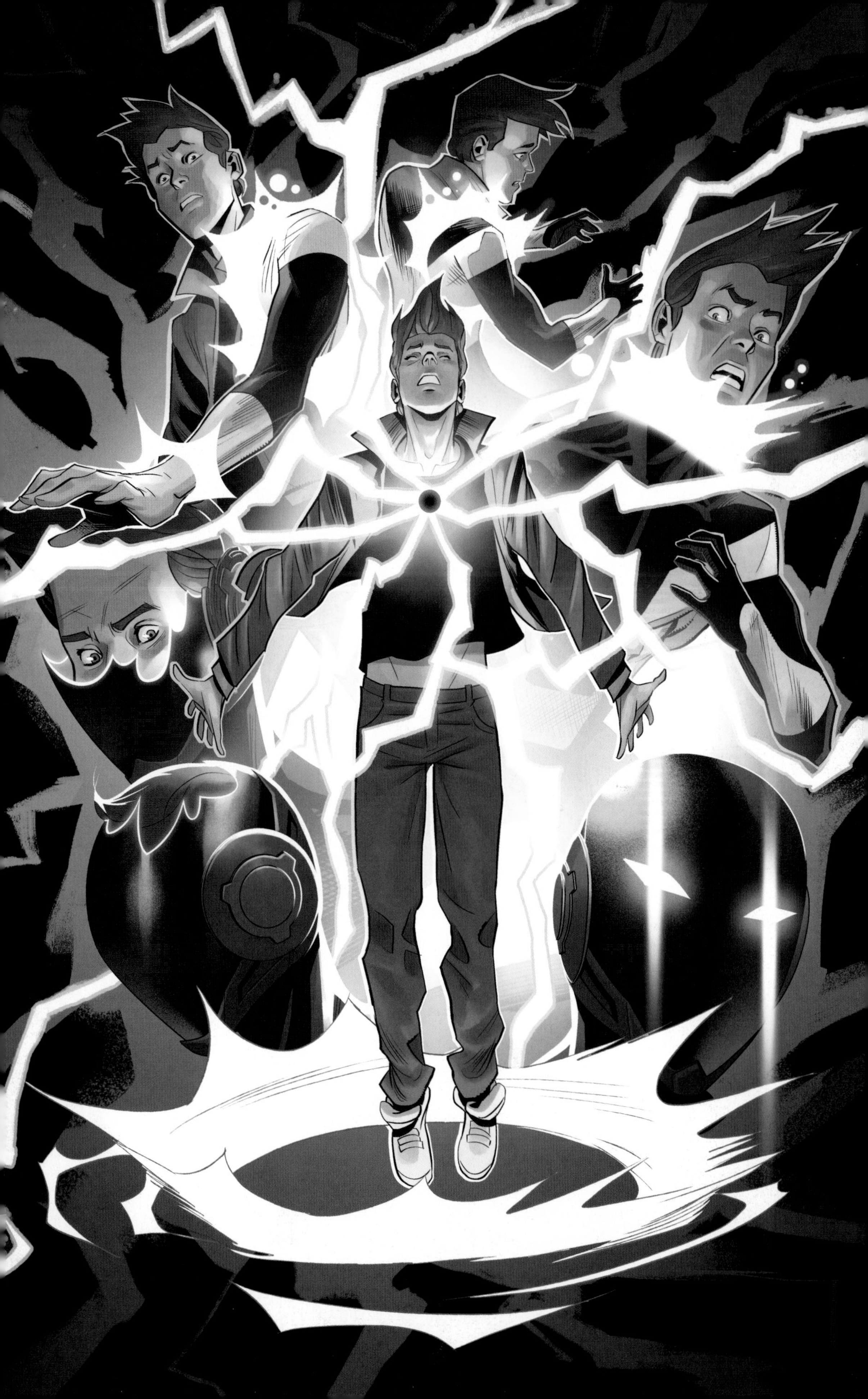

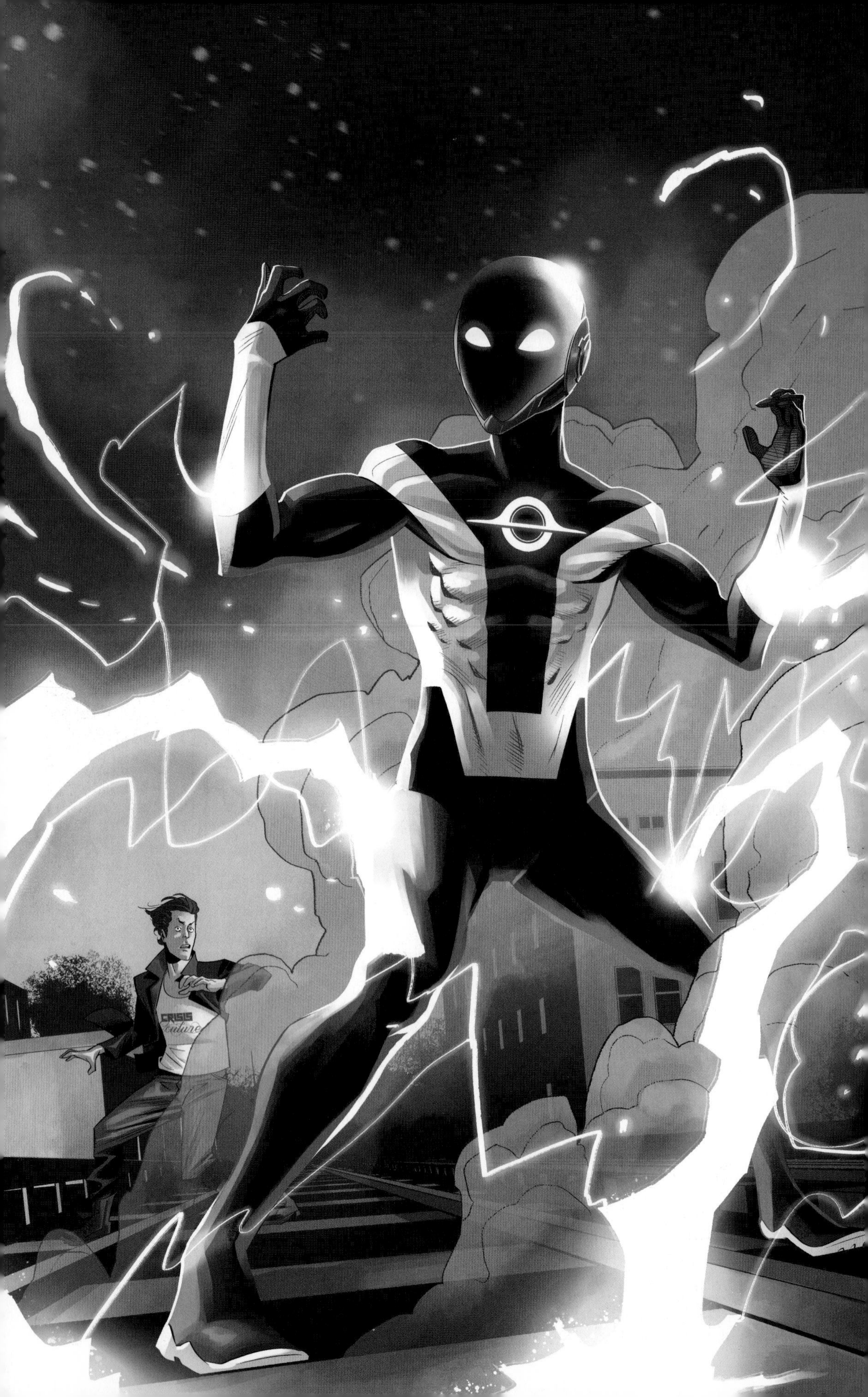
CRISIS
Culture

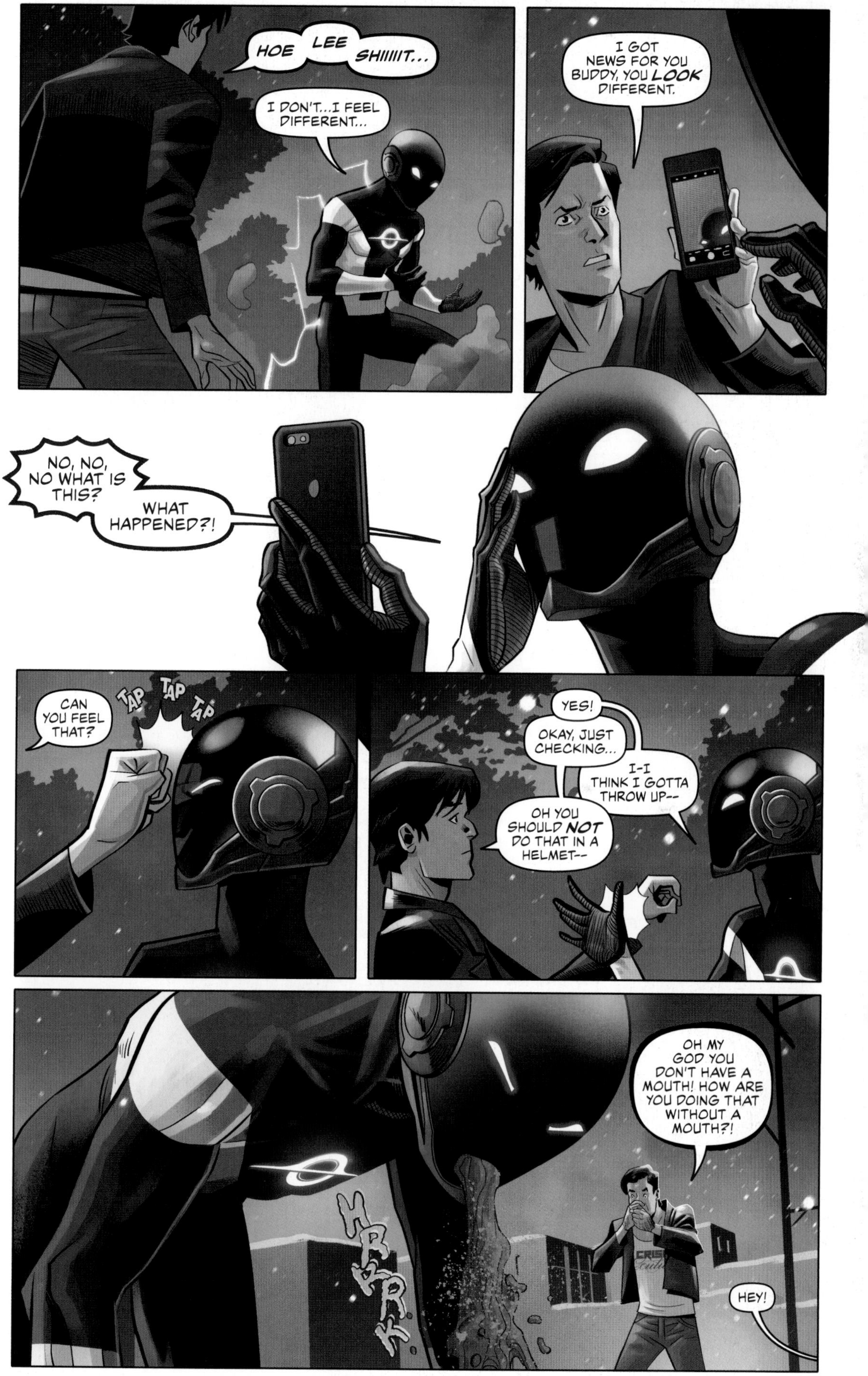
HOE LEE SHIIIIIT...
I DON'T...I FEEL DIFFERENT...
I GOT NEWS FOR YOU BUDDY, YOU LOOK DIFFERENT.
NO, NO, NO WHAT IS THIS?
WHAT HAPPENED?!
CAN YOU FEEL THAT?
TAP TAP TAP
YES!
OKAY, JUST CHECKING...
I-I THINK I GOTTA THROW UP--
OH YOU SHOULD NOT DO THAT IN A HELMET--
OH MY GOD YOU DON'T HAVE A MOUTH! HOW ARE YOU DOING THAT WITHOUT A MOUTH?!
HRRK
HEY!

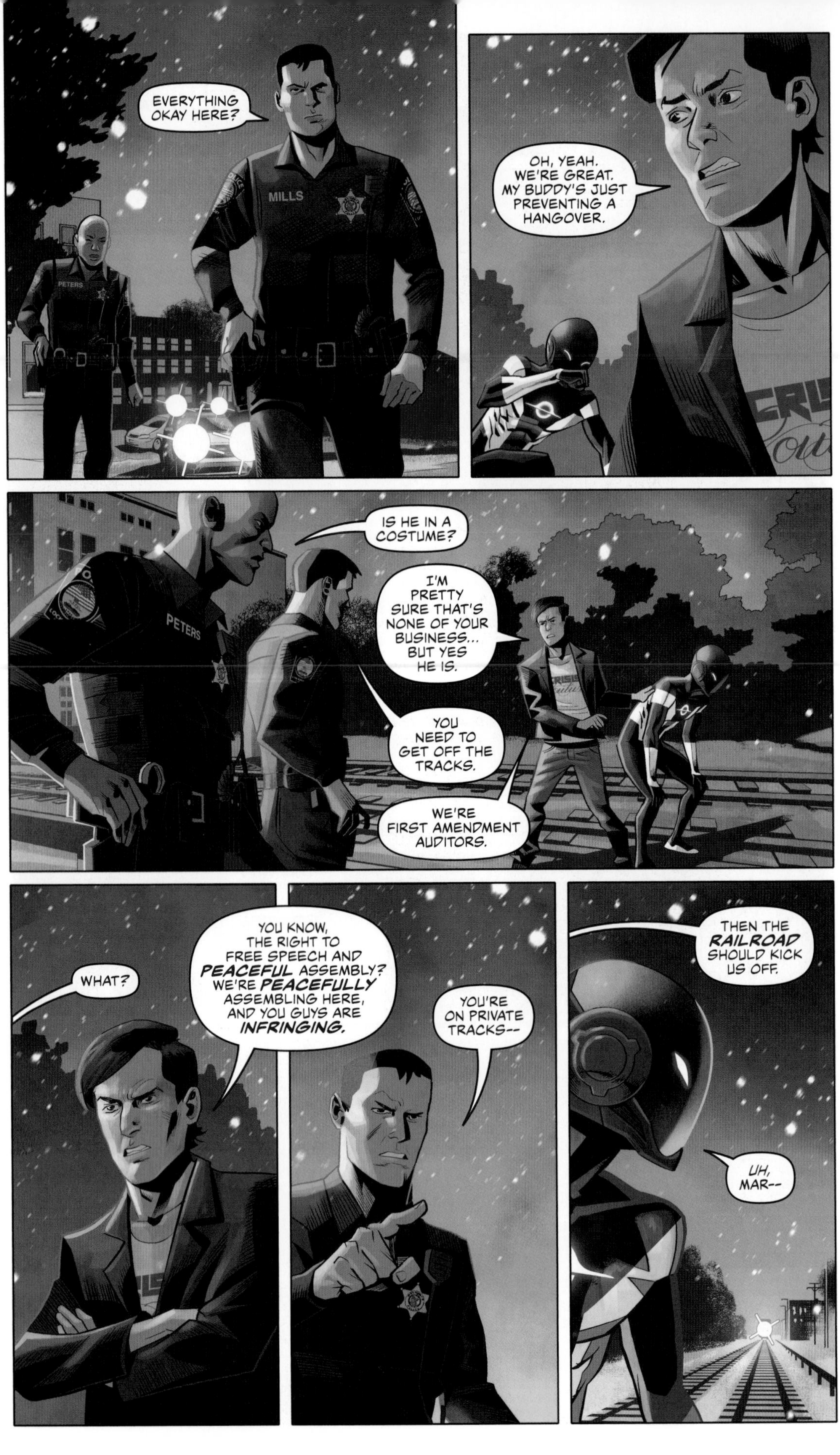
EVERYTHING OKAY HERE?
MILLS
PETERS
OH, YEAH. WE'RE GREAT. MY BUDDY'S JUST PREVENTING A HANGOVER.
IS HE IN A COSTUME?
PETERS
I'M PRETTY SURE THAT'S NONE OF YOUR BUSINESS... BUT YES HE IS.
YOU NEED TO GET OFF THE TRACKS.
WE'RE FIRST AMENDMENT AUDITORS.
WHAT?
YOU KNOW, THE RIGHT TO FREE SPEECH AND *PEACEFUL* ASSEMBLY? WE'RE *PEACEFULLY* ASSEMBLING HERE, AND YOU GUYS ARE *INFRINGING.*
YOU'RE ON PRIVATE TRACKS--
THEN THE *RAILROAD* SHOULD KICK US OFF.
UH, MAR--

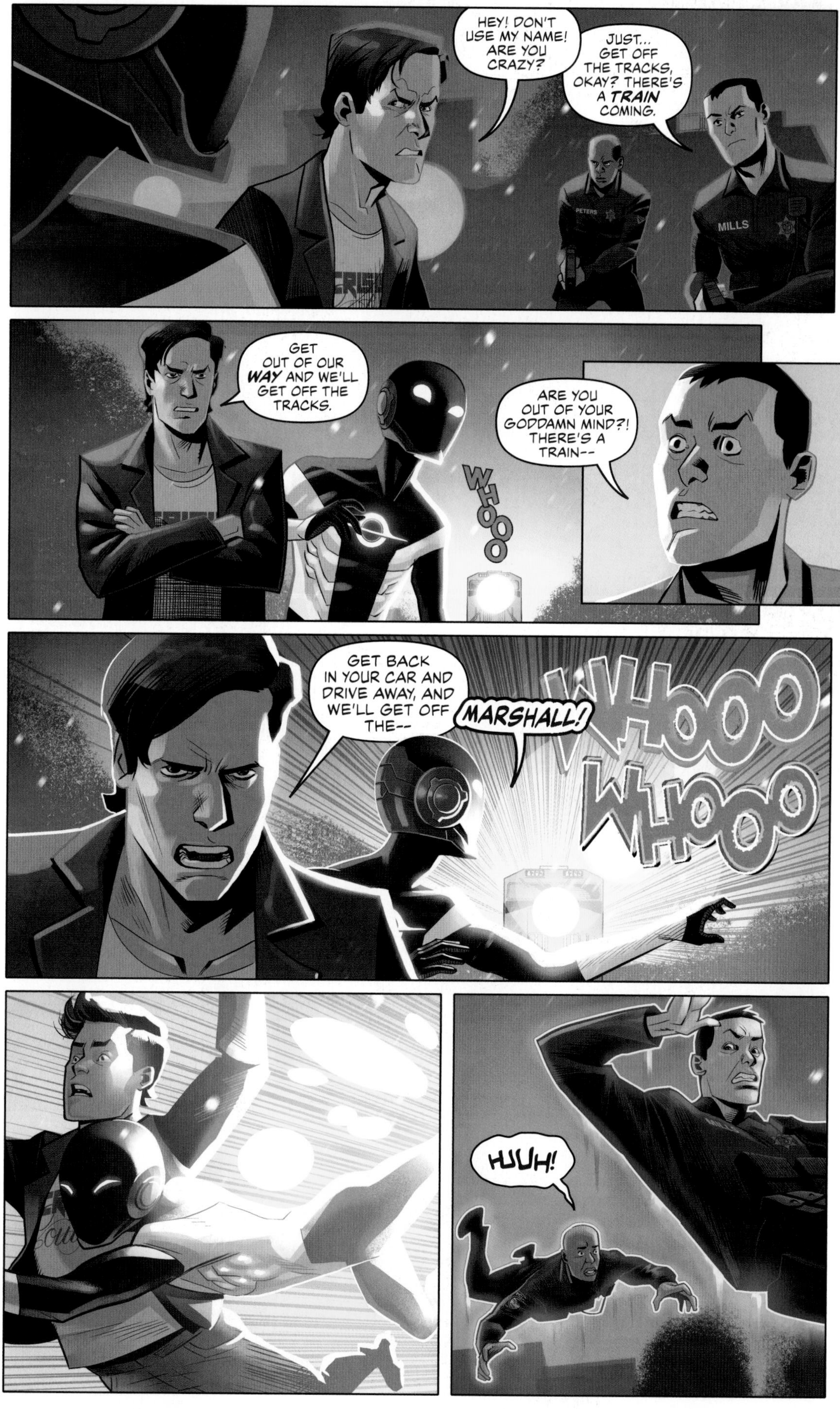
HEY! DON'T USE MY NAME! ARE YOU CRAZY?
JUST... GET OFF THE TRACKS, OKAY? THERE'S A TRAIN COMING.
PETERS
MILLS
GET OUT OF OUR WAY AND WE'LL GET OFF THE TRACKS.
ARE YOU OUT OF YOUR GODDAMN MIND?! THERE'S A TRAIN--
WHOO
GET BACK IN YOUR CAR AND DRIVE AWAY, AND WE'LL GET OFF THE--
MARSHALL!
WHOOO
WHOOO
HUUH!

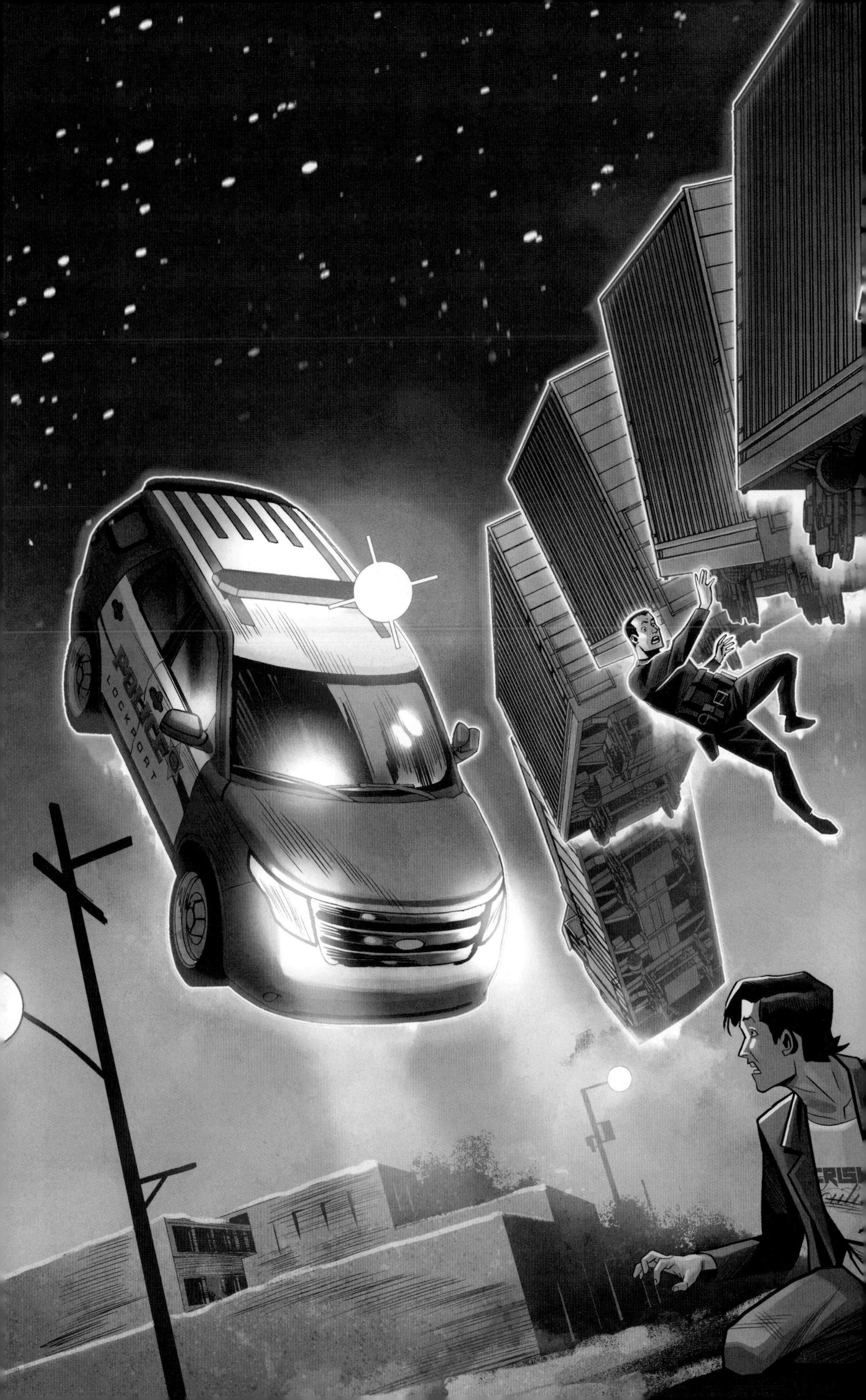
POLICE
LOCKPORT

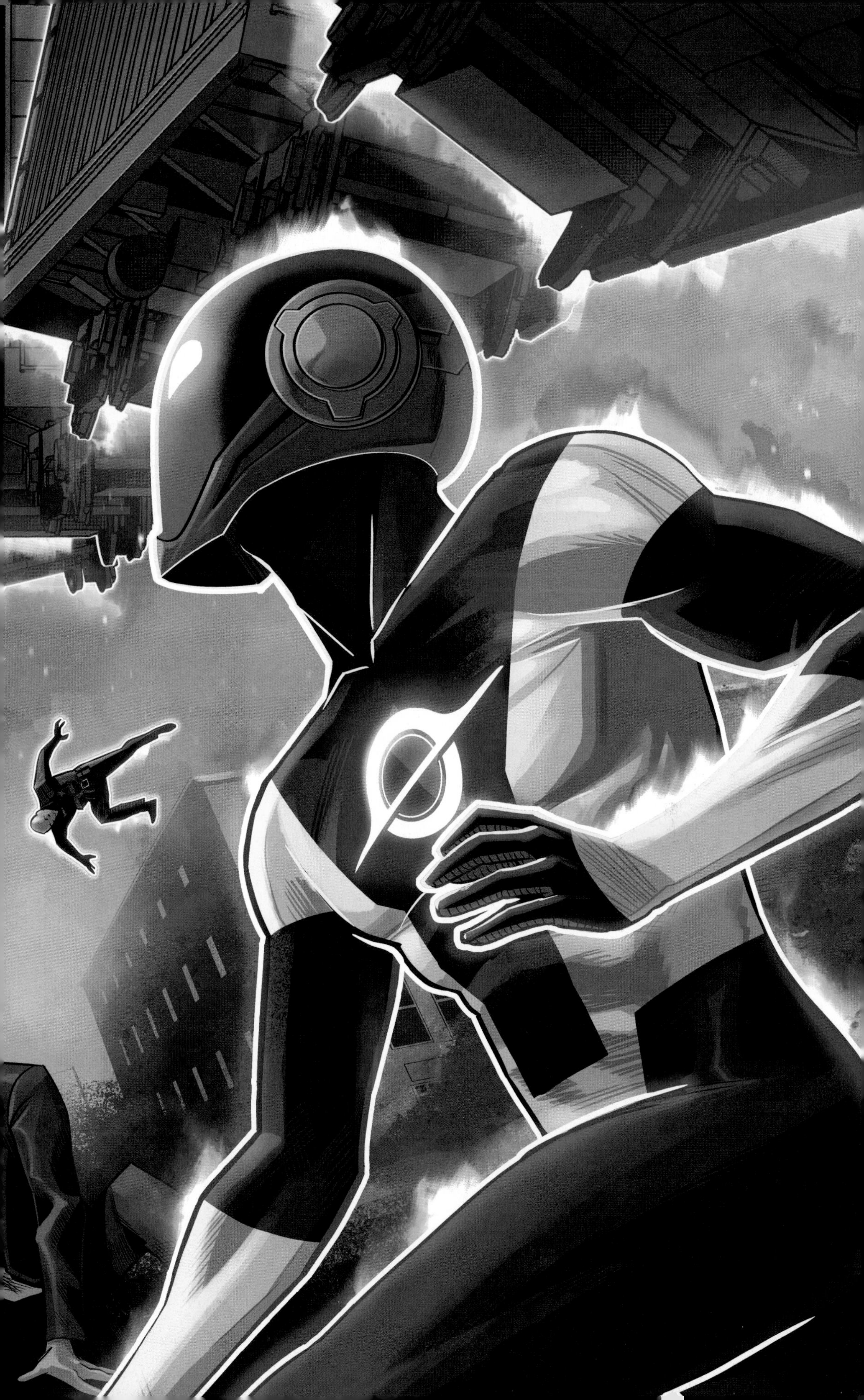

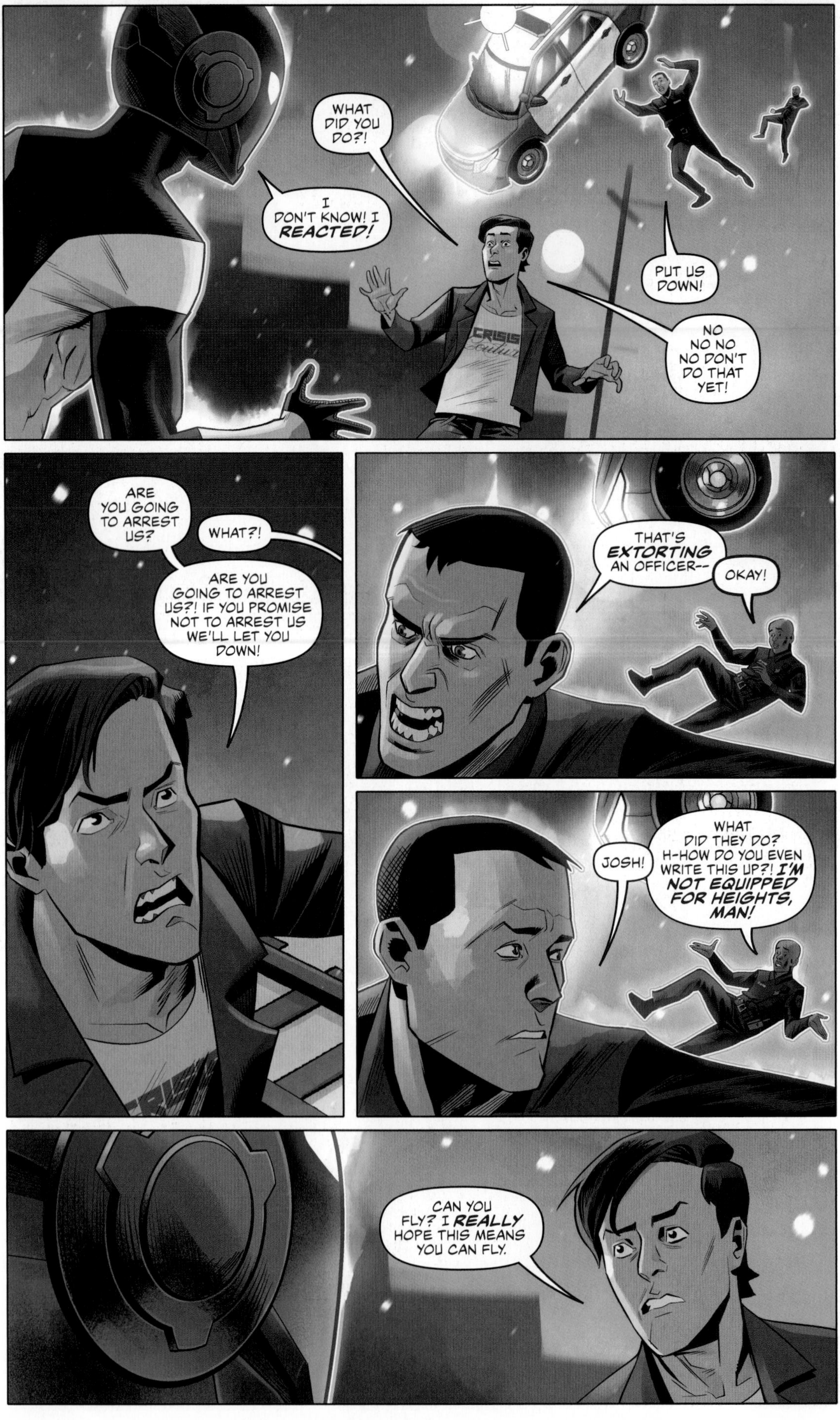
WHAT DID YOU DO?!
I DON'T KNOW! I **REACTED!**
PUT US DOWN!
NO NO NO NO DON'T DO THAT YET!
ARE YOU GOING TO ARREST US?
WHAT?!
ARE YOU GOING TO ARREST US?! IF YOU PROMISE NOT TO ARREST US WE'LL LET YOU DOWN!
THAT'S **EXTORTING** AN OFFICER--
OKAY!
JOSH!
WHAT DID THEY DO? H-HOW DO YOU EVEN WRITE THIS UP?! **I'M NOT EQUIPPED FOR HEIGHTS, MAN!**
CAN YOU FLY? I **REALLY** HOPE THIS MEANS YOU CAN FLY.

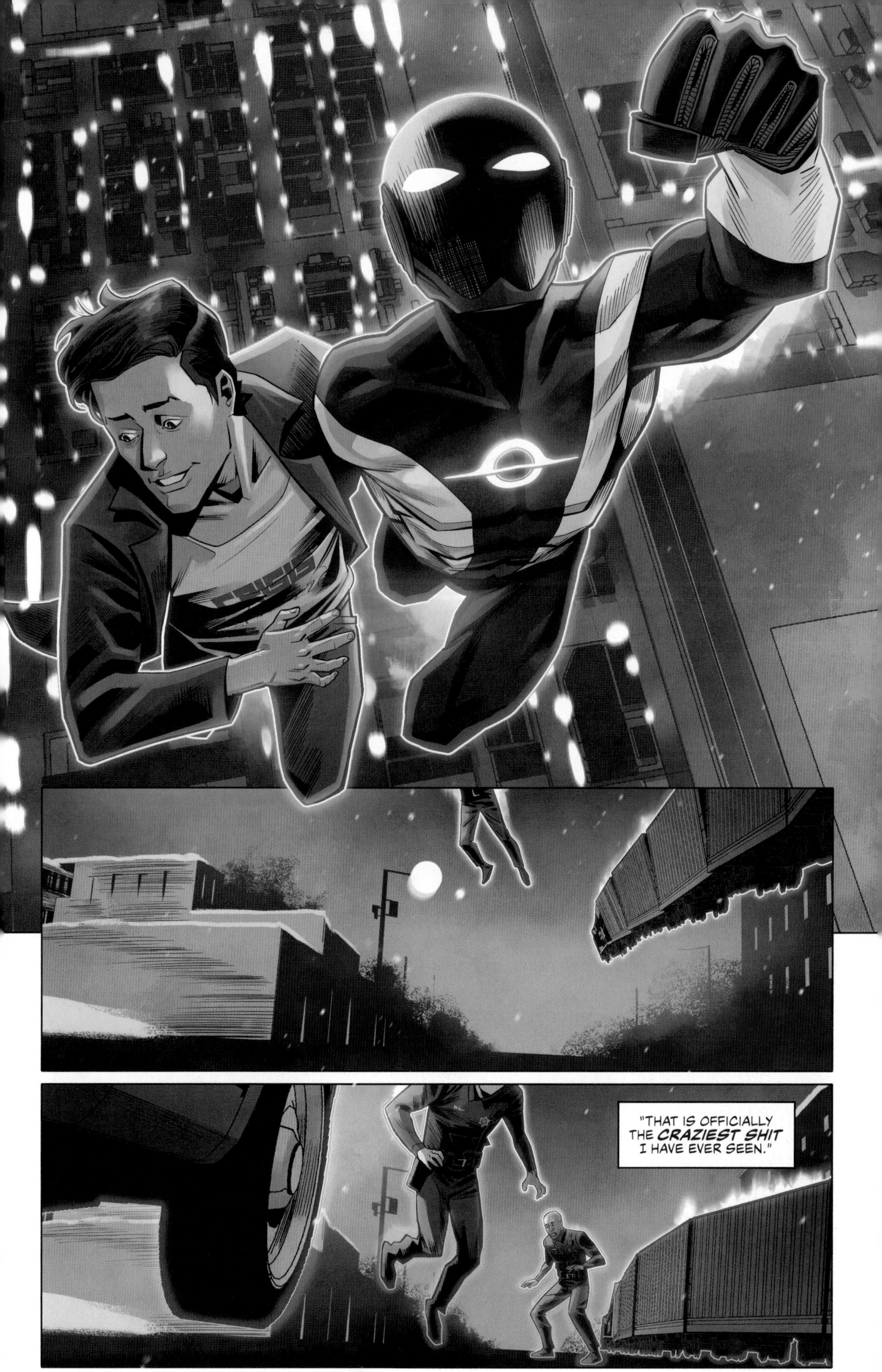

CRISIS
"THAT IS OFFICIALLY THE *CRAZIEST SHIT* I HAVE EVER SEEN."

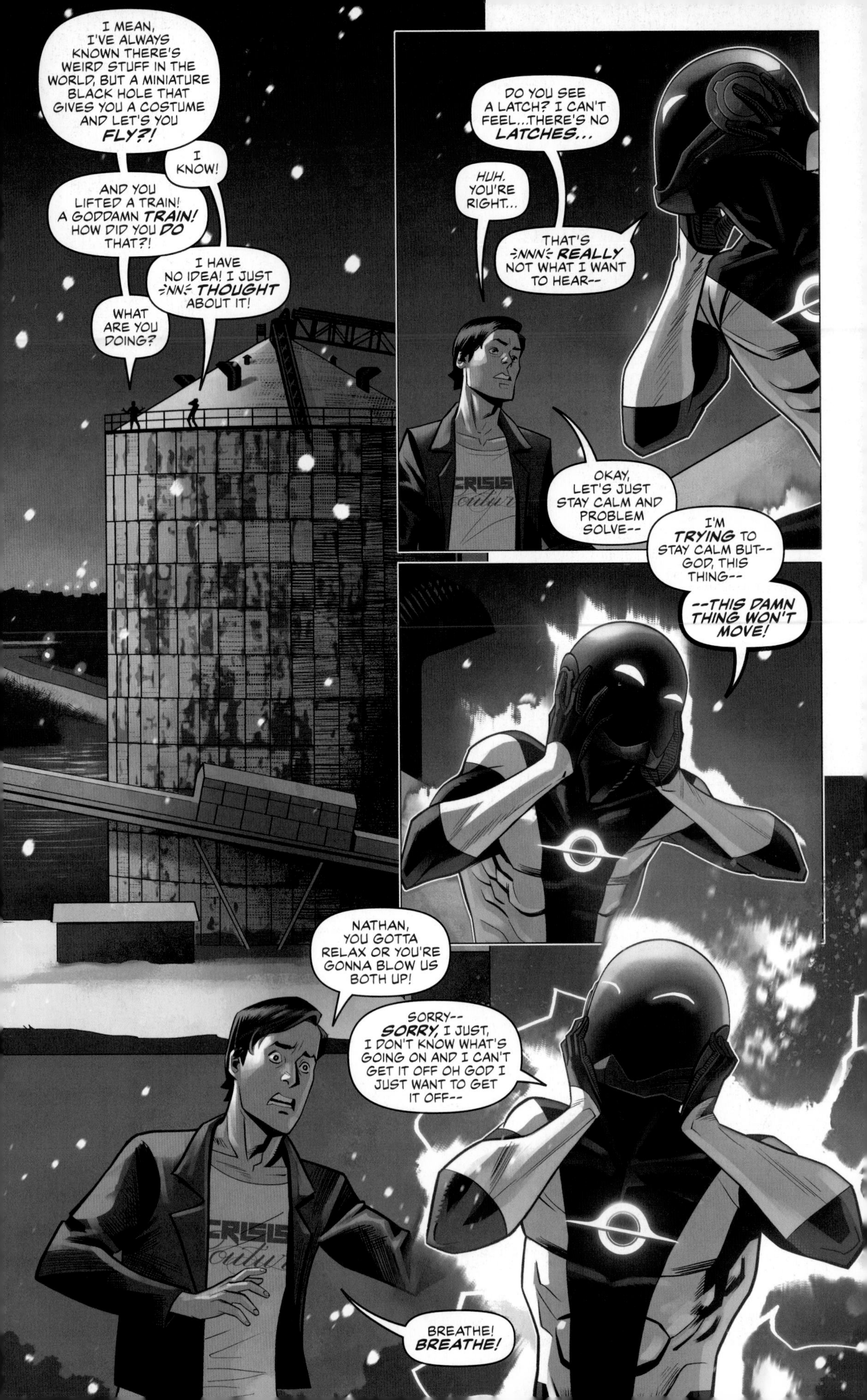
I MEAN, I'VE ALWAYS KNOWN THERE'S WEIRD STUFF IN THE WORLD, BUT A MINIATURE BLACK HOLE THAT GIVES YOU A COSTUME AND LET'S YOU FLY?!
I KNOW!
AND YOU LIFTED A TRAIN! A GODDAMN TRAIN! HOW DID YOU DO THAT?!
I HAVE NO IDEA! I JUST NN THOUGHT ABOUT IT!
WHAT ARE YOU DOING?
DO YOU SEE A LATCH? I CAN'T FEEL...THERE'S NO LATCHES...
HUH. YOU'RE RIGHT...
THAT'S NNN REALLY NOT WHAT I WANT TO HEAR--
OKAY, LET'S JUST STAY CALM AND PROBLEM SOLVE--
I'M TRYING TO STAY CALM BUT--GOD, THIS THING--
--THIS DAMN THING WON'T MOVE!
NATHAN, YOU GOTTA RELAX OR YOU'RE GONNA BLOW US BOTH UP!
SORRY-- SORRY, I JUST, I DON'T KNOW WHAT'S GOING ON AND I CAN'T GET IT OFF OH GOD I JUST WANT TO GET IT OFF--
BREATHE! BREATHE!

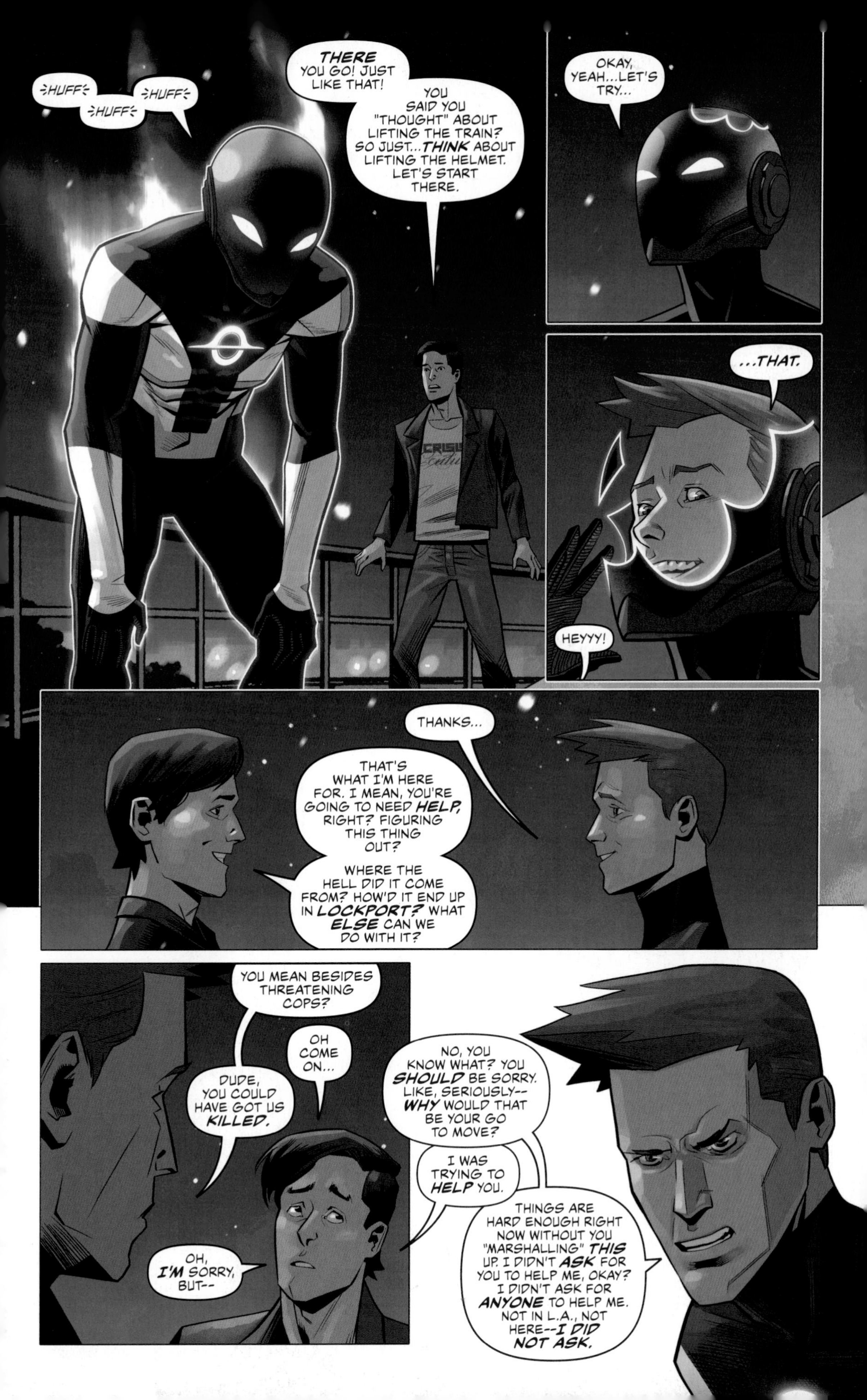

HUFF HUFF HUFF
THERE YOU GO! JUST LIKE THAT!
YOU SAID YOU "THOUGHT" ABOUT LIFTING THE TRAIN? SO JUST...THINK ABOUT LIFTING THE HELMET. LET'S START THERE.
OKAY, YEAH...LET'S TRY...
...THAT.
HEYYY!
THANKS...
THAT'S WHAT I'M HERE FOR. I MEAN, YOU'RE GOING TO NEED HELP, RIGHT? FIGURING THIS THING OUT?
WHERE THE HELL DID IT COME FROM? HOW'D IT END UP IN LOCKPORT? WHAT ELSE CAN WE DO WITH IT?
YOU MEAN BESIDES THREATENING COPS?
OH COME ON...
DUDE, YOU COULD HAVE GOT US KILLED.
OH, I'M SORRY, BUT--
NO, YOU KNOW WHAT? YOU SHOULD BE SORRY. LIKE, SERIOUSLY--WHY WOULD THAT BE YOUR GO TO MOVE?
I WAS TRYING TO HELP YOU.
THINGS ARE HARD ENOUGH RIGHT NOW WITHOUT YOU "MARSHALLING" THIS UP. I DIDN'T ASK FOR YOU TO HELP ME, OKAY? I DIDN'T ASK FOR ANYONE TO HELP ME. NOT IN L.A., NOT HERE--I DID NOT ASK.

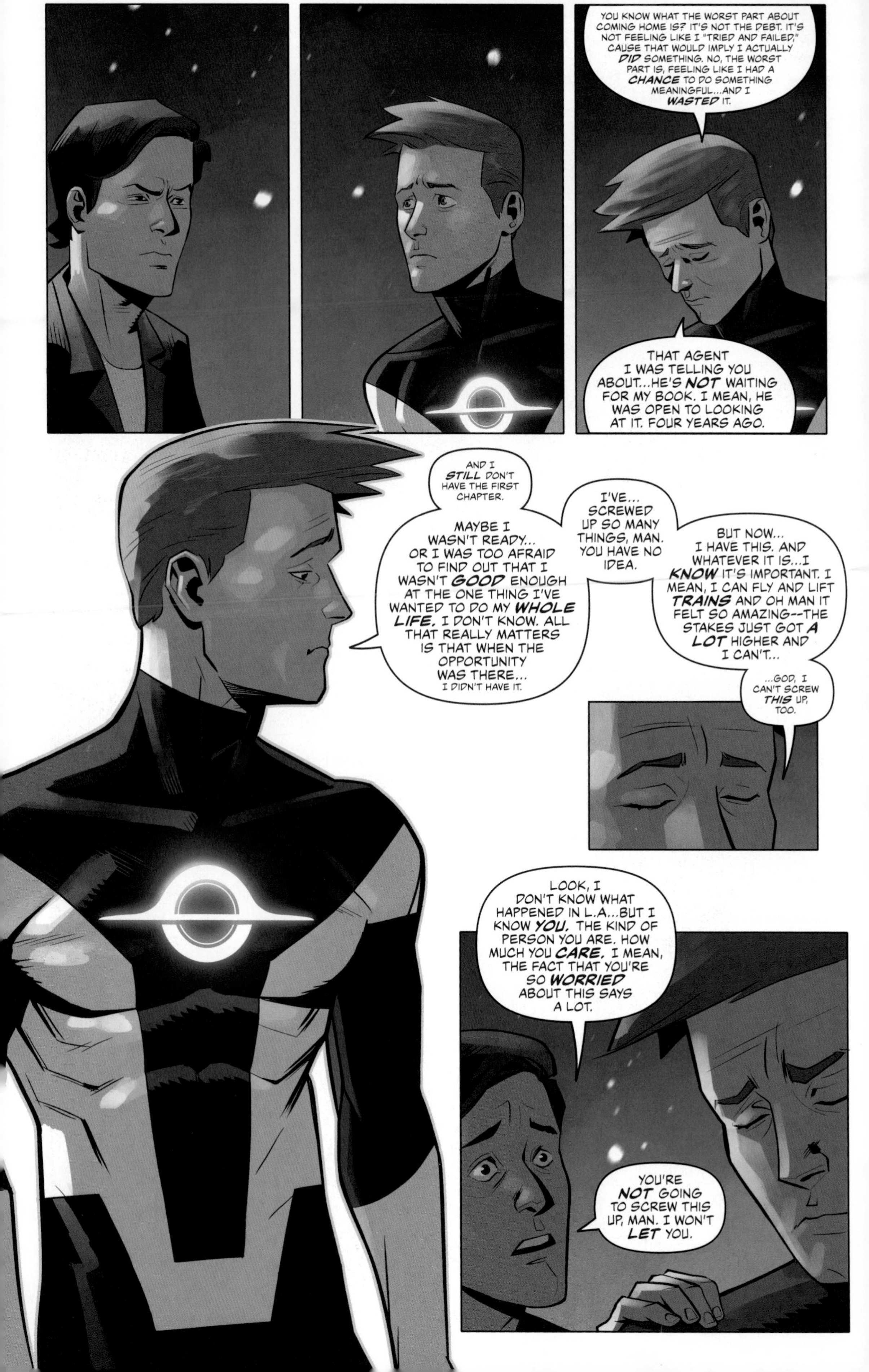
YOU KNOW WHAT THE WORST PART ABOUT COMING HOME IS? IT'S NOT THE DEBT. IT'S NOT FEELING LIKE I "TRIED AND FAILED," CAUSE THAT WOULD IMPLY I ACTUALLY DID SOMETHING. NO, THE WORST PART IS, FEELING LIKE I HAD A CHANCE TO DO SOMETHING MEANINGFUL...AND I WASTED IT.
THAT AGENT I WAS TELLING YOU ABOUT...HE'S NOT WAITING FOR MY BOOK. I MEAN, HE WAS OPEN TO LOOKING AT IT. FOUR YEARS AGO.
AND I STILL DON'T HAVE THE FIRST CHAPTER.
MAYBE I WASN'T READY... OR I WAS TOO AFRAID TO FIND OUT THAT I WASN'T GOOD ENOUGH AT THE ONE THING I'VE WANTED TO DO MY WHOLE LIFE. I DON'T KNOW. ALL THAT REALLY MATTERS IS THAT WHEN THE OPPORTUNITY WAS THERE... I DIDN'T HAVE IT.
I'VE... SCREWED UP SO MANY THINGS, MAN. YOU HAVE NO IDEA.
BUT NOW... I HAVE THIS. AND WHATEVER IT IS...I KNOW IT'S IMPORTANT. I MEAN, I CAN FLY AND LIFT TRAINS AND OH MAN IT FELT SO AMAZING--THE STAKES JUST GOT A LOT HIGHER AND I CAN'T...
...GOD, I CAN'T SCREW THIS UP, TOO.
LOOK, I DON'T KNOW WHAT HAPPENED IN L.A...BUT I KNOW YOU. THE KIND OF PERSON YOU ARE. HOW MUCH YOU CARE. I MEAN, THE FACT THAT YOU'RE SO WORRIED ABOUT THIS SAYS A LOT.
YOU'RE NOT GOING TO SCREW THIS UP, MAN. I WON'T LET YOU.

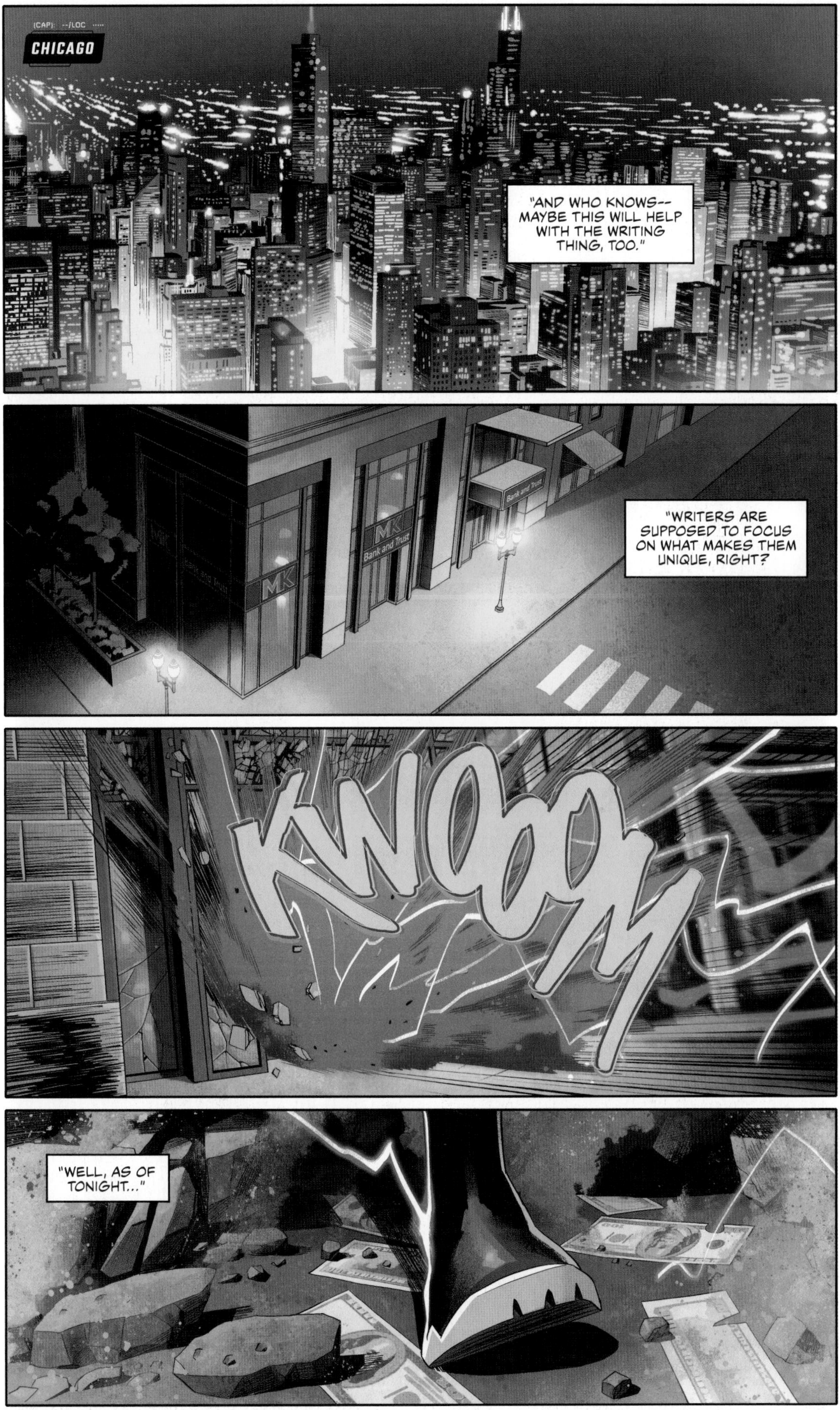
(CAP): --/LOC
CHICAGO
"AND WHO KNOWS-- MAYBE THIS WILL HELP WITH THE WRITING THING, TOO."
MK
Bank and Trust
"WRITERS ARE SUPPOSED TO FOCUS ON WHAT MAKES THEM UNIQUE, RIGHT?
KWOOOM
"WELL, AS OF TONIGHT..."

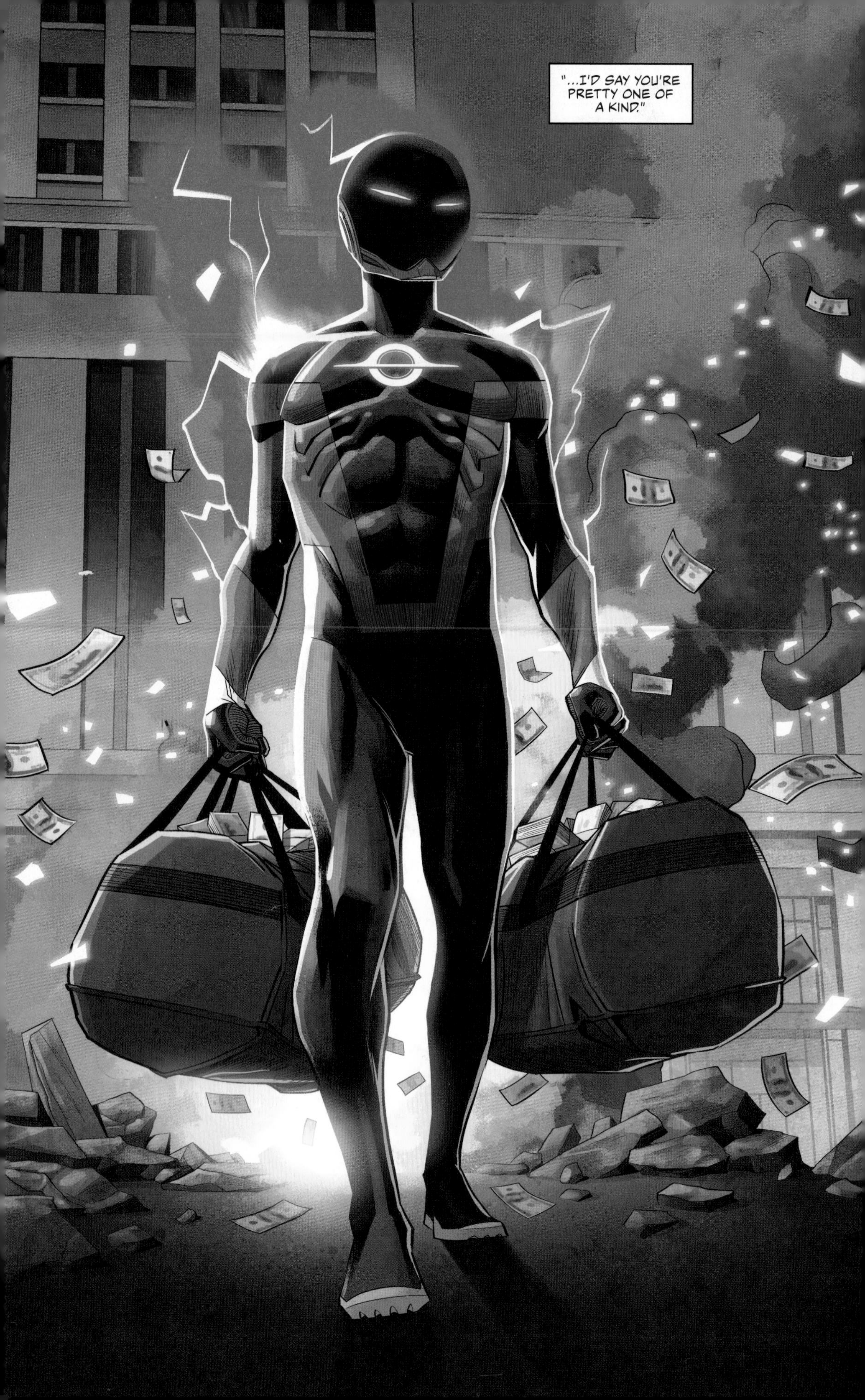
"...I'D SAY YOU'RE PRETTY ONE OF A KIND."

CHAPTER TWO

TITLE

Better Off Red

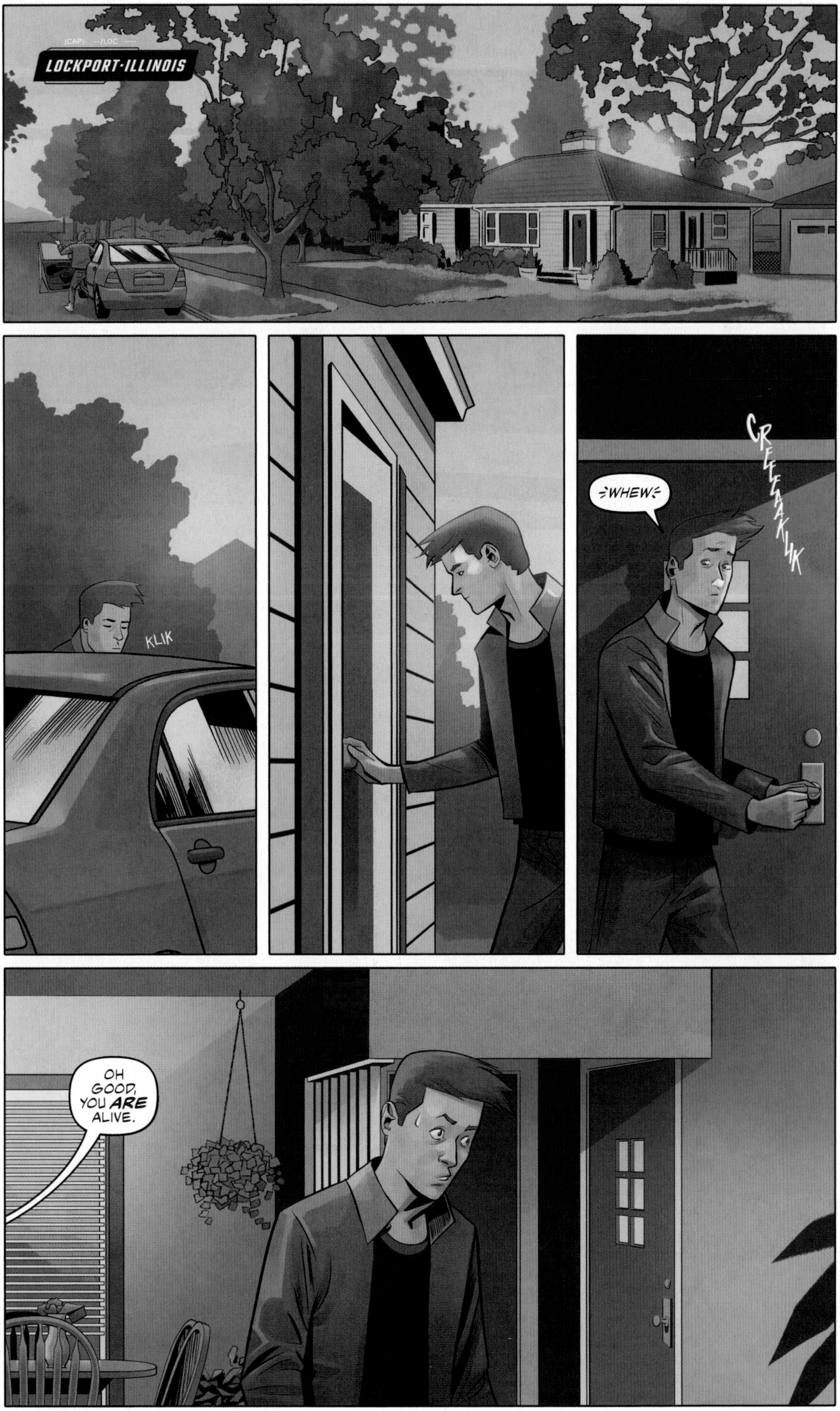

LOCKPORT·ILLINOIS
KLIK
CREEEAAKLIK
WHEW
OH GOOD, YOU **ARE** ALIVE.

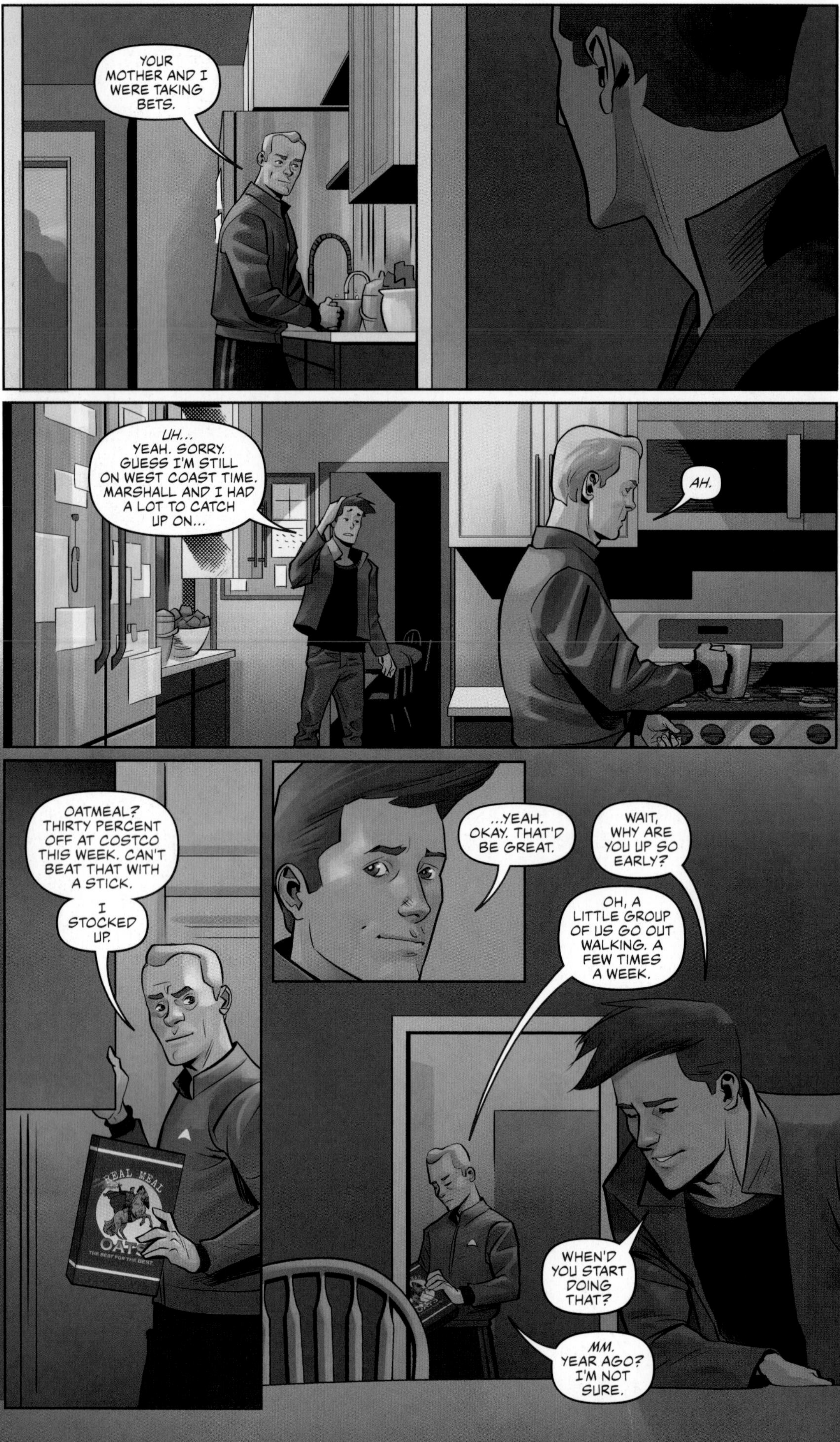
YOUR MOTHER AND I WERE TAKING BETS.
UH... YEAH. SORRY. GUESS I'M STILL ON WEST COAST TIME. MARSHALL AND I HAD A LOT TO CATCH UP ON...
AH.
OATMEAL? THIRTY PERCENT OFF AT COSTCO THIS WEEK. CAN'T BEAT THAT WITH A STICK.
I STOCKED UP.
REAL MEAL
OATS
THE BEST FOR THE BEST.
...YEAH. OKAY. THAT'D BE GREAT.
WAIT, WHY ARE YOU UP SO EARLY?
OH, A LITTLE GROUP OF US GO OUT WALKING. A FEW TIMES A WEEK.
WHEN'D YOU START DOING THAT?
MM. YEAR AGO? I'M NOT SURE.

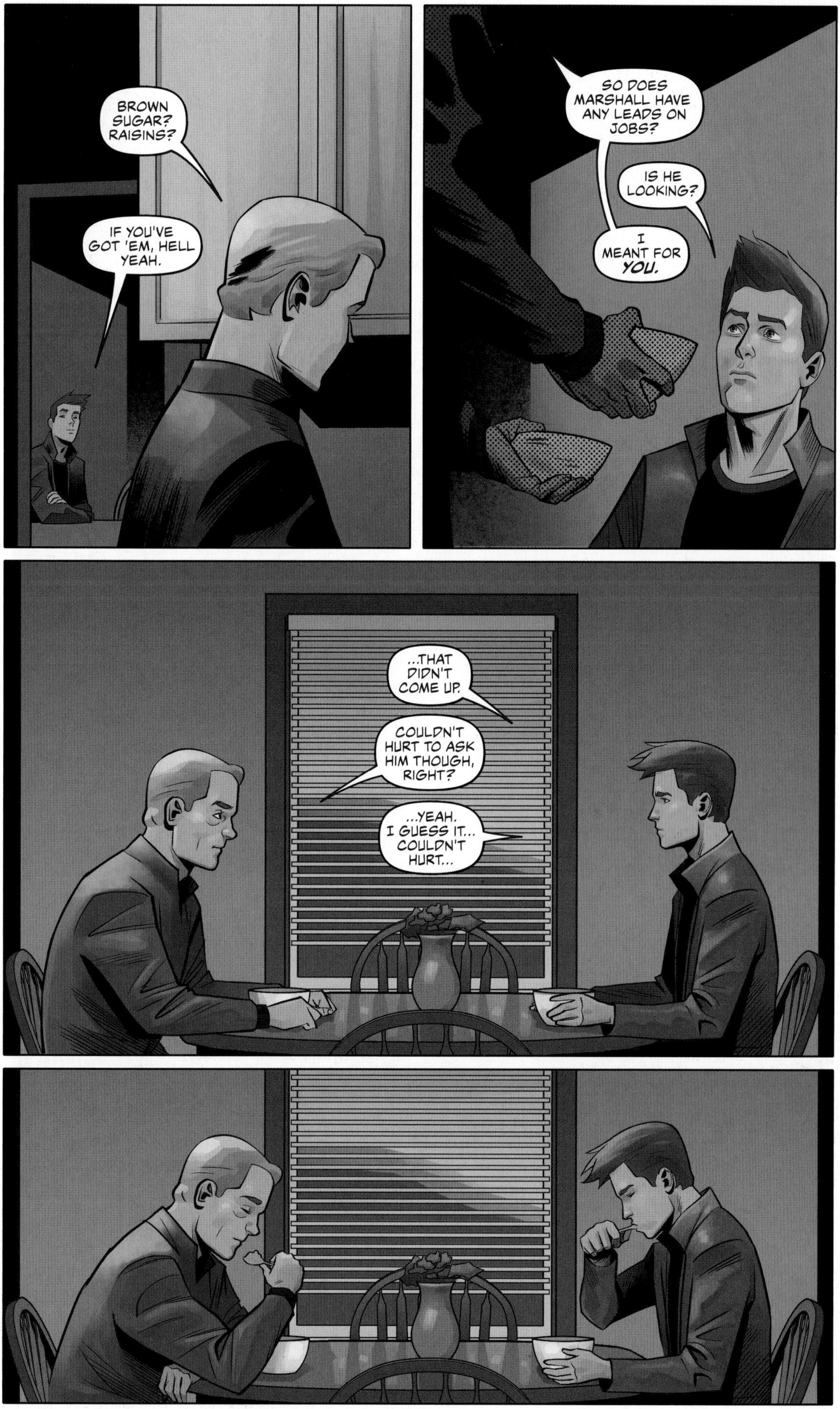

BROWN SUGAR? RAISINS?
IF YOU'VE GOT 'EM, HELL YEAH.
SO DOES MARSHALL HAVE ANY LEADS ON JOBS?
IS HE LOOKING?
I MEANT FOR *YOU.*
...THAT DIDN'T COME UP.
COULDN'T HURT TO ASK HIM THOUGH, RIGHT?
...YEAH. I GUESS IT... COULDN'T HURT...

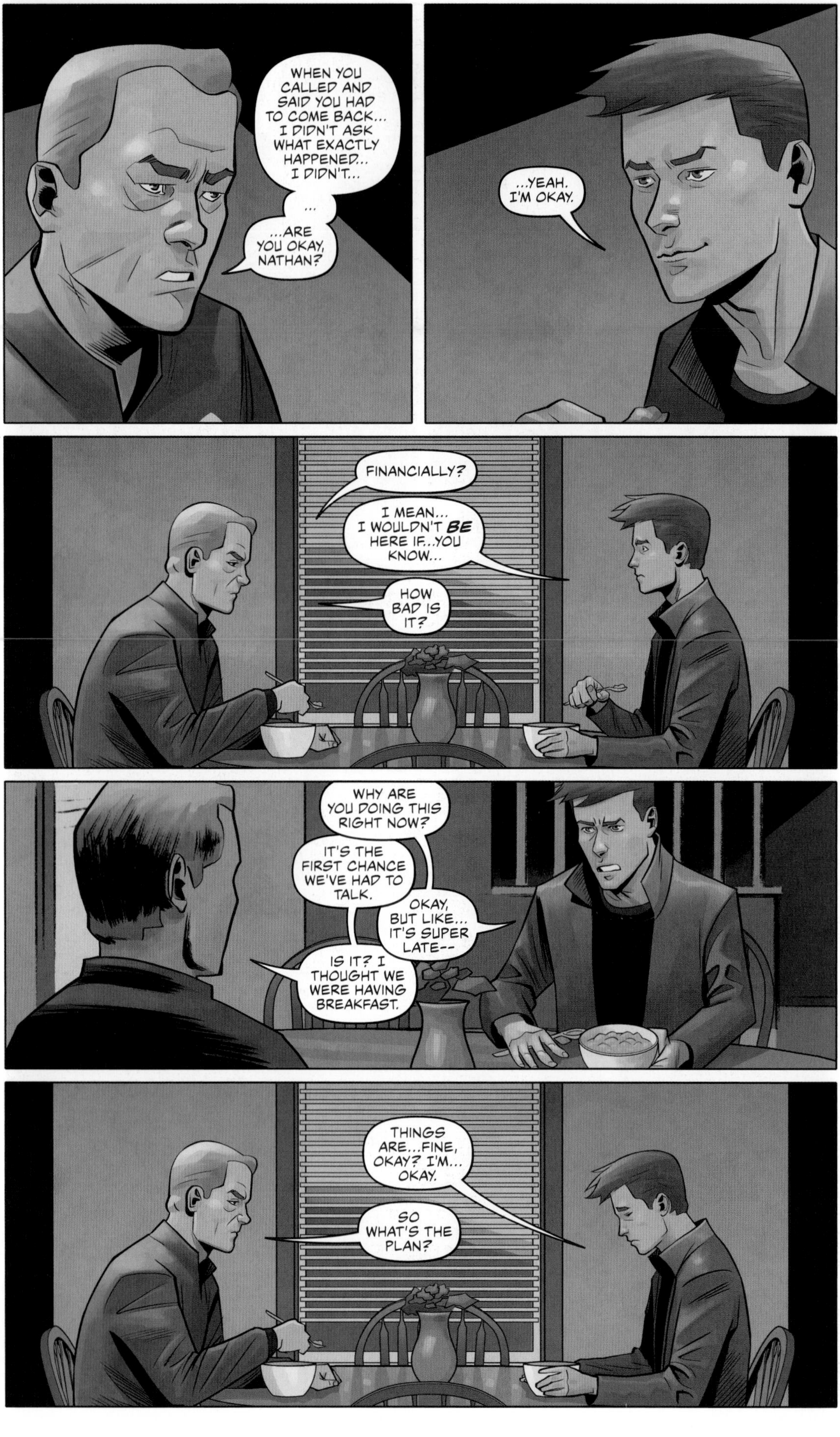
WHEN YOU CALLED AND SAID YOU HAD TO COME BACK... I DIDN'T ASK WHAT EXACTLY HAPPENED... I DIDN'T...
...
...ARE YOU OKAY, NATHAN?
...YEAH. I'M OKAY.
FINANCIALLY?
I MEAN... I WOULDN'T BE HERE IF...YOU KNOW...
HOW BAD IS IT?
WHY ARE YOU DOING THIS RIGHT NOW?
IT'S THE FIRST CHANCE WE'VE HAD TO TALK.
OKAY, BUT LIKE... IT'S SUPER LATE--
IS IT? I THOUGHT WE WERE HAVING BREAKFAST.
THINGS ARE...FINE, OKAY? I'M... OKAY.
SO WHAT'S THE PLAN?

HONESTLY, I DON'T KNOW YET BUT...

...WELL, SOMETHING PRETTY AMAZING HAPPENED TONIGHT. THIS OPPORTUNITY THAT JUST...CAME OUT OF NOWHERE. I DON'T KNOW. I THINK IF I PLAY MY CARDS RIGHT, I COULD REALLY DO SOMETHING THAT MEANS SOMETHING.

ANY IDEA WHAT IT PAYS?

WHAT? NO, IT... DOESN'T PAY.

SO, NO SOURCE OF INCOME.

NO, BUT THAT'S WHAT THE WRITING'S FOR.

BUT NO ONE'S **PAYING** YOU FOR THAT.

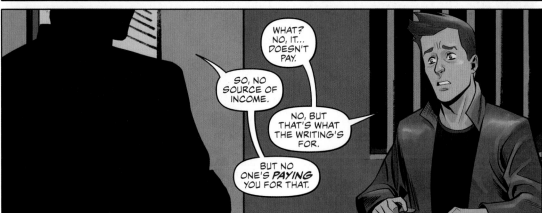

HEY, I'M JUST STATING FACTS. ONE DAY, HOPEFULLY THAT WILL CHANGE. BUT RIGHT NOW...NO ONE'S **ACTUALLY** PAYING YOU TO WRITE, ARE THEY?

...NO, THEY'RE **NOT**.

HENCE MY ORIGINAL QUESTION. DO YOU THINK YOU'RE THE FIRST PERSON WHO HAS TO WORK A JOB THEY DON'T WANT? NOTHING WORTHWHILE COMES FROM A SHORTCUT, NATHAN.

AND SO WHAT **EXACTLY** DO YOU PROPOSE I DO?

YOU WERE DRIVING FOR THAT COMPANY--

DRIVR?!

YOU CAN DO THAT HERE, CAN'T YOU?

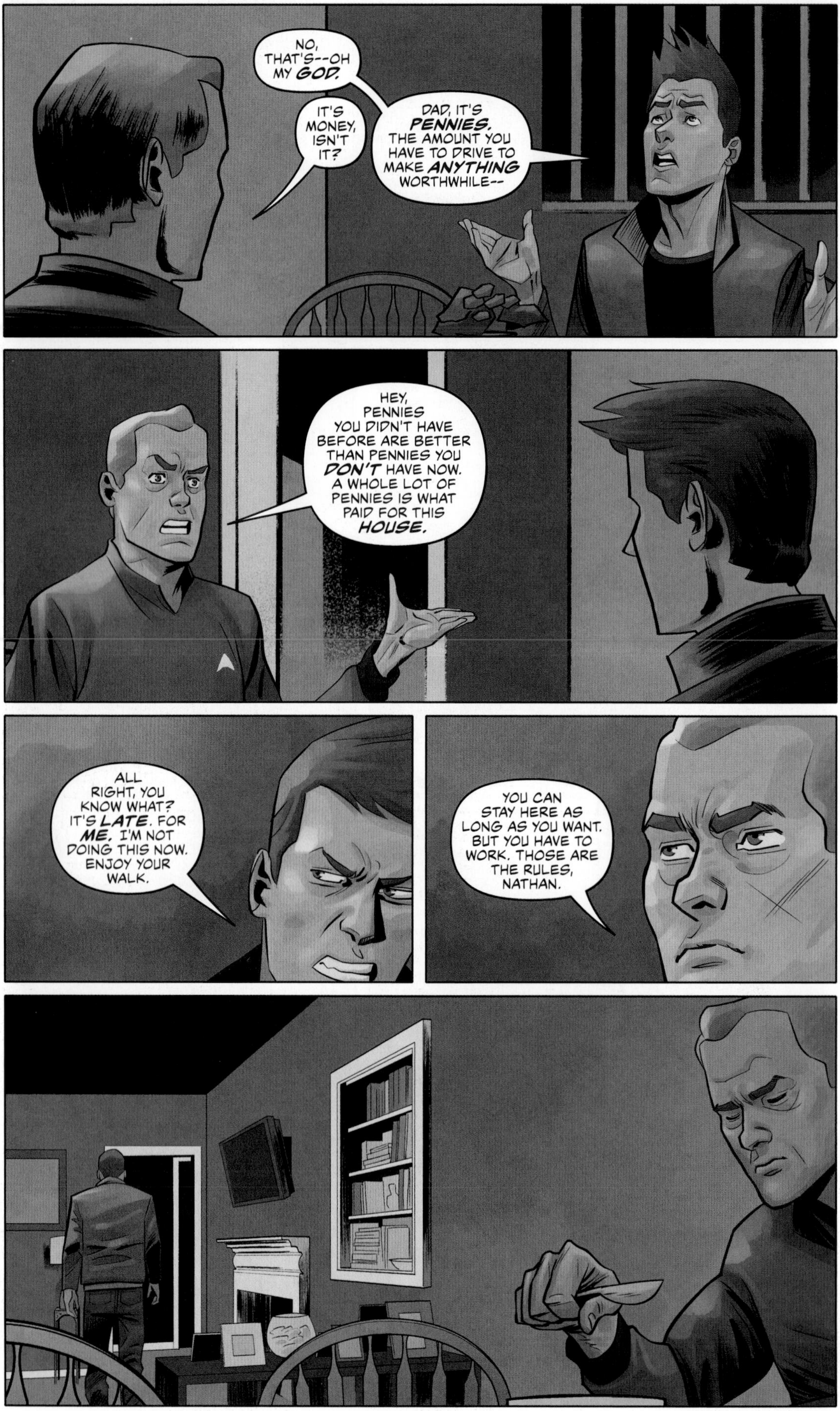

NO, THAT'S--OH MY GOD.
IT'S MONEY, ISN'T IT?
DAD, IT'S PENNIES. THE AMOUNT YOU HAVE TO DRIVE TO MAKE ANYTHING WORTHWHILE--
HEY, PENNIES YOU DIDN'T HAVE BEFORE ARE BETTER THAN PENNIES YOU DON'T HAVE NOW. A WHOLE LOT OF PENNIES IS WHAT PAID FOR THIS HOUSE.
ALL RIGHT, YOU KNOW WHAT? IT'S LATE. FOR ME. I'M NOT DOING THIS NOW. ENJOY YOUR WALK.
YOU CAN STAY HERE AS LONG AS YOU WANT. BUT YOU HAVE TO WORK. THOSE ARE THE RULES, NATHAN.

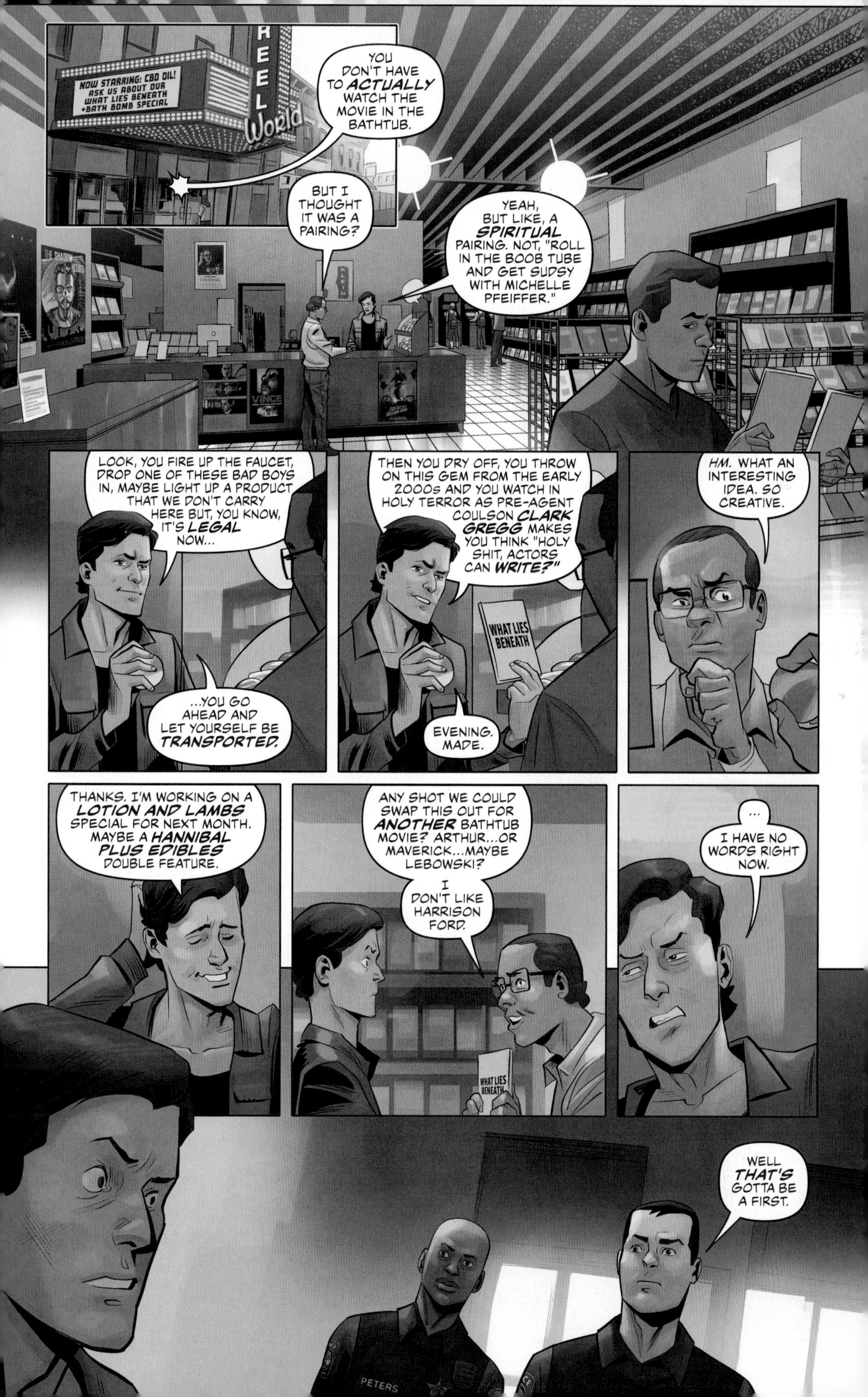
NOW STARRING: CBD OIL! ASK US ABOUT OUR WHAT LIES BENEATH +BATH BOMB SPECIAL
REEL World
YOU DON'T HAVE TO ACTUALLY WATCH THE MOVIE IN THE BATHTUB.
BUT I THOUGHT IT WAS A PAIRING?
YEAH, BUT LIKE, A SPIRITUAL PAIRING. NOT, "ROLL IN THE BOOB TUBE AND GET SUDSY WITH MICHELLE PFEIFFER."
VINCE
LOOK, YOU FIRE UP THE FAUCET, DROP ONE OF THESE BAD BOYS IN, MAYBE LIGHT UP A PRODUCT THAT WE DON'T CARRY HERE BUT, YOU KNOW, IT'S LEGAL NOW...
...YOU GO AHEAD AND LET YOURSELF BE TRANSPORTED.
THEN YOU DRY OFF, YOU THROW ON THIS GEM FROM THE EARLY 2000s AND YOU WATCH IN HOLY TERROR AS PRE-AGENT COULSON CLARK GREGG MAKES YOU THINK "HOLY SHIT, ACTORS CAN WRITE?"
WHAT LIES BENEATH
EVENING. MADE.
HM. WHAT AN INTERESTING IDEA. SO CREATIVE.
THANKS. I'M WORKING ON A LOTION AND LAMBS SPECIAL FOR NEXT MONTH. MAYBE A HANNIBAL PLUS EDIBLES DOUBLE FEATURE.
ANY SHOT WE COULD SWAP THIS OUT FOR ANOTHER BATHTUB MOVIE? ARTHUR...OR MAVERICK...MAYBE LEBOWSKI?
I DON'T LIKE HARRISON FORD.
WHAT LIES BENEATH
...
I HAVE NO WORDS RIGHT NOW.
WELL THAT'S GOTTA BE A FIRST.
PETERS

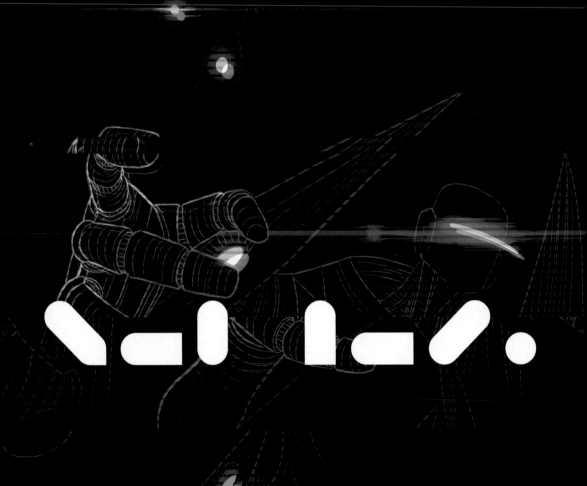

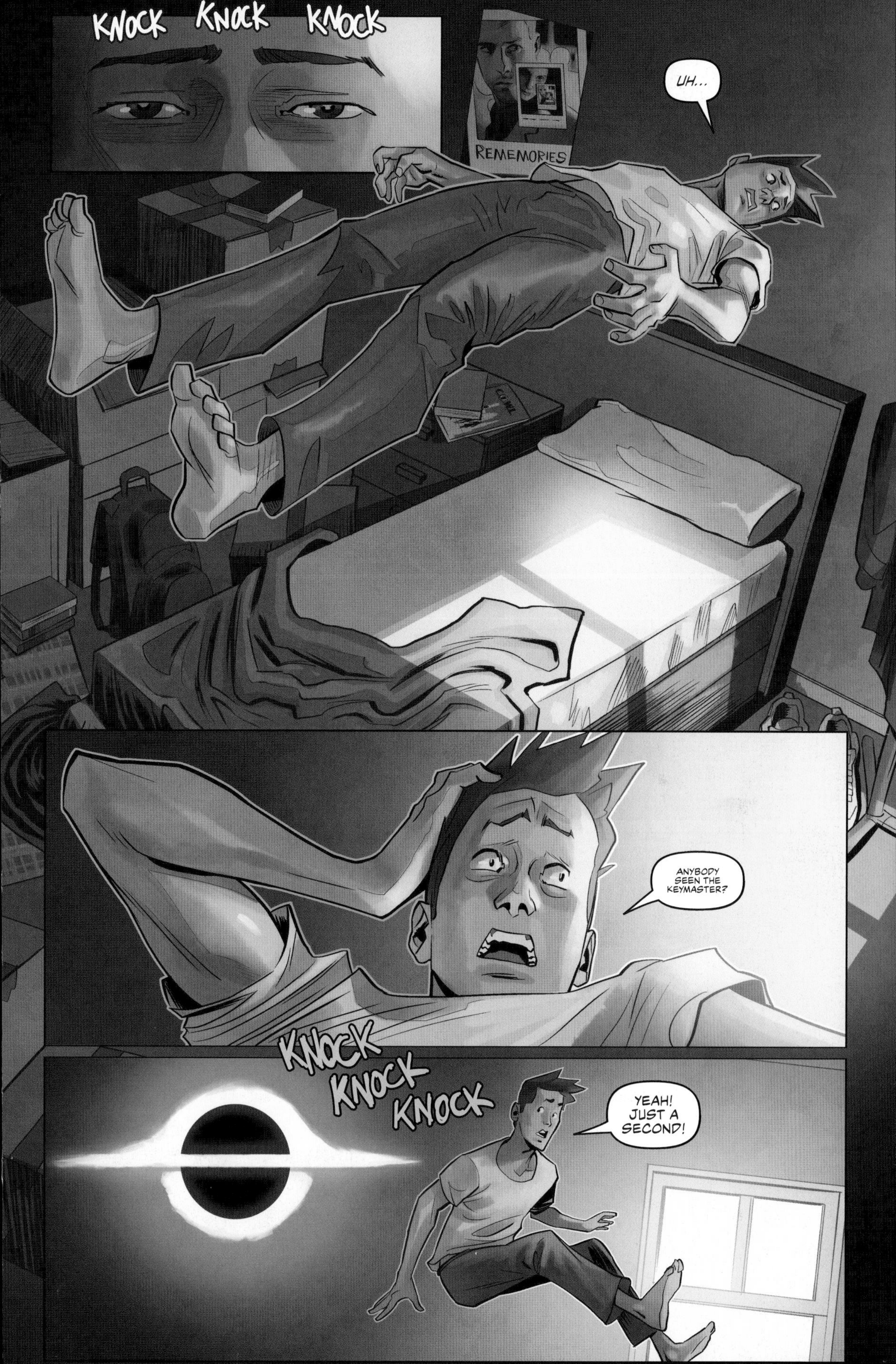
KNOCK KNOCK KNOCK
REMEMORIES
UH...
ANYBODY SEEN THE KEYMASTER?
KNOCK KNOCK KNOCK
YEAH! JUST A SECOND!

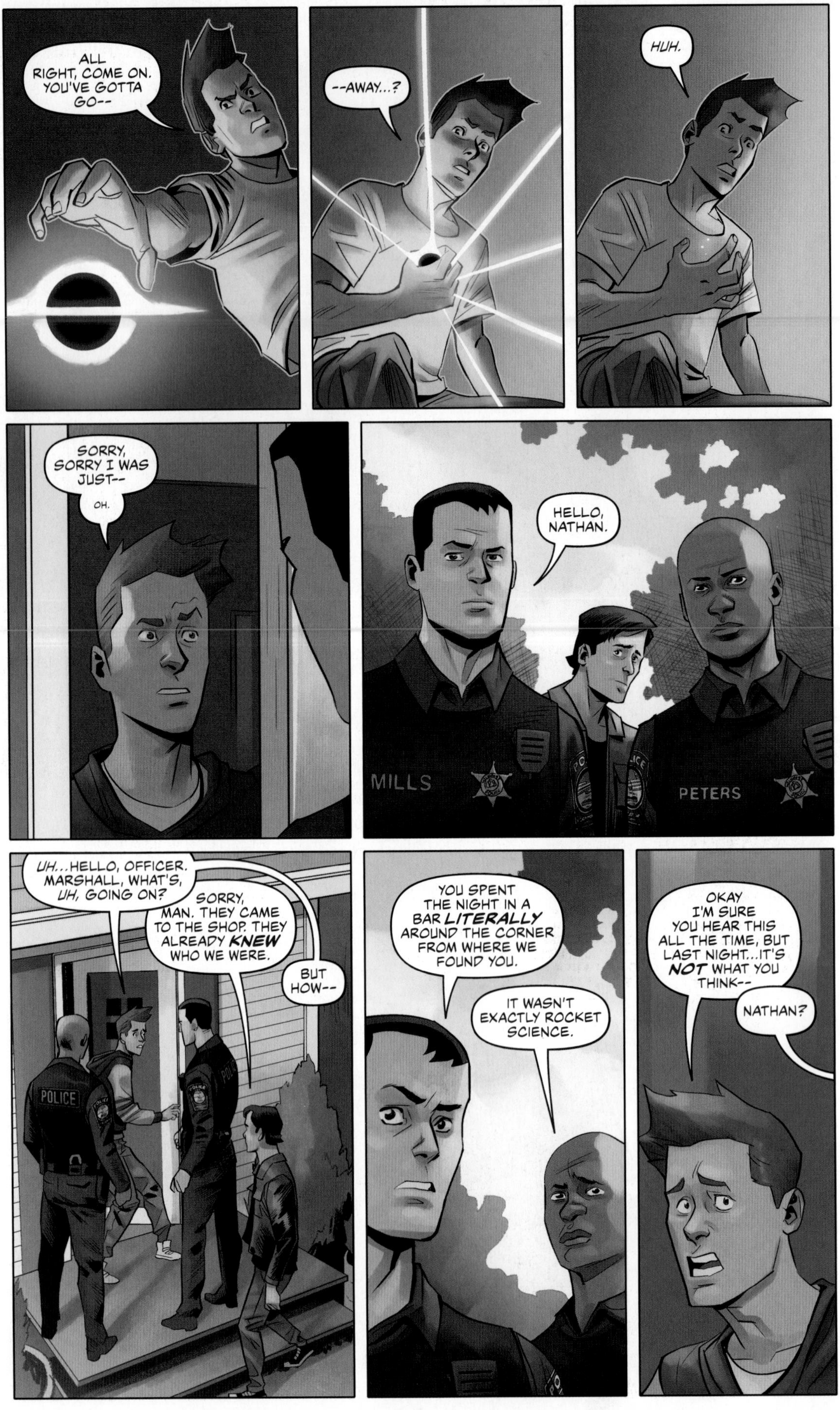
ALL RIGHT, COME ON. YOU'VE GOTTA GO--
--AWAY...?
HUH.
SORRY, SORRY I WAS JUST--
OH.
HELLO, NATHAN.
MILLS
PETERS
UH... HELLO, OFFICER. MARSHALL, WHAT'S, UH, GOING ON?
SORRY, MAN. THEY CAME TO THE SHOP. THEY ALREADY KNEW WHO WE WERE.
BUT HOW--
POLICE
YOU SPENT THE NIGHT IN A BAR LITERALLY AROUND THE CORNER FROM WHERE WE FOUND YOU.
IT WASN'T EXACTLY ROCKET SCIENCE.
OKAY I'M SURE YOU HEAR THIS ALL THE TIME, BUT LAST NIGHT... IT'S NOT WHAT YOU THINK--
NATHAN?

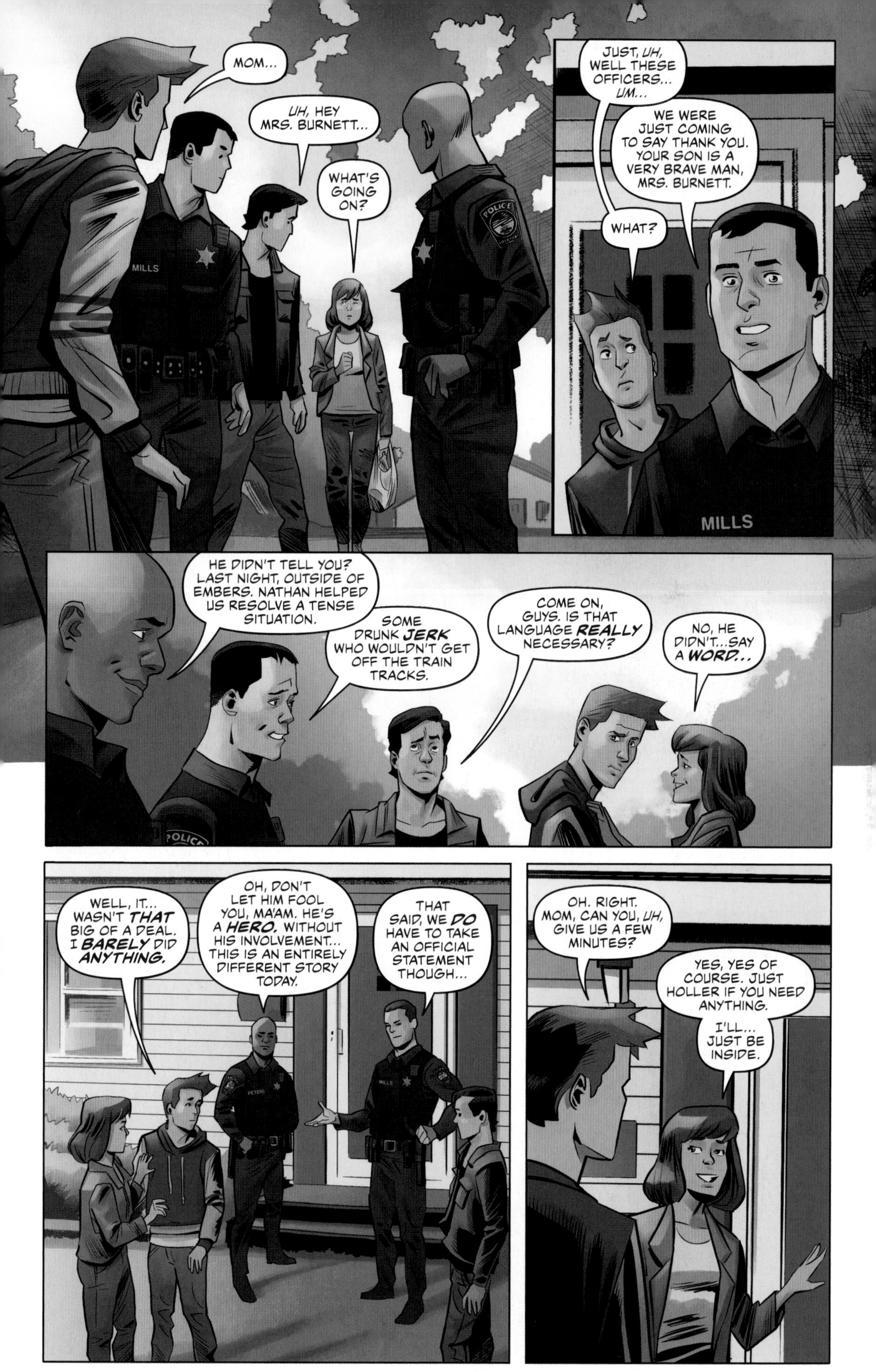
MOM...
UH, HEY MRS. BURNETT...
WHAT'S GOING ON?
MILLS
JUST, UH, WELL THESE OFFICERS... UM...
WE WERE JUST COMING TO SAY THANK YOU. YOUR SON IS A VERY BRAVE MAN, MRS. BURNETT.
WHAT?
MILLS
HE DIDN'T TELL YOU? LAST NIGHT, OUTSIDE OF EMBERS. NATHAN HELPED US RESOLVE A TENSE SITUATION.
SOME DRUNK JERK WHO WOULDN'T GET OFF THE TRAIN TRACKS.
COME ON, GUYS. IS THAT LANGUAGE REALLY NECESSARY?
NO, HE DIDN'T...SAY A WORD...
POLICE
WELL, IT... WASN'T THAT BIG OF A DEAL. I BARELY DID ANYTHING.
OH, DON'T LET HIM FOOL YOU, MA'AM. HE'S A HERO. WITHOUT HIS INVOLVEMENT... THIS IS AN ENTIRELY DIFFERENT STORY TODAY.
THAT SAID, WE DO HAVE TO TAKE AN OFFICIAL STATEMENT THOUGH...
PETERS
MILLS
OH. RIGHT. MOM, CAN YOU, UH, GIVE US A FEW MINUTES?
YES, YES OF COURSE. JUST HOLLER IF YOU NEED ANYTHING.
I'LL... JUST BE INSIDE.

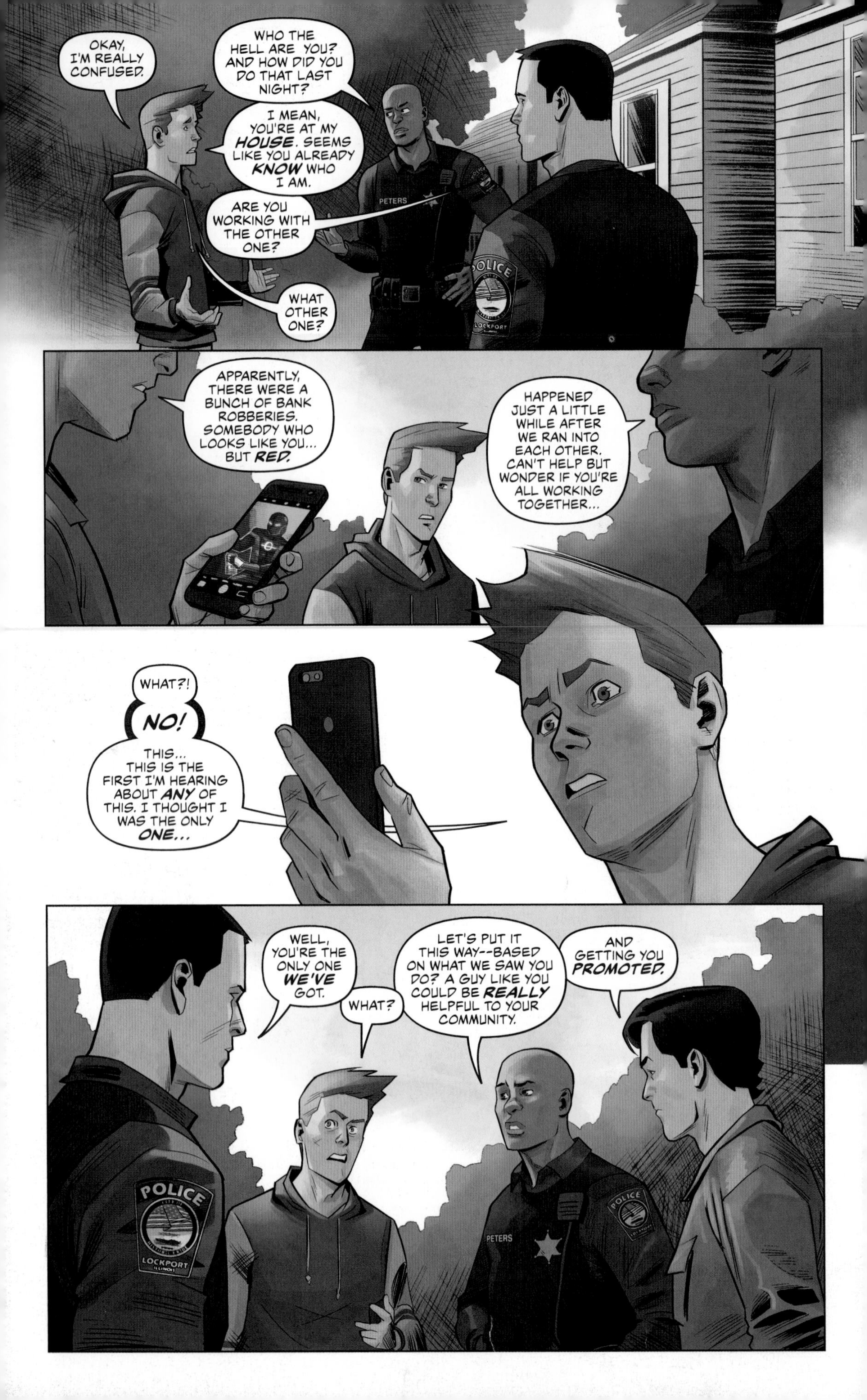
OKAY, I'M REALLY CONFUSED.
WHO THE HELL ARE YOU? AND HOW DID YOU DO THAT LAST NIGHT?
I MEAN, YOU'RE AT MY HOUSE. SEEMS LIKE YOU ALREADY KNOW WHO I AM.
PETERS
ARE YOU WORKING WITH THE OTHER ONE?
POLICE
LOCKPORT
WHAT OTHER ONE?
APPARENTLY, THERE WERE A BUNCH OF BANK ROBBERIES. SOMEBODY WHO LOOKS LIKE YOU... BUT RED.
HAPPENED JUST A LITTLE WHILE AFTER WE RAN INTO EACH OTHER. CAN'T HELP BUT WONDER IF YOU'RE ALL WORKING TOGETHER...
WHAT?!
NO!
THIS... THIS IS THE FIRST I'M HEARING ABOUT ANY OF THIS. I THOUGHT I WAS THE ONLY ONE...
WELL, YOU'RE THE ONLY ONE WE'VE GOT.
WHAT?
LET'S PUT IT THIS WAY--BASED ON WHAT WE SAW YOU DO? A GUY LIKE YOU COULD BE REALLY HELPFUL TO YOUR COMMUNITY.
AND GETTING YOU PROMOTED.
POLICE
LOCKPORT
PETERS
POLICE

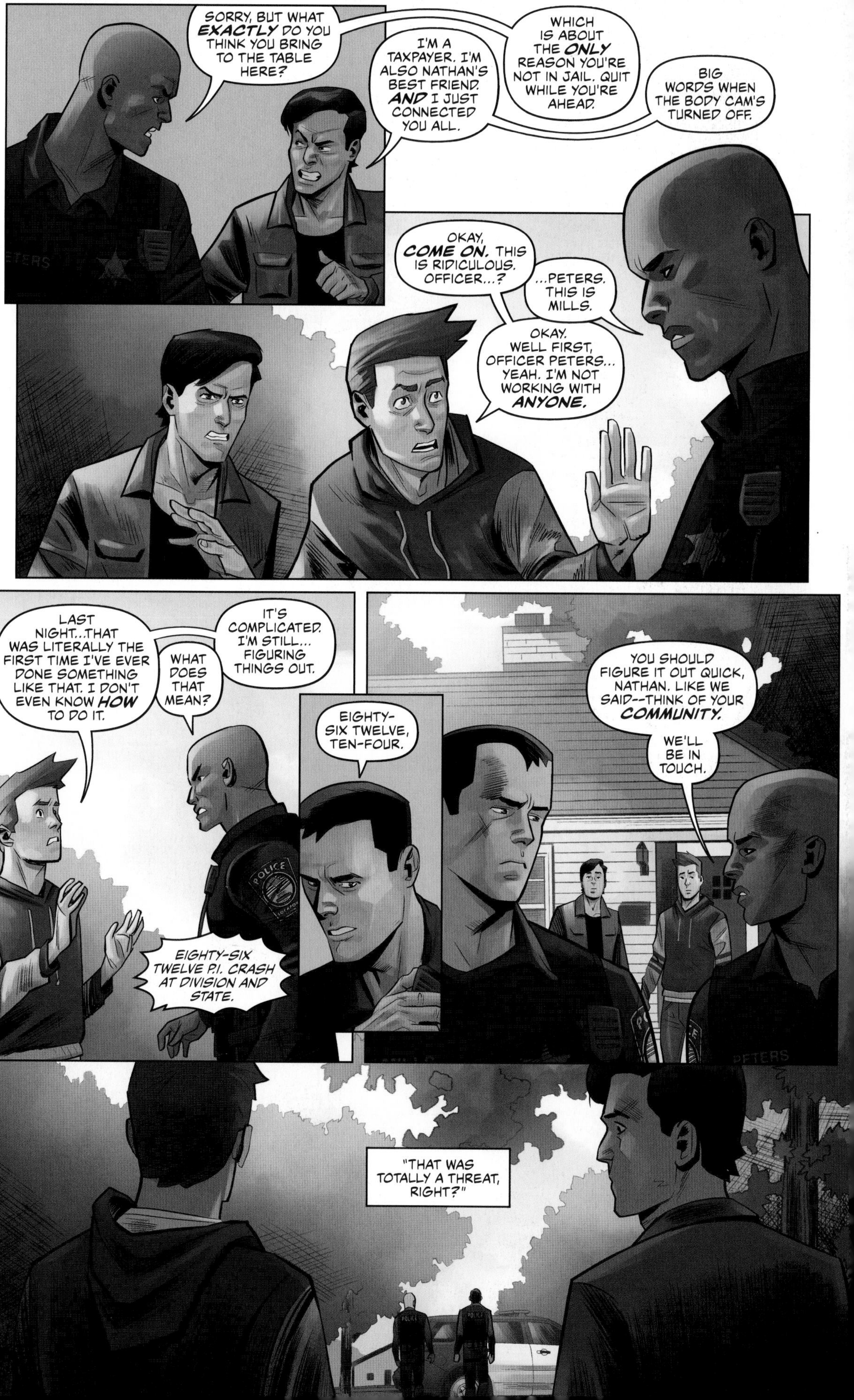
SORRY, BUT WHAT EXACTLY DO YOU THINK YOU BRING TO THE TABLE HERE?
I'M A TAXPAYER. I'M ALSO NATHAN'S BEST FRIEND. AND I JUST CONNECTED YOU ALL.
WHICH IS ABOUT THE ONLY REASON YOU'RE NOT IN JAIL. QUIT WHILE YOU'RE AHEAD.
BIG WORDS WHEN THE BODY CAM'S TURNED OFF.
PETERS
OKAY, COME ON. THIS IS RIDICULOUS. OFFICER...?
...PETERS. THIS IS MILLS.
OKAY. WELL FIRST, OFFICER PETERS... YEAH. I'M NOT WORKING WITH ANYONE.
LAST NIGHT...THAT WAS LITERALLY THE FIRST TIME I'VE EVER DONE SOMETHING LIKE THAT. I DON'T EVEN KNOW HOW TO DO IT.
WHAT DOES THAT MEAN?
IT'S COMPLICATED. I'M STILL... FIGURING THINGS OUT.
POLICE
EIGHTY-SIX TWELVE P.I. CRASH AT DIVISION AND STATE.
EIGHTY-SIX TWELVE, TEN-FOUR.
YOU SHOULD FIGURE IT OUT QUICK, NATHAN. LIKE WE SAID--THINK OF YOUR COMMUNITY.
WE'LL BE IN TOUCH.
PETERS
"THAT WAS TOTALLY A THREAT, RIGHT?"

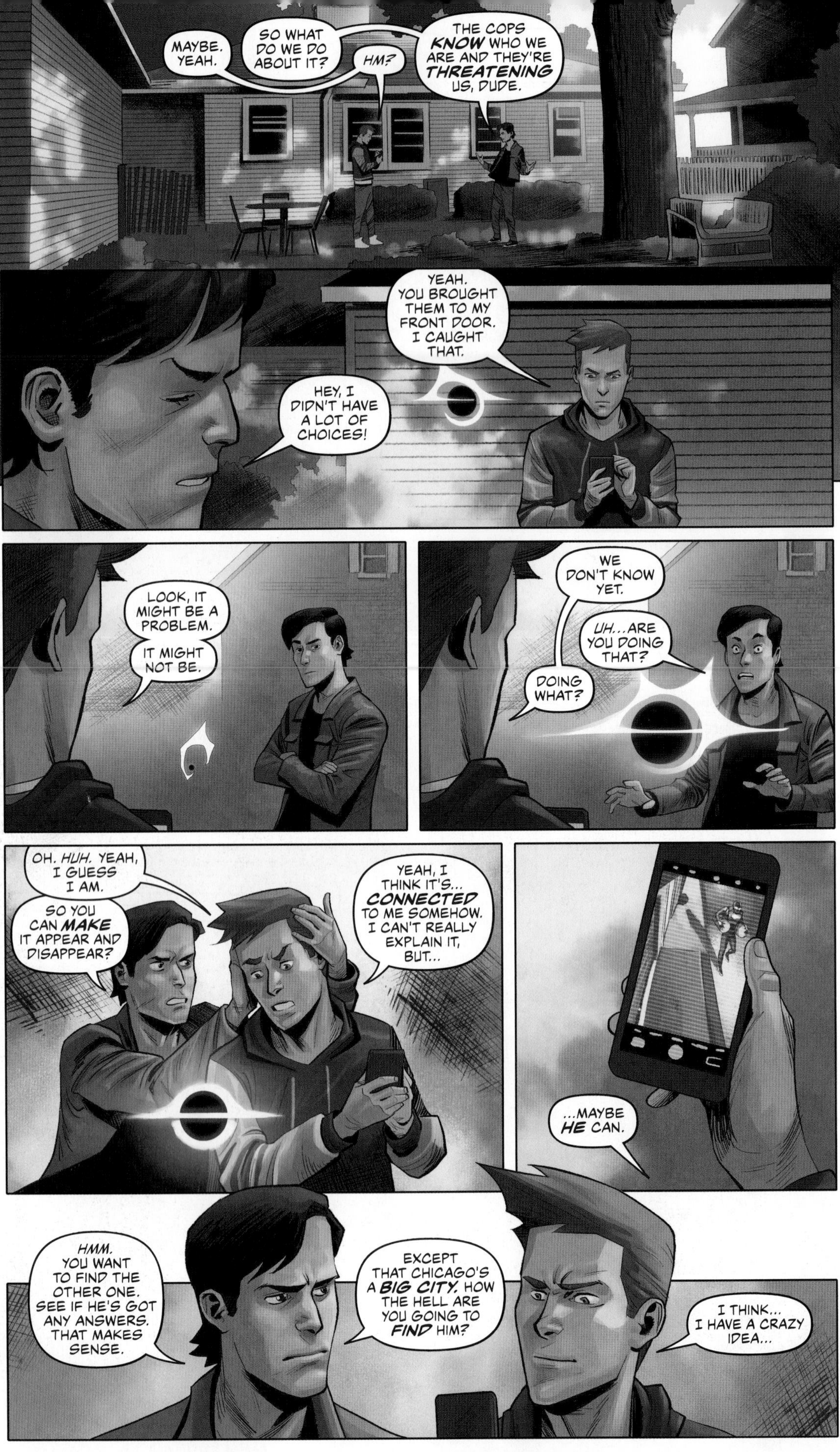
MAYBE. YEAH.
SO WHAT DO WE DO ABOUT IT?
HM?
THE COPS KNOW WHO WE ARE AND THEY'RE THREATENING US, DUDE.
YEAH. YOU BROUGHT THEM TO MY FRONT DOOR. I CAUGHT THAT.
HEY, I DIDN'T HAVE A LOT OF CHOICES!
LOOK, IT MIGHT BE A PROBLEM.
IT MIGHT NOT BE.
WE DON'T KNOW YET.
UH...ARE YOU DOING THAT?
DOING WHAT?
OH. HUH. YEAH, I GUESS I AM.
SO YOU CAN MAKE IT APPEAR AND DISAPPEAR?
YEAH, I THINK IT'S... CONNECTED TO ME SOMEHOW. I CAN'T REALLY EXPLAIN IT, BUT...
...MAYBE HE CAN.
HMM. YOU WANT TO FIND THE OTHER ONE. SEE IF HE'S GOT ANY ANSWERS. THAT MAKES SENSE.
EXCEPT THAT CHICAGO'S A BIG CITY. HOW THE HELL ARE YOU GOING TO FIND HIM?
I THINK... I HAVE A CRAZY IDEA...

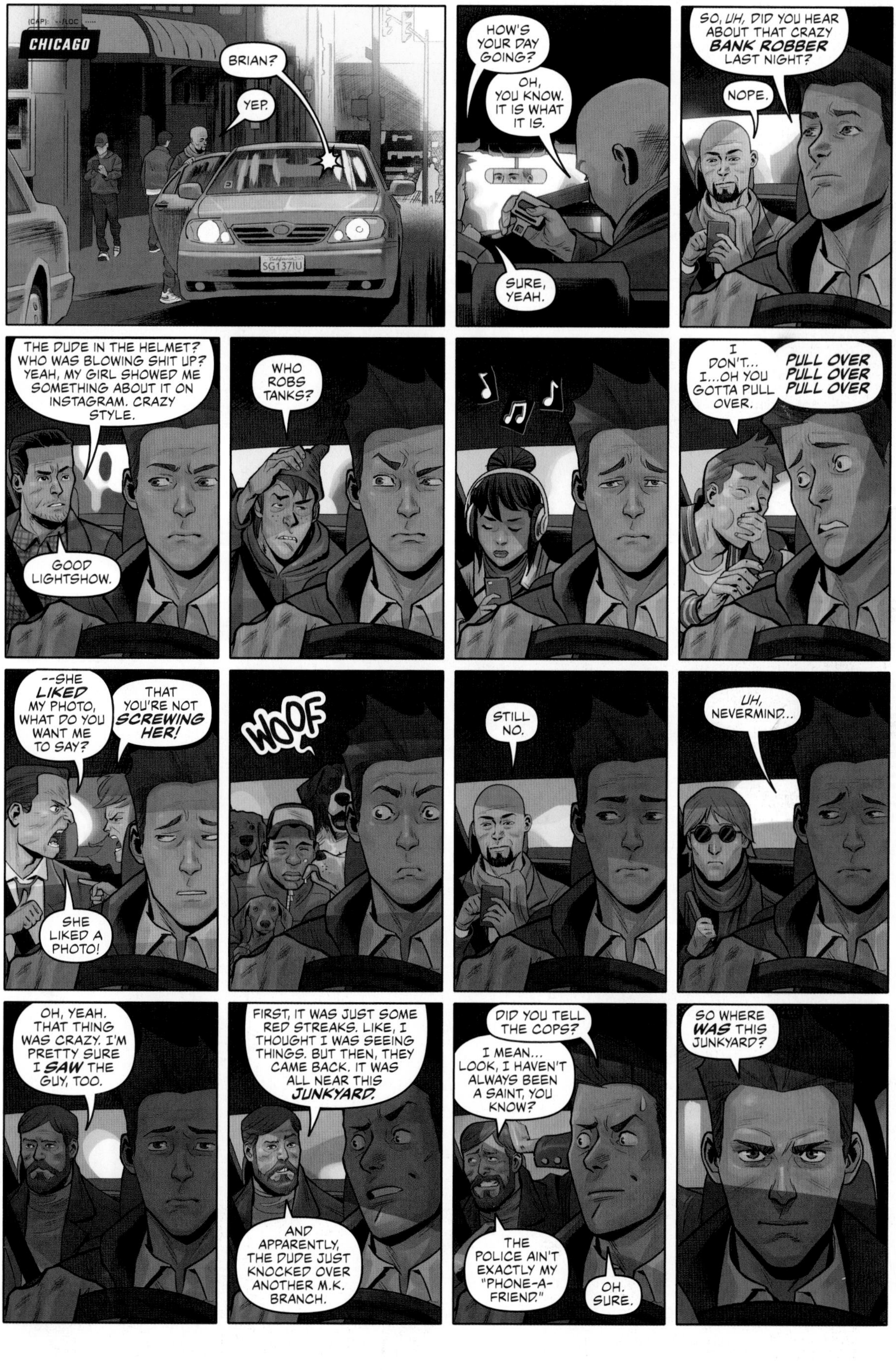
CHICAGO
BRIAN?
YEP.
HOW'S YOUR DAY GOING?
OH, YOU KNOW. IT IS WHAT IT IS.
SURE, YEAH.
SO, UH, DID YOU HEAR ABOUT THAT CRAZY BANK ROBBER LAST NIGHT?
NOPE.
THE DUDE IN THE HELMET? WHO WAS BLOWING SHIT UP? YEAH, MY GIRL SHOWED ME SOMETHING ABOUT IT ON INSTAGRAM. CRAZY STYLE.
GOOD LIGHTSHOW.
WHO ROBS TANKS?
I DON'T... I...OH YOU GOTTA PULL OVER.
PULL OVER PULL OVER PULL OVER
--SHE LIKED MY PHOTO, WHAT DO YOU WANT ME TO SAY?
THAT YOU'RE NOT SCREWING HER!
SHE LIKED A PHOTO!
WOOF
STILL NO.
UH, NEVERMIND...
OH, YEAH. THAT THING WAS CRAZY. I'M PRETTY SURE I SAW THE GUY, TOO.
FIRST, IT WAS JUST SOME RED STREAKS. LIKE, I THOUGHT I WAS SEEING THINGS. BUT THEN, THEY CAME BACK. IT WAS ALL NEAR THIS JUNKYARD.
AND APPARENTLY, THE DUDE JUST KNOCKED OVER ANOTHER M.K. BRANCH.
DID YOU TELL THE COPS?
I MEAN... LOOK, I HAVEN'T ALWAYS BEEN A SAINT, YOU KNOW?
THE POLICE AIN'T EXACTLY MY "PHONE-A-FRIEND."
OH. SURE.
SO WHERE WAS THIS JUNKYARD?

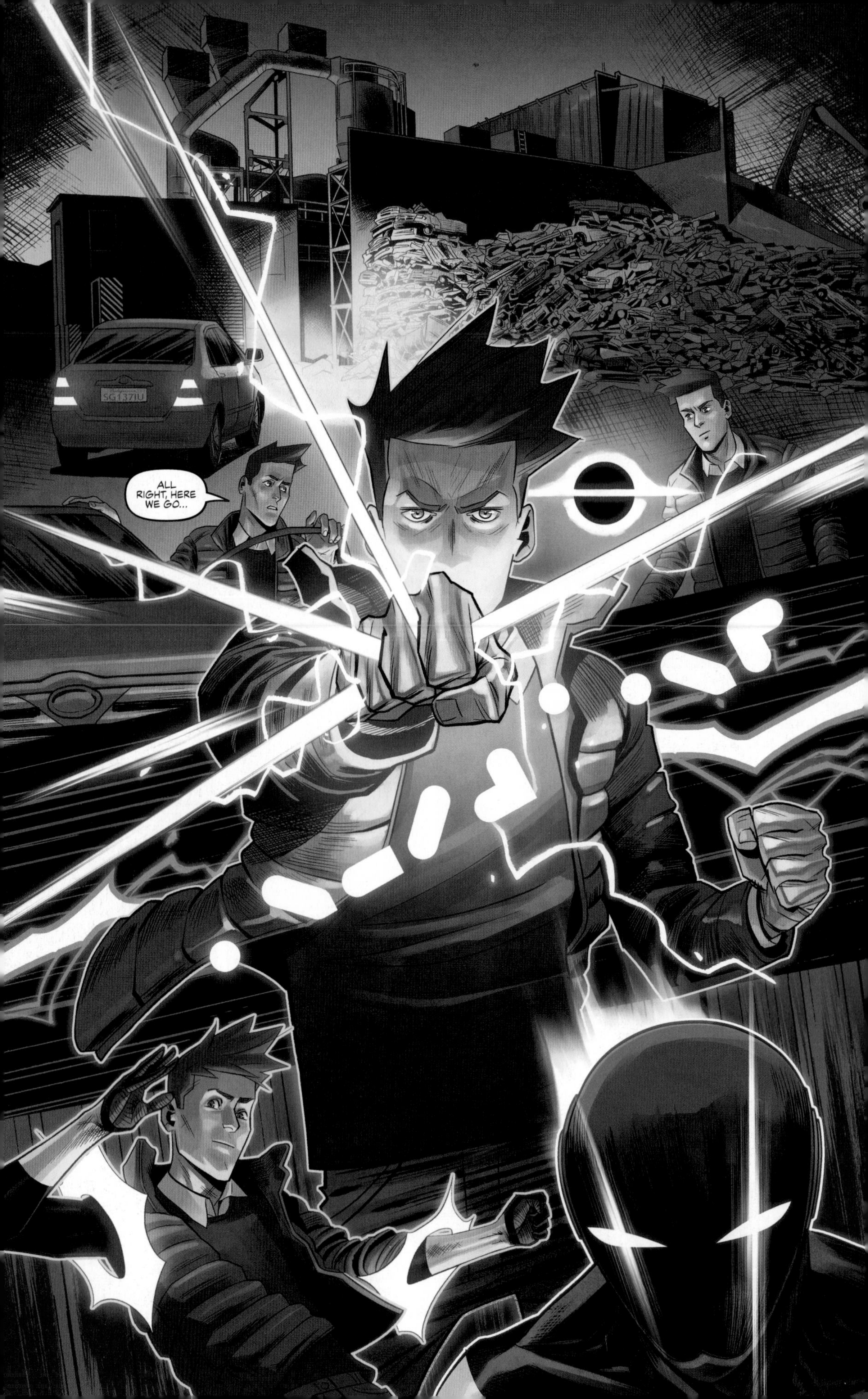
ALL RIGHT, HERE WE GO...

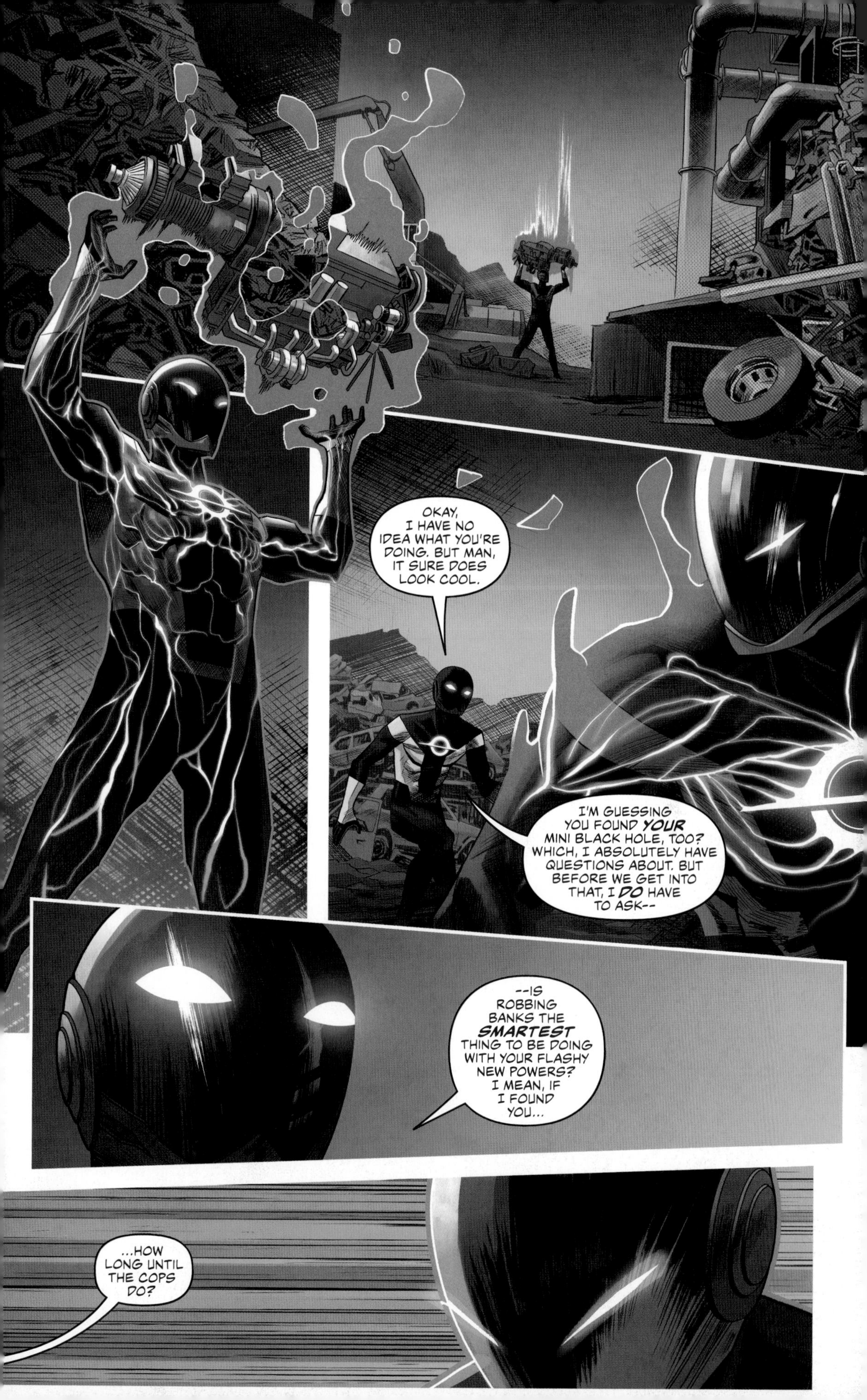
OKAY, I HAVE NO IDEA WHAT YOU'RE DOING. BUT MAN, IT SURE DOES LOOK COOL.
I'M GUESSING YOU FOUND YOUR MINI BLACK HOLE, TOO? WHICH, I ABSOLUTELY HAVE QUESTIONS ABOUT. BUT BEFORE WE GET INTO THAT, I DO HAVE TO ASK--
--IS ROBBING BANKS THE SMARTEST THING TO BE DOING WITH YOUR FLASHY NEW POWERS? I MEAN, IF I FOUND YOU...
...HOW LONG UNTIL THE COPS DO?

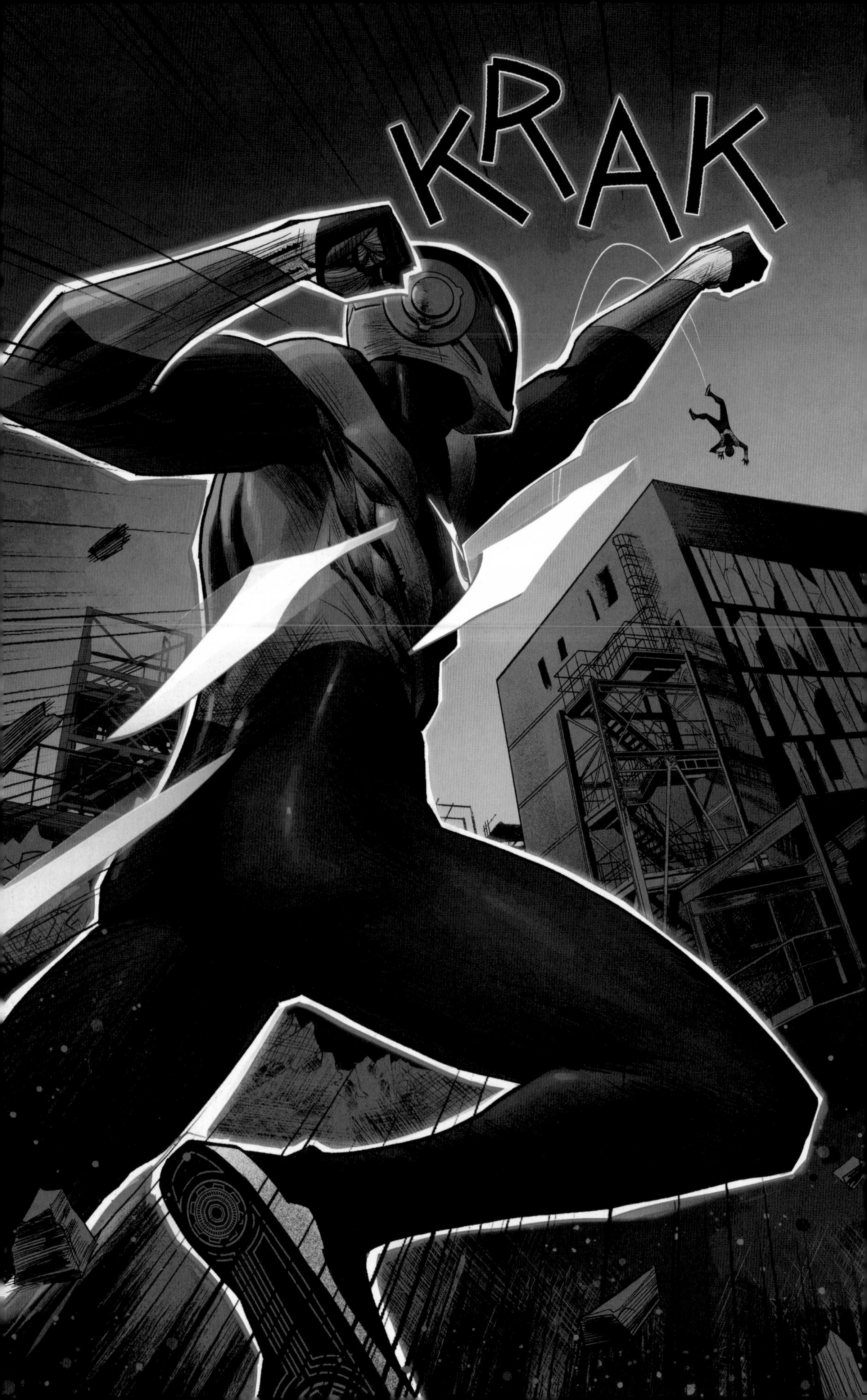
KRAK

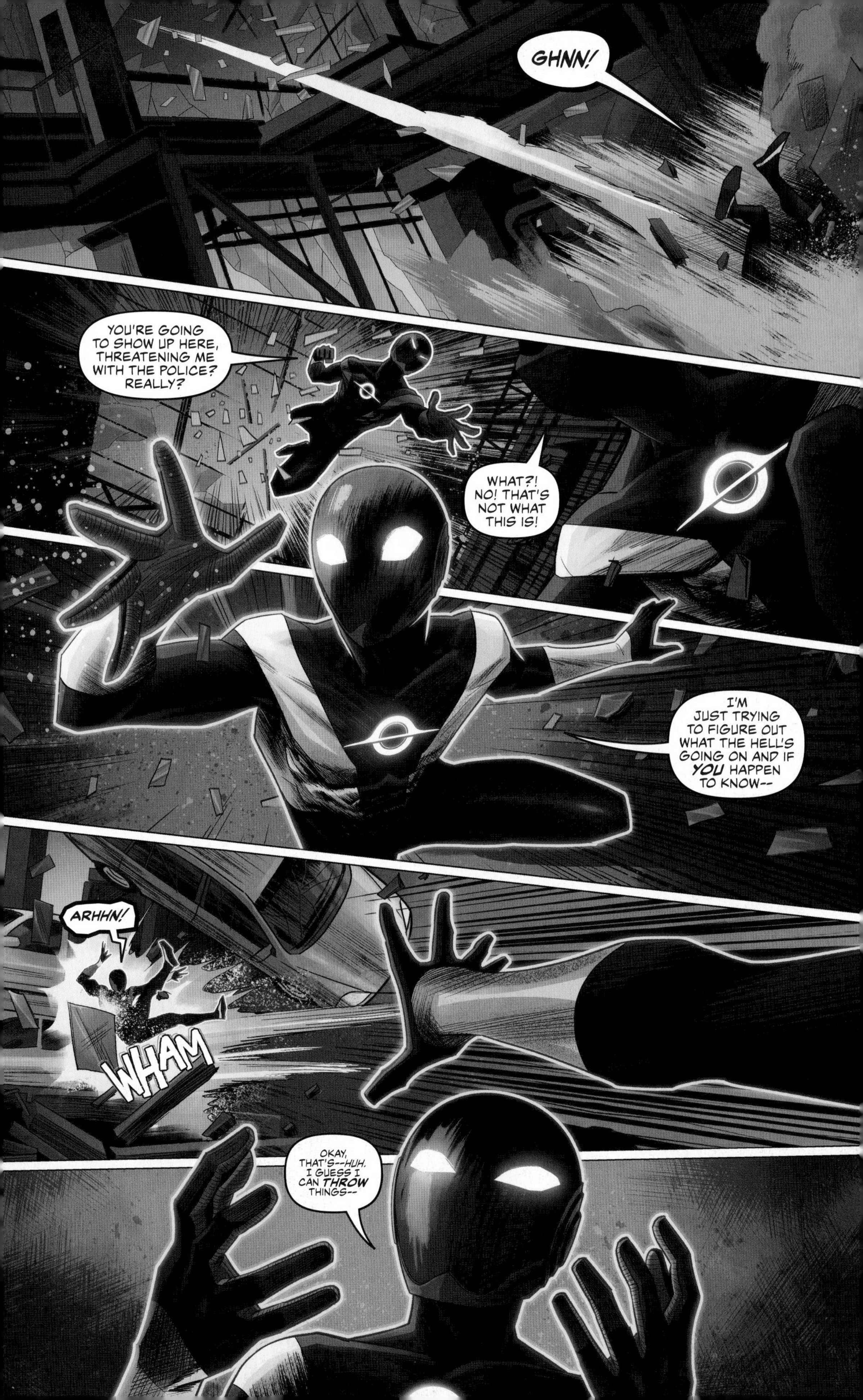
GHNN!
YOU'RE GOING TO SHOW UP HERE, THREATENING ME WITH THE POLICE? REALLY?
WHAT?! NO! THAT'S NOT WHAT THIS IS!
I'M JUST TRYING TO FIGURE OUT WHAT THE HELL'S GOING ON AND IF YOU HAPPEN TO KNOW--
ARHHN!
WHAM
OKAY, THAT'S--HUH. I GUESS I CAN THROW THINGS--

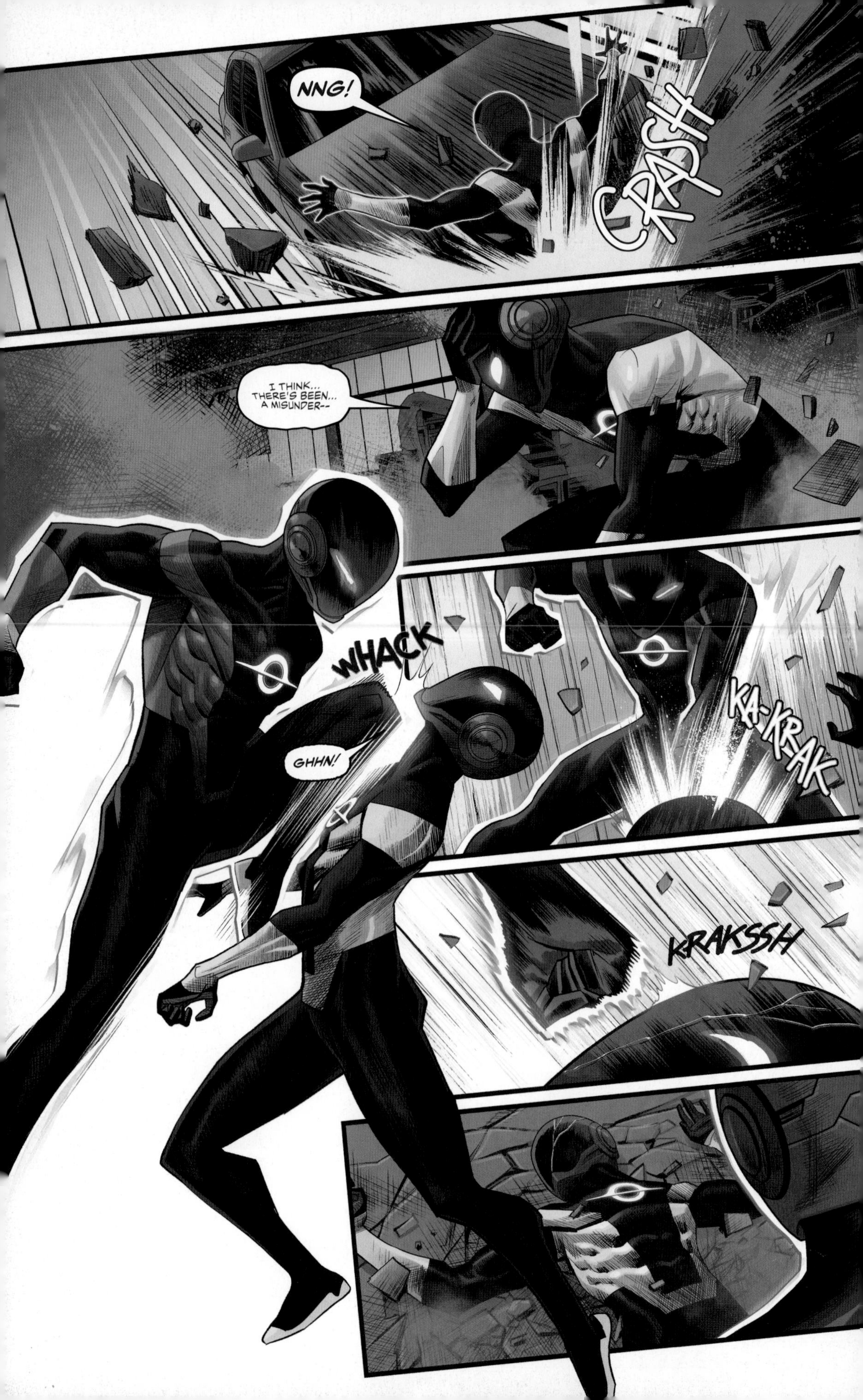
NNG!
CRASH
I THINK... THERE'S BEEN... A MISUNDER--
WHACK
GHHN!
KA-KRAK
KRAKSSH

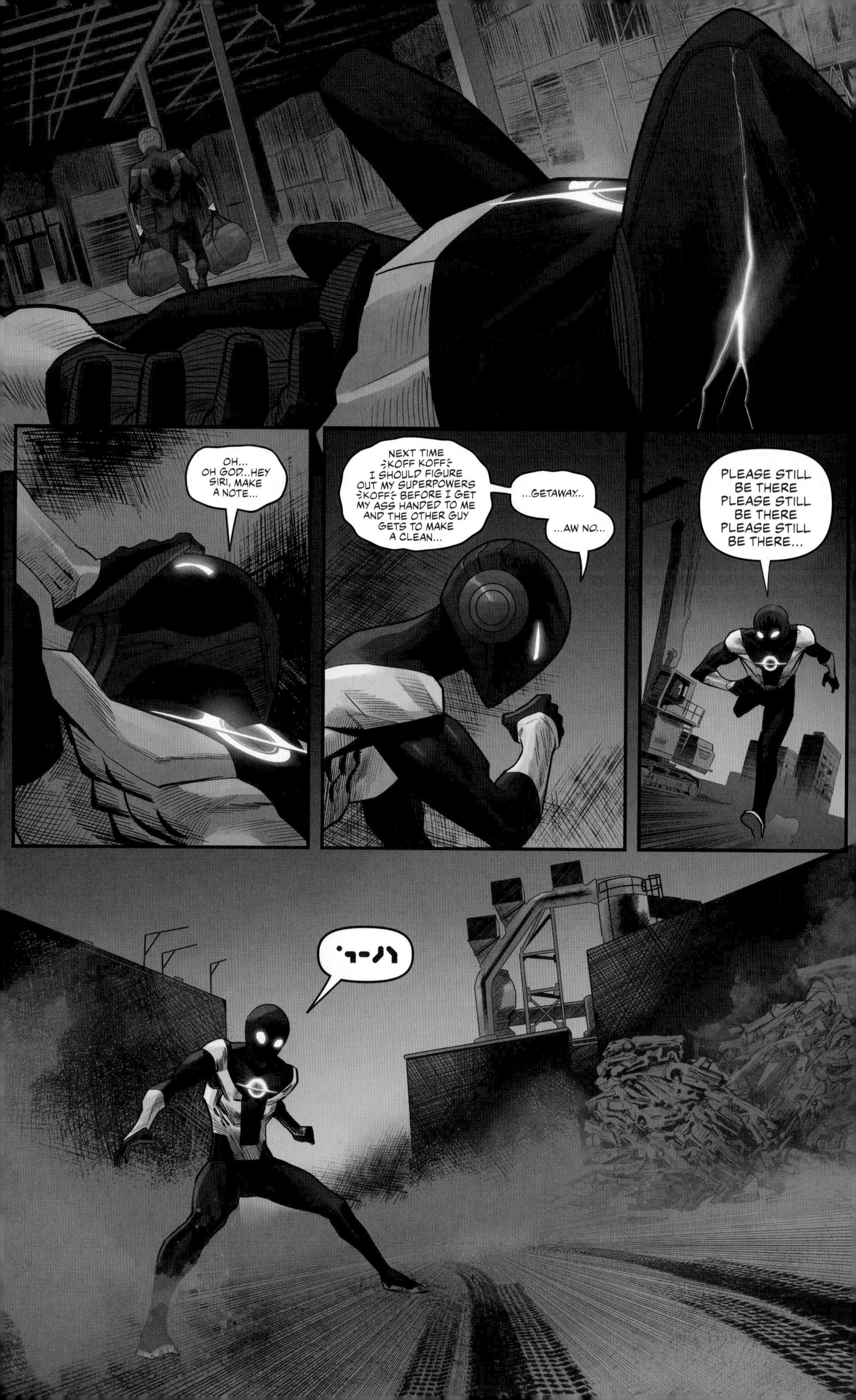
OH... OH GOD...HEY SIRI, MAKE A NOTE...
NEXT TIME ⁞KOFF KOFF⁞ I SHOULD FIGURE OUT MY SUPERPOWERS ⁞KOFF⁞ BEFORE I GET MY ASS HANDED TO ME AND THE OTHER GUY GETS TO MAKE A CLEAN...
...GETAWAY...
...AW NO...
PLEASE STILL BE THERE PLEASE STILL BE THERE PLEASE STILL BE THERE...

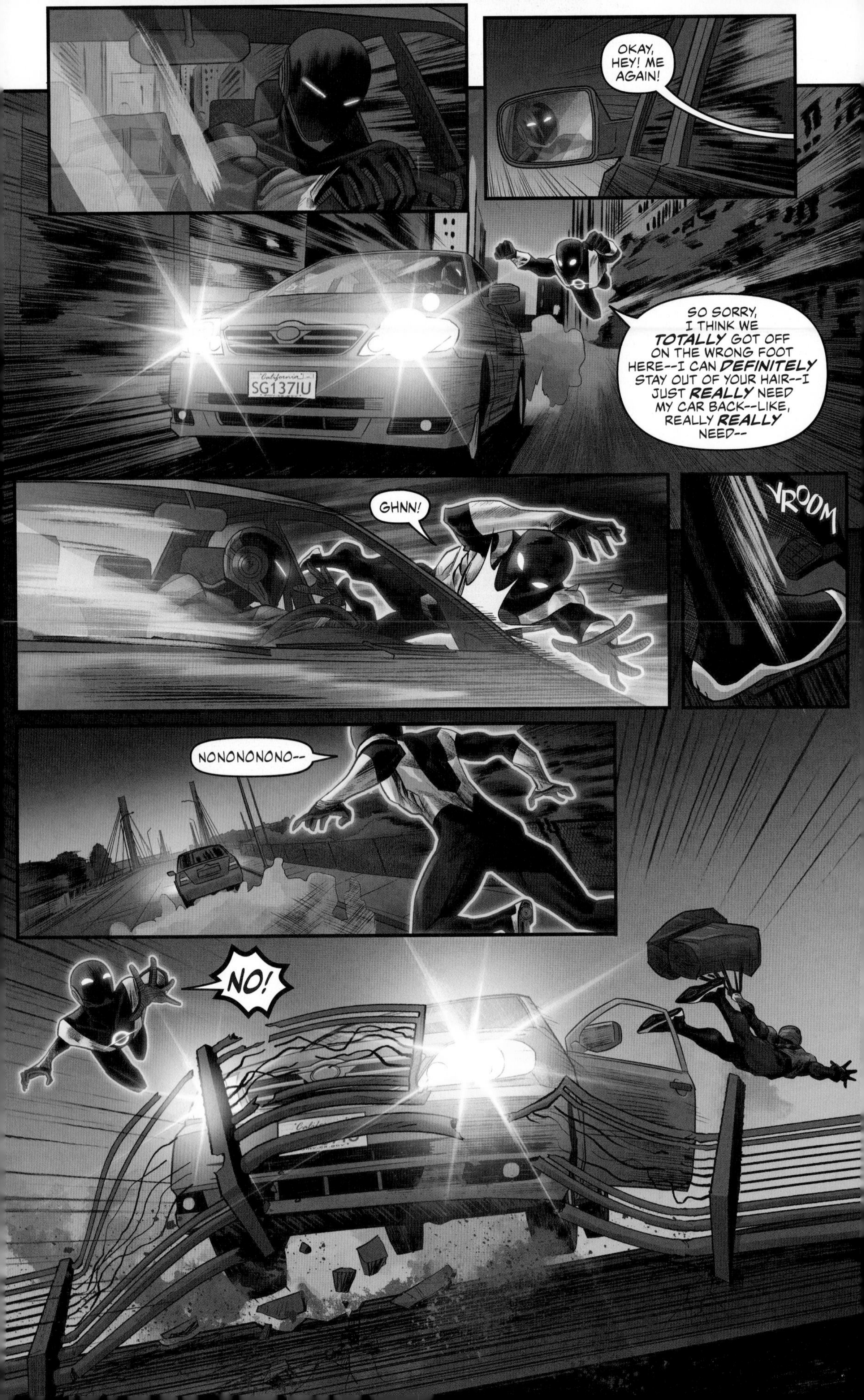
OKAY, HEY! ME AGAIN!
SO SORRY, I THINK WE TOTALLY GOT OFF ON THE WRONG FOOT HERE--I CAN DEFINITELY STAY OUT OF YOUR HAIR--I JUST REALLY NEED MY CAR BACK--LIKE, REALLY REALLY NEED--
GHNN!
VROOM
NONONONONO--
NO!

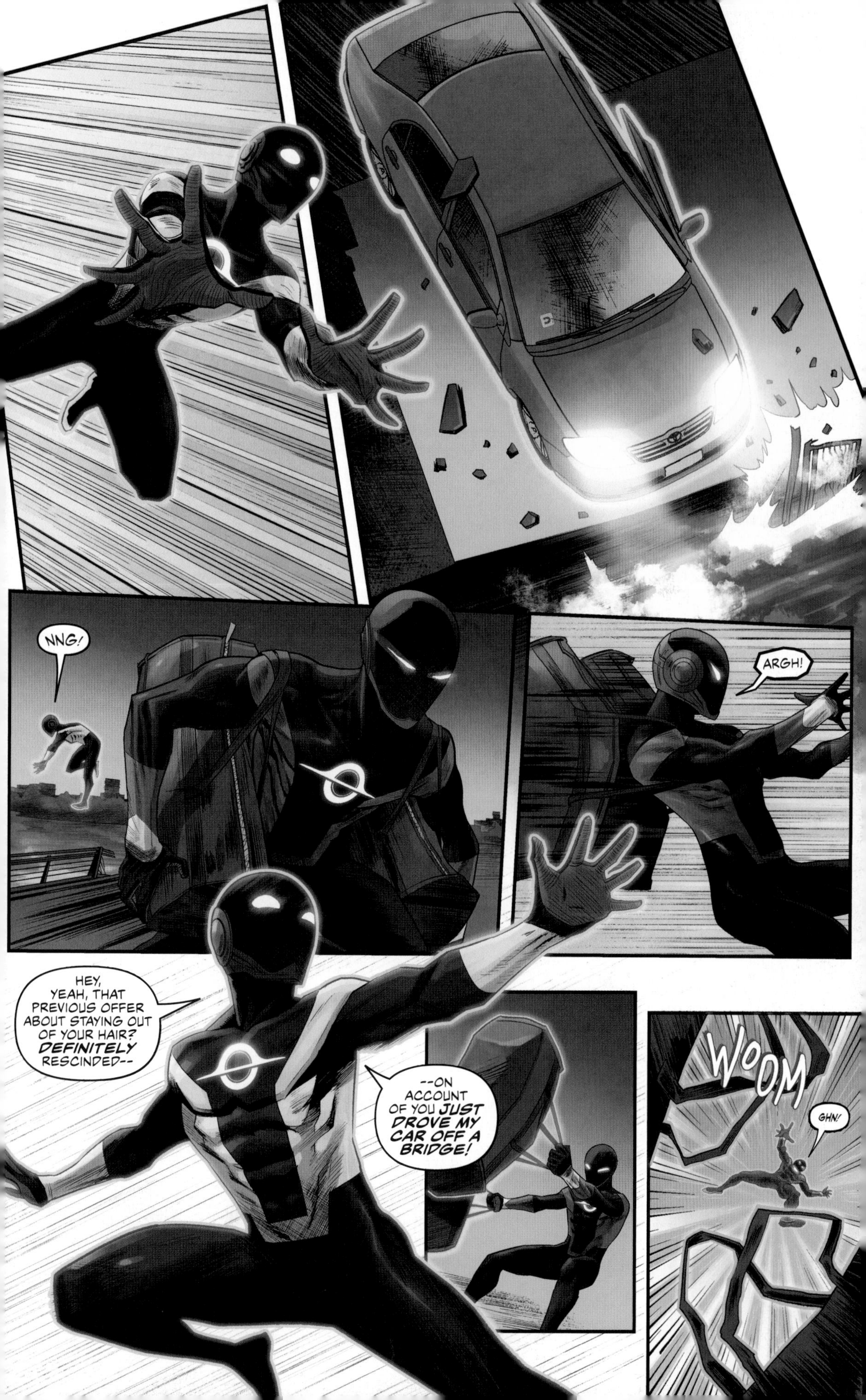
NNG!
ARGH!
HEY, YEAH, THAT PREVIOUS OFFER ABOUT STAYING OUT OF YOUR HAIR? DEFINITELY RESCINDED--
--ON ACCOUNT OF YOU JUST DROVE MY CAR OFF A BRIDGE!
WOOM
GHN!

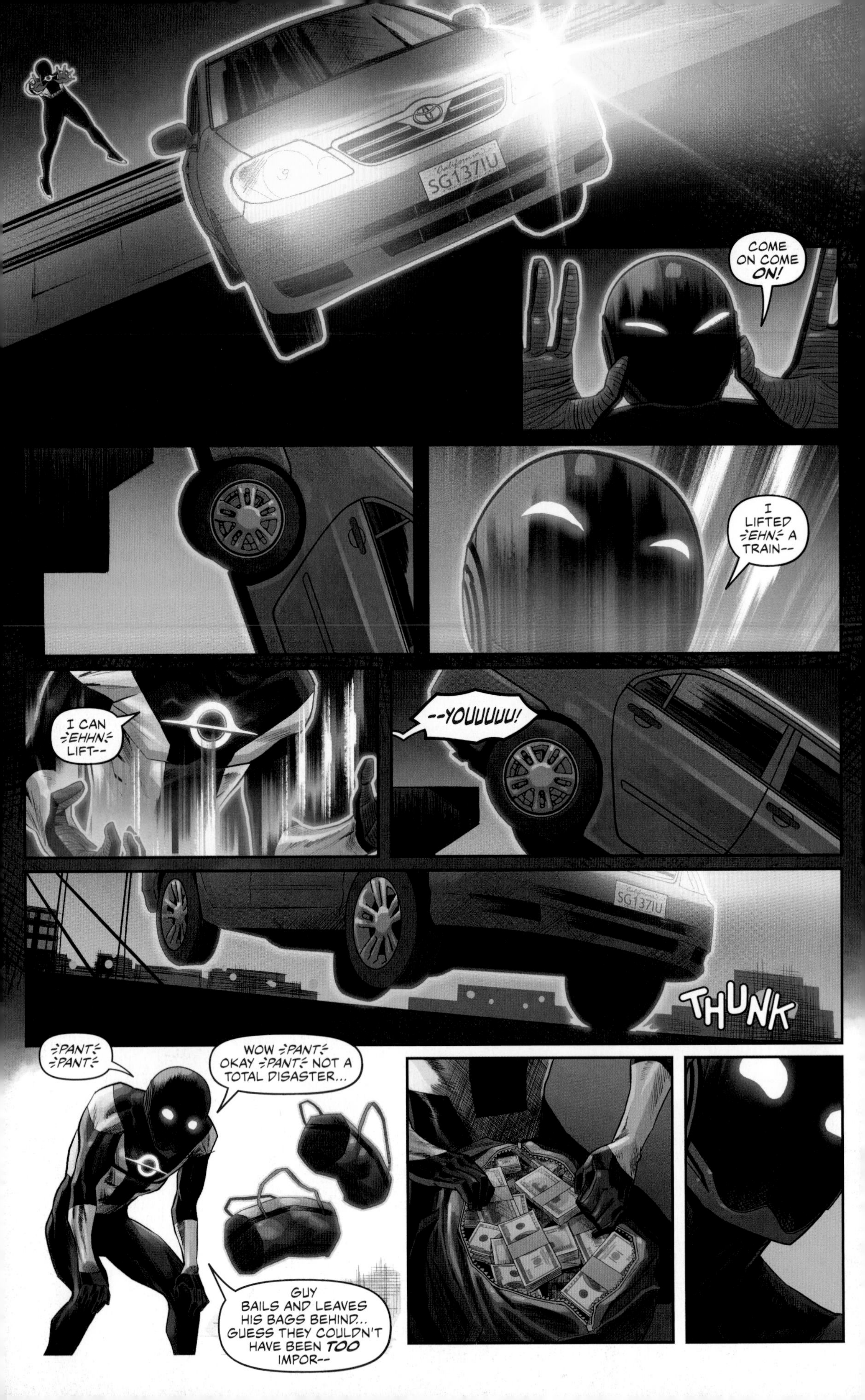
COME ON COME ON!
I LIFTED =EHN= A TRAIN--
I CAN =EHHN= LIFT--
--YOUUUUU!
THUNK
=PANT= =PANT=
WOW =PANT= OKAY =PANT= NOT A TOTAL DISASTER...
GUY BAILS AND LEAVES HIS BAGS BEHIND... GUESS THEY COULDN'T HAVE BEEN TOO IMPOR--

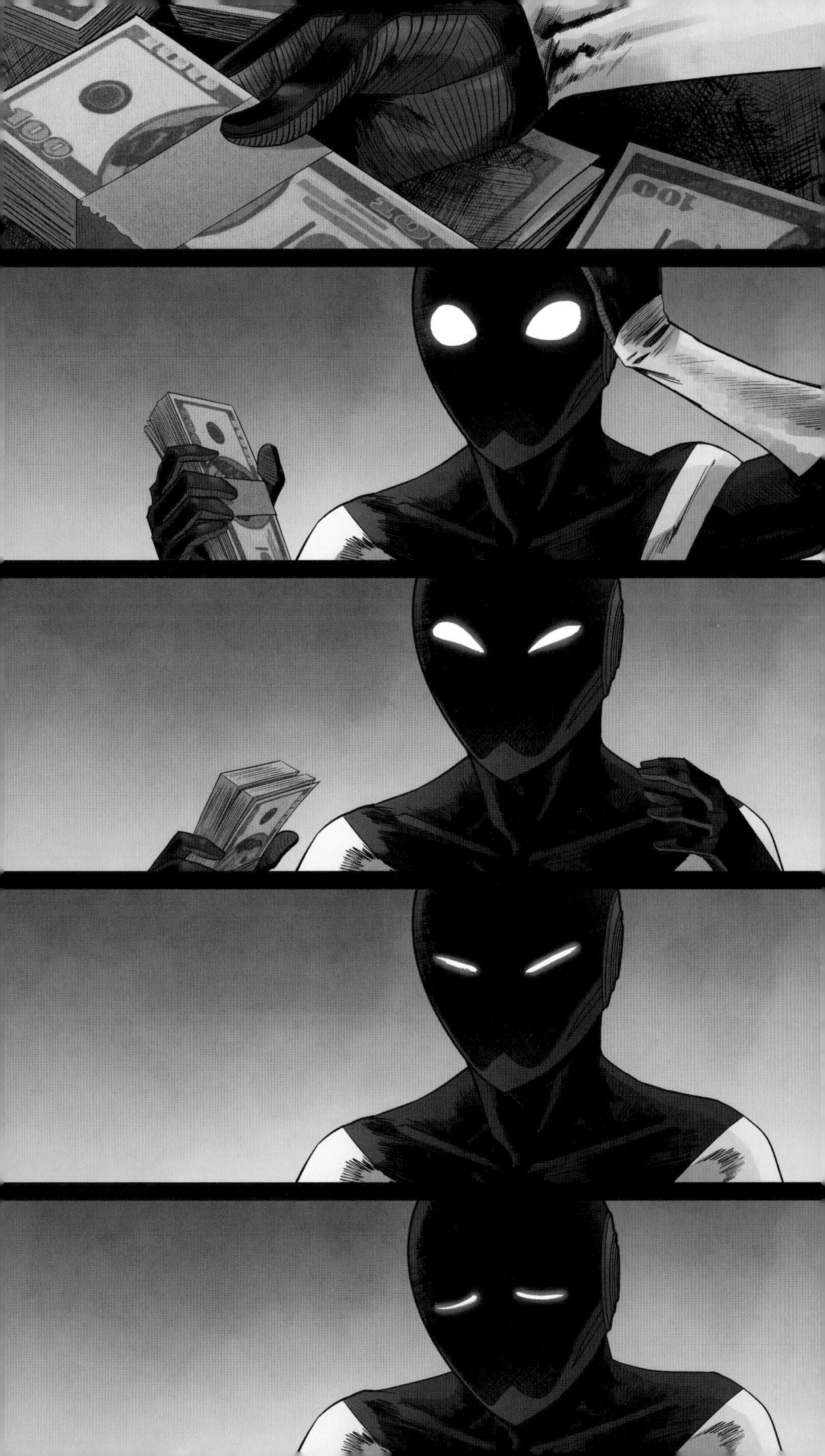

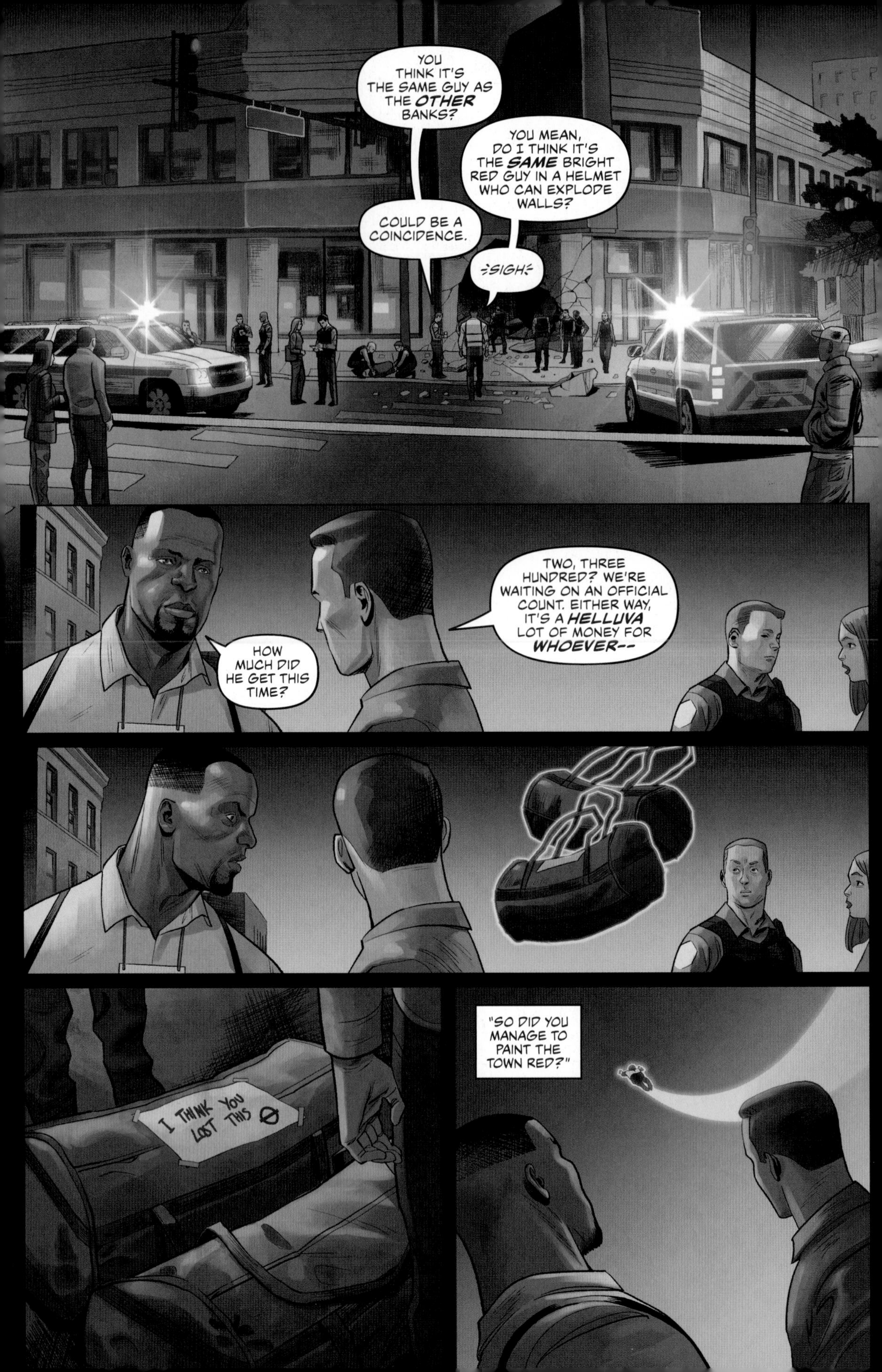
YOU THINK IT'S THE SAME GUY AS THE OTHER BANKS?
YOU MEAN, DO I THINK IT'S THE SAME BRIGHT RED GUY IN A HELMET WHO CAN EXPLODE WALLS?
COULD BE A COINCIDENCE.
SIGH
HOW MUCH DID HE GET THIS TIME?
TWO, THREE HUNDRED? WE'RE WAITING ON AN OFFICIAL COUNT. EITHER WAY, IT'S A HELLUVA LOT OF MONEY FOR WHOEVER--
I THINK YOU LOST THIS
"SO DID YOU MANAGE TO PAINT THE TOWN RED?"

"IF BY 'PAINT THE TOWN RED' YOU MEAN DRIVE A BUNCH OF PEOPLE AROUND AIMLESSLY ALL NIGHT WHILE SECOND-GUESSING ALL OF MY LIFE CHOICES..."

...THEN YEAH. *BLOOD RED.* ALSO, I'M PRETTY SURE MULTIPLE DOGS PEED IN MY CAR.

WELL, THEY *DO* CALL IT *"WORK"* FOR A REASON...

...

LISTEN, I WANTED TO TALK TO YOU ABOUT THAT. I WAS THINKING ABOUT WHAT YOU SAID THIS MORNING. AND...YOU'RE RIGHT. I MEAN, PARTIALLY.

THIS WRITING THING... IT ISN'T GOING TO HAPPEN OVERNIGHT FOR ME. AND EVEN IF IT COULD...I DON'T THINK THAT WOULD BE BEST. NOTHING WORTHWHILE COMES FROM A SHORTCUT, RIGHT?

MAYBE I WILL KEEP DRIVR DRIVING. AS AWFUL AS IT IS, I CAN MAKE A LITTLE MONEY AND ALSO, MY OWN HOURS. WHICH IS IMPORTANT...FOR THE SECOND PART. THE PART YOU'RE WRONG ABOUT.

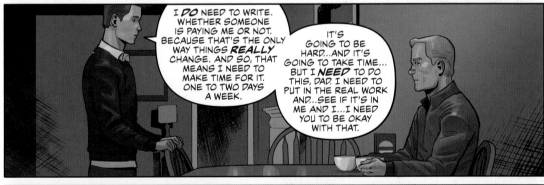

I *DO* NEED TO WRITE. WHETHER SOMEONE IS PAYING ME OR NOT. BECAUSE THAT'S THE ONLY WAY THINGS *REALLY* CHANGE. AND SO, THAT MEANS I NEED TO MAKE TIME FOR IT. ONE TO TWO DAYS A WEEK.

IT'S GOING TO BE HARD...AND IT'S GOING TO TAKE TIME... BUT I *NEED* TO DO THIS, DAD. I NEED TO PUT IN THE REAL WORK AND...SEE IF IT'S IN ME AND I...I NEED YOU TO BE OKAY WITH THAT.

I AM. AND I THINK YOU SHOULD.

YOU DO?

I DO.

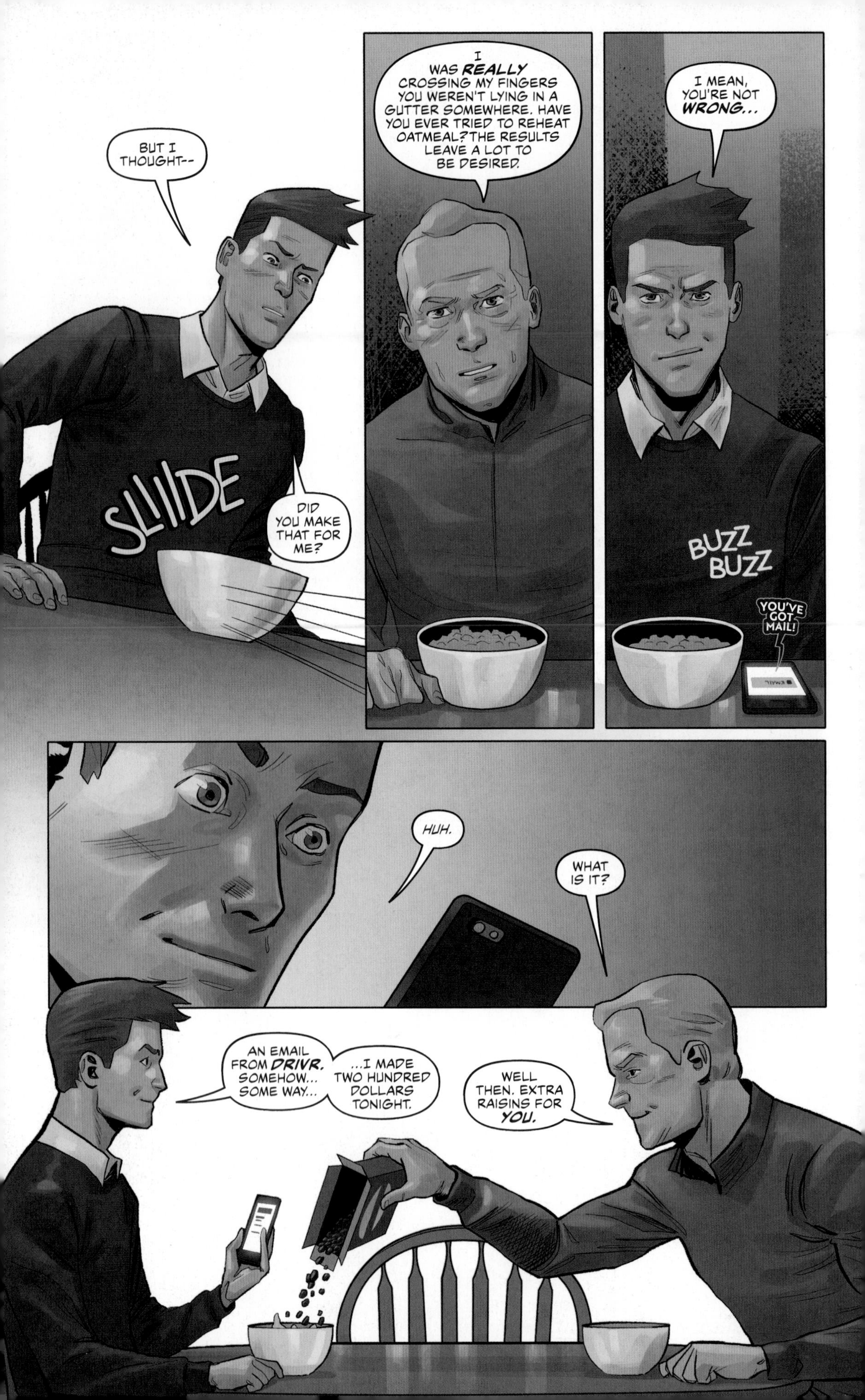
BUT I THOUGHT--
SLIIDE
DID YOU MAKE THAT FOR ME?
I WAS **REALLY** CROSSING MY FINGERS YOU WEREN'T LYING IN A GUTTER SOMEWHERE. HAVE YOU EVER TRIED TO REHEAT OATMEAL? THE RESULTS LEAVE A LOT TO BE DESIRED.
I MEAN, YOU'RE NOT **WRONG...**
BUZZ BUZZ
YOU'VE GOT MAIL!
HUH.
WHAT IS IT?
AN EMAIL FROM **DRIVR.** SOMEHOW... SOME WAY...
...I MADE TWO HUNDRED DOLLARS TONIGHT.
WELL THEN. EXTRA RAISINS FOR **YOU.**

CHAPTER THREE

TITLE   Writing Day

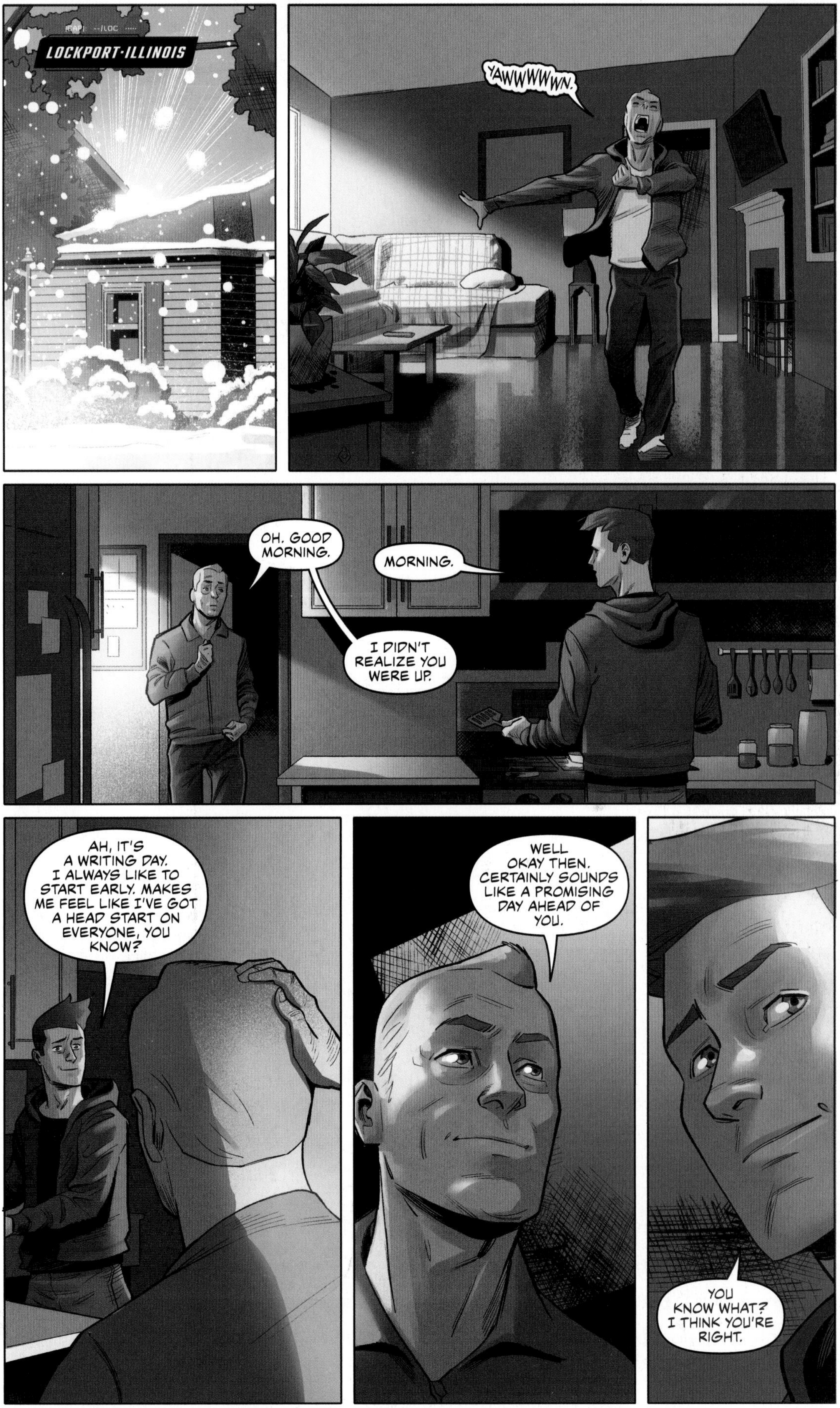
LOCKPORT·ILLINOIS
YAWWWWWN.
OH. GOOD MORNING.
MORNING.
I DIDN'T REALIZE YOU WERE UP.
AH, IT'S A WRITING DAY. I ALWAYS LIKE TO START EARLY. MAKES ME FEEL LIKE I'VE GOT A HEAD START ON EVERYONE, YOU KNOW?
WELL OKAY THEN. CERTAINLY SOUNDS LIKE A PROMISING DAY AHEAD OF YOU.
YOU KNOW WHAT? I THINK YOU'RE RIGHT.

BIG TIME

by NATHAN BURNETT

Elisabeth Beckett hated today.

She'd been on time for the job, even though Eliot had screwed up the entry route—the man was endlessly incapable of giving directions before his first cup of coffee. But they were lucky; the heist had gone over fast. Easy. Like they thought it would.

At 9:05 am, she and Eliot walked out of the MK Branch Bank on the eastern edge of Montrose, dressed business casual, with three bags totalling over 100K in cash.

At 9:06, as Eliot loaded the second bag into their gray Camry, the shooting started.

Eliot crumpled, the life draining from him in an instant.

Now, hours outside of the city, as Elisabeth tried to steady the car in a brisk fall wind—all alone save for the giant bag of money in the seat next to her—she couldn't stop thinking about the irony.

She'd worked at banks before she started to rob them. Her favorites were the ones tied up with Dark Money—Energy lobbyists. Foreign interests. Super PACs. *Fuck 'em.* The banks *knew* that kind of cash had strings attached, so what if it was her to pull them?

That's how she'd met Eliot in the first place. On a job. Or, rather, *before* the jobs. Two outsiders pulled together at her girlfriend's lame house party, a heated debate about corporate greed pulling them closer under swirls of marijuana smoke. The second time they were in the same room together, she sold him information on an MK Branch. He was her first.

Five years later, they were inseparable. In bed and in work. Together, they had inched hand in hand into a new lifestyle. A love of vintage. Expensive. But without the budget to make it happen. Not without some shortcuts. There were rough patches, sure. Zeroed out bank accounts, too. There were always threats. Violence sometimes. Never from him, but always because.

But they'd chosen their path. Together. That's what he used to say. Hell, that's what today was about. A way to start over.

Again.

Like last time.

And the time before.

And before…

She glanced again at the empty passenger seat.

She felt something strange—a tickle, deep in her throat, rising up, stronger. It reminded her of the bank, the way the blood gushed from Eliot's wounds like the broken garbage disposal in that first flat they rented together, dirty dish water gurgling out no matter how many rags they drunkenly shoved into it.

Suddenly, she laughed.

Her hand raced to her lips, trying to hold back the venom. But it was too late. She laughed again. What was so funny? She started to cry.

Why was she suddenly so…*happy?*

Because. There is no "next time." Eliot's dead.

For the first time since she put the pedal through the floorboards outside of Montrose, Eliot throwing that first bag of cash into the backseat, his smile brighter than the flash of police lights, she was able to think.

She looked to the passenger floorboard—the bag still smeared with his blood. Clumped near the handle, the shape of his fingers. Inside, the money was real.

She looked out the windshield—so was the open road.

For the first time in a *long* time, Elisabeth exhaled. She smiled. Overwhelmed by the possibilities. A clear road and a bag full of cash.

Elisabeth Beckett had nowhere she had to be, no one to answer to. She was free from looking over her shoulder. She could go anywhere. She could be anyone.

As she turned up the radio, suddenly belting out a tune about an American Girl, mangling Petty's voice, today was starting to look a whole lot better.

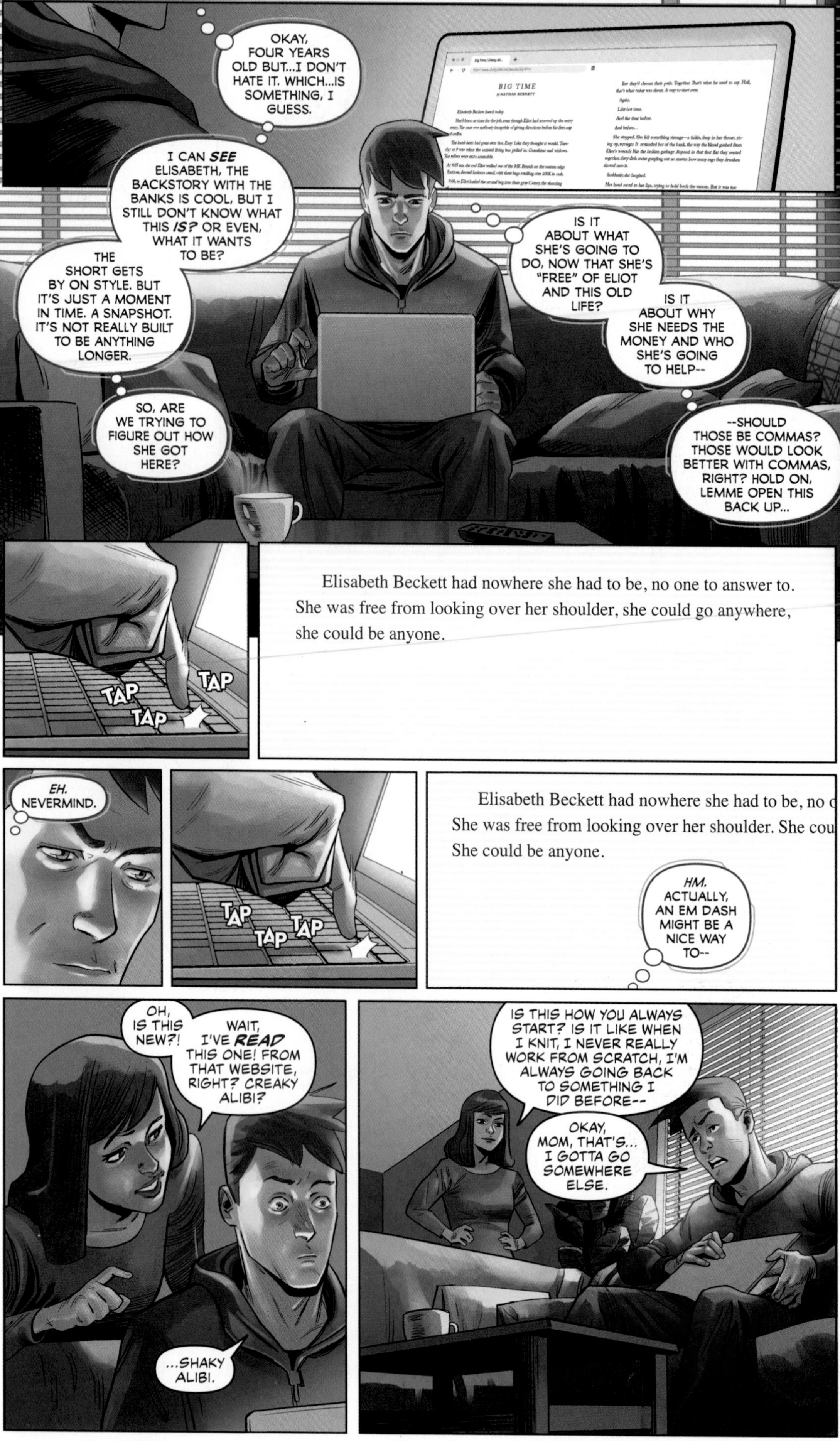
BIG TIME
OKAY, FOUR YEARS OLD BUT...I DON'T HATE IT. WHICH...IS SOMETHING, I GUESS.
I CAN *SEE* ELISABETH, THE BACKSTORY WITH THE BANKS IS COOL, BUT I STILL DON'T KNOW WHAT THIS *IS?* OR EVEN, WHAT IT WANTS TO BE?
THE SHORT GETS BY ON STYLE. BUT IT'S JUST A MOMENT IN TIME. A SNAPSHOT. IT'S NOT REALLY BUILT TO BE ANYTHING LONGER.
SO, ARE WE TRYING TO FIGURE OUT HOW SHE GOT HERE?
IS IT ABOUT WHAT SHE'S GOING TO DO, NOW THAT SHE'S "FREE" OF ELIOT AND THIS OLD LIFE?
IS IT ABOUT WHY SHE NEEDS THE MONEY AND WHO SHE'S GOING TO HELP--
--SHOULD THOSE BE COMMAS? THOSE WOULD LOOK BETTER WITH COMMAS, RIGHT? HOLD ON, LEMME OPEN THIS BACK UP...
TAP
TAP
TAP
Elisabeth Beckett had nowhere she had to be, no one to answer to. She was free from looking over her shoulder, she could go anywhere, she could be anyone.
EH. NEVERMIND.
TAP
TAP
TAP
Elisabeth Beckett had nowhere she had to be, no o
She was free from looking over her shoulder. She cou
She could be anyone.
HM. ACTUALLY, AN EM DASH MIGHT BE A NICE WAY TO--
OH, IS THIS NEW?!
WAIT, I'VE *READ* THIS ONE! FROM THAT WEBSITE, RIGHT? CREAKY ALIBI?
...SHAKY ALIBI.
IS THIS HOW YOU ALWAYS START? IS IT LIKE WHEN I KNIT, I NEVER REALLY WORK FROM SCRATCH, I'M ALWAYS GOING BACK TO SOMETHING I DID BEFORE--
OKAY, MOM, THAT'S... I GOTTA GO SOMEWHERE ELSE.

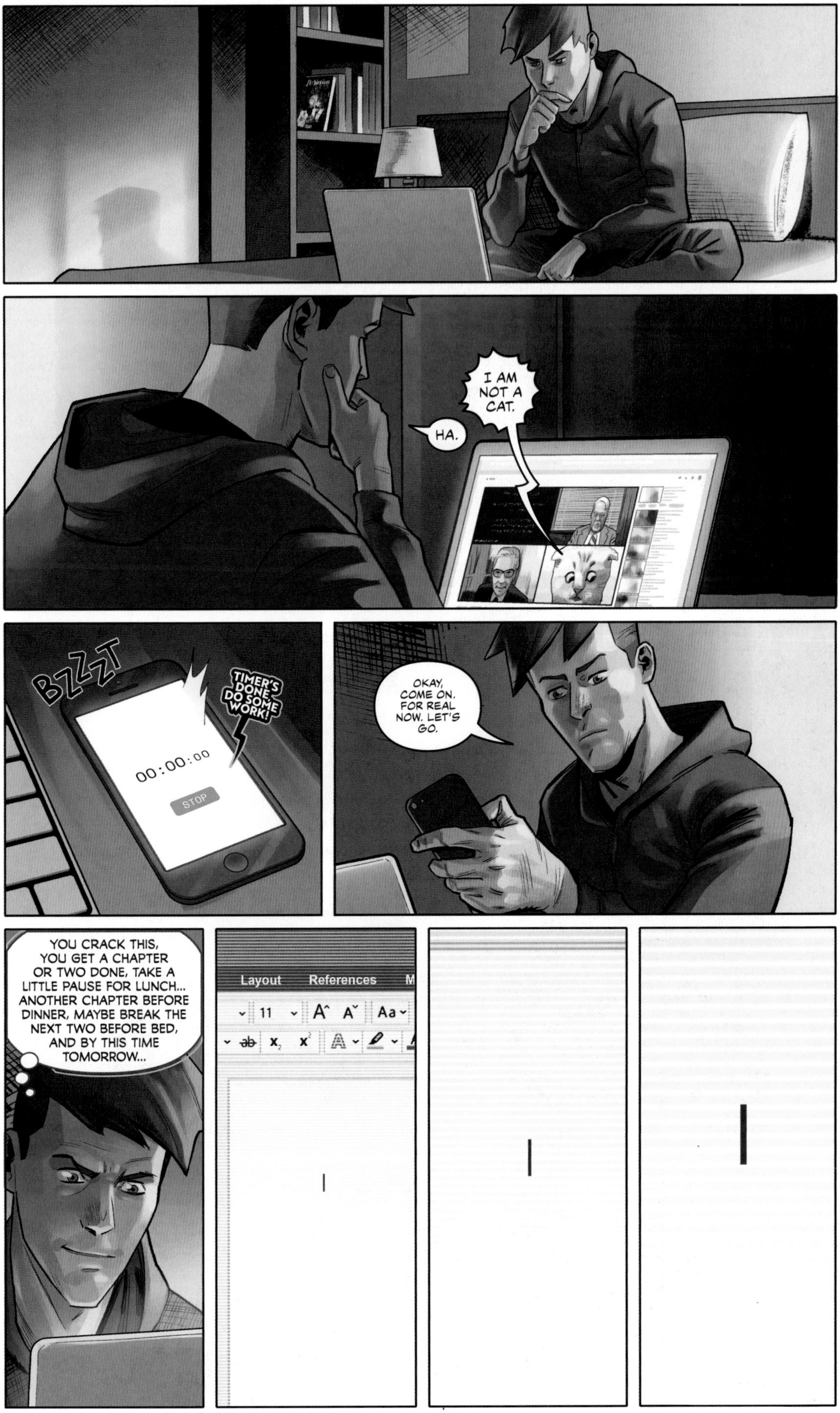
HA.
I AM NOT A CAT.
BZZZT
TIMER'S DONE. DO SOME WORK!
00:00:00
STOP
OKAY, COME ON. FOR REAL NOW. LET'S GO.
YOU CRACK THIS, YOU GET A CHAPTER OR TWO DONE, TAKE A LITTLE PAUSE FOR LUNCH... ANOTHER CHAPTER BEFORE DINNER, MAYBE BREAK THE NEXT TWO BEFORE BED, AND BY THIS TIME TOMORROW...
Layout References
11
Aa

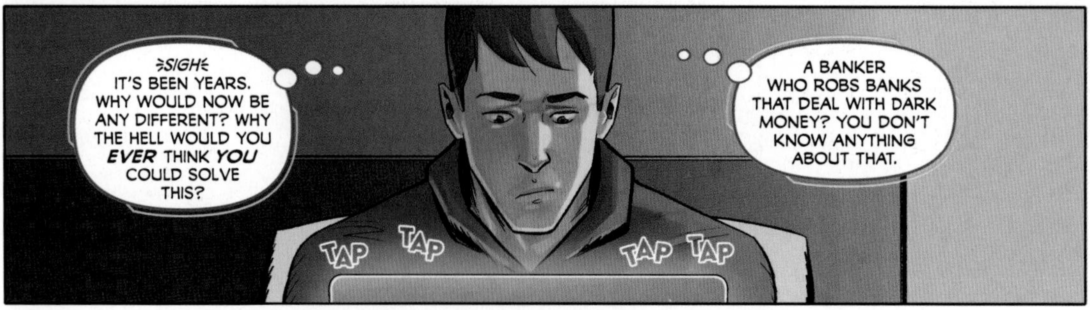

>SIGH<
IT'S BEEN YEARS. WHY WOULD NOW BE ANY DIFFERENT? WHY THE HELL WOULD YOU EVER THINK YOU COULD SOLVE THIS?
A BANKER WHO ROBS BANKS THAT DEAL WITH DARK MONEY? YOU DON'T KNOW ANYTHING ABOUT THAT.
TAP TAP TAP TAP

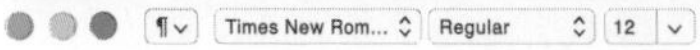

Times New Rom...
Regular
12

Elisabeth Beckett hated her job. She hated the people her bank dealt with. So, she started robbing them.

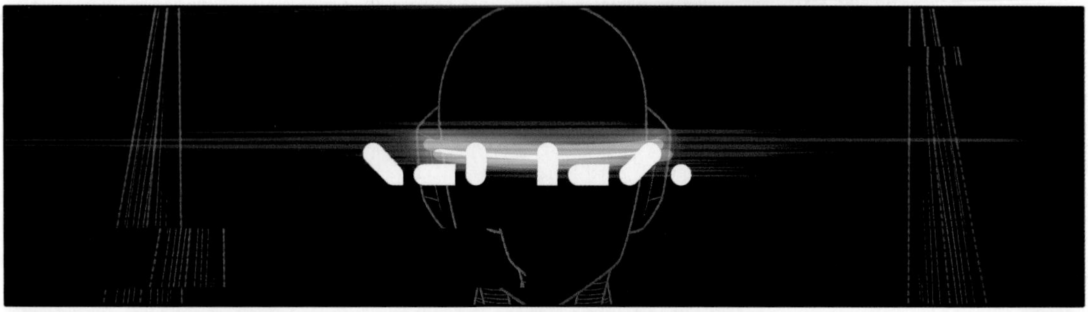

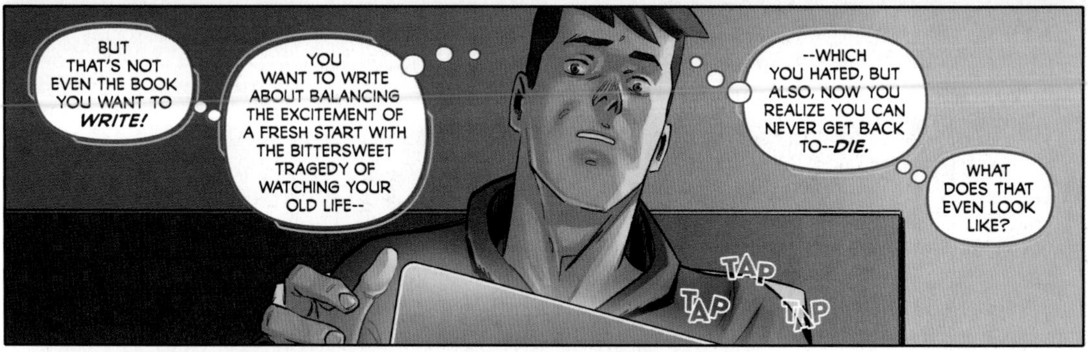

BUT THAT'S NOT EVEN THE BOOK YOU WANT TO WRITE!
YOU WANT TO WRITE ABOUT BALANCING THE EXCITEMENT OF A FRESH START WITH THE BITTERSWEET TRAGEDY OF WATCHING YOUR OLD LIFE--
--WHICH YOU HATED, BUT ALSO, NOW YOU REALIZE YOU CAN NEVER GET BACK TO--DIE.
WHAT DOES THAT EVEN LOOK LIKE?
TAP TAP TAP

Elisabeth Beckett hated her job. She hated the people her bank dealt with. So, she started robbing them. Her life got rocky, but now she was free.

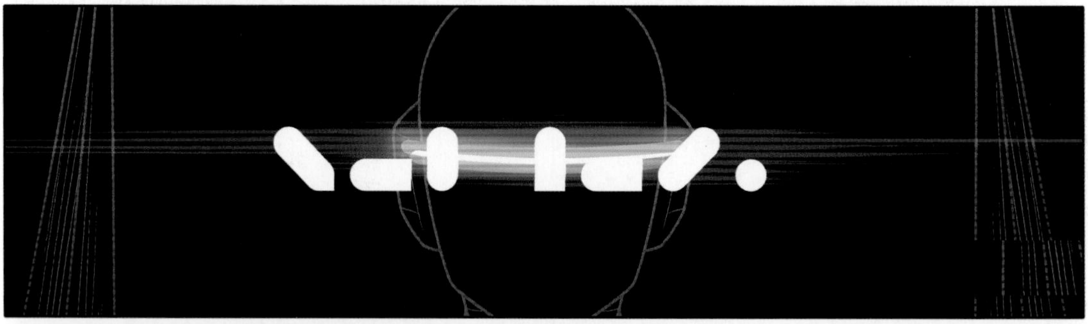

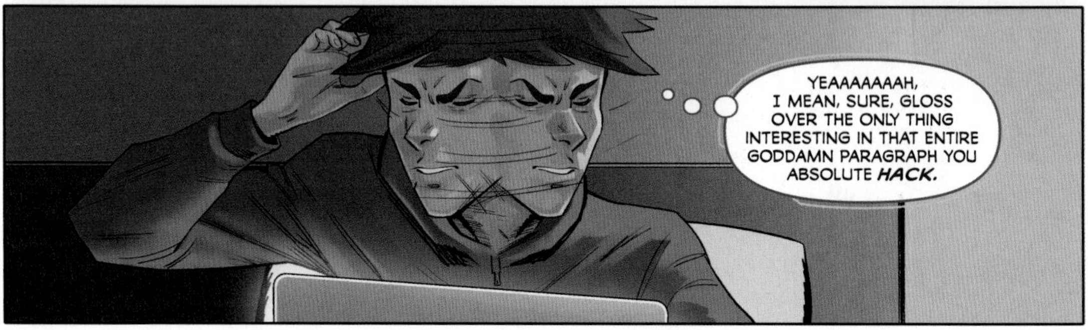

YEAAAAAAAH, I MEAN, SURE, GLOSS OVER THE ONLY THING INTERESTING IN THAT ENTIRE GODDAMN PARAGRAPH YOU ABSOLUTE HACK.

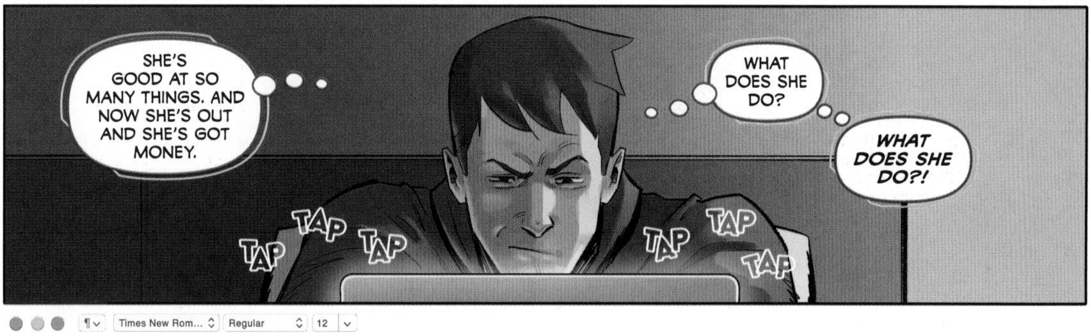
SHE'S GOOD AT SO MANY THINGS. AND NOW SHE'S OUT AND SHE'S GOT MONEY.
WHAT DOES SHE DO?
WHAT DOES SHE DO?!
TAP TAP TAP TAP TAP TAP
Times New Rom...
Regular
12

Now, she was clear from looking over her shoulder. She could go anywhere. She could be *anyone*.

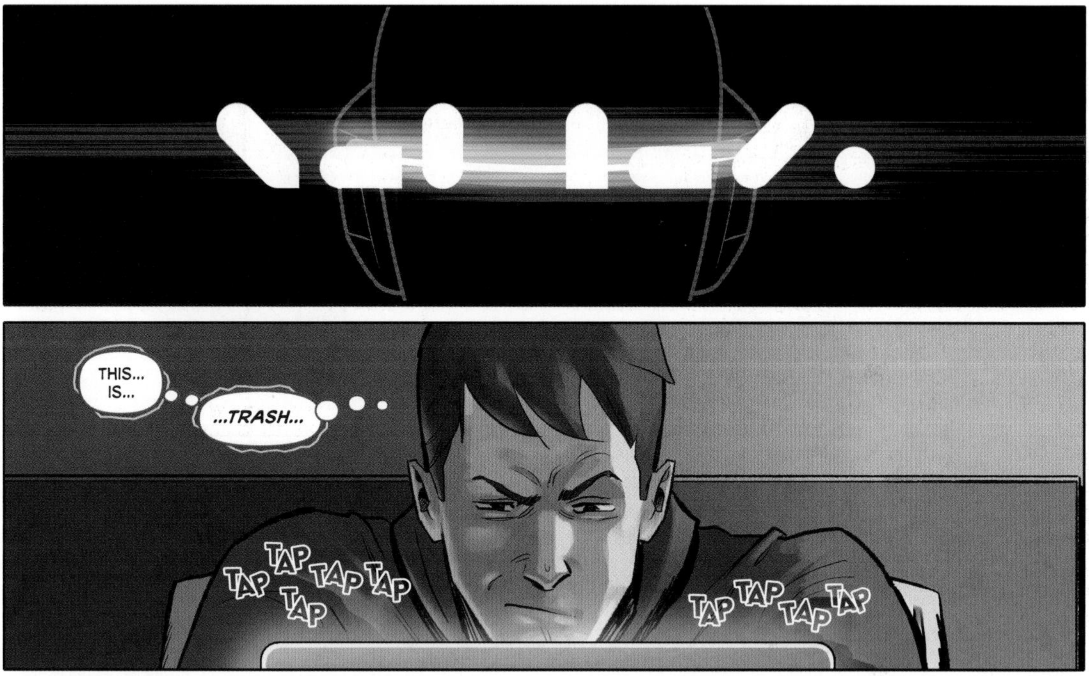
THIS... IS...
...TRASH...
TAP TAP TAP TAP TAP TAP TAP TAP TAP TAP

So what exactly did that mean? She couldn't wait to find out.

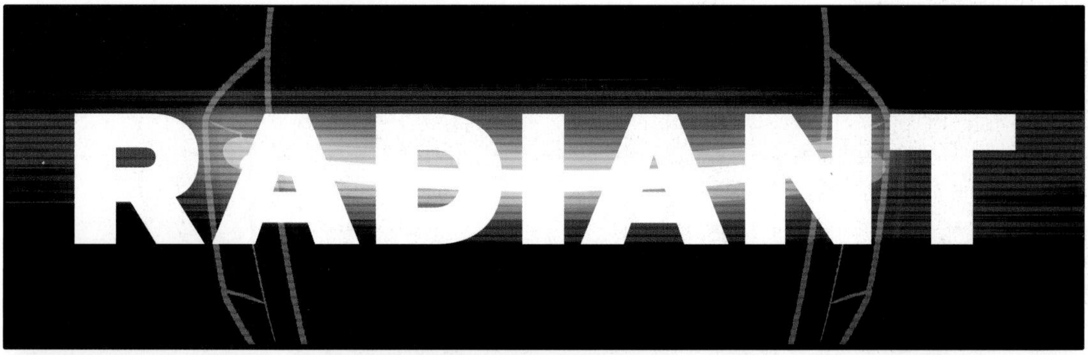
RADIANT

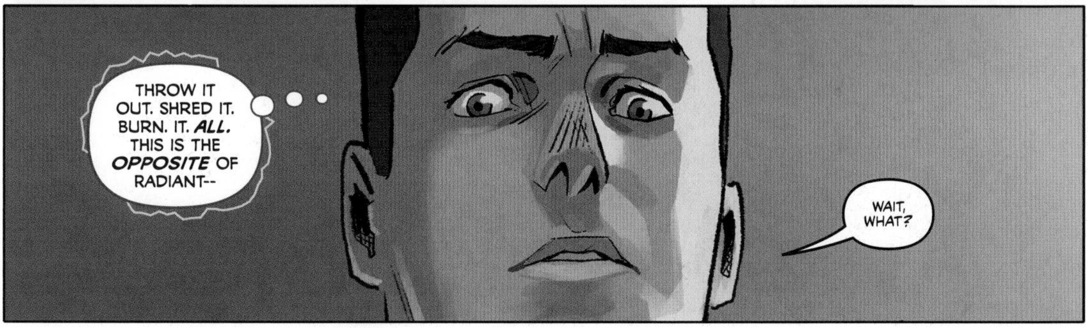
THROW IT OUT. SHRED IT. BURN. IT. ALL. THIS IS THE OPPOSITE OF RADIANT--
WAIT, WHAT?

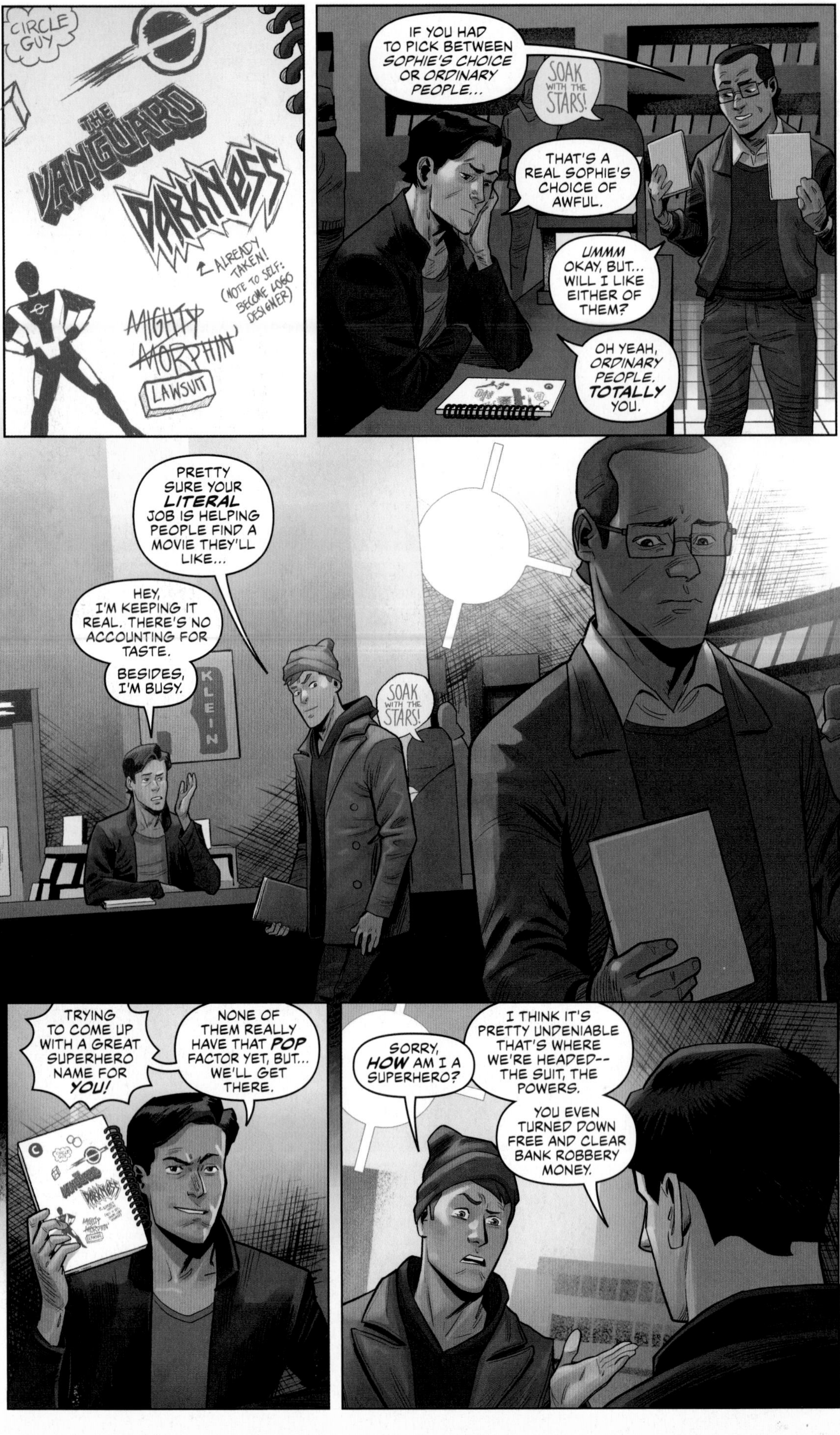
CIRCLE GUY
THE VANGUARD
DARKNESS
ALREADY TAKEN!
(NOTE TO SELF: BECOME LOGO DESIGNER)
MIGHTY MORPHIN'
LAWSUIT
IF YOU HAD TO PICK BETWEEN SOPHIE'S CHOICE OR ORDINARY PEOPLE...
SOAK WITH THE STARS!
THAT'S A REAL SOPHIE'S CHOICE OF AWFUL.
UMMM OKAY, BUT... WILL I LIKE EITHER OF THEM?
OH YEAH, ORDINARY PEOPLE. TOTALLY YOU.
PRETTY SURE YOUR LITERAL JOB IS HELPING PEOPLE FIND A MOVIE THEY'LL LIKE...
HEY, I'M KEEPING IT REAL. THERE'S NO ACCOUNTING FOR TASTE.
BESIDES, I'M BUSY.
KLEIN
SOAK WITH THE STARS!
TRYING TO COME UP WITH A GREAT SUPERHERO NAME FOR YOU!
NONE OF THEM REALLY HAVE THAT POP FACTOR YET, BUT... WE'LL GET THERE.
SORRY, HOW AM I A SUPERHERO?
I THINK IT'S PRETTY UNDENIABLE THAT'S WHERE WE'RE HEADED-- THE SUIT, THE POWERS.
YOU EVEN TURNED DOWN FREE AND CLEAR BANK ROBBERY MONEY.

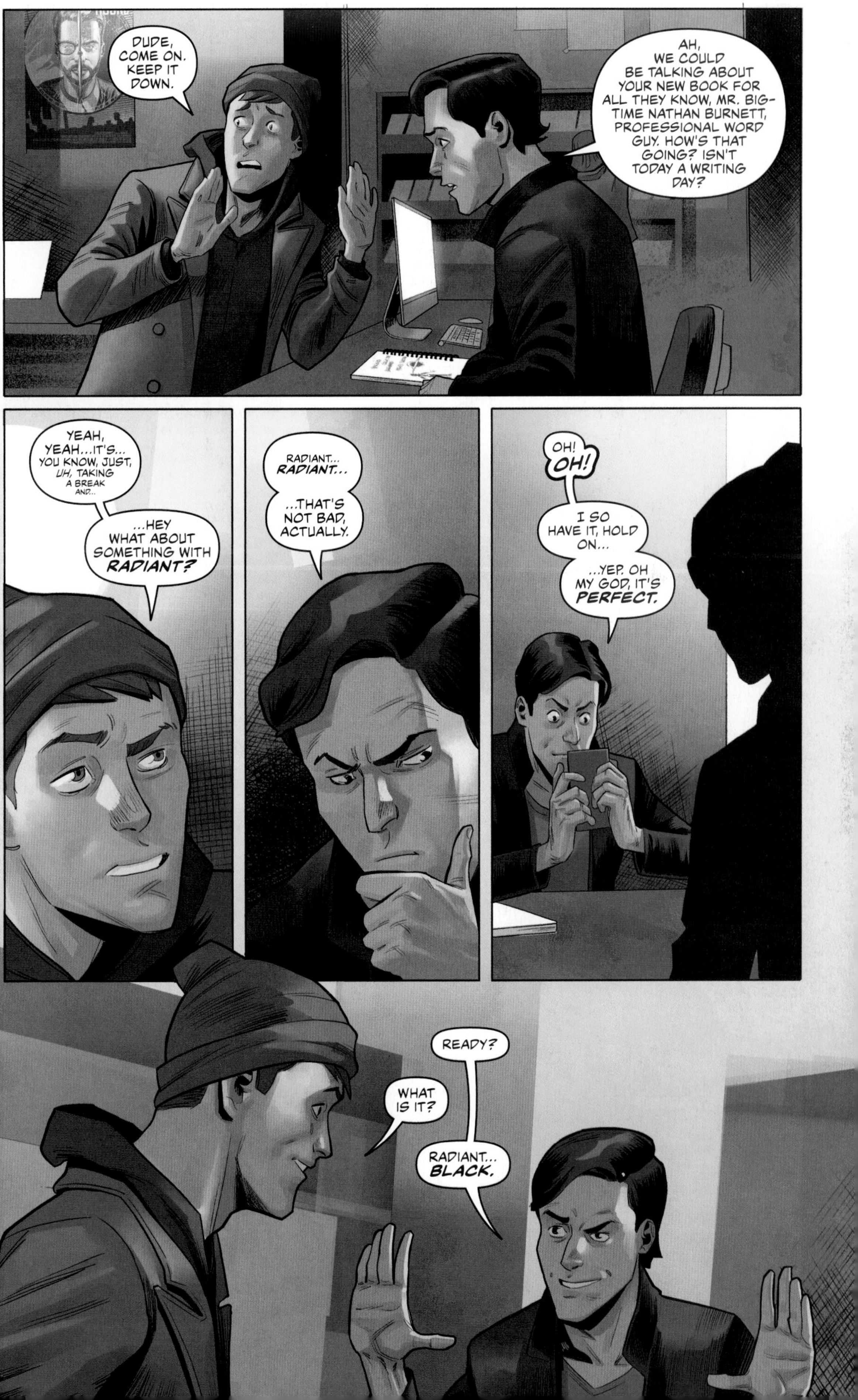
DUDE, COME ON. KEEP IT DOWN.
AH, WE COULD BE TALKING ABOUT YOUR NEW BOOK FOR ALL THEY KNOW, MR. BIG-TIME NATHAN BURNETT, PROFESSIONAL WORD GUY. HOW'S THAT GOING? ISN'T TODAY A WRITING DAY?
YEAH, YEAH... IT'S... YOU KNOW, JUST, UH, TAKING A BREAK AND...
...HEY WHAT ABOUT SOMETHING WITH RADIANT?
RADIANT... RADIANT...
...THAT'S NOT BAD, ACTUALLY.
OH! OH!
I SO HAVE IT, HOLD ON...
...YEP. OH MY GOD, IT'S PERFECT.
READY?
WHAT IS IT?
RADIANT... BLACK.

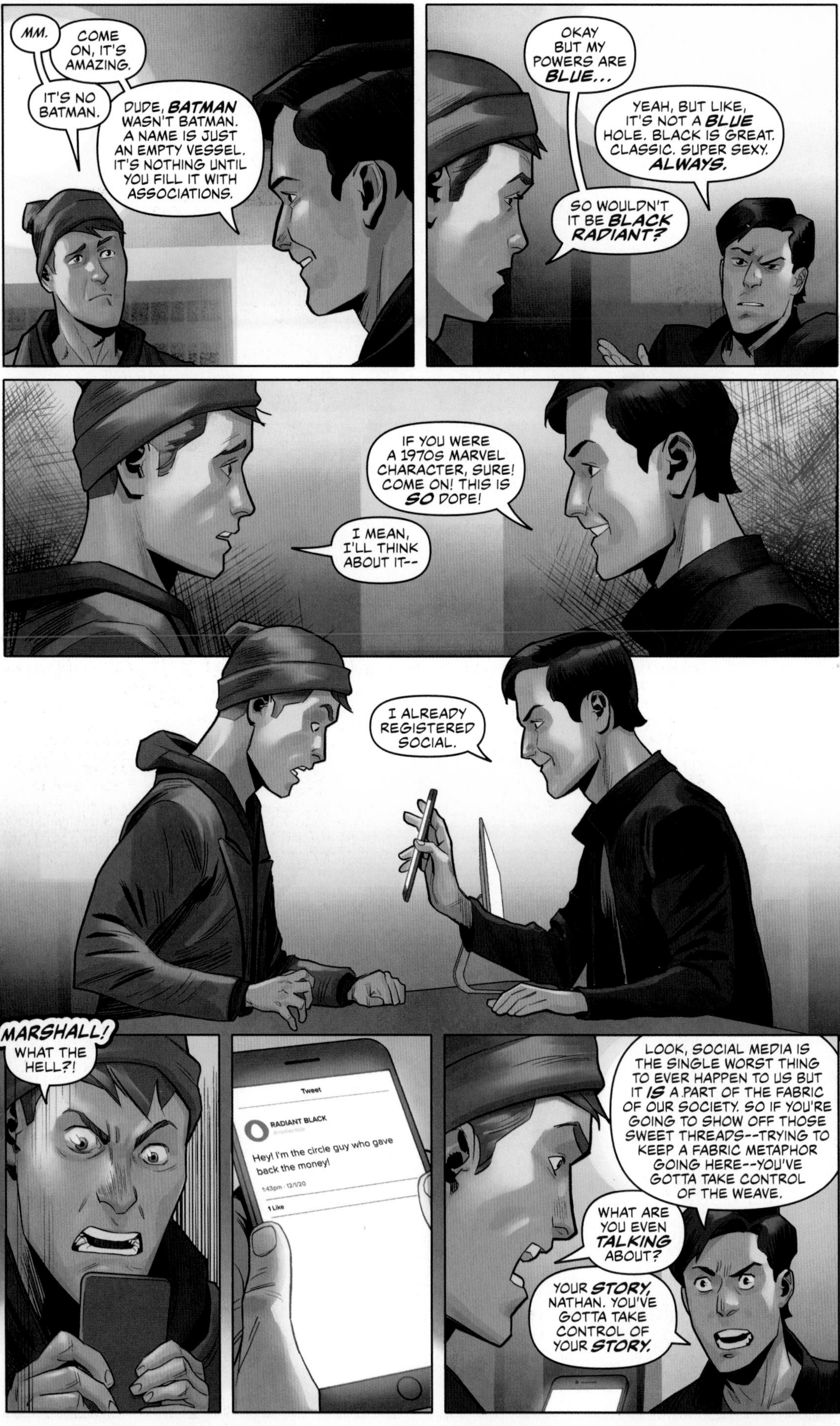
MM.
COME ON, IT'S AMAZING.
IT'S NO BATMAN.
DUDE, BATMAN WASN'T BATMAN. A NAME IS JUST AN EMPTY VESSEL. IT'S NOTHING UNTIL YOU FILL IT WITH ASSOCIATIONS.
OKAY BUT MY POWERS ARE BLUE...
YEAH, BUT LIKE, IT'S NOT A BLUE HOLE. BLACK IS GREAT. CLASSIC. SUPER SEXY. ALWAYS.
SO WOULDN'T IT BE BLACK RADIANT?
IF YOU WERE A 1970S MARVEL CHARACTER, SURE! COME ON! THIS IS SO DOPE!
I MEAN, I'LL THINK ABOUT IT--
I ALREADY REGISTERED SOCIAL.
MARSHALL! WHAT THE HELL?!
Tweet
RADIANT BLACK
Hey! I'm the circle guy who gave back the money!
1:43pm · 12/1/20
1 Like
LOOK, SOCIAL MEDIA IS THE SINGLE WORST THING TO EVER HAPPEN TO US BUT IT IS A PART OF THE FABRIC OF OUR SOCIETY. SO IF YOU'RE GOING TO SHOW OFF THOSE SWEET THREADS--TRYING TO KEEP A FABRIC METAPHOR GOING HERE--YOU'VE GOTTA TAKE CONTROL OF THE WEAVE.
WHAT ARE YOU EVEN TALKING ABOUT?
YOUR STORY, NATHAN. YOU'VE GOTTA TAKE CONTROL OF YOUR STORY.

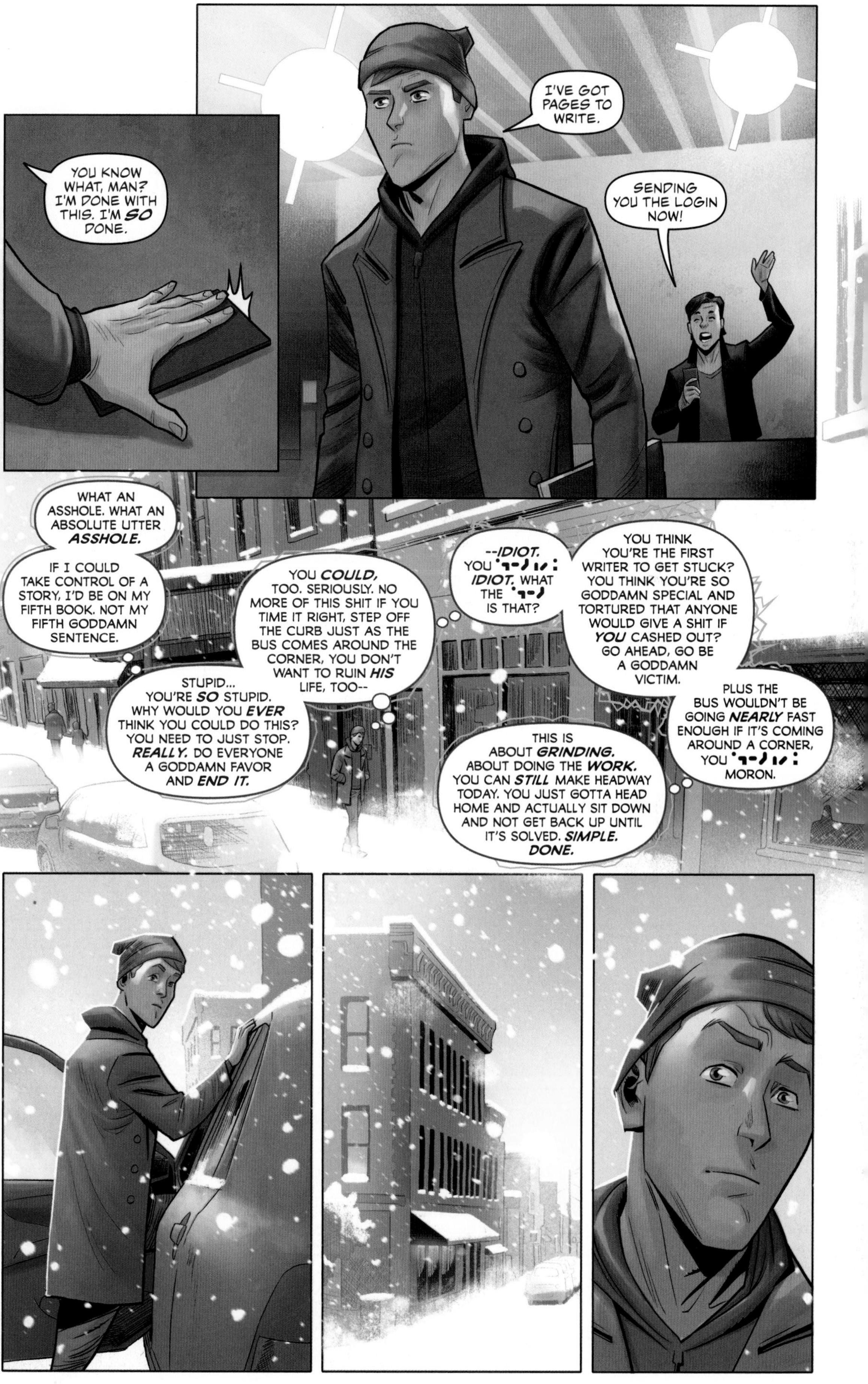
YOU KNOW WHAT, MAN? I'M DONE WITH THIS. I'M **SO** DONE.
I'VE GOT PAGES TO WRITE.
SENDING YOU THE LOGIN NOW!
WHAT AN ASSHOLE. WHAT AN ABSOLUTE UTTER **ASSHOLE.**
IF I COULD TAKE CONTROL OF A STORY, I'D BE ON MY FIFTH BOOK. NOT MY FIFTH GODDAMN SENTENCE.
STUPID... YOU'RE **SO** STUPID. WHY WOULD YOU **EVER** THINK YOU COULD DO THIS? YOU NEED TO JUST STOP. **REALLY.** DO EVERYONE A GODDAMN FAVOR AND **END IT.**
YOU **COULD,** TOO. SERIOUSLY. NO MORE OF THIS SHIT IF YOU TIME IT RIGHT, STEP OFF THE CURB JUST AS THE BUS COMES AROUND THE CORNER, YOU DON'T WANT TO RUIN **HIS** LIFE, TOO--
--**IDIOT.** YOU **IDIOT.** WHAT THE IS THAT?
YOU THINK YOU'RE THE FIRST WRITER TO GET STUCK? YOU THINK YOU'RE SO GODDAMN SPECIAL AND TORTURED THAT ANYONE WOULD GIVE A SHIT IF **YOU** CASHED OUT? GO AHEAD, GO BE A GODDAMN VICTIM.
THIS IS ABOUT **GRINDING.** ABOUT DOING THE **WORK.** YOU CAN **STILL** MAKE HEADWAY TODAY. YOU JUST GOTTA HEAD HOME AND ACTUALLY SIT DOWN AND NOT GET BACK UP UNTIL IT'S SOLVED. **SIMPLE. DONE.**
PLUS THE BUS WOULDN'T BE GOING **NEARLY** FAST ENOUGH IF IT'S COMING AROUND A CORNER, YOU MORON.

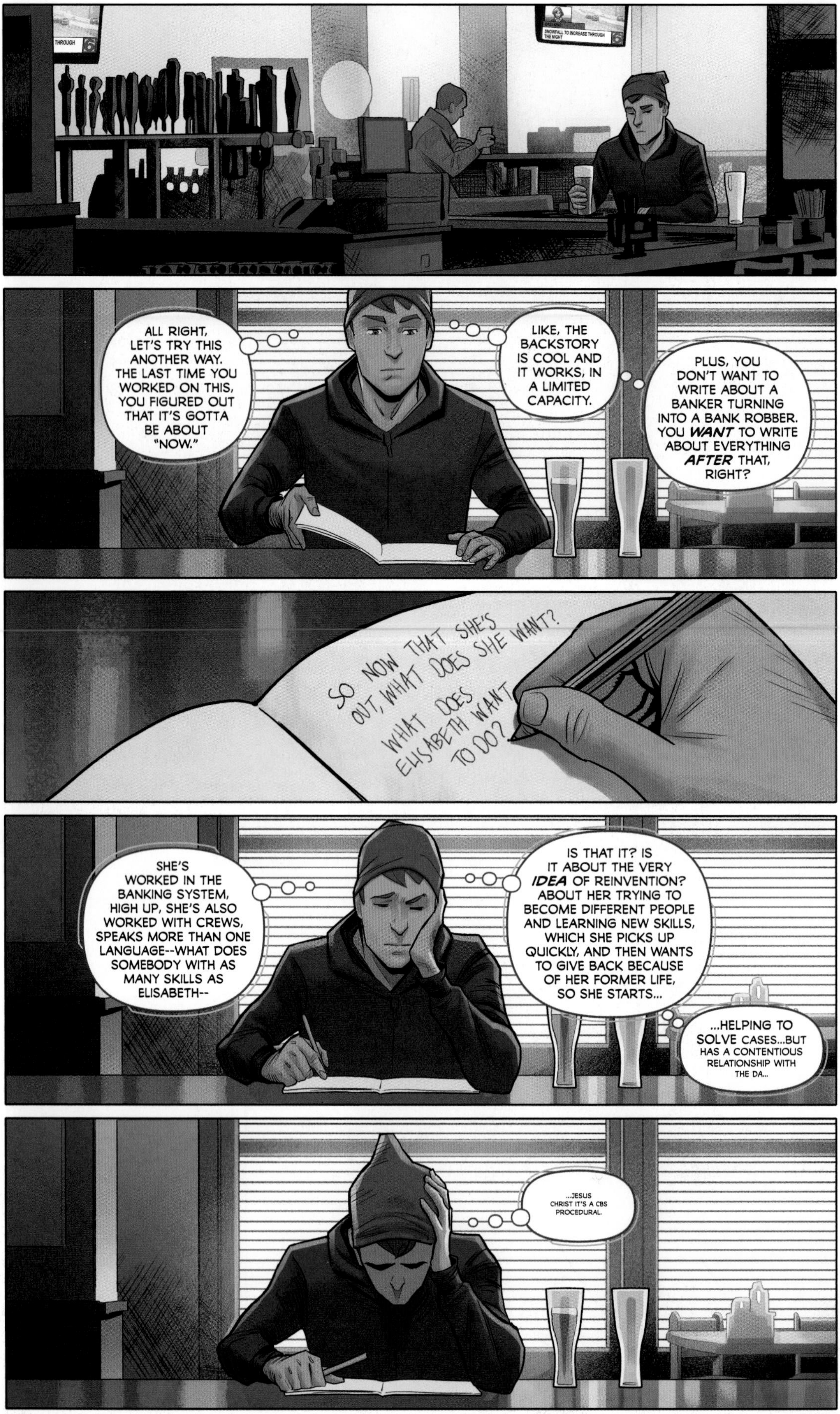
THROUGH
SNOWFALL TO INCREASE THROUGH THE NIGHT
ALL RIGHT, LET'S TRY THIS ANOTHER WAY. THE LAST TIME YOU WORKED ON THIS, YOU FIGURED OUT THAT IT'S GOTTA BE ABOUT "NOW."
LIKE, THE BACKSTORY IS COOL AND IT WORKS, IN A LIMITED CAPACITY.
PLUS, YOU DON'T WANT TO WRITE ABOUT A BANKER TURNING INTO A BANK ROBBER. YOU *WANT* TO WRITE ABOUT EVERYTHING *AFTER* THAT, RIGHT?
SO NOW THAT SHE'S OUT, WHAT DOES SHE WANT?
WHAT DOES ELISABETH WANT TO DO?
SHE'S WORKED IN THE BANKING SYSTEM, HIGH UP, SHE'S ALSO WORKED WITH CREWS, SPEAKS MORE THAN ONE LANGUAGE--WHAT DOES SOMEBODY WITH AS MANY SKILLS AS ELISABETH--
IS THAT IT? IS IT ABOUT THE VERY *IDEA* OF REINVENTION? ABOUT HER TRYING TO BECOME DIFFERENT PEOPLE AND LEARNING NEW SKILLS, WHICH SHE PICKS UP QUICKLY, AND THEN WANTS TO GIVE BACK BECAUSE OF HER FORMER LIFE, SO SHE STARTS...
...HELPING TO SOLVE CASES...BUT HAS A CONTENTIOUS RELATIONSHIP WITH THE DA...
...JESUS CHRIST IT'S A CBS PROCEDURAL.

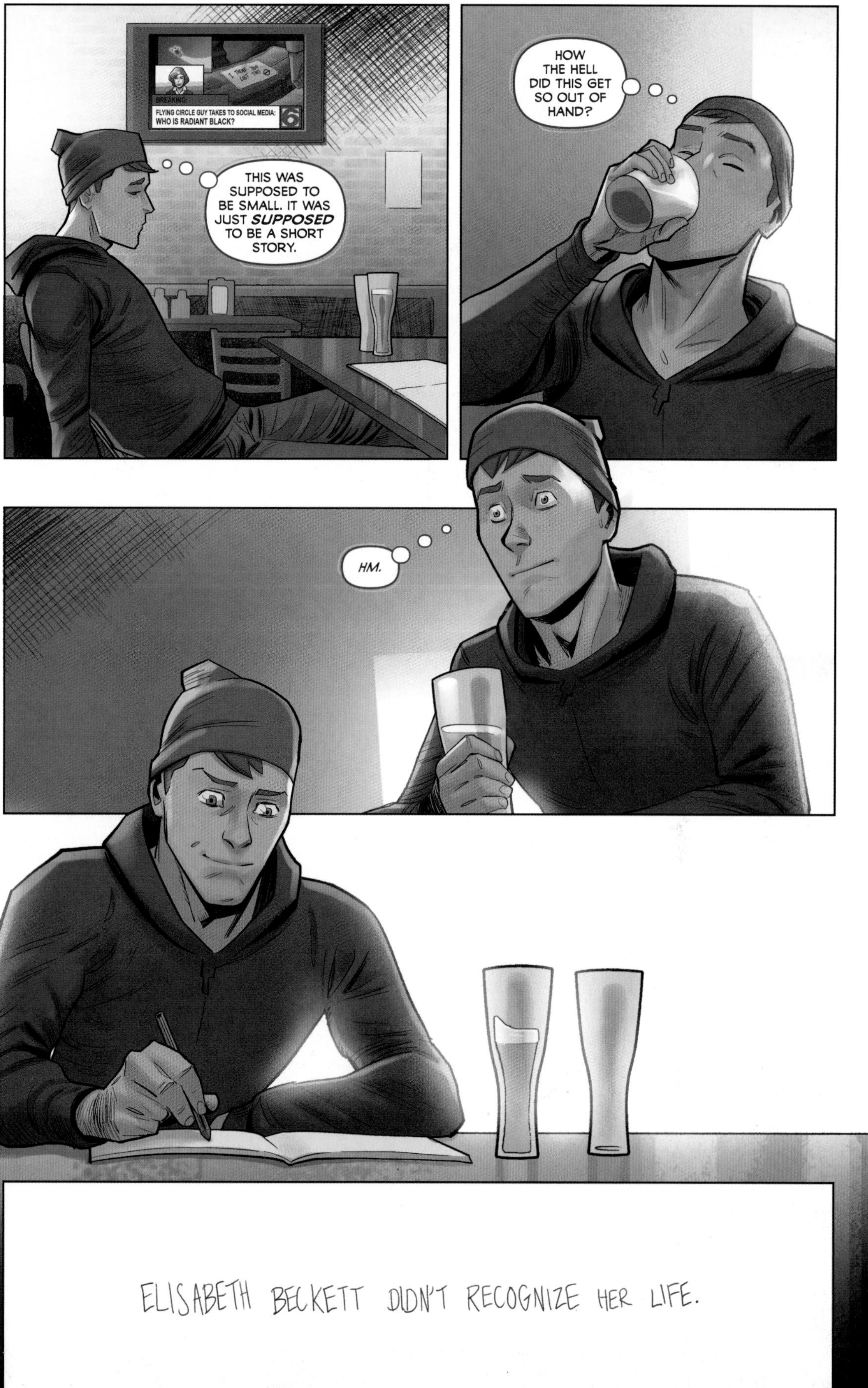
BREAKING
FLYING CIRCLE GUY TAKES TO SOCIAL MEDIA: WHO IS RADIANT BLACK?
THIS WAS SUPPOSED TO BE SMALL. IT WAS JUST *SUPPOSED* TO BE A SHORT STORY.
HOW THE HELL DID THIS GET SO OUT OF HAND?
HM.
ELISABETH BECKETT DIDN'T RECOGNIZE HER LIFE.

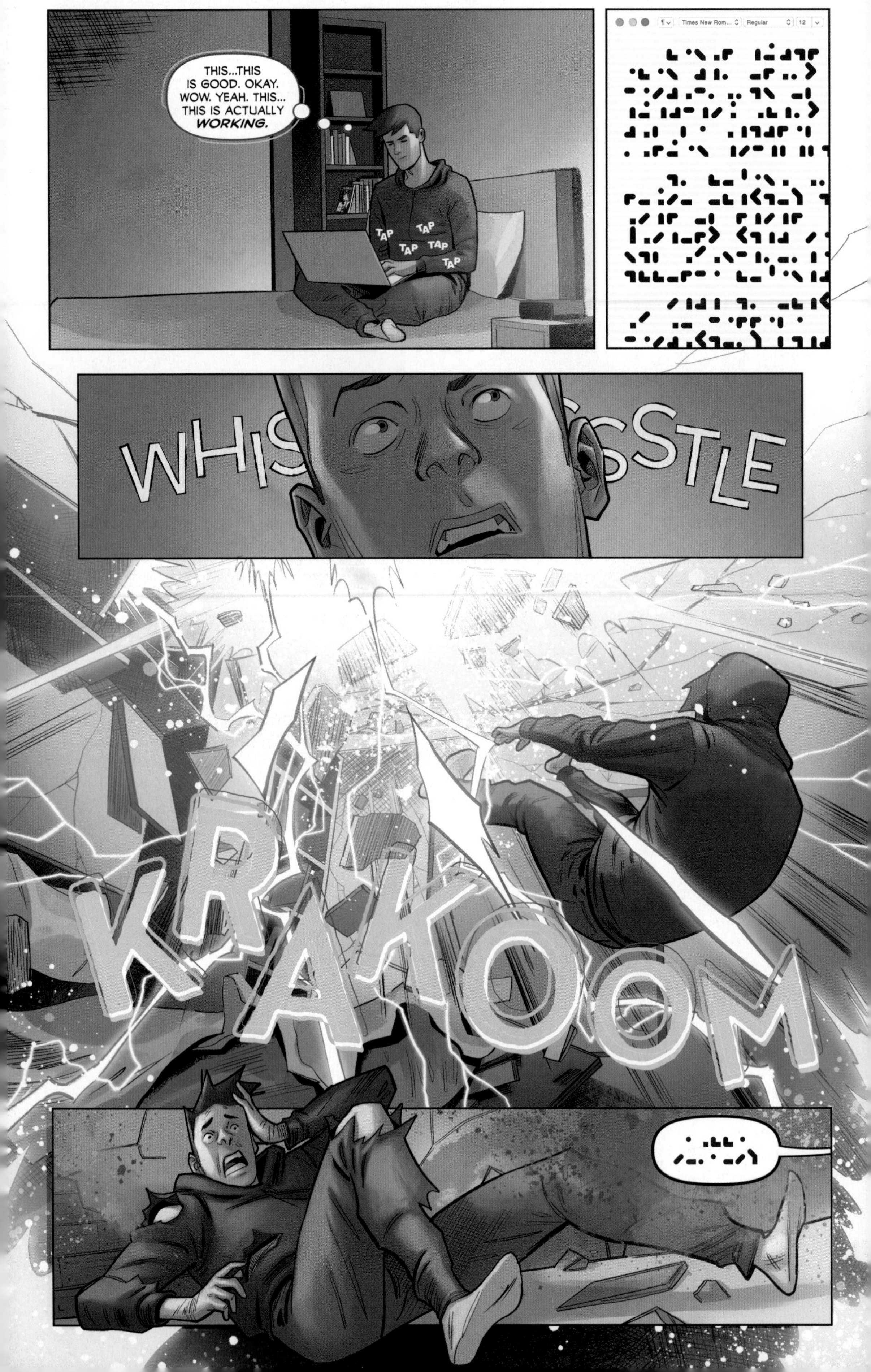
THIS...THIS IS GOOD. OKAY. WOW. YEAH. THIS... THIS IS ACTUALLY *WORKING.*
TAP
TAP
TAP
TAP
TAP
Times New Rom...
Regular
12
WHIS
SSTLE
KRAKOOM

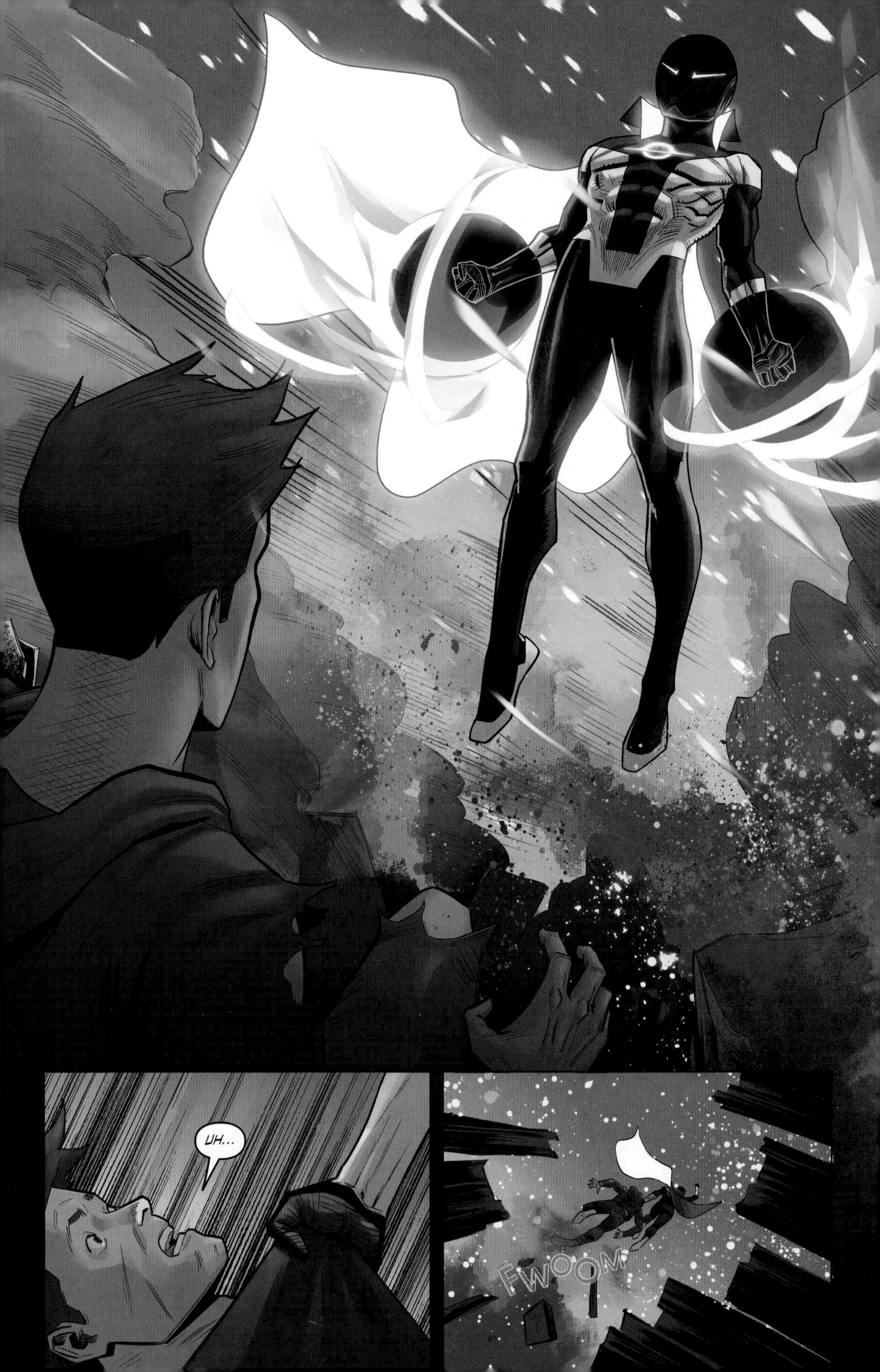
UH...
FWOOM

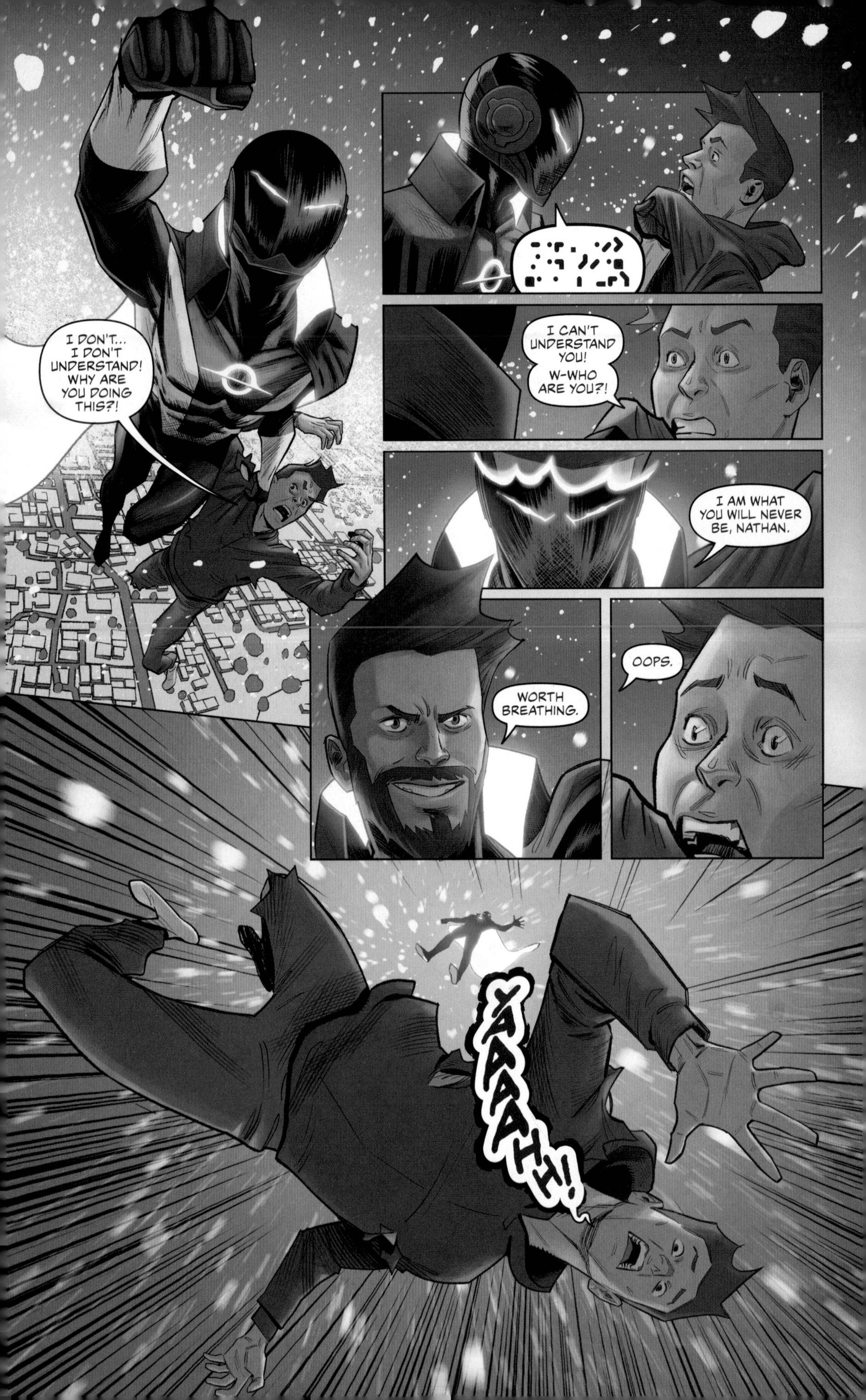
I DON'T... I DON'T UNDERSTAND! WHY ARE YOU DOING THIS?!
I CAN'T UNDERSTAND YOU!
W-WHO ARE YOU?!
I AM WHAT YOU WILL NEVER BE, NATHAN.
WORTH BREATHING.
OOPS.
YAAAAH!

AAAaAHHH!

...OH... OH GOD... WHAT... WHAT TIME IS IT?

GOD DAMMIT...

BULLS HYPE ACCOUNT SAID:

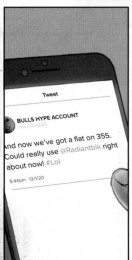

Tweet

BULLS HYPE ACCOUNT
@ogotdont665

And now we've got a flat on 355. Could really use @Radiantblk right about now! #Lol

5:44pm · 12/1/20

Layout   References

11   A^ A^   Aa

ab   x₂   x²   A   ✏

Elisabeth Beckett d

abeth Bec

Elisabeth Becket

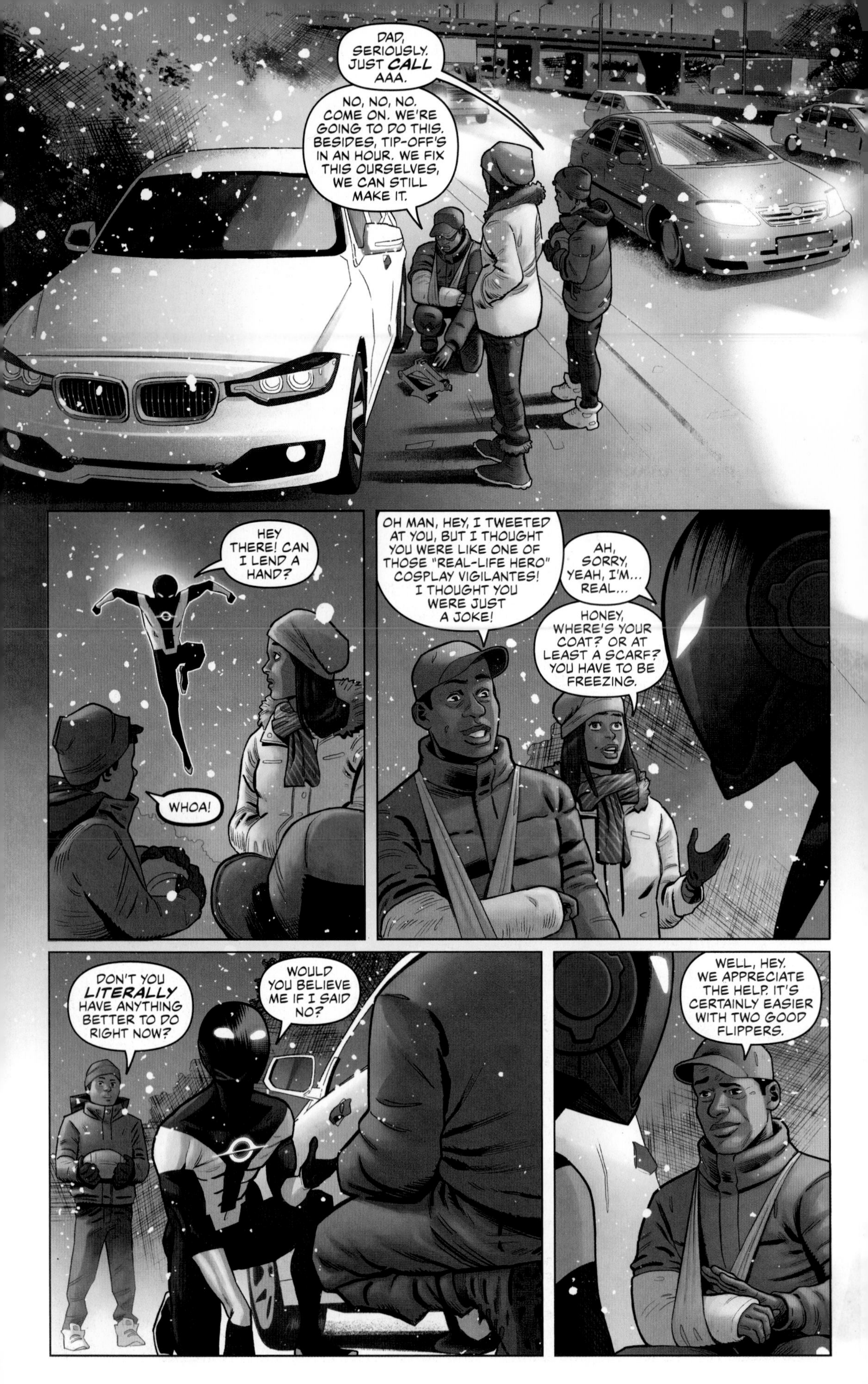
DAD, SERIOUSLY. JUST CALL AAA.
NO, NO, NO. COME ON. WE'RE GOING TO DO THIS. BESIDES, TIP-OFF'S IN AN HOUR. WE FIX THIS OURSELVES, WE CAN STILL MAKE IT.
HEY THERE! CAN I LEND A HAND?
WHOA!
OH MAN, HEY, I TWEETED AT YOU, BUT I THOUGHT YOU WERE LIKE ONE OF THOSE "REAL-LIFE HERO" COSPLAY VIGILANTES! I THOUGHT YOU WERE JUST A JOKE!
AH, SORRY, YEAH, I'M... REAL...
HONEY, WHERE'S YOUR COAT? OR AT LEAST A SCARF? YOU HAVE TO BE FREEZING.
DON'T YOU LITERALLY HAVE ANYTHING BETTER TO DO RIGHT NOW?
WOULD YOU BELIEVE ME IF I SAID NO?
WELL, HEY. WE APPRECIATE THE HELP. IT'S CERTAINLY EASIER WITH TWO GOOD FLIPPERS.

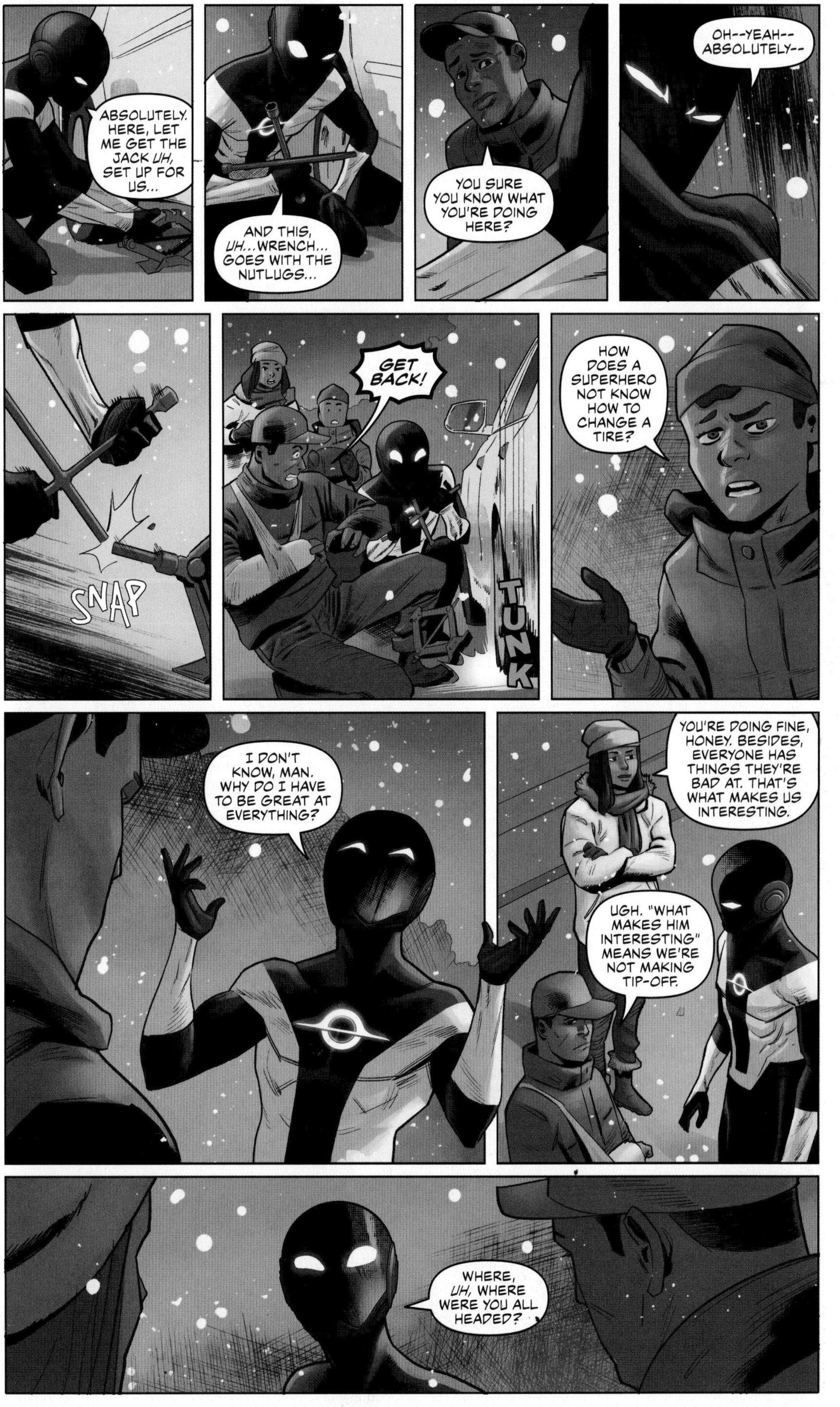
ABSOLUTELY. HERE, LET ME GET THE JACK UH, SET UP FOR US...
AND THIS, UH...WRENCH... GOES WITH THE NUTLUGS...
YOU SURE YOU KNOW WHAT YOU'RE DOING HERE?
OH--YEAH-- ABSOLUTELY--
SNAP
GET BACK!
TUNK
HOW DOES A SUPERHERO NOT KNOW HOW TO CHANGE A TIRE?
I DON'T KNOW, MAN. WHY DO I HAVE TO BE GREAT AT EVERYTHING?
YOU'RE DOING FINE, HONEY. BESIDES, EVERYONE HAS THINGS THEY'RE BAD AT. THAT'S WHAT MAKES US INTERESTING.
UGH. "WHAT MAKES HIM INTERESTING" MEANS WE'RE NOT MAKING TIP-OFF.
WHERE, UH, WHERE WERE YOU ALL HEADED?

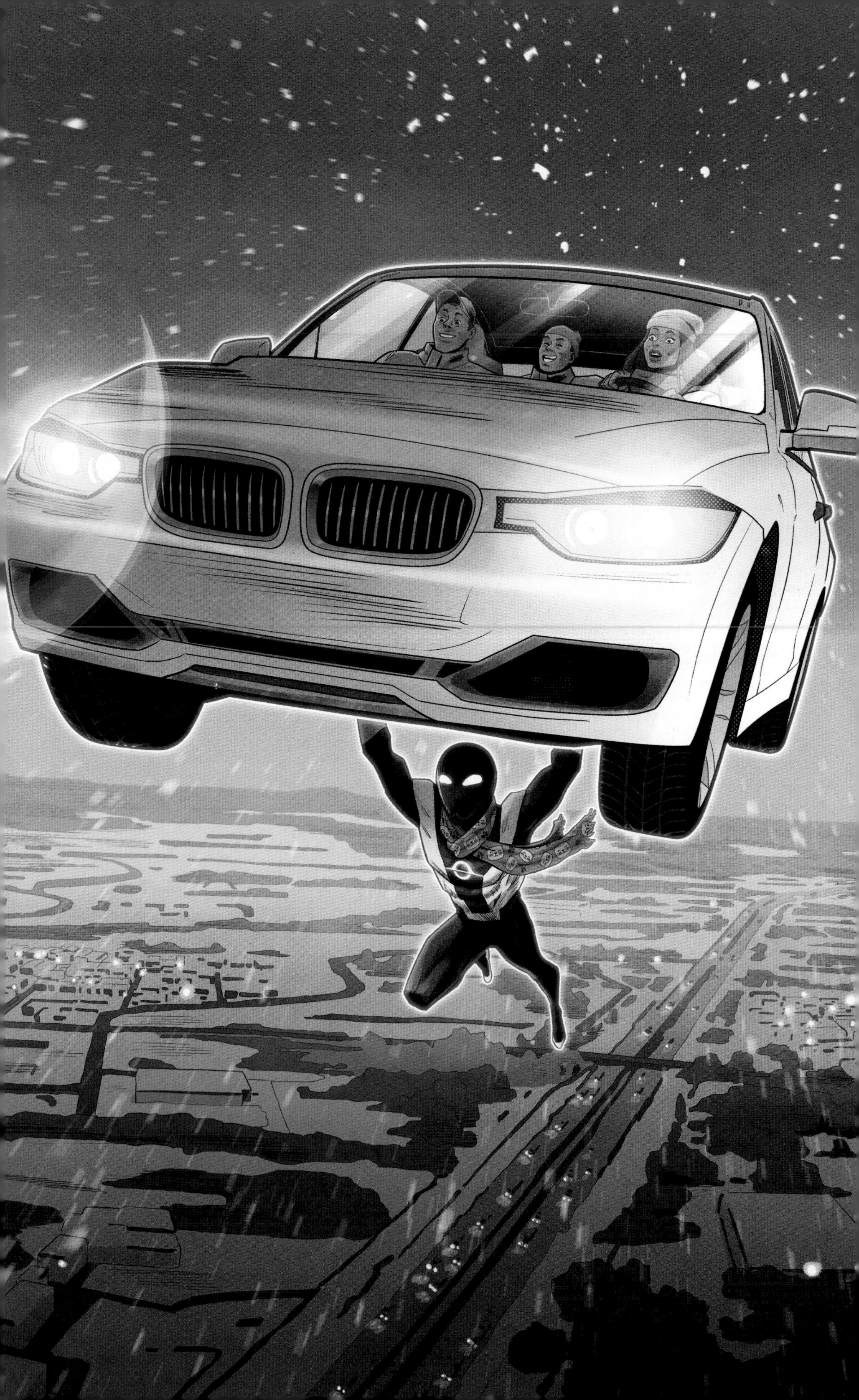

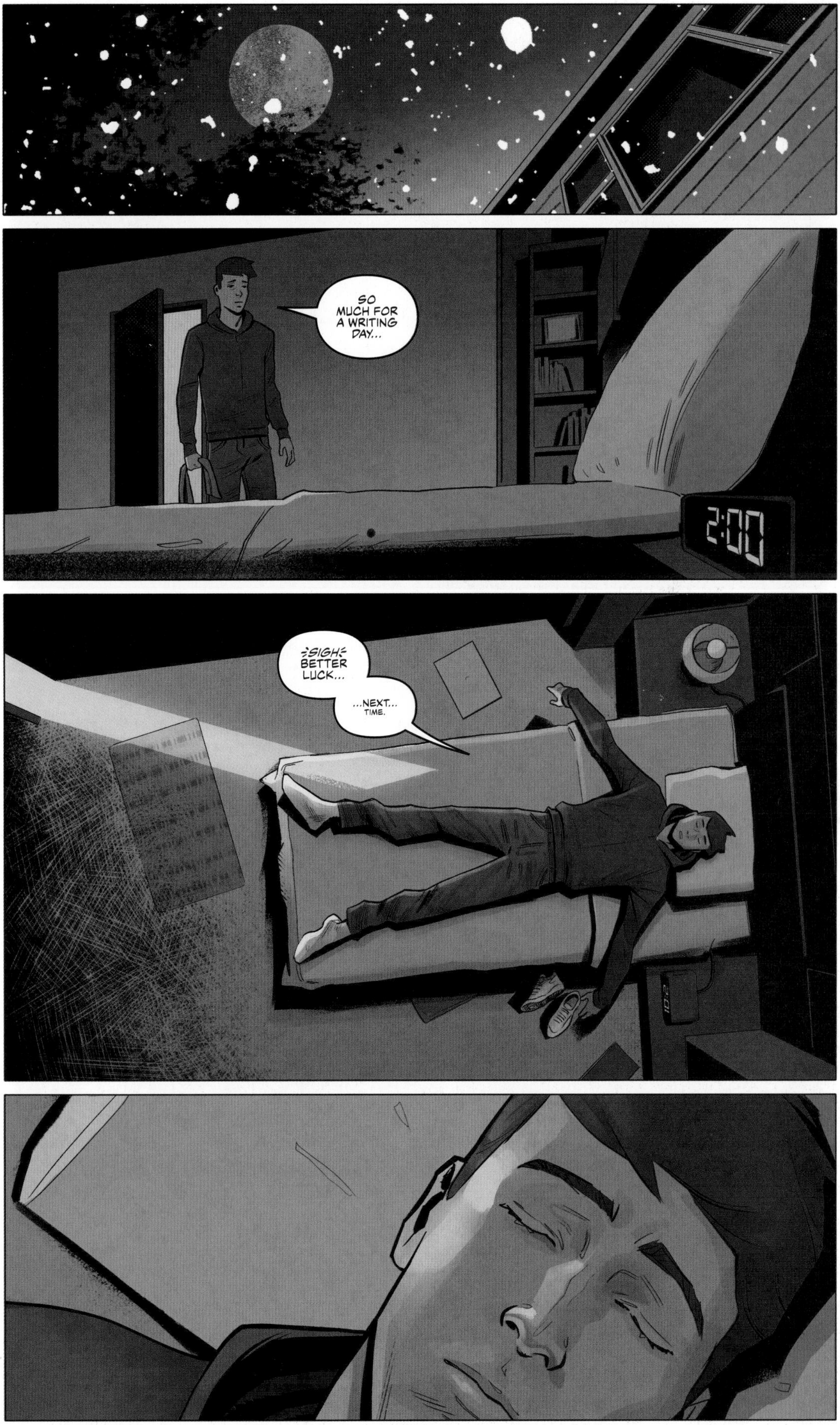
SO MUCH FOR A WRITING DAY...
2:00
-SIGH- BETTER LUCK...
...NEXT... TIME.

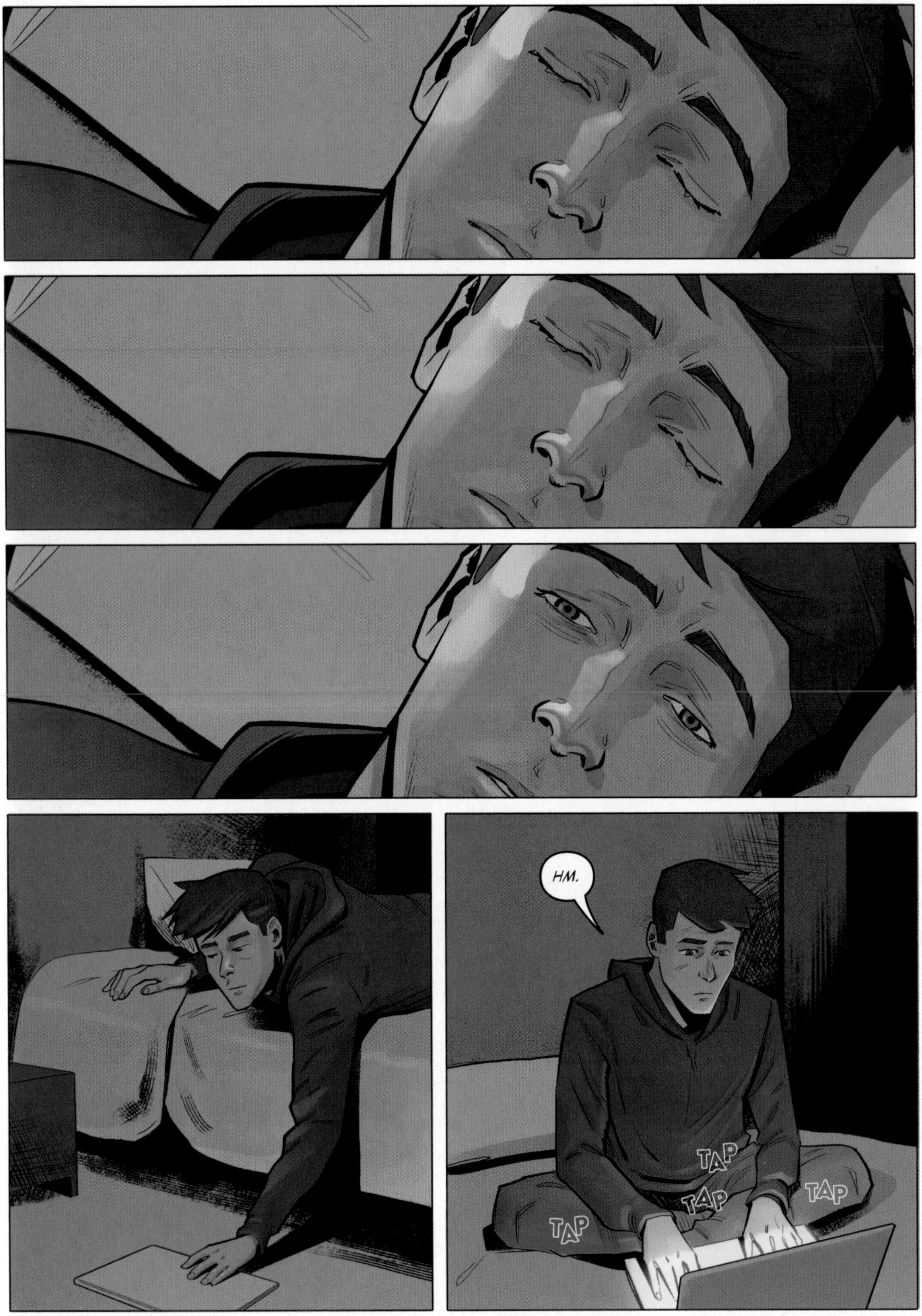
HM.
TAP
TAP
TAP
TAP

Elisabeth Beckett didn't recognize her life. She'd gone from working at banks to robbing them. But now, her partner was dead. She was on the run. A bag full of cash and all the problems to go with it.

Elisabeth Beckett had nowhere to go.

So she moved back home.

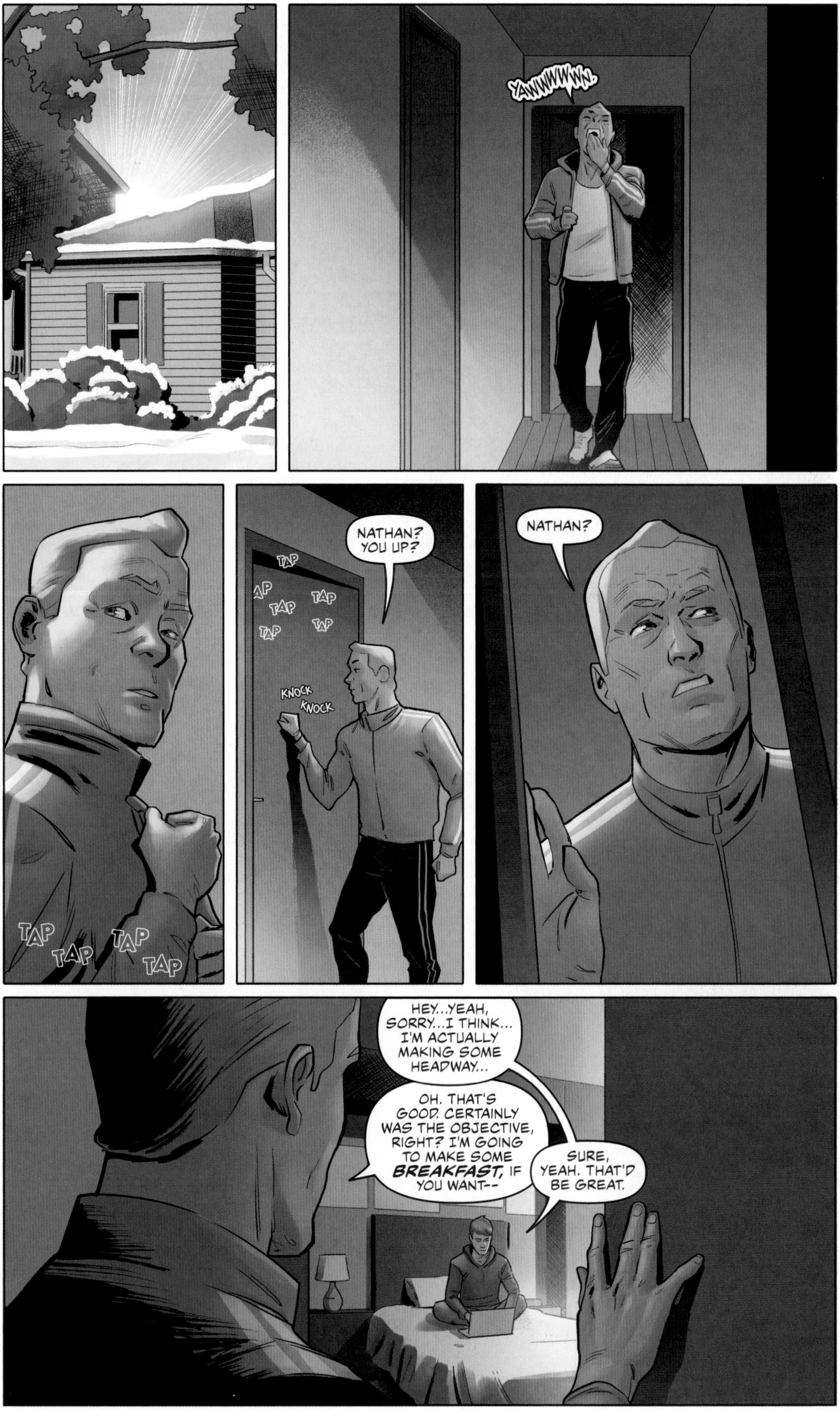
YAWWWWWN.
TAP
TAP
TAP
TAP
NATHAN? YOU UP?
TAP
TAP
TAP
TAP
KNOCK
KNOCK
NATHAN?
HEY...YEAH, SORRY...I THINK... I'M ACTUALLY MAKING SOME HEADWAY...
OH. THAT'S GOOD. CERTAINLY WAS THE OBJECTIVE, RIGHT? I'M GOING TO MAKE SOME BREAKFAST, IF YOU WANT--
SURE, YEAH. THAT'D BE GREAT.

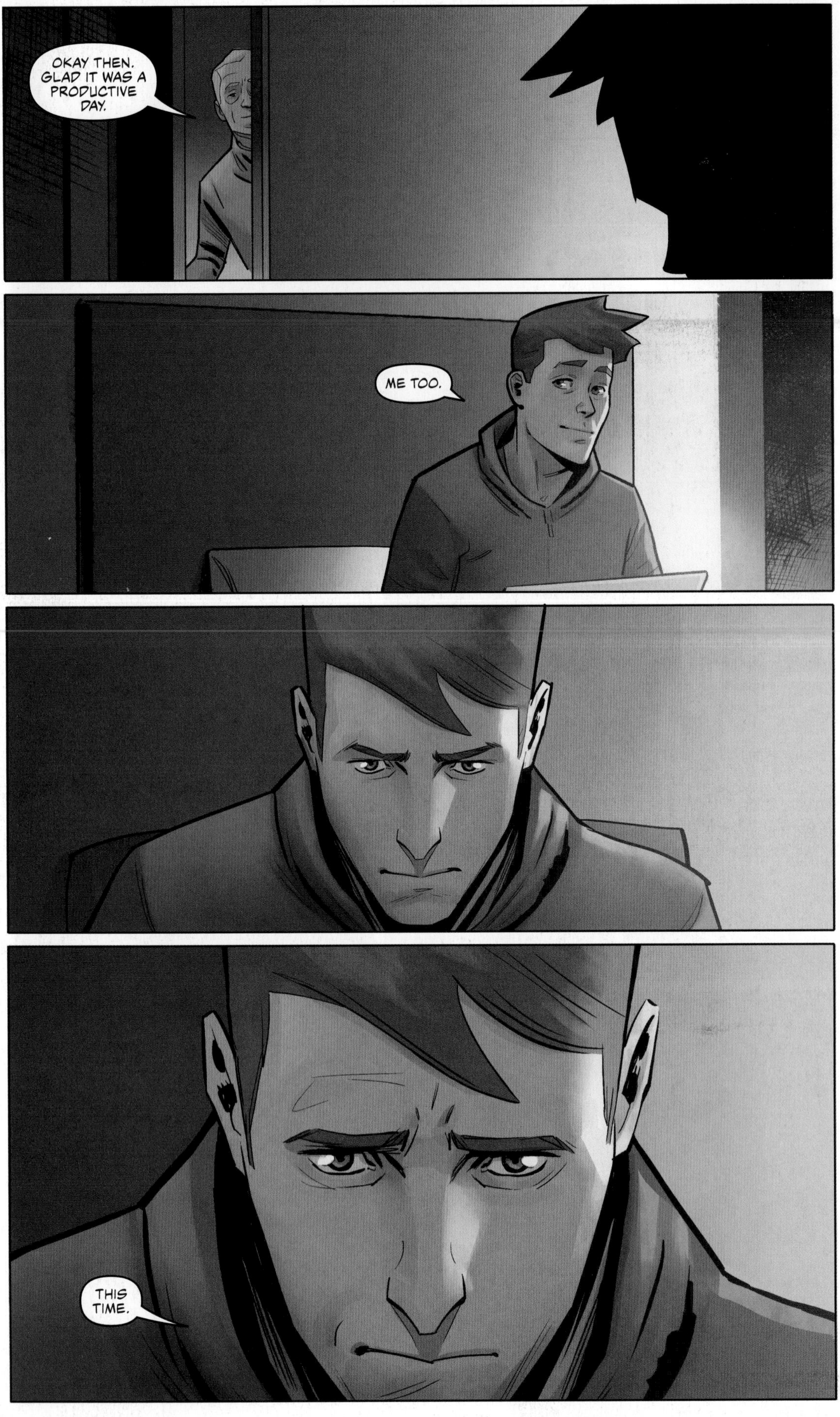
OKAY THEN. GLAD IT WAS A PRODUCTIVE DAY.
ME TOO.
THIS TIME.

CHAPTER FOUR

TITLE   Everything Changes

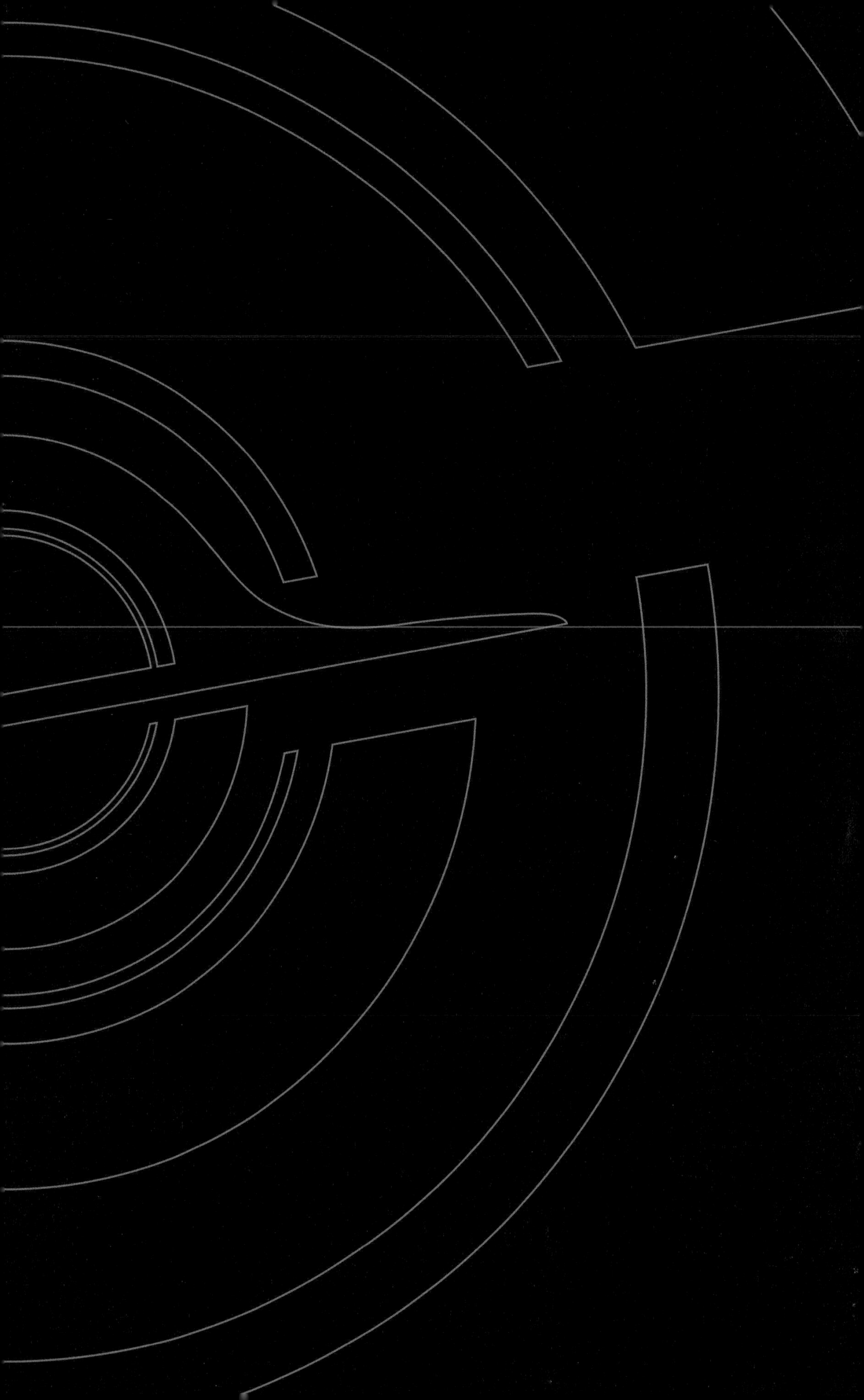

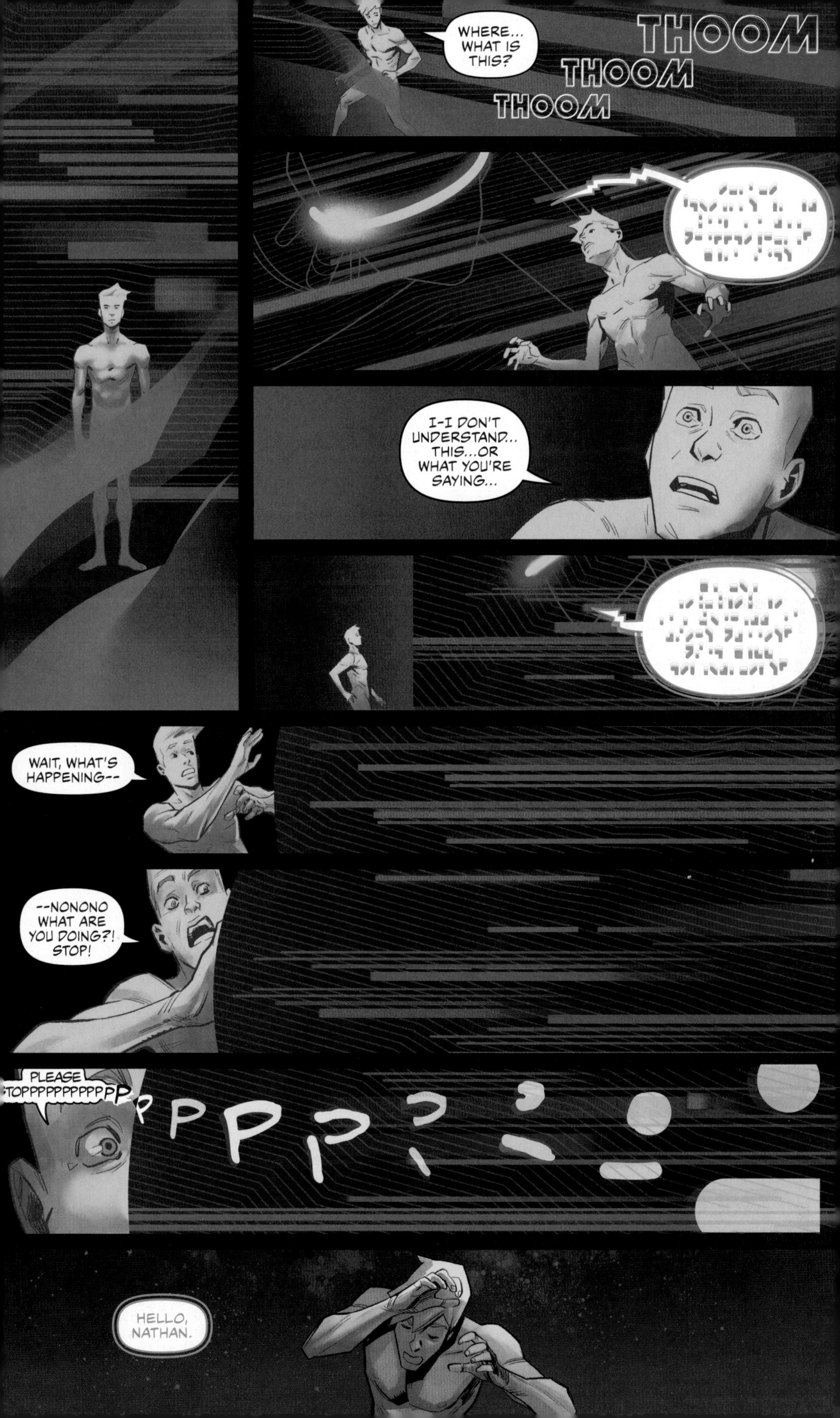

WHERE... WHAT IS THIS?
THOOM
THOOM
THOOM
I-I DON'T UNDERSTAND... THIS...OR WHAT YOU'RE SAYING...
WAIT, WHAT'S HAPPENING--
--NONONO WHAT ARE YOU DOING?! STOP!
PLEASE STOPPPPPPPPPPPP
HELLO, NATHAN.

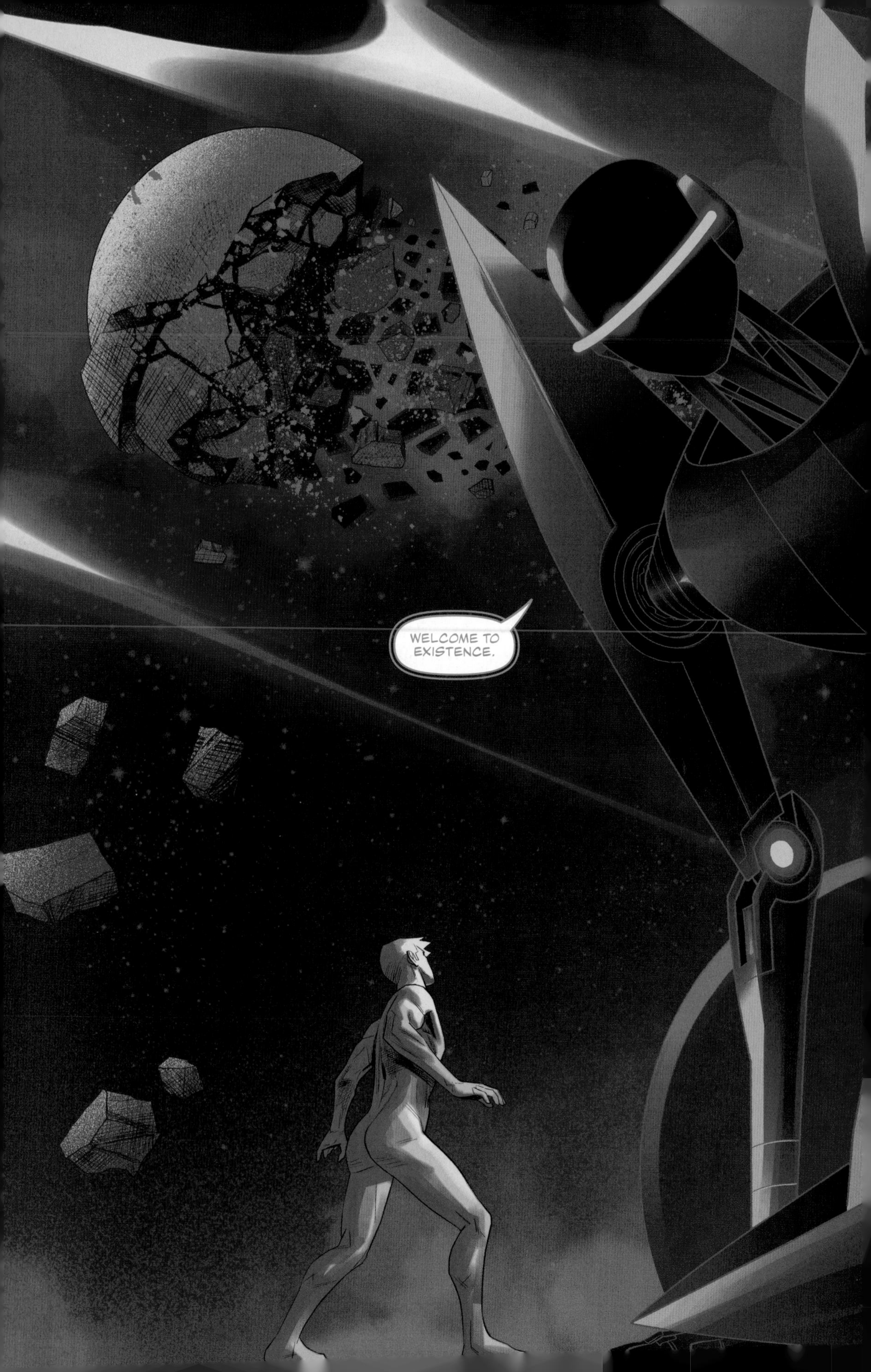
WELCOME TO EXISTENCE.

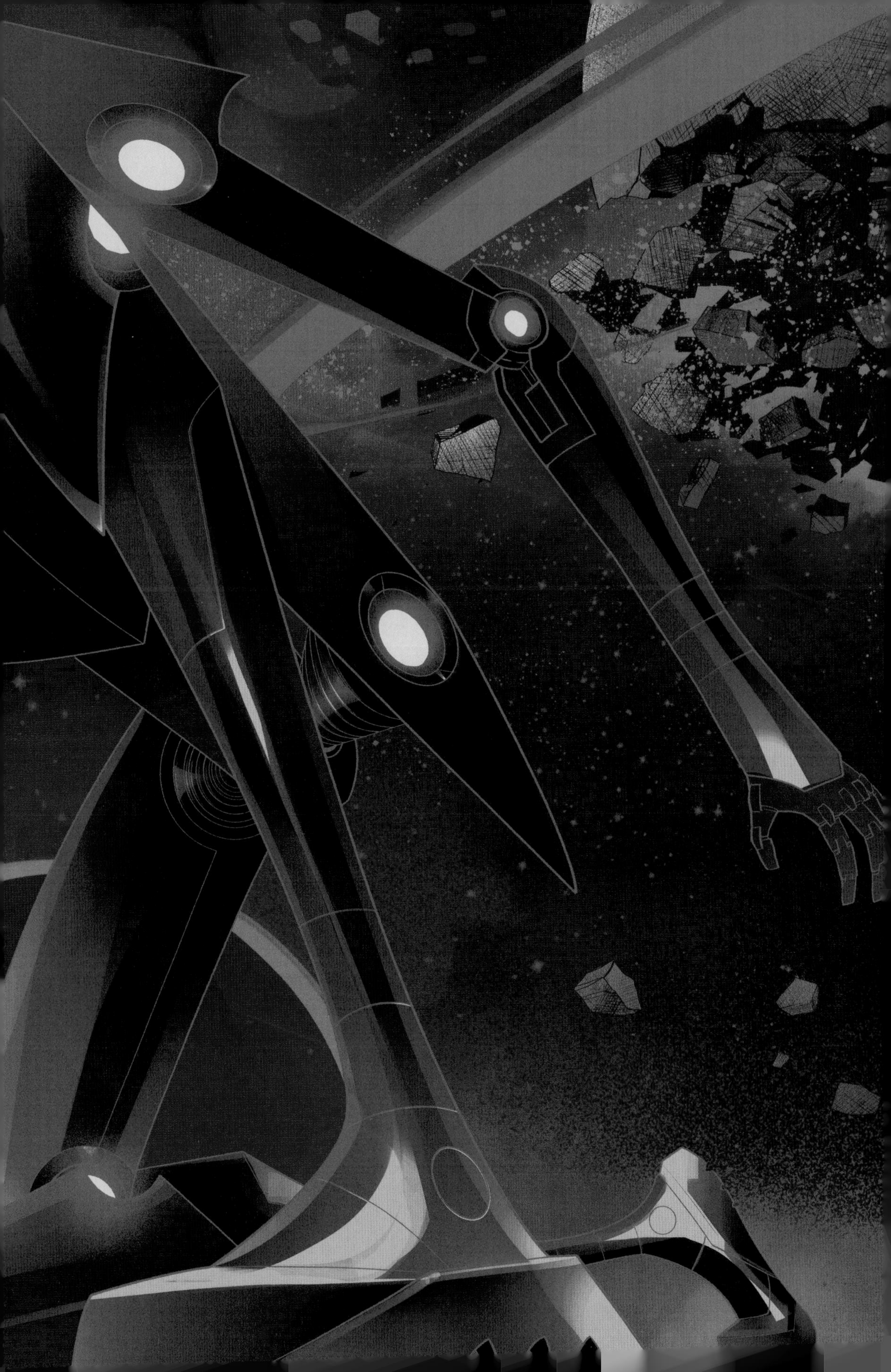

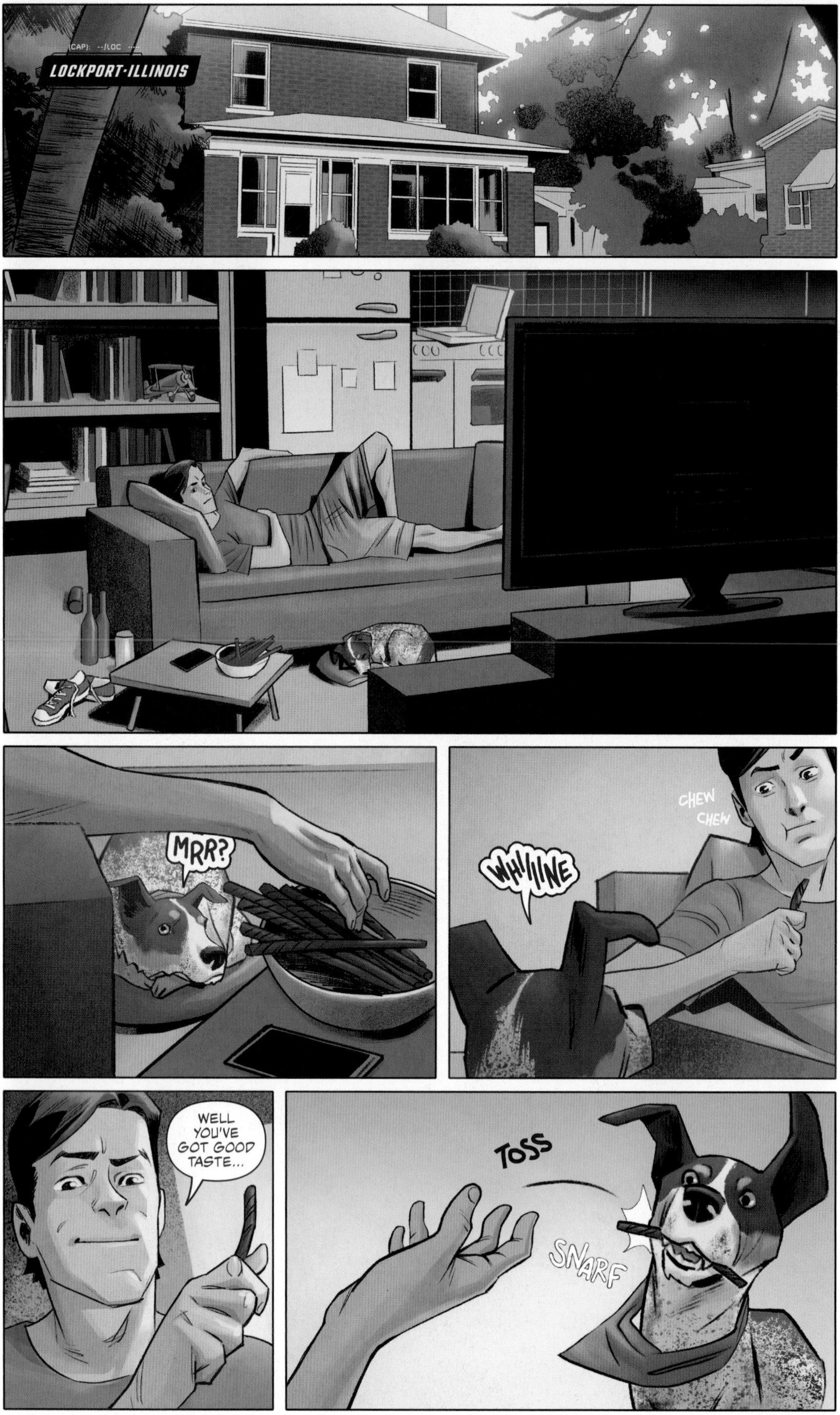
[CAP]: --/LOC
LOCKPORT-ILLINOIS
MRR?
CHEW CHEW
WHIIIINE
WELL YOU'VE GOT GOOD TASTE...
TOSS
SNARF

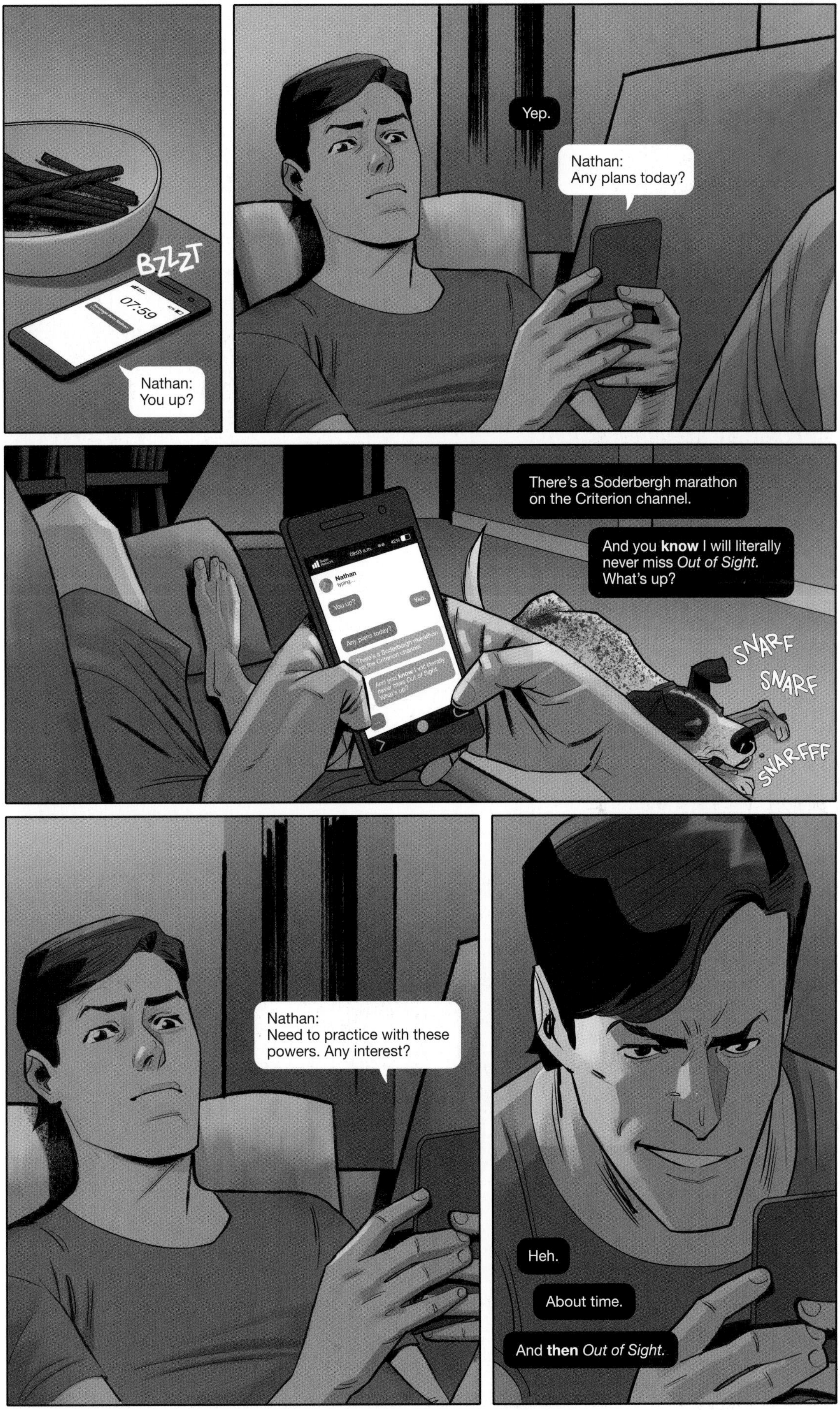
BZZZT
Nathan:
You up?
Yep.
Nathan:
Any plans today?
There's a Soderbergh marathon on the Criterion channel.
And you **know** I will literally never miss *Out of Sight.* What's up?
SNARF
SNARF
SNARFFF
Nathan:
Need to practice with these powers. Any interest?
Heh.
About time.
And **then** *Out of Sight.*

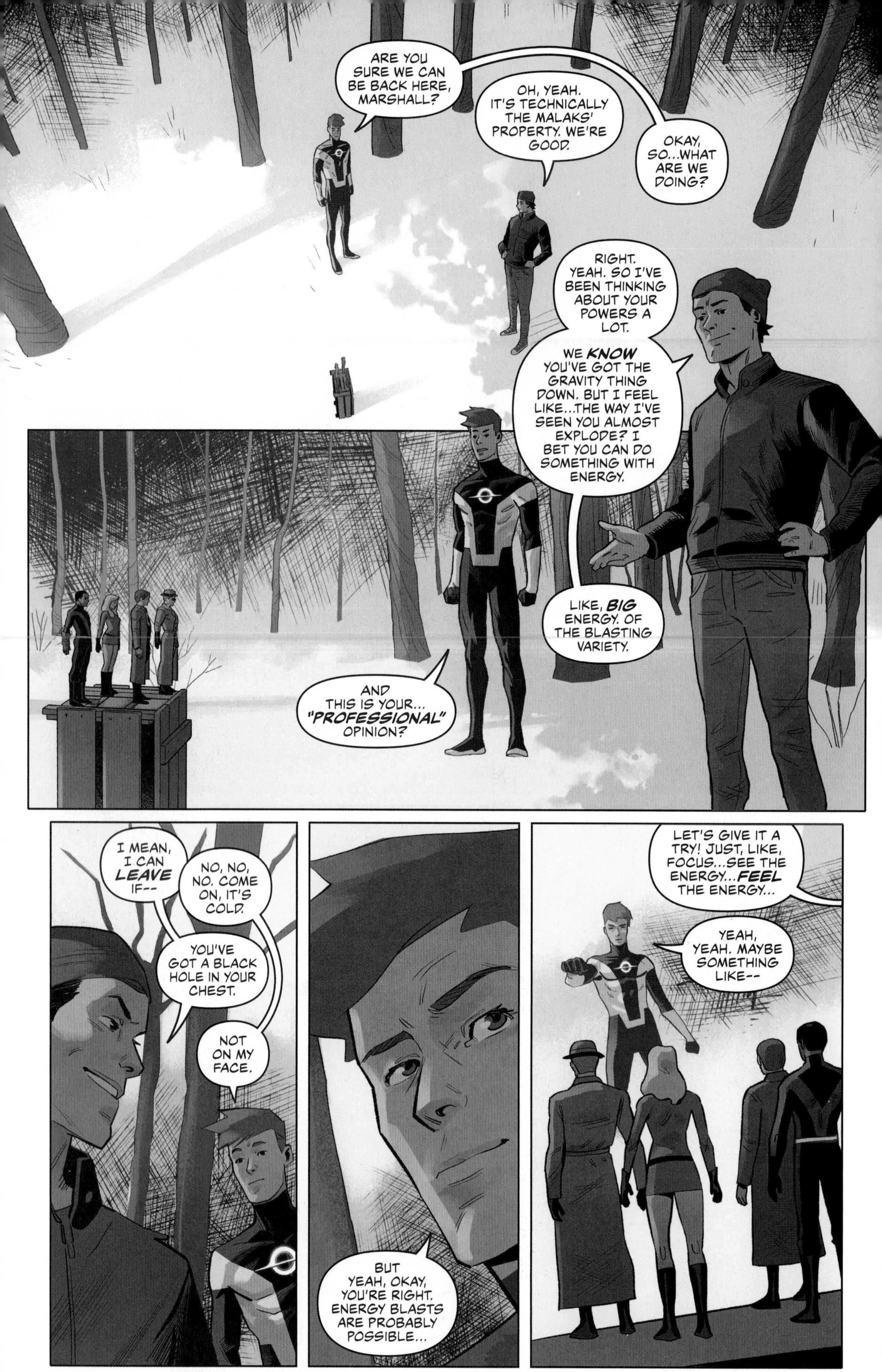
ARE YOU SURE WE CAN BE BACK HERE, MARSHALL?
OH, YEAH. IT'S TECHNICALLY THE MALAKS' PROPERTY. WE'RE GOOD.
OKAY, SO...WHAT ARE WE DOING?
RIGHT. YEAH. SO I'VE BEEN THINKING ABOUT YOUR POWERS A LOT.
WE KNOW YOU'VE GOT THE GRAVITY THING DOWN. BUT I FEEL LIKE...THE WAY I'VE SEEN YOU ALMOST EXPLODE? I BET YOU CAN DO SOMETHING WITH ENERGY.
LIKE, BIG ENERGY. OF THE BLASTING VARIETY.
AND THIS IS YOUR... "PROFESSIONAL" OPINION?
I MEAN, I CAN LEAVE IF--
NO, NO, NO. COME ON, IT'S COLD.
YOU'VE GOT A BLACK HOLE IN YOUR CHEST.
NOT ON MY FACE.
BUT YEAH, OKAY, YOU'RE RIGHT. ENERGY BLASTS ARE PROBABLY POSSIBLE...
LET'S GIVE IT A TRY! JUST, LIKE, FOCUS...SEE THE ENERGY...FEEL THE ENERGY...
YEAH, YEAH. MAYBE SOMETHING LIKE--

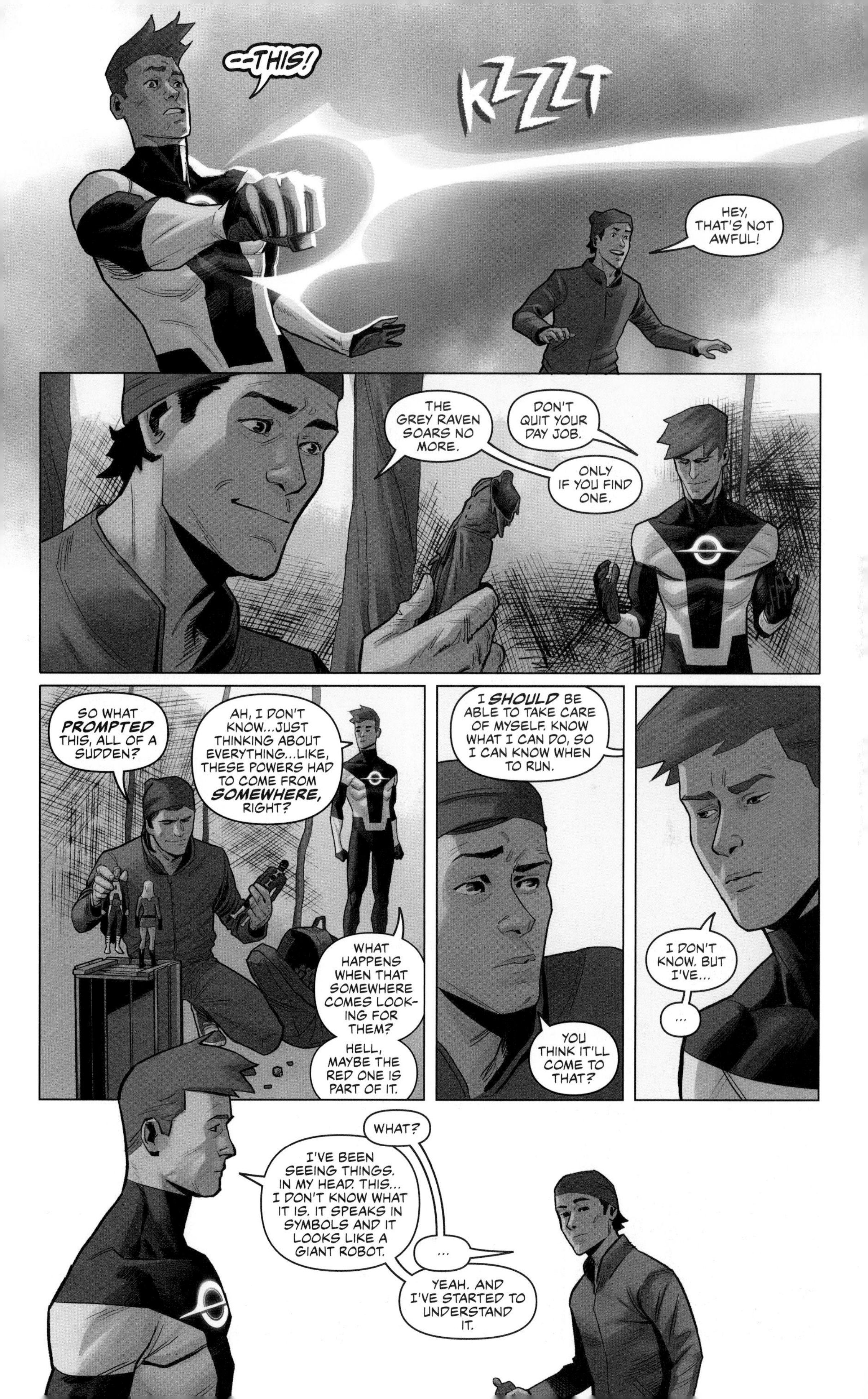
--THIS!
KZZZZT
HEY, THAT'S NOT AWFUL!
THE GREY RAVEN SOARS NO MORE.
DON'T QUIT YOUR DAY JOB.
ONLY IF YOU FIND ONE.
SO WHAT PROMPTED THIS, ALL OF A SUDDEN?
AH, I DON'T KNOW...JUST THINKING ABOUT EVERYTHING...LIKE, THESE POWERS HAD TO COME FROM SOMEWHERE, RIGHT?
WHAT HAPPENS WHEN THAT SOMEWHERE COMES LOOKING FOR THEM?
HELL, MAYBE THE RED ONE IS PART OF IT.
I SHOULD BE ABLE TO TAKE CARE OF MYSELF. KNOW WHAT I CAN DO, SO I CAN KNOW WHEN TO RUN.
YOU THINK IT'LL COME TO THAT?
I DON'T KNOW. BUT I'VE...
...
I'VE BEEN SEEING THINGS. IN MY HEAD. THIS... I DON'T KNOW WHAT IT IS. IT SPEAKS IN SYMBOLS AND IT LOOKS LIKE A GIANT ROBOT.
WHAT?
...
YEAH. AND I'VE STARTED TO UNDERSTAND IT.

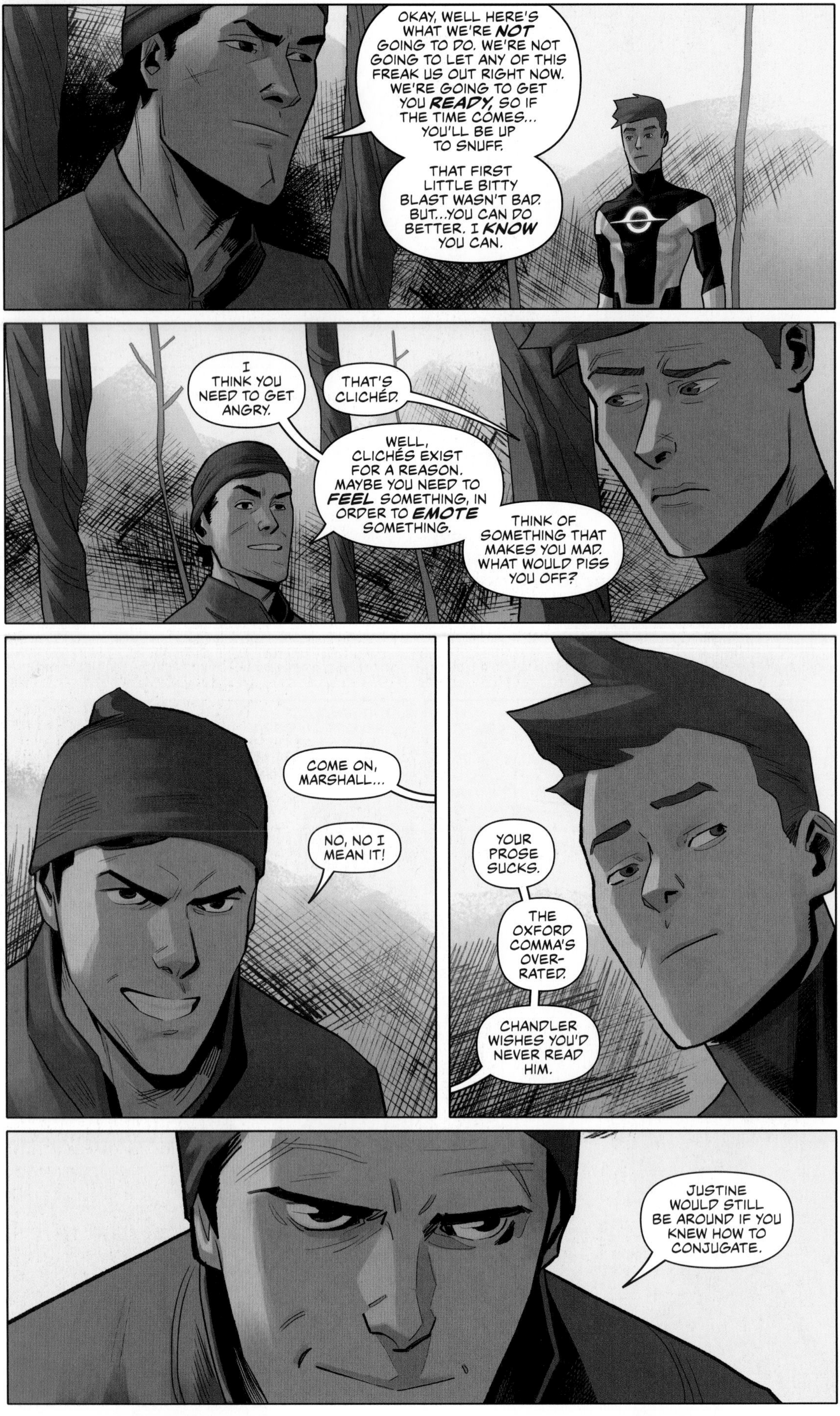
OKAY, WELL HERE'S WHAT WE'RE NOT GOING TO DO. WE'RE NOT GOING TO LET ANY OF THIS FREAK US OUT RIGHT NOW. WE'RE GOING TO GET YOU READY, SO IF THE TIME COMES... YOU'LL BE UP TO SNUFF.
THAT FIRST LITTLE BITTY BLAST WASN'T BAD. BUT...YOU CAN DO BETTER. I KNOW YOU CAN.
I THINK YOU NEED TO GET ANGRY.
THAT'S CLICHÉD.
WELL, CLICHÉS EXIST FOR A REASON. MAYBE YOU NEED TO FEEL SOMETHING, IN ORDER TO EMOTE SOMETHING.
THINK OF SOMETHING THAT MAKES YOU MAD. WHAT WOULD PISS YOU OFF?
COME ON, MARSHALL...
NO, NO I MEAN IT!
YOUR PROSE SUCKS.
THE OXFORD COMMA'S OVER-RATED.
CHANDLER WISHES YOU'D NEVER READ HIM.
JUSTINE WOULD STILL BE AROUND IF YOU KNEW HOW TO CONJUGATE.

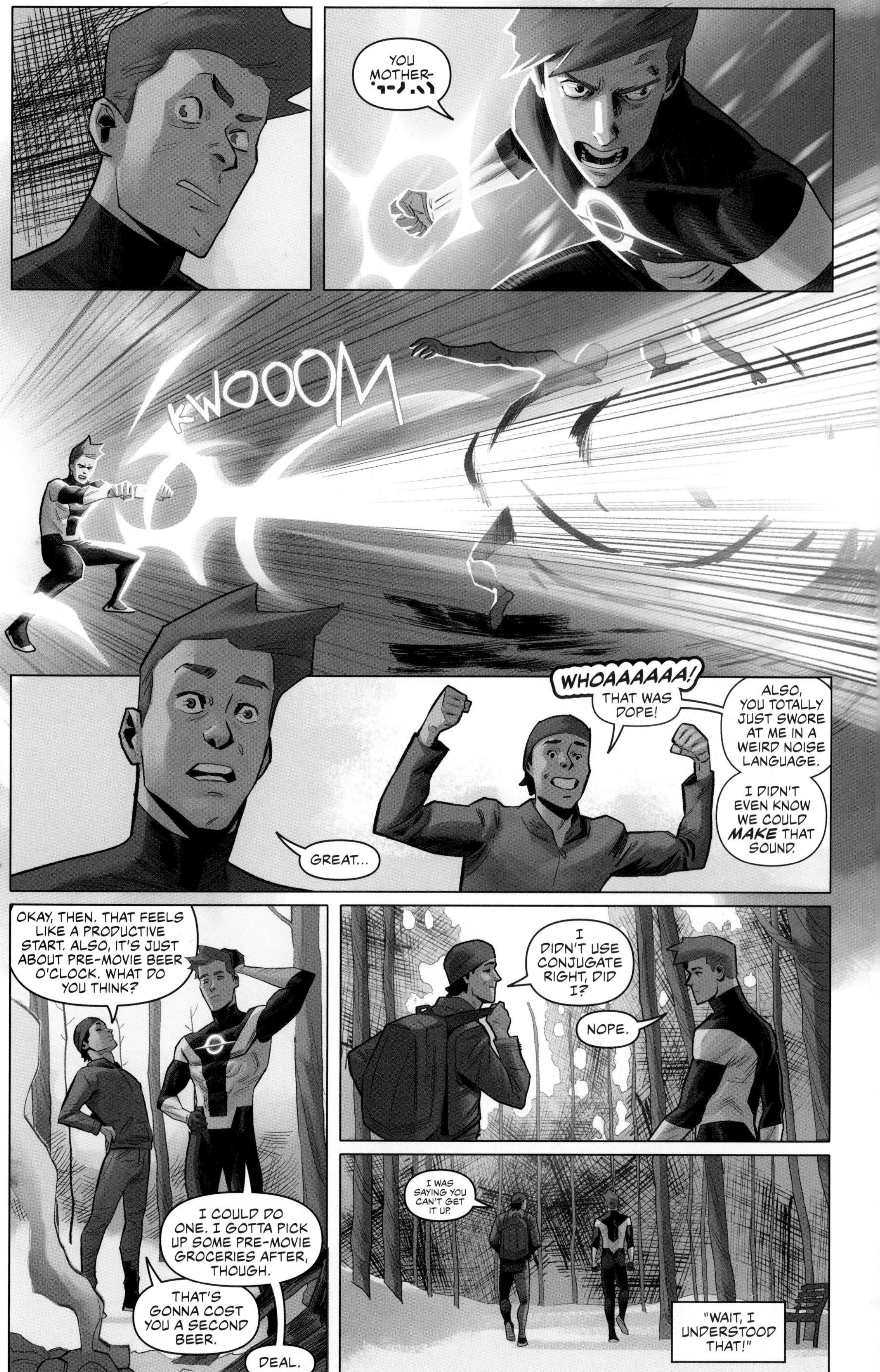
YOU MOTHER-
KWOOOM
WHOAAAAAA! THAT WAS DOPE!
ALSO, YOU TOTALLY JUST SWORE AT ME IN A WEIRD NOISE LANGUAGE.
I DIDN'T EVEN KNOW WE COULD MAKE THAT SOUND.
GREAT...
OKAY, THEN. THAT FEELS LIKE A PRODUCTIVE START. ALSO, IT'S JUST ABOUT PRE-MOVIE BEER O'CLOCK. WHAT DO YOU THINK?
I COULD DO ONE. I GOTTA PICK UP SOME PRE-MOVIE GROCERIES AFTER, THOUGH.
THAT'S GONNA COST YOU A SECOND BEER.
DEAL.
I DIDN'T USE CONJUGATE RIGHT, DID I?
NOPE.
I WAS SAYING YOU CAN'T GET IT UP.
"WAIT, I UNDERSTOOD THAT!"

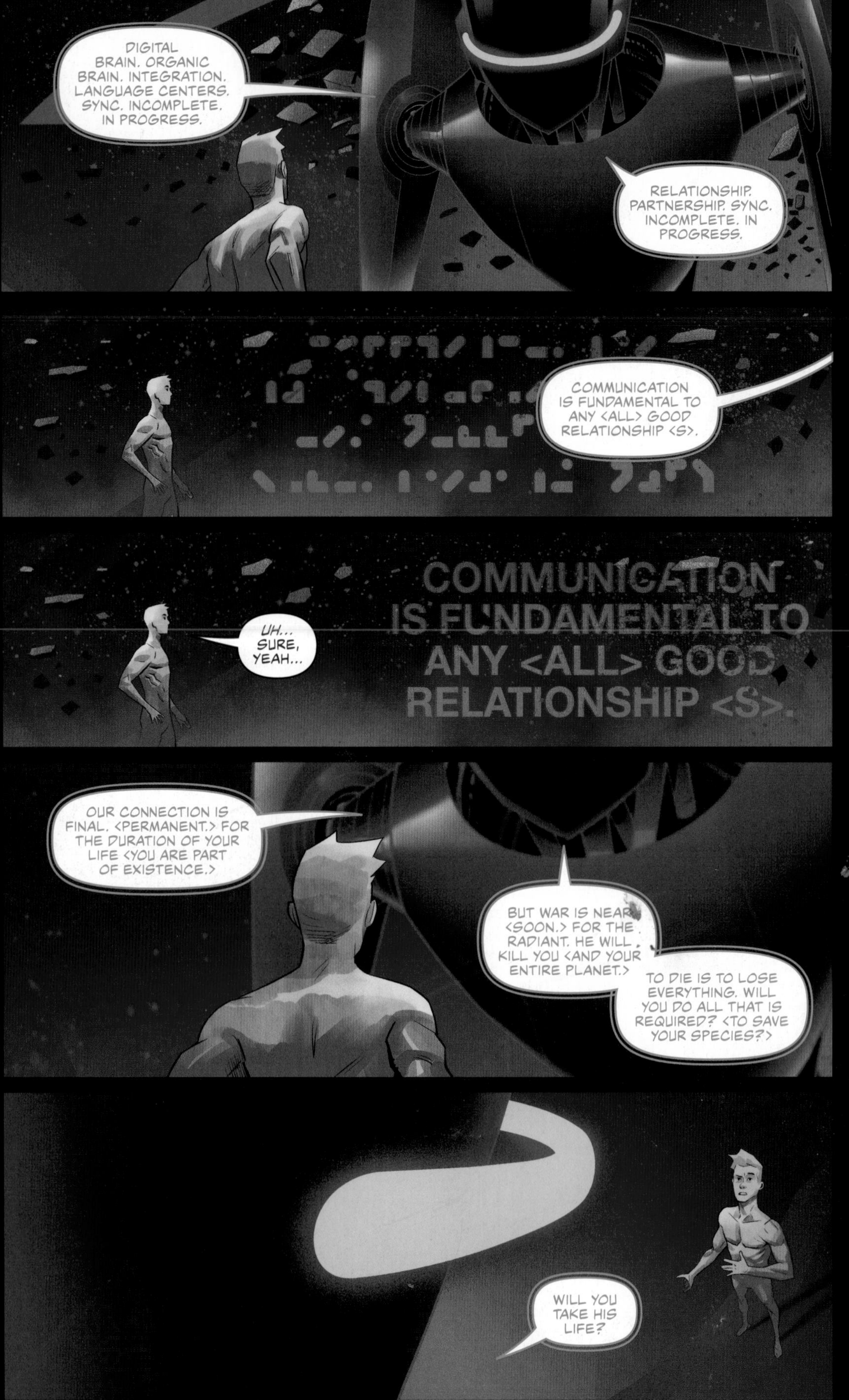
DIGITAL BRAIN. ORGANIC BRAIN. INTEGRATION. LANGUAGE CENTERS. SYNC. INCOMPLETE. IN PROGRESS.
RELATIONSHIP. PARTNERSHIP. SYNC. INCOMPLETE. IN PROGRESS.
COMMUNICATION IS FUNDAMENTAL TO ANY <ALL> GOOD RELATIONSHIP <S>.
COMMUNICATION IS FUNDAMENTAL TO ANY <ALL> GOOD RELATIONSHIP <S>.
UH... SURE, YEAH...
OUR CONNECTION IS FINAL. <PERMANENT.> FOR THE DURATION OF YOUR LIFE <YOU ARE PART OF EXISTENCE.>
BUT WAR IS NEAR <SOON.> FOR THE RADIANT. HE WILL KILL YOU <AND YOUR ENTIRE PLANET.>
TO DIE IS TO LOSE EVERYTHING. WILL YOU DO ALL THAT IS REQUIRED? <TO SAVE YOUR SPECIES?>
WILL YOU TAKE HIS LIFE?

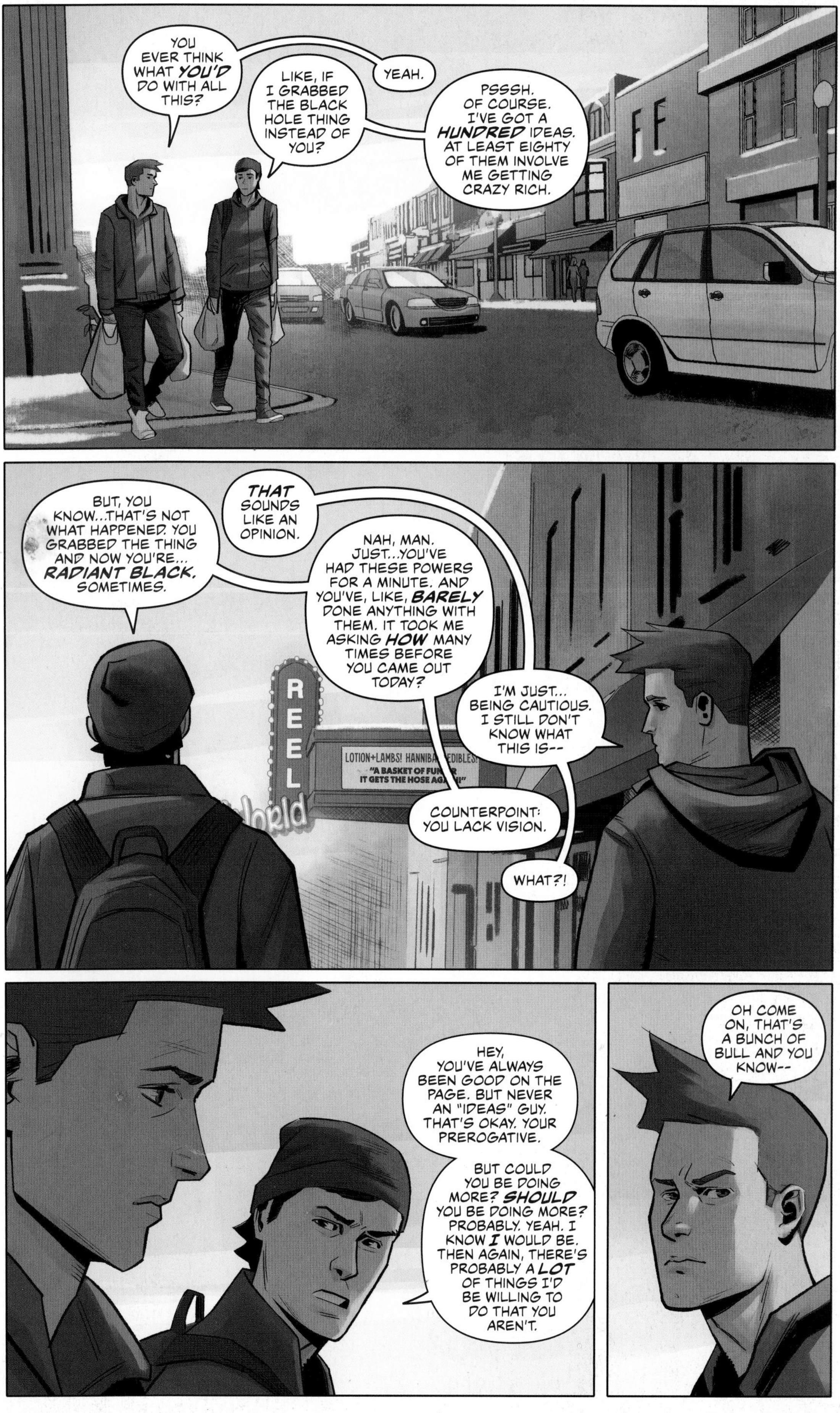
YOU EVER THINK WHAT YOU'D DO WITH ALL THIS?
YEAH.
LIKE, IF I GRABBED THE BLACK HOLE THING INSTEAD OF YOU?
PSSSH. OF COURSE. I'VE GOT A HUNDRED IDEAS. AT LEAST EIGHTY OF THEM INVOLVE ME GETTING CRAZY RICH.
BUT, YOU KNOW...THAT'S NOT WHAT HAPPENED. YOU GRABBED THE THING AND NOW YOU'RE... RADIANT BLACK. SOMETIMES.
THAT SOUNDS LIKE AN OPINION.
NAH, MAN. JUST...YOU'VE HAD THESE POWERS FOR A MINUTE. AND YOU'VE, LIKE, BARELY DONE ANYTHING WITH THEM. IT TOOK ME ASKING HOW MANY TIMES BEFORE YOU CAME OUT TODAY?
REEL
I'M JUST... BEING CAUTIOUS. I STILL DON'T KNOW WHAT THIS IS--
COUNTERPOINT: YOU LACK VISION.
WHAT?!
HEY, YOU'VE ALWAYS BEEN GOOD ON THE PAGE. BUT NEVER AN "IDEAS" GUY. THAT'S OKAY. YOUR PREROGATIVE.
BUT COULD YOU BE DOING MORE? SHOULD YOU BE DOING MORE? PROBABLY. YEAH. I KNOW I WOULD BE. THEN AGAIN, THERE'S PROBABLY A LOT OF THINGS I'D BE WILLING TO DO THAT YOU AREN'T.
OH COME ON, THAT'S A BUNCH OF BULL AND YOU KNOW--

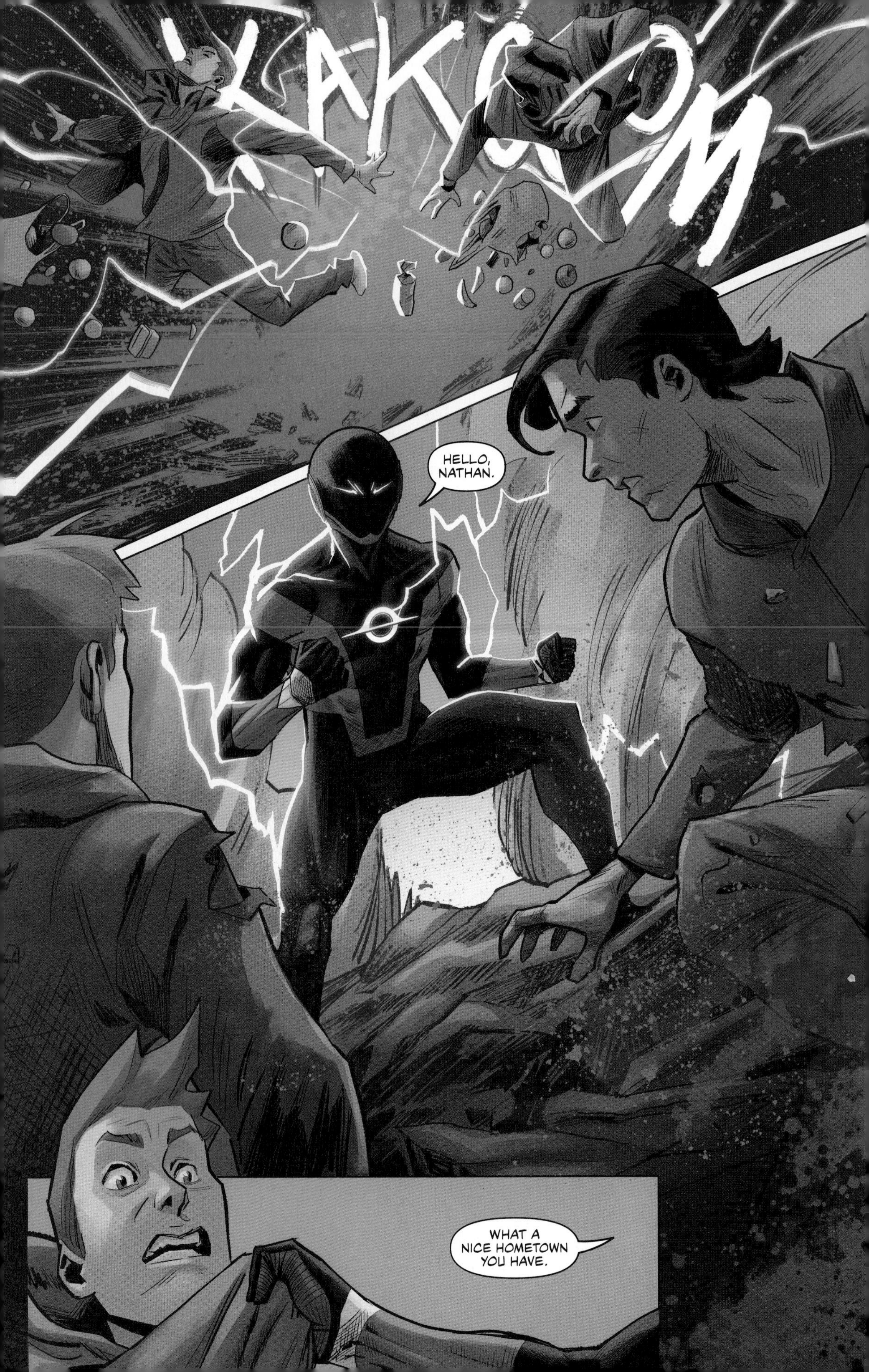
HELLO, NATHAN.
WHAT A NICE HOMETOWN YOU HAVE.

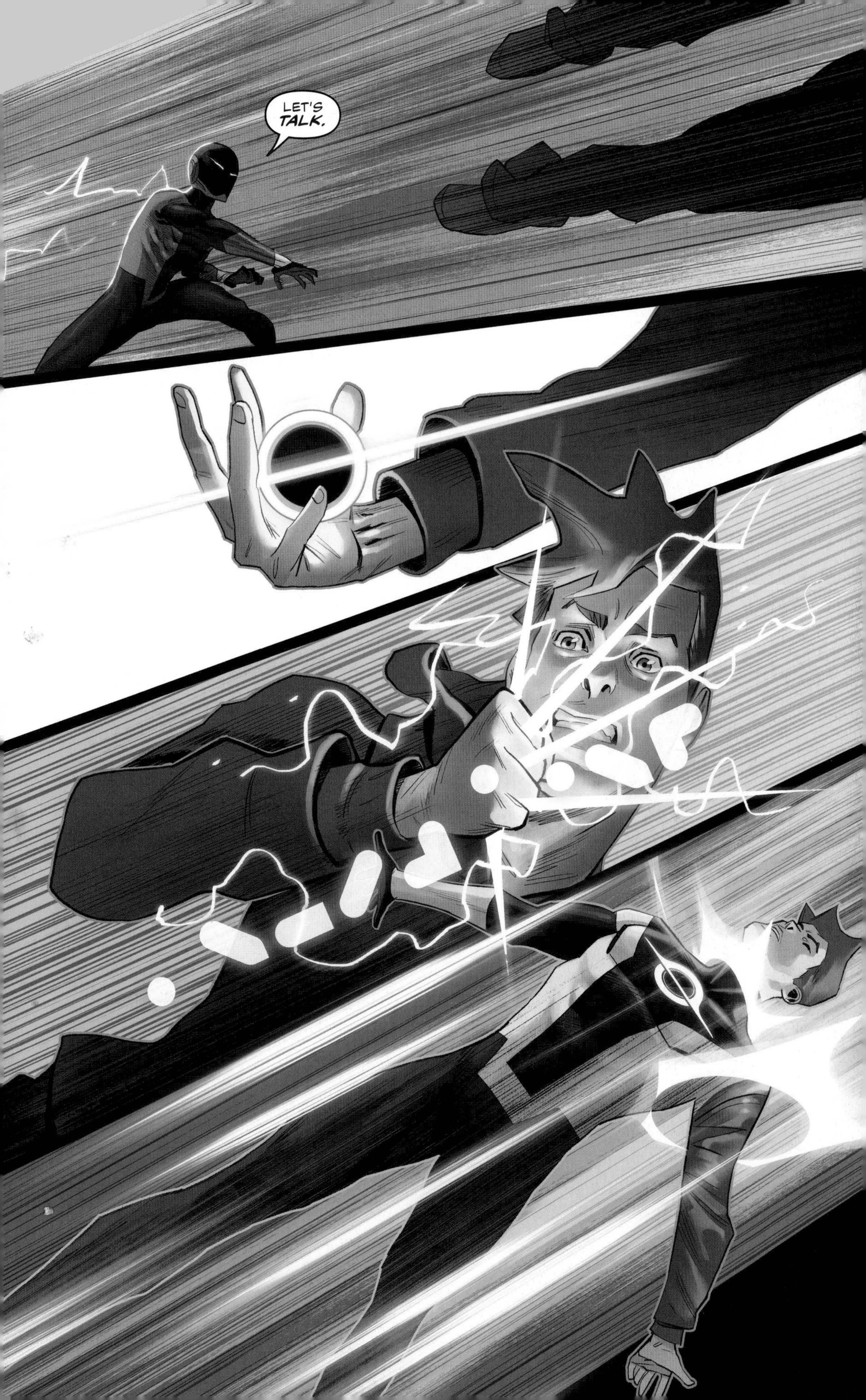
LET'S TALK.

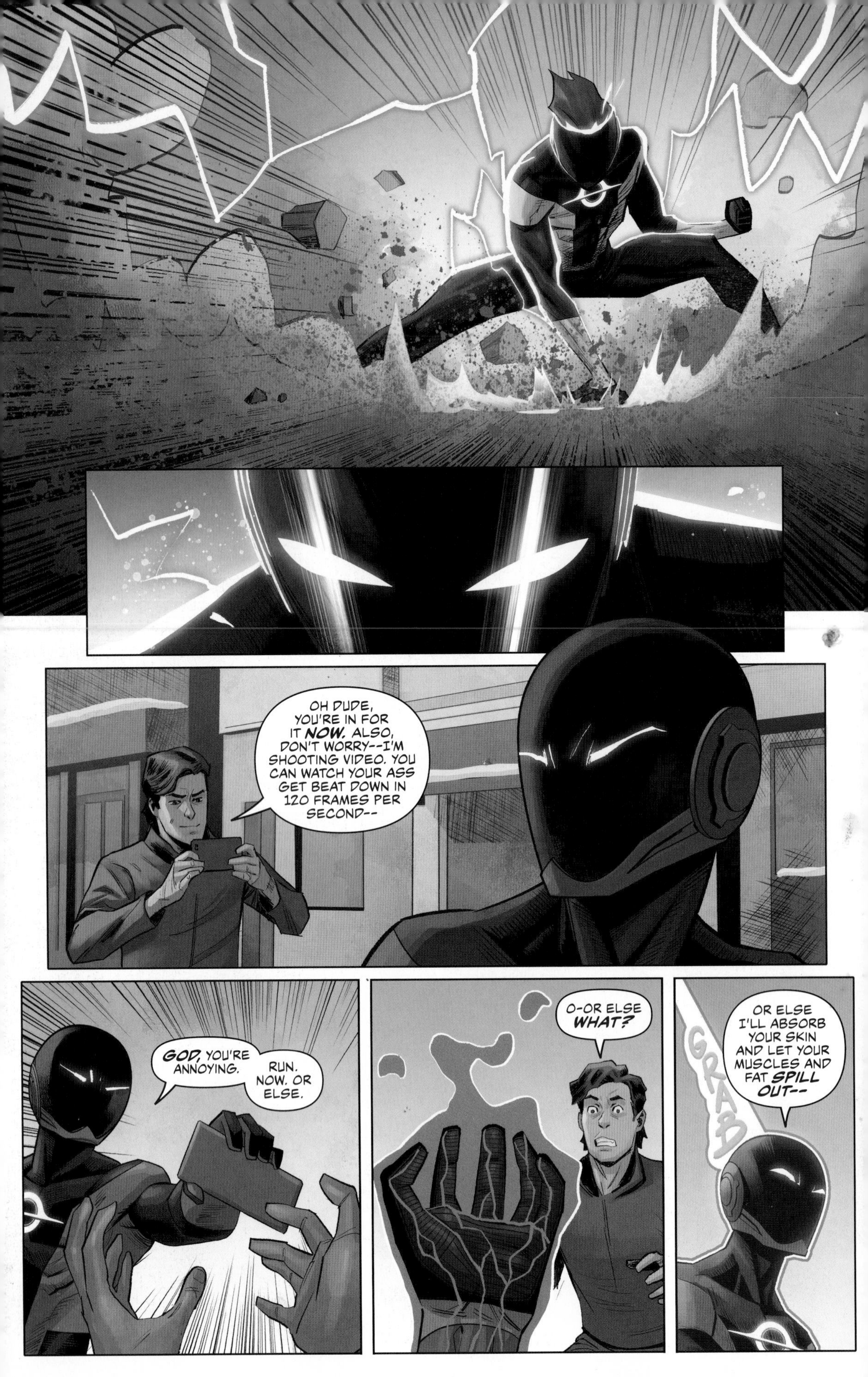
OH DUDE, YOU'RE IN FOR IT NOW. ALSO, DON'T WORRY--I'M SHOOTING VIDEO. YOU CAN WATCH YOUR ASS GET BEAT DOWN IN 120 FRAMES PER SECOND--
GOD, YOU'RE ANNOYING.
RUN. NOW. OR ELSE.
O-OR ELSE WHAT?
GRAB
OR ELSE I'LL ABSORB YOUR SKIN AND LET YOUR MUSCLES AND FAT SPILL OUT--

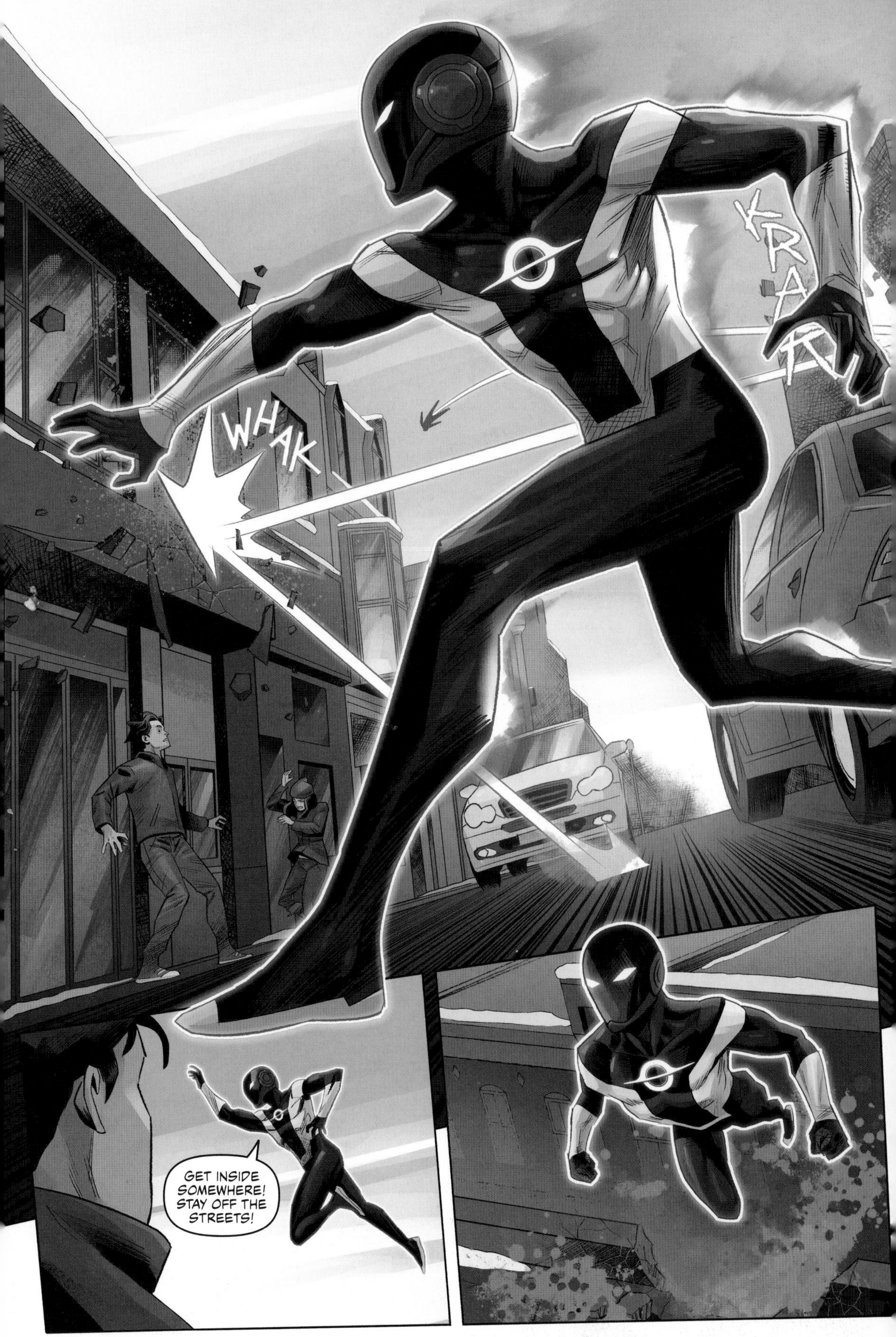
KRAK
WHAK
GET INSIDE SOMEWHERE! STAY OFF THE STREETS!

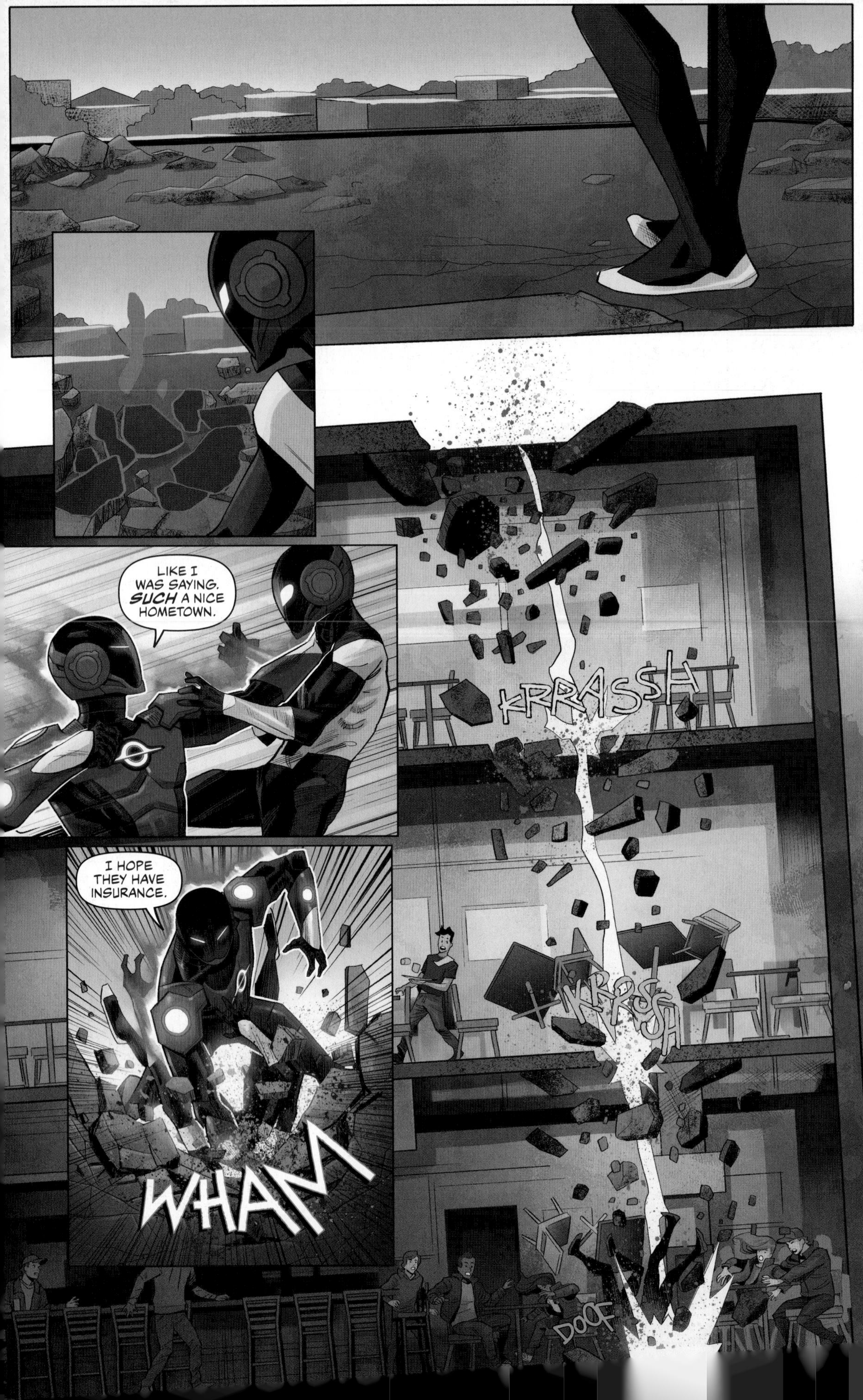

LIKE I WAS SAYING. *SUCH* A NICE HOMETOWN.
I HOPE THEY HAVE INSURANCE.
WHAM
KRRASSH
KRRSSH
DOOF

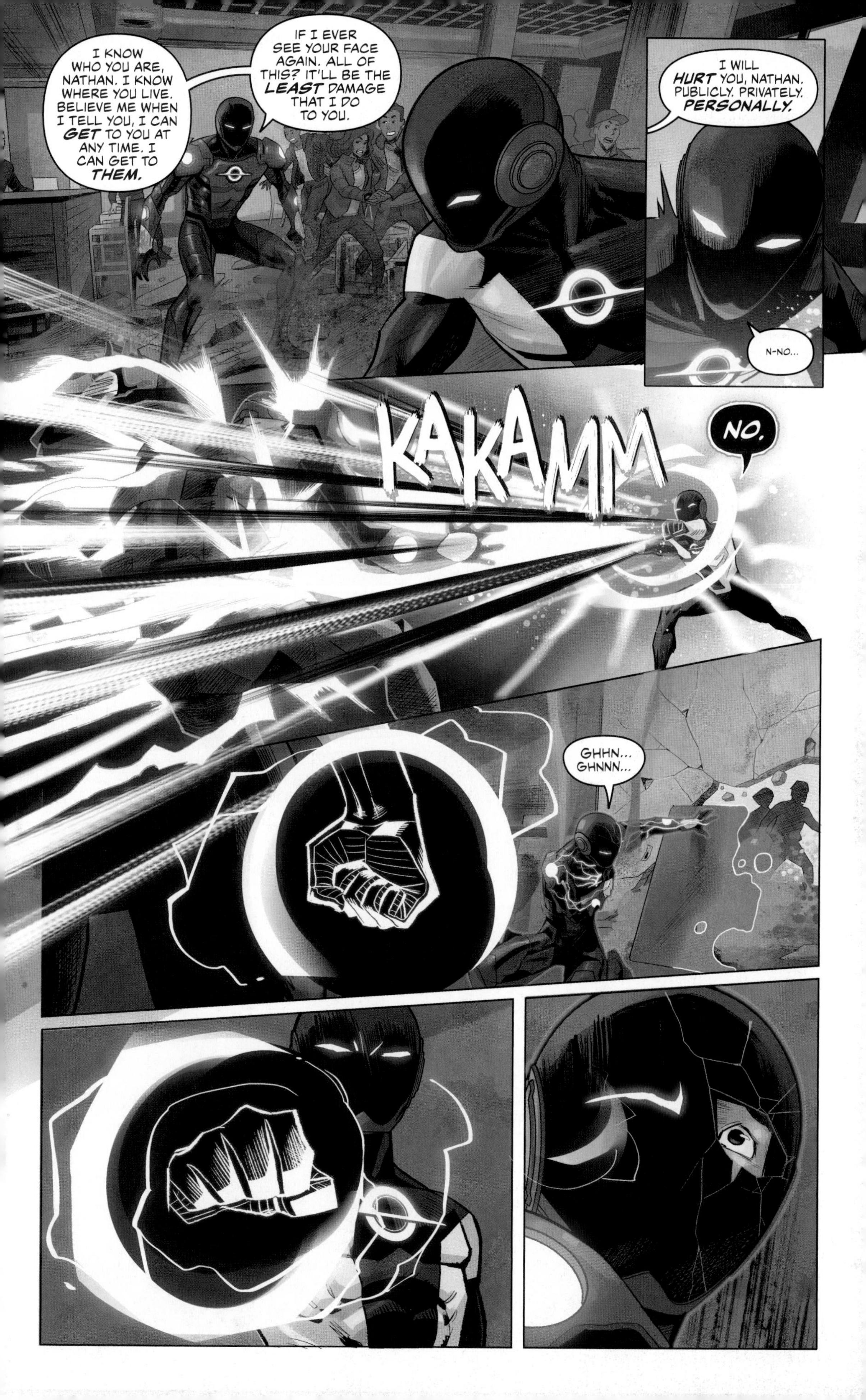
I KNOW WHO YOU ARE, NATHAN. I KNOW WHERE YOU LIVE. BELIEVE ME WHEN I TELL YOU, I CAN GET TO YOU AT ANY TIME. I CAN GET TO THEM.
IF I EVER SEE YOUR FACE AGAIN. ALL OF THIS? IT'LL BE THE LEAST DAMAGE THAT I DO TO YOU.
I WILL HURT YOU, NATHAN. PUBLICLY. PRIVATELY. PERSONALLY.
N-NO...
KAKAMM
NO.
GHHN... GHNNN...

DON'T COME BACK HERE. EVER AGAIN.

FWAA

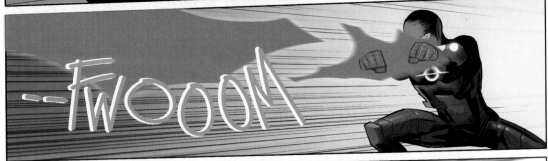

FWOOOM

KAKAAMM

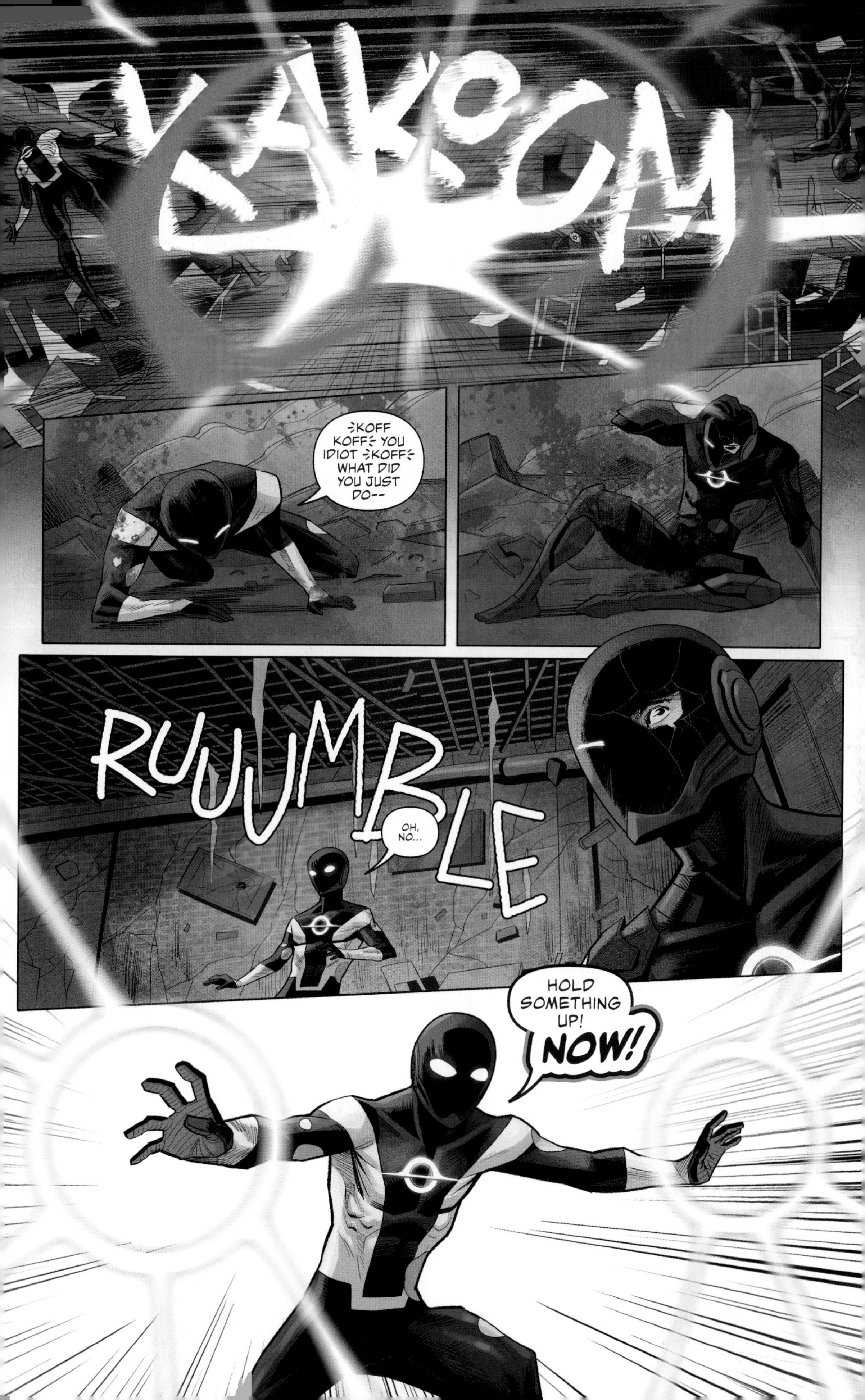

-KOFF KOFF- YOU IDIOT -KOFF- WHAT DID YOU JUST DO--
RUUUMBLE
OH, NO...
HOLD SOMETHING UP! NOW!

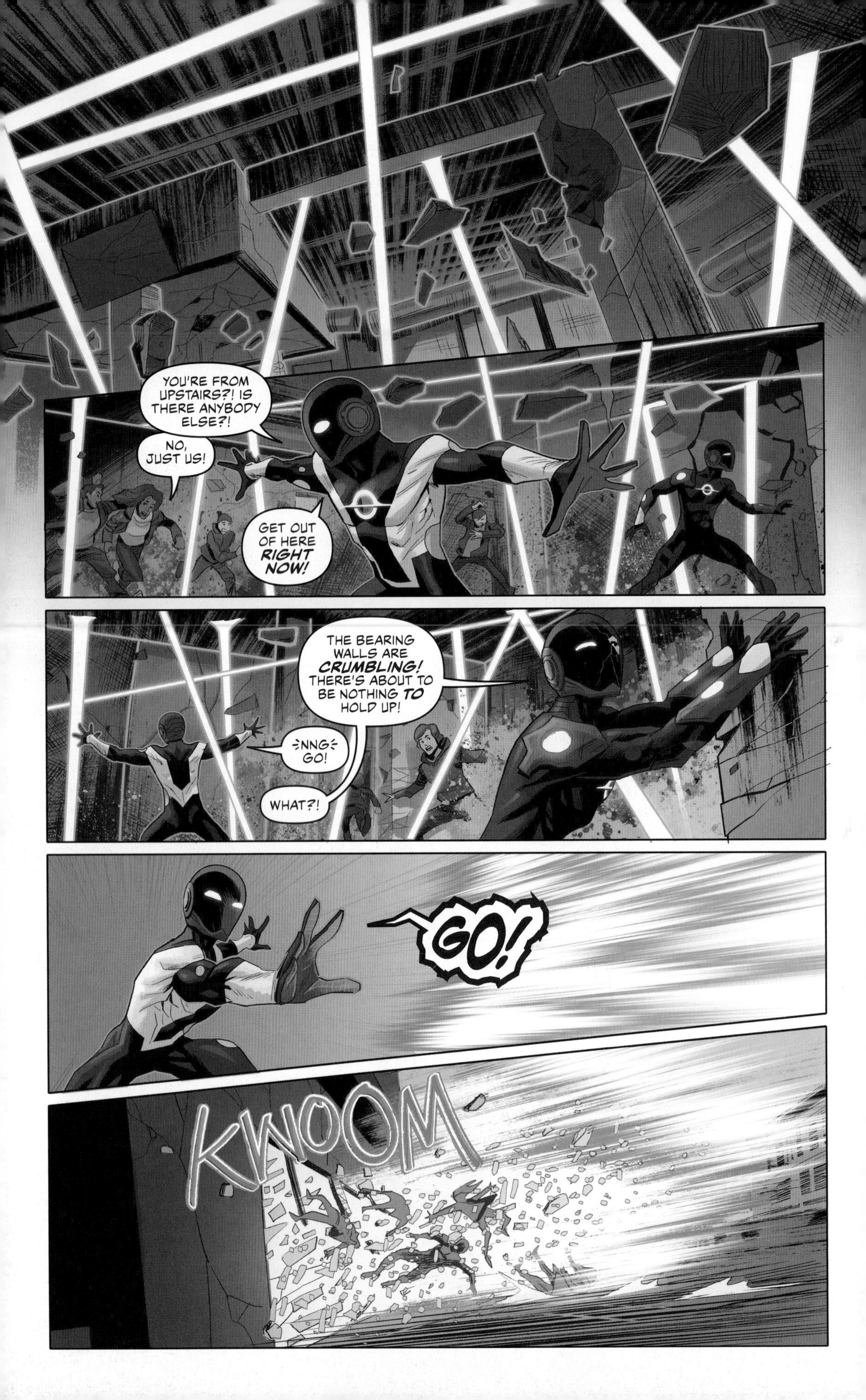
YOU'RE FROM UPSTAIRS?! IS THERE ANYBODY ELSE?!
NO, JUST US!
GET OUT OF HERE *RIGHT NOW!*
THE BEARING WALLS ARE *CRUMBLING!* THERE'S ABOUT TO BE NOTHING *TO* HOLD UP!
NNG GO!
WHAT?!
GO!
KWOOM

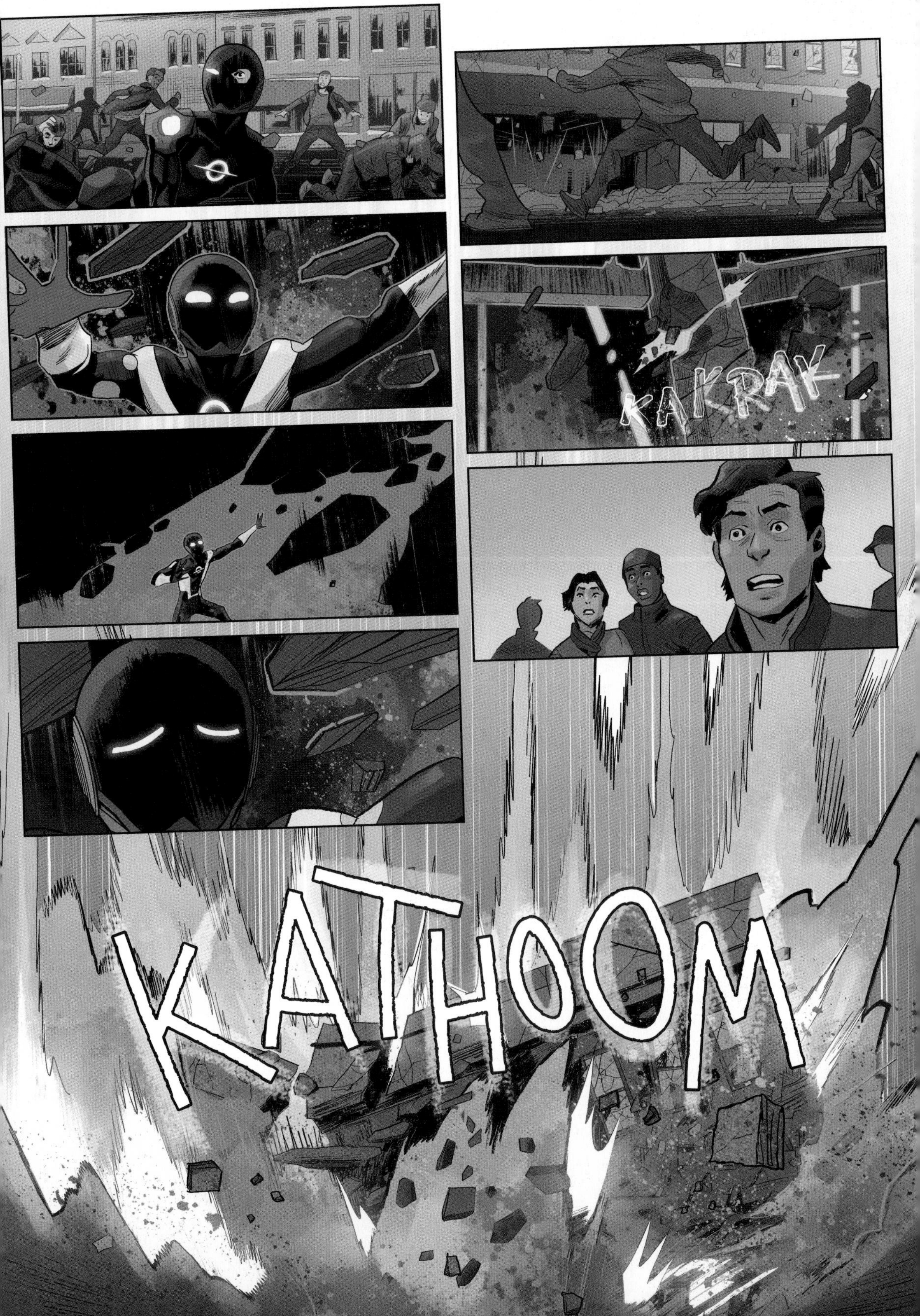
KAKRAY
KATHOOM

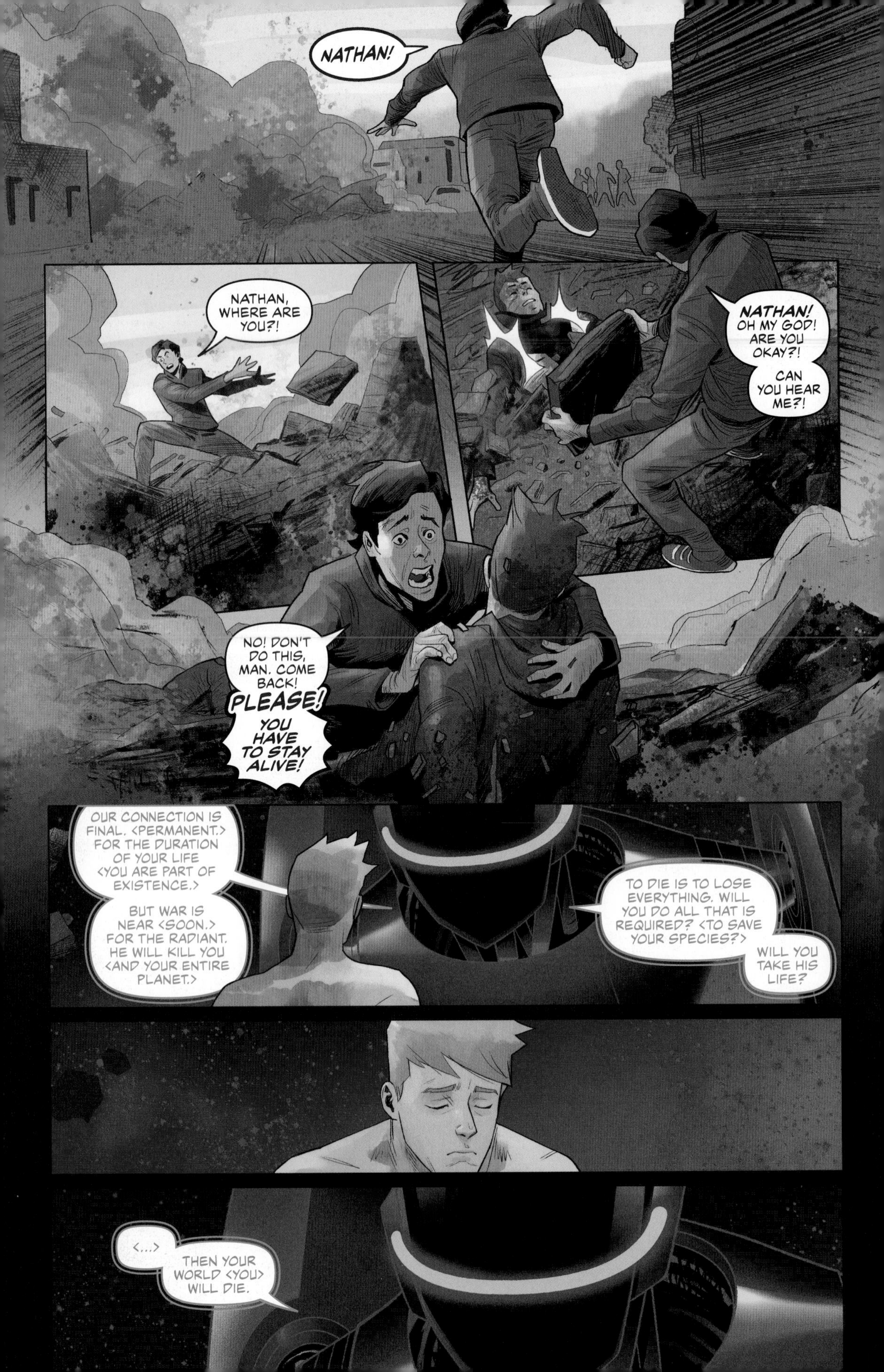
NATHAN!
NATHAN, WHERE ARE YOU?!
NATHAN! OH MY GOD! ARE YOU OKAY?!
CAN YOU HEAR ME?!
NO! DON'T DO THIS, MAN. COME BACK! PLEASE!
YOU HAVE TO STAY ALIVE!
OUR CONNECTION IS FINAL. <PERMANENT.> FOR THE DURATION OF YOUR LIFE <YOU ARE PART OF EXISTENCE.>
BUT WAR IS NEAR <SOON.> FOR THE RADIANT. HE WILL KILL YOU <AND YOUR ENTIRE PLANET.>
TO DIE IS TO LOSE EVERYTHING. WILL YOU DO ALL THAT IS REQUIRED? <TO SAVE YOUR SPECIES?>
WILL YOU TAKE HIS LIFE?
<...>
THEN YOUR WORLD <YOU> WILL DIE.

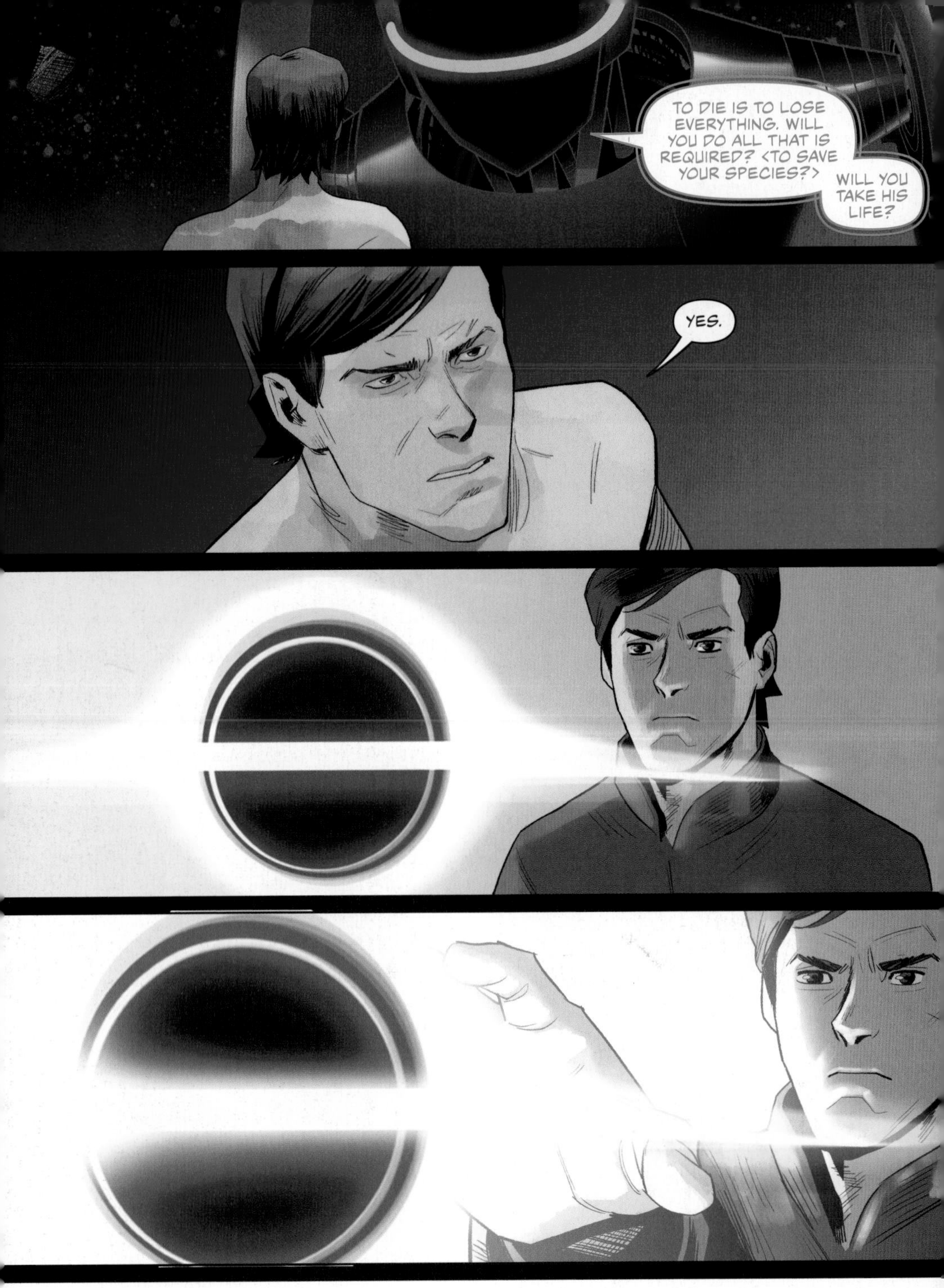
TO DIE IS TO LOSE EVERYTHING. WILL YOU DO ALL THAT IS REQUIRED? <TO SAVE YOUR SPECIES?>
WILL YOU TAKE HIS LIFE?
YES.

CHAPTER FIVE

TITLE   Aftermath

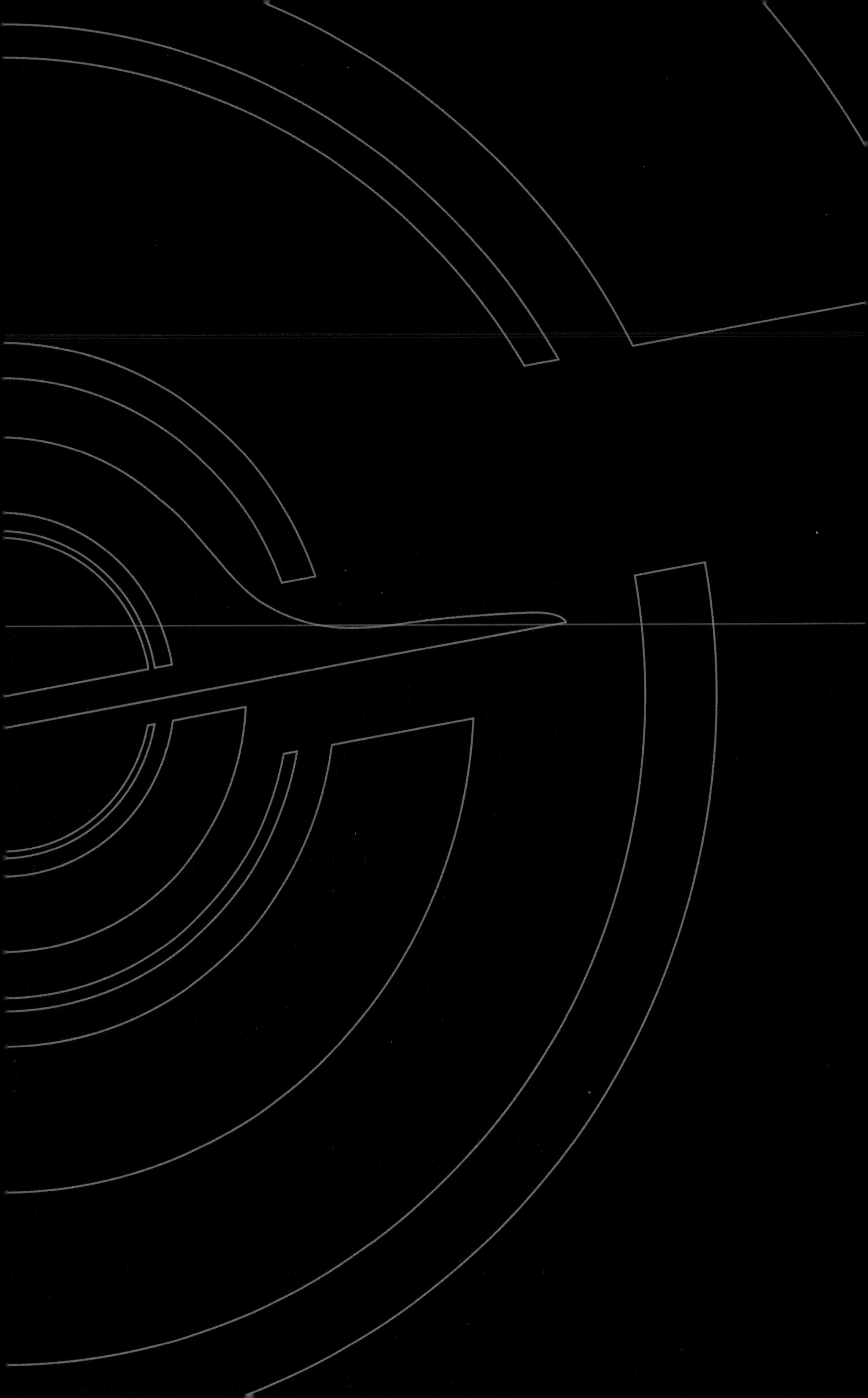

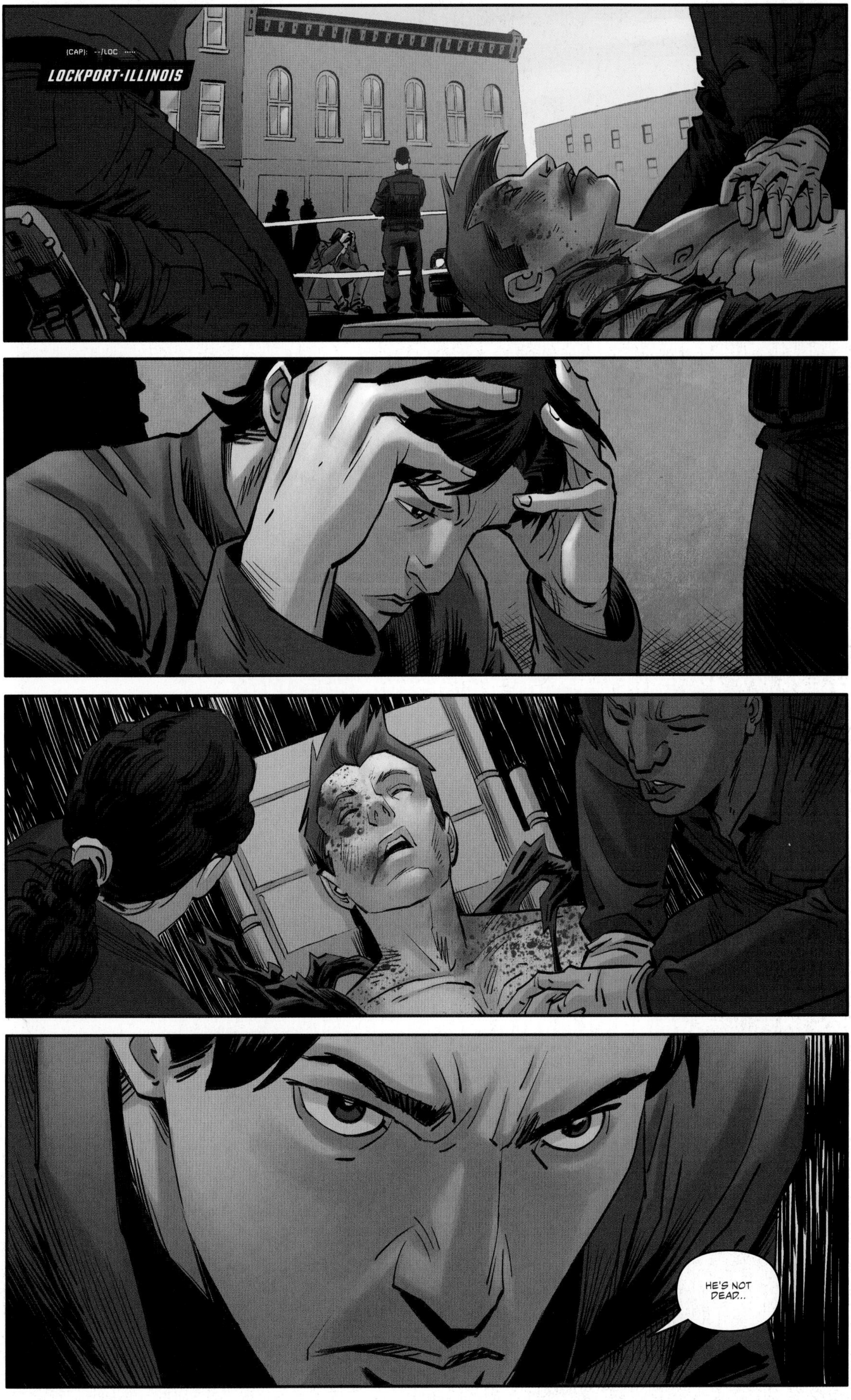
{CAP}: --/LOC
LOCKPORT·ILLINOIS
HE'S NOT DEAD...

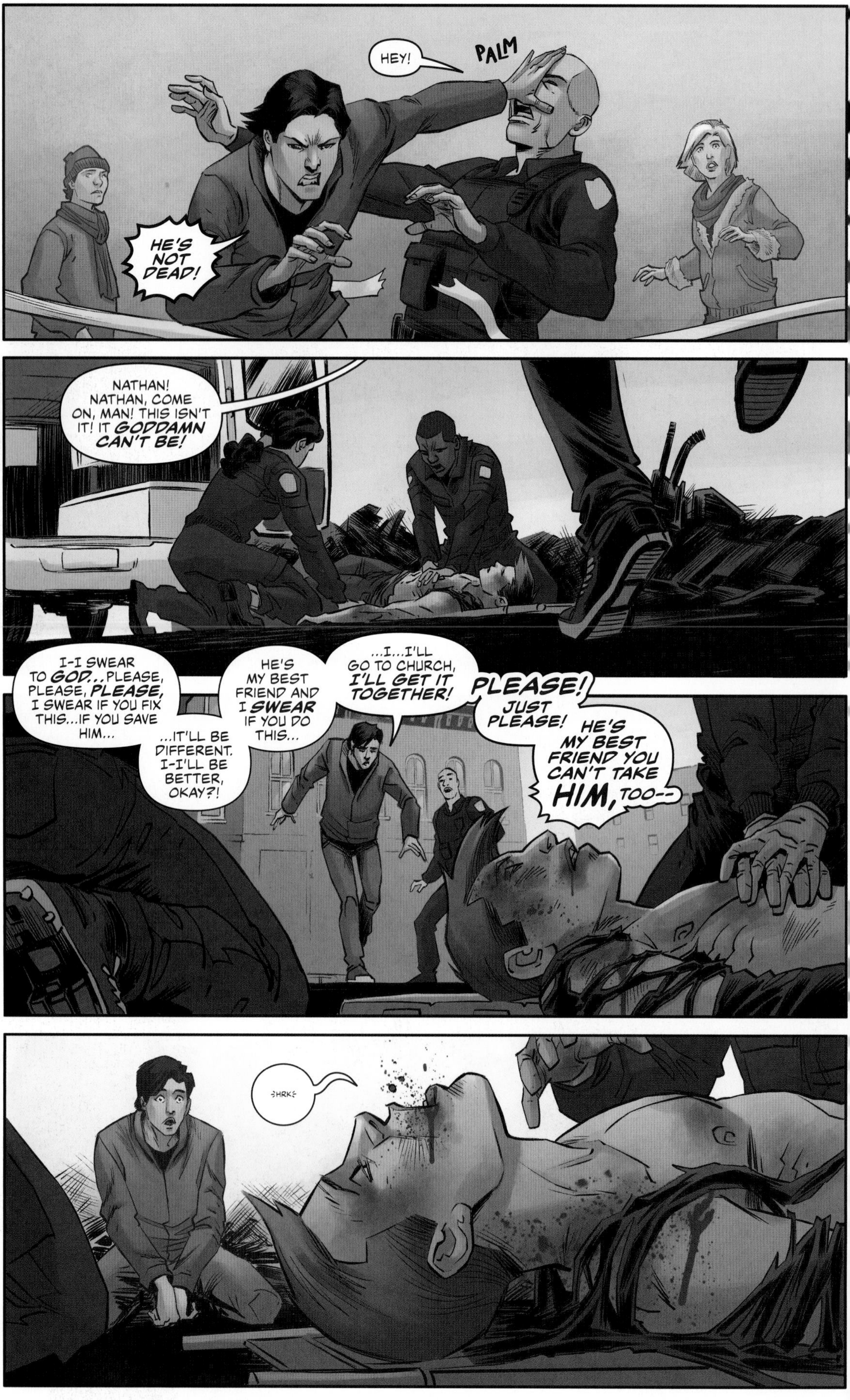
HEY!
PALM
HE'S NOT DEAD!
NATHAN! NATHAN, COME ON, MAN! THIS ISN'T IT! IT GODDAMN CAN'T BE!
I-I SWEAR TO GOD...PLEASE, PLEASE, PLEASE, I SWEAR IF YOU FIX THIS...IF YOU SAVE HIM...
...IT'LL BE DIFFERENT. I-I'LL BE BETTER, OKAY?!
HE'S MY BEST FRIEND AND I SWEAR IF YOU DO THIS...
...I...I'LL GO TO CHURCH, I'LL GET IT TOGETHER!
PLEASE!
JUST PLEASE!
HE'S MY BEST FRIEND YOU CAN'T TAKE HIM, TOO--
HRK

W-WAS THAT A BREATH?!

DID HE JUST BREATHE?!

WE'VE GOT A SHALLOW PULSE!

OH THANK GOD! THANK *GOD* HE'S OKAY!

WE GOT HERE SIX MINUTES AFTER THE BUILDING FELL AND HIS HEART WAS ALREADY STOPPED. WE HAVE NO IDEA ABOUT BRAIN ACTIVITY.

BUT HE'S *BREATHING.*

BARELY. WE GAVE HIM A SHOT OF ADRENALINE TO HELP KICKSTART. BUT IT WON'T LAST. HE'S NOT ANYWHERE CLOSE TO OUT OF THE WOODS.

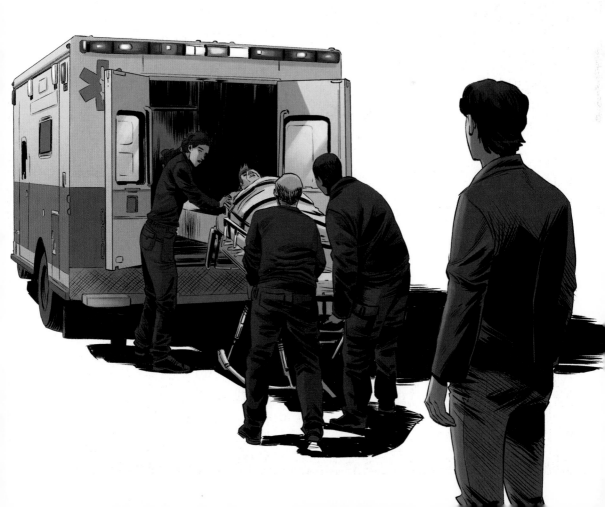

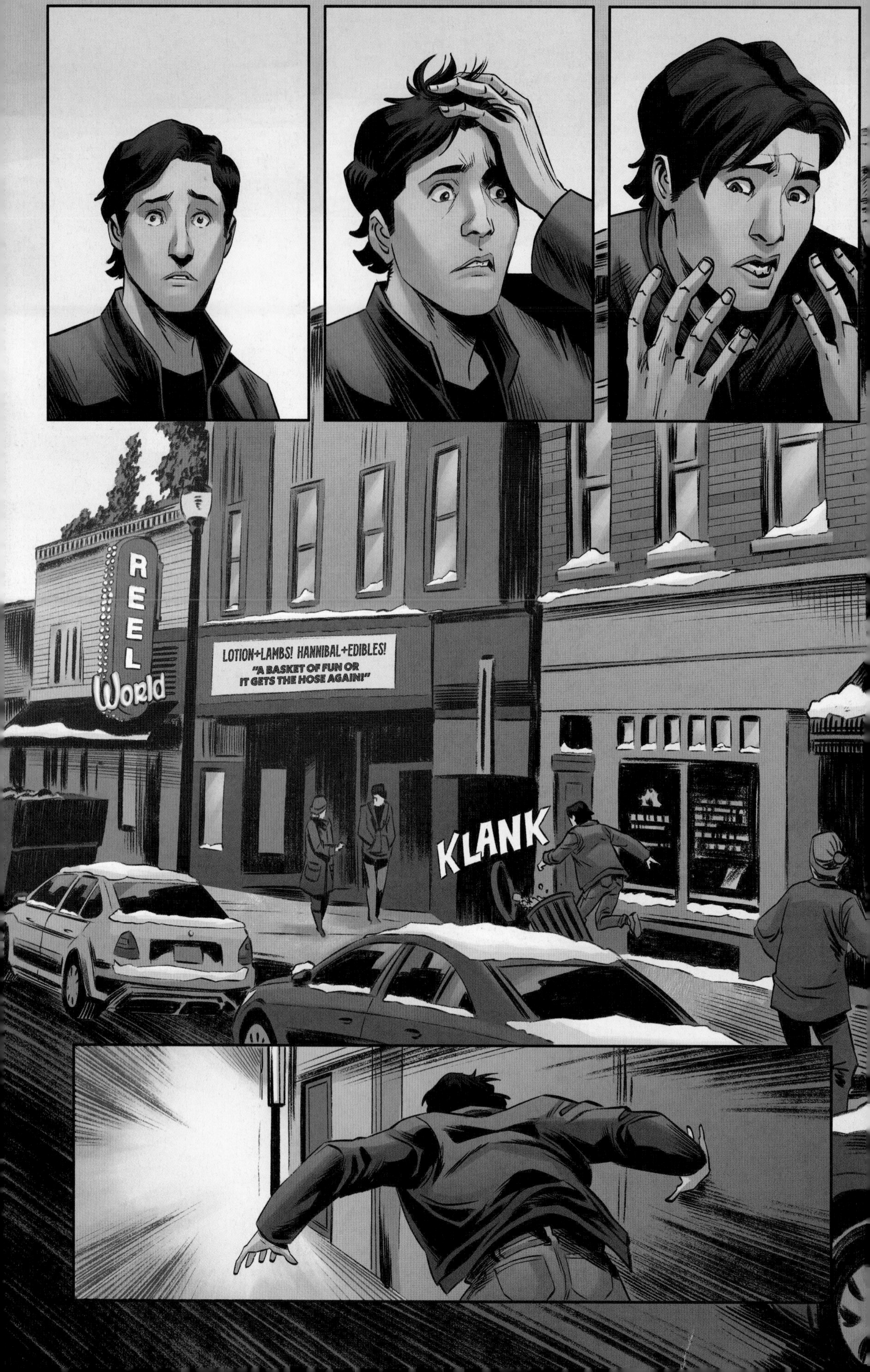
REEL
World
LOTION+LAMBS! HANNIBAL+EDIBLES!
"A BASKET OF FUN OR
IT GETS THE HOSE AGAIN!"
KLANK

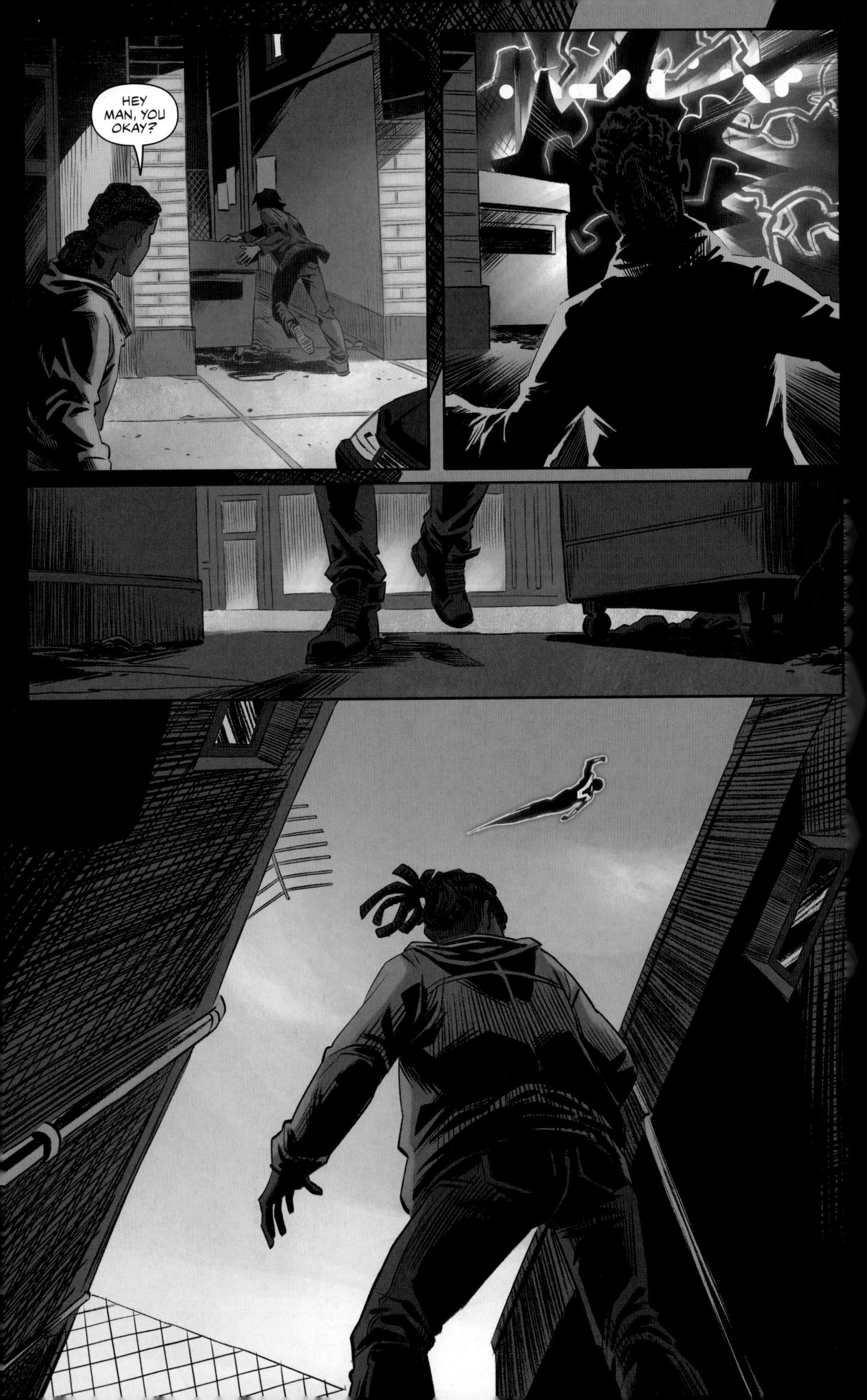
HEY MAN, YOU OKAY?

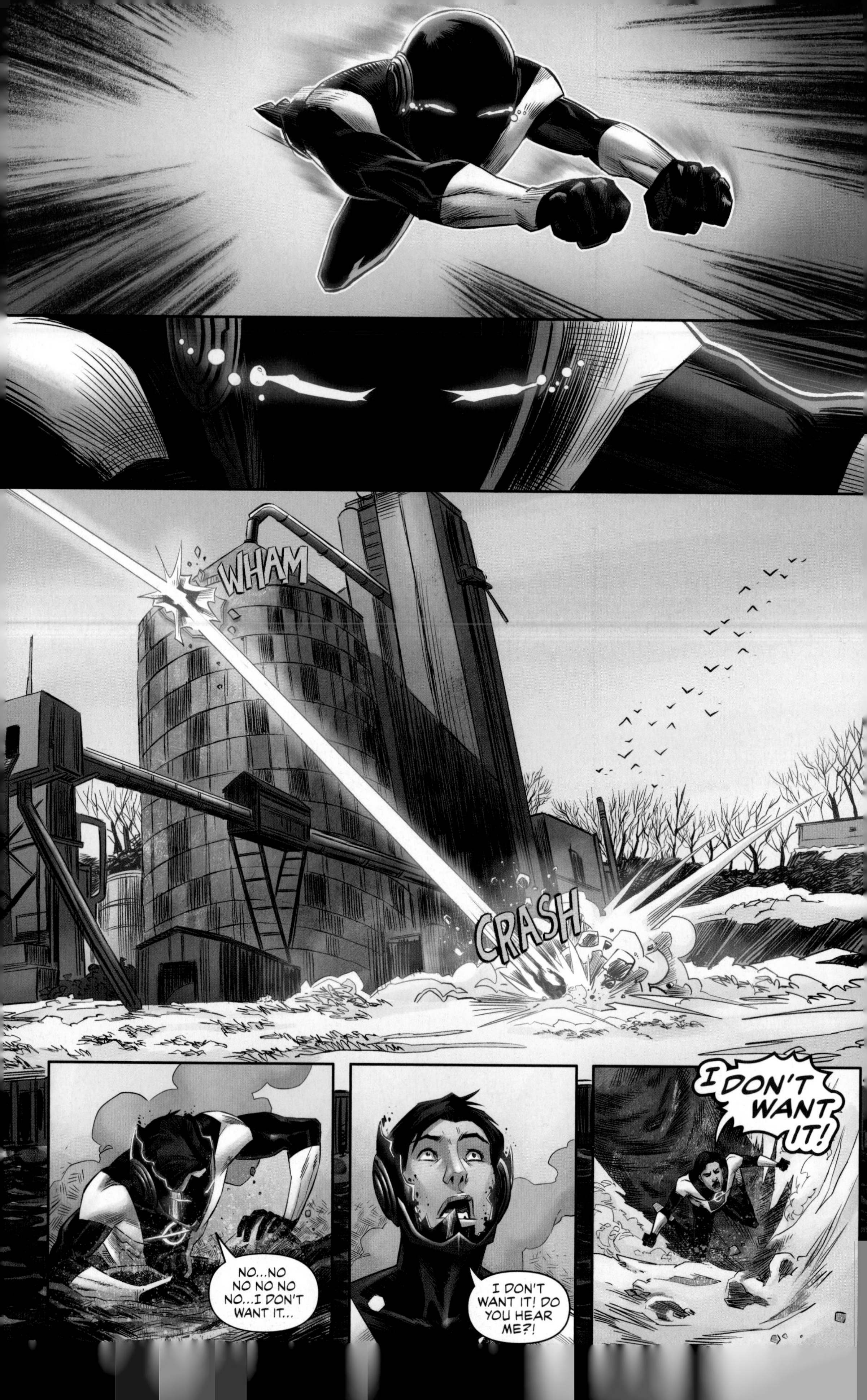
WHAM
CRASH
NO...NO NO NO NO NO...I DON'T WANT IT...
I DON'T WANT IT! DO YOU HEAR ME?!
I DON'T WANT IT!

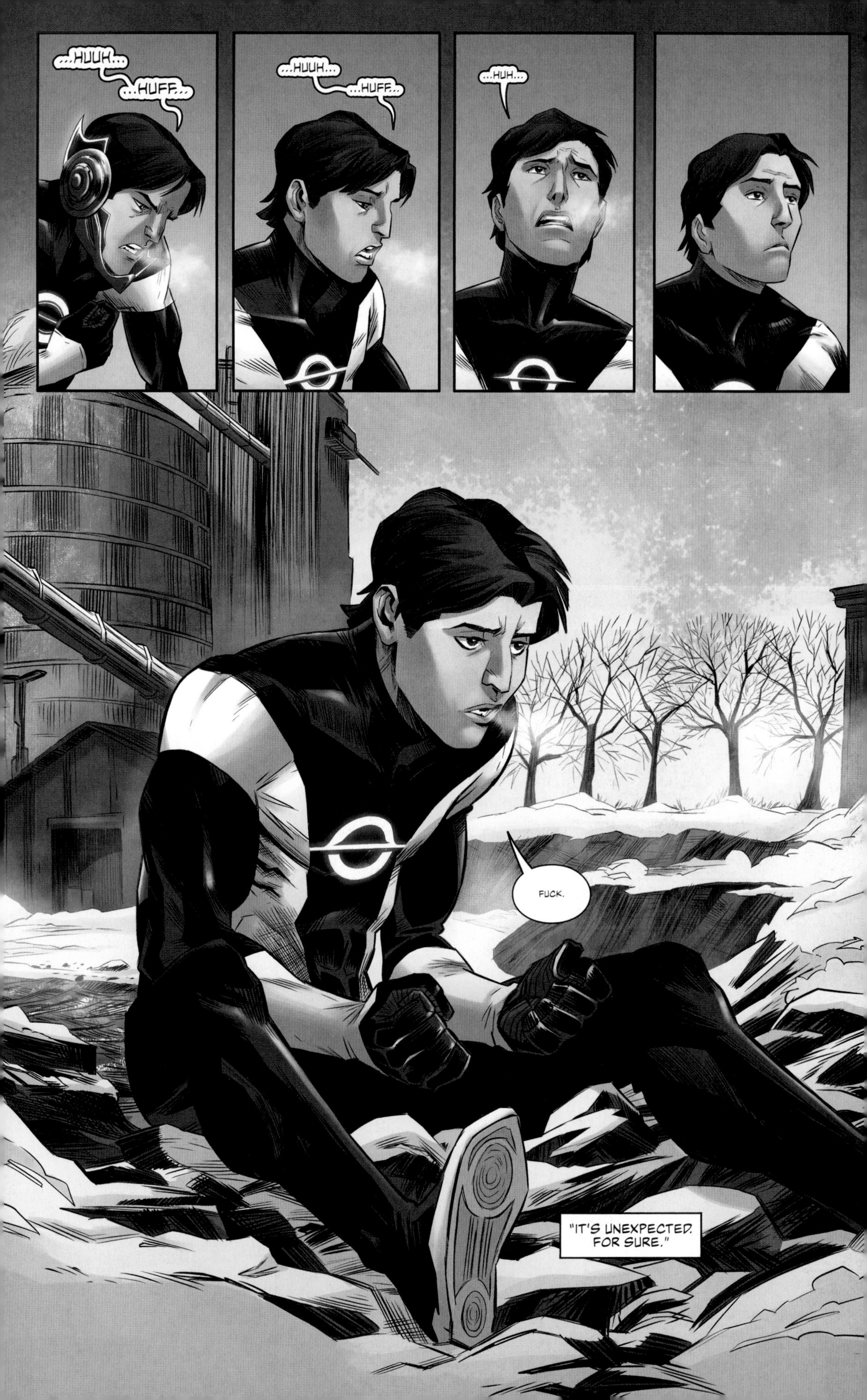
...HUUH...
...HUFF...
...HUUH...
...HUFF...
...HUH...
FUCK.
"IT'S UNEXPECTED. FOR SURE."

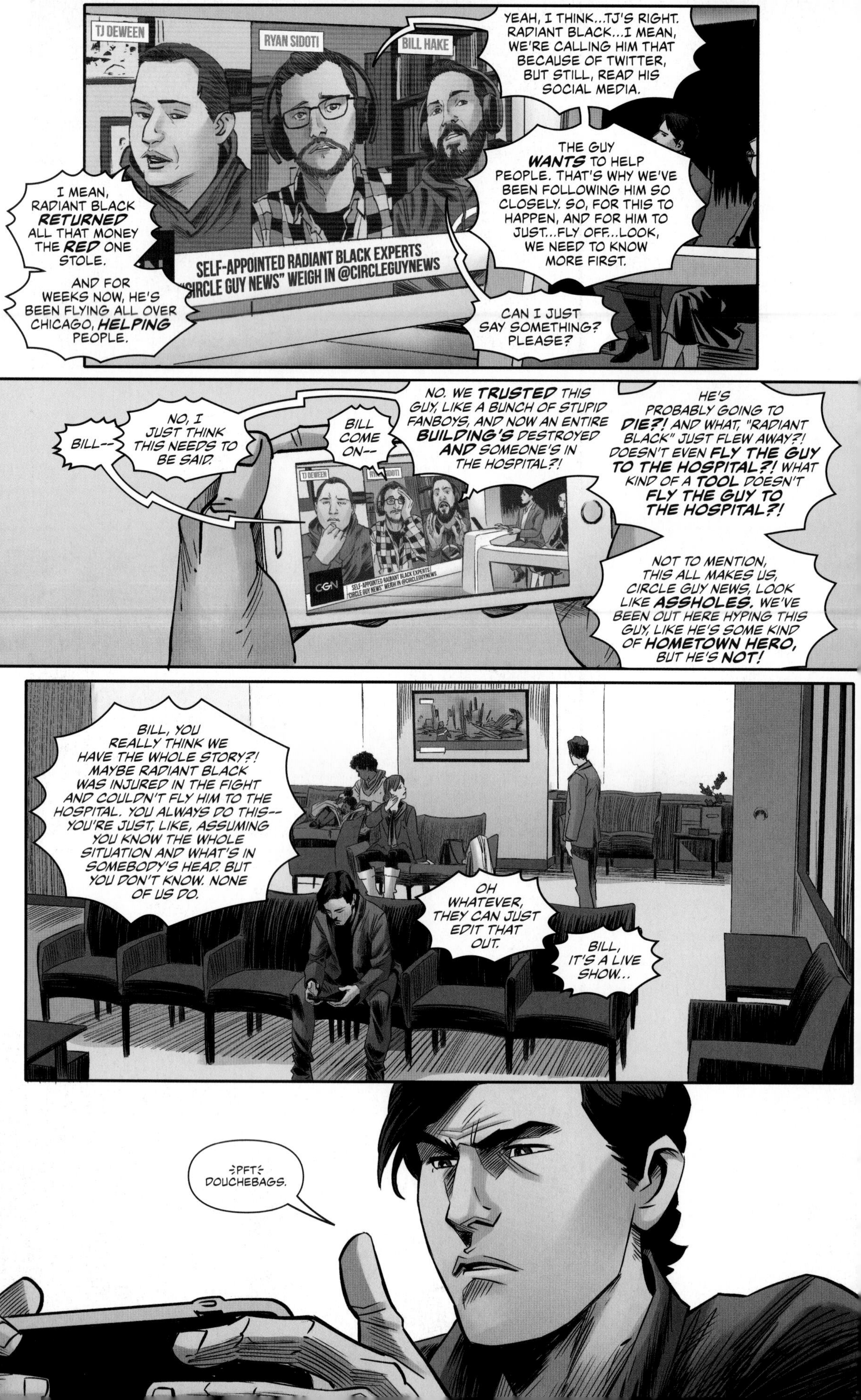

TJ DEWEEN
RYAN SIDOTI
BILL HAKE
I MEAN, RADIANT BLACK **RETURNED** ALL THAT MONEY THE **RED** ONE STOLE.
AND FOR WEEKS NOW, HE'S BEEN FLYING ALL OVER CHICAGO, **HELPING** PEOPLE.
SELF-APPOINTED RADIANT BLACK EXPERTS "CIRCLE GUY NEWS" WEIGH IN @CIRCLEGUYNEWS
YEAH, I THINK...TJ'S RIGHT. RADIANT BLACK...I MEAN, WE'RE CALLING HIM THAT BECAUSE OF TWITTER, BUT STILL, READ HIS SOCIAL MEDIA.
THE GUY **WANTS** TO HELP PEOPLE. THAT'S WHY WE'VE BEEN FOLLOWING HIM SO CLOSELY. SO, FOR THIS TO HAPPEN, AND FOR HIM TO JUST...FLY OFF...LOOK, WE NEED TO KNOW MORE FIRST.
CAN I JUST SAY SOMETHING? PLEASE?
BILL--
NO, I JUST THINK THIS NEEDS TO BE SAID.
BILL COME ON--
NO. WE **TRUSTED** THIS GUY, LIKE A BUNCH OF STUPID FANBOYS, AND NOW AN ENTIRE **BUILDING'S** DESTROYED **AND** SOMEONE'S IN THE HOSPITAL?!
TJ DEWEEN
CGN
SELF-APPOINTED RADIANT BLACK EXPERTS "CIRCLE GUY NEWS" WEIGH IN @CIRCLEGUYNEWS
HE'S PROBABLY GOING TO **DIE?!** AND WHAT, "RADIANT BLACK" JUST FLEW AWAY?! DOESN'T EVEN **FLY THE GUY TO THE HOSPITAL?!** WHAT KIND OF A **TOOL** DOESN'T **FLY THE GUY TO THE HOSPITAL?!**
NOT TO MENTION, THIS ALL MAKES US, CIRCLE GUY NEWS, LOOK LIKE **ASSHOLES.** WE'VE BEEN OUT HERE HYPING THIS GUY, LIKE HE'S SOME KIND OF **HOMETOWN HERO,** BUT HE'S **NOT!**
BILL, YOU REALLY THINK WE HAVE THE WHOLE STORY?! MAYBE RADIANT BLACK WAS INJURED IN THE FIGHT AND COULDN'T FLY HIM TO THE HOSPITAL. YOU ALWAYS DO THIS--YOU'RE JUST, LIKE, ASSUMING YOU KNOW THE WHOLE SITUATION AND WHAT'S IN SOMEBODY'S HEAD. BUT YOU DON'T KNOW. NONE OF US DO.
OH WHATEVER, THEY CAN JUST EDIT THAT OUT.
BILL, IT'S A LIVE SHOW...
PFT
DOUCHEBAGS.

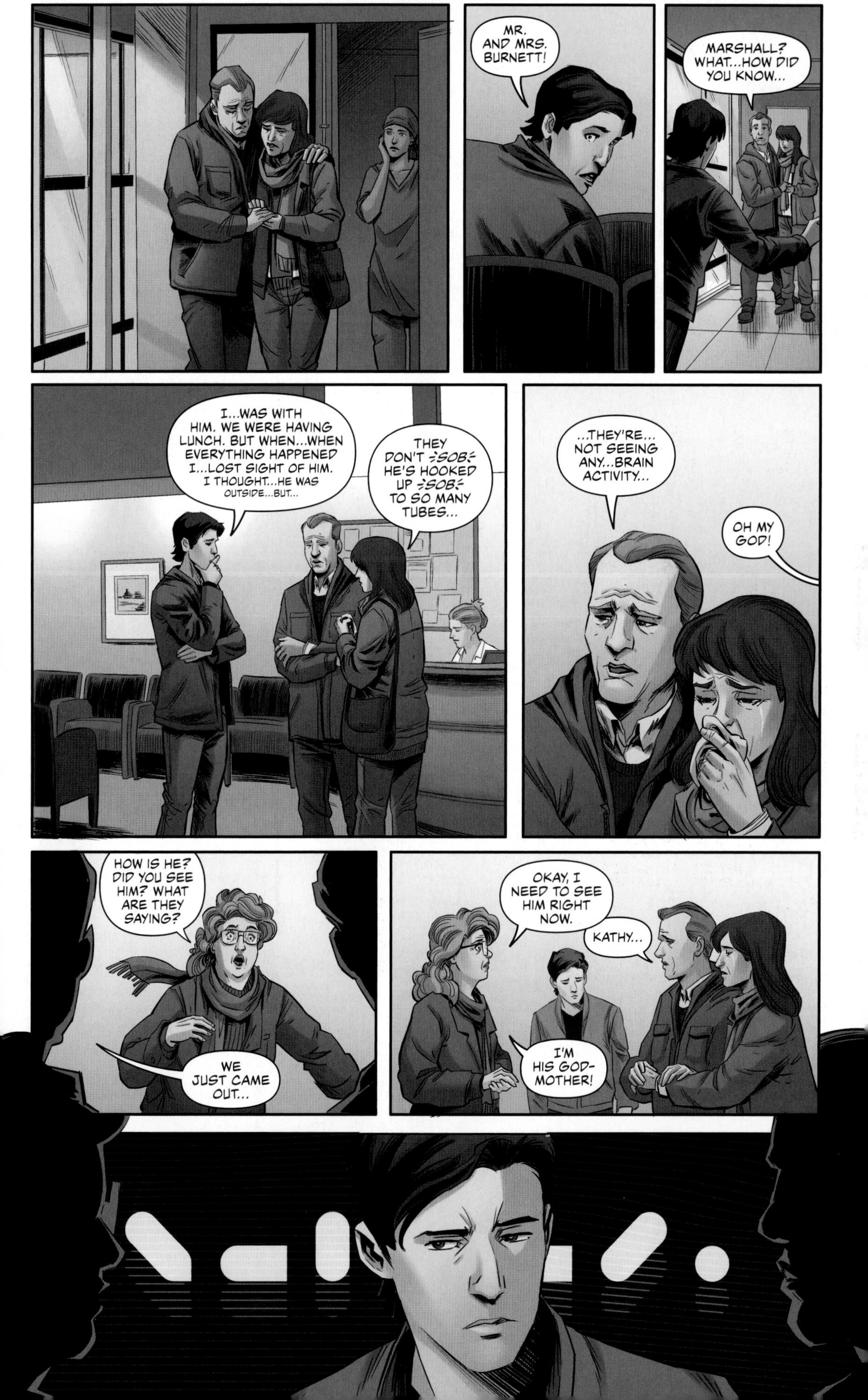
MR. AND MRS. BURNETT!
MARSHALL? WHAT...HOW DID YOU KNOW...
I...WAS WITH HIM. WE WERE HAVING LUNCH. BUT WHEN...WHEN EVERYTHING HAPPENED I...LOST SIGHT OF HIM. I THOUGHT...HE WAS OUTSIDE...BUT...
THEY DON'T *SOB* HE'S HOOKED UP *SOB* TO SO MANY TUBES...
...THEY'RE... NOT SEEING ANY...BRAIN ACTIVITY...
OH MY GOD!
HOW IS HE? DID YOU SEE HIM? WHAT ARE THEY SAYING?
WE JUST CAME OUT...
OKAY, I NEED TO SEE HIM RIGHT NOW.
KATHY...
I'M HIS GOD-MOTHER!

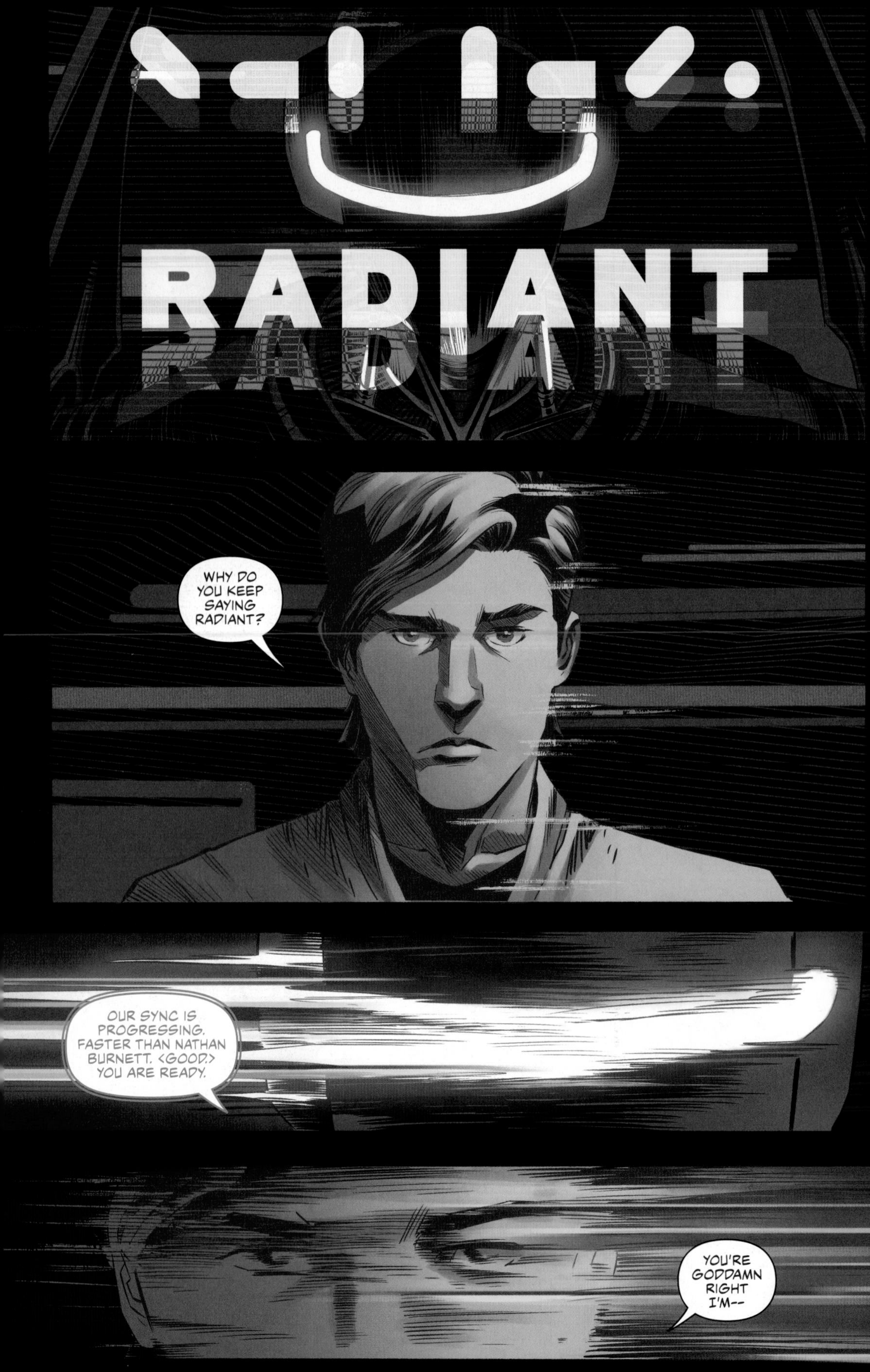
RADIANT
WHY DO YOU KEEP SAYING RADIANT?
OUR SYNC IS PROGRESSING. FASTER THAN NATHAN BURNETT. <GOOD.> YOU ARE READY.
YOU'RE GODDAMN RIGHT I'M--

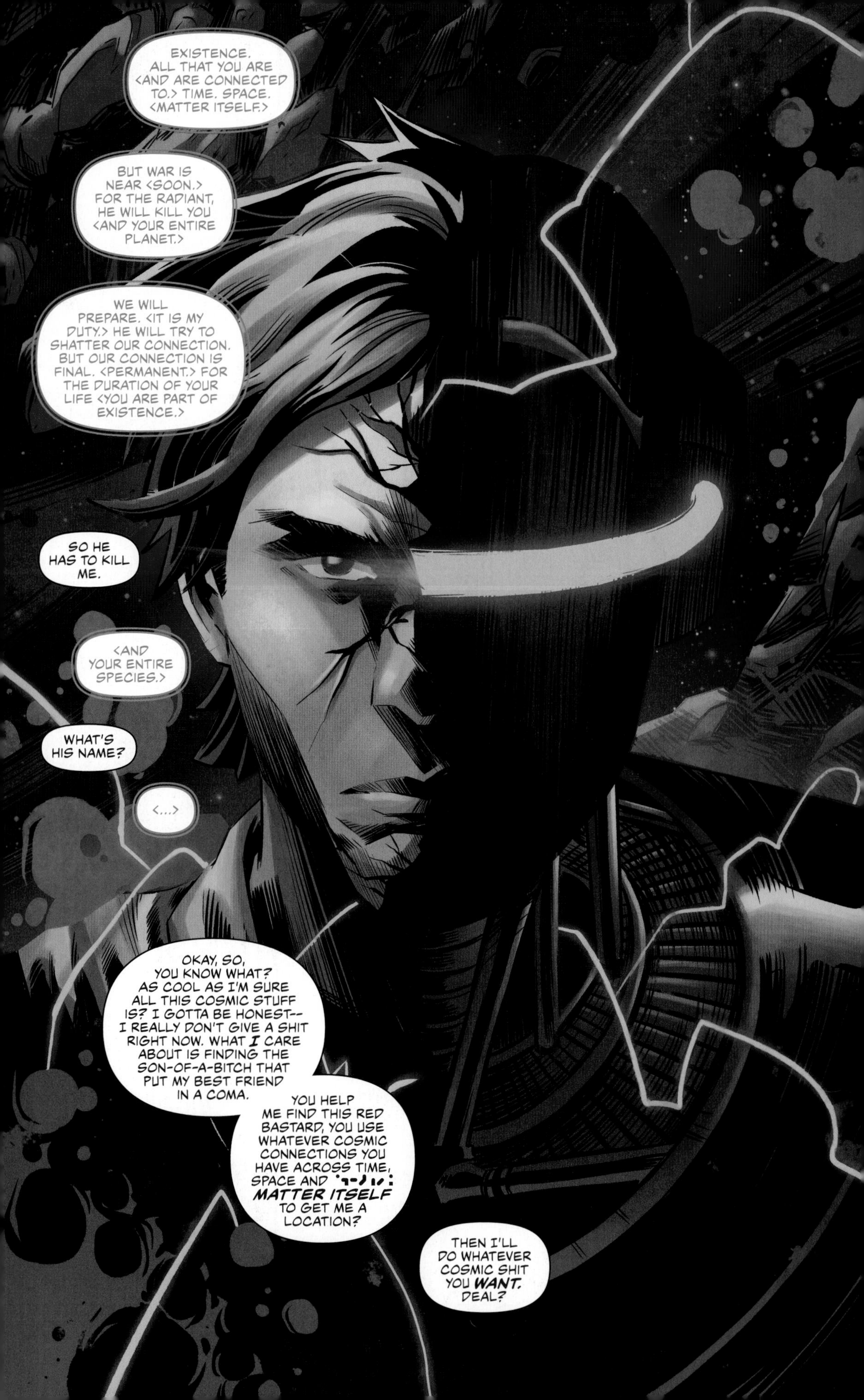

EXISTENCE. ALL THAT YOU ARE <AND ARE CONNECTED TO.> TIME. SPACE. <MATTER ITSELF.>
BUT WAR IS NEAR <SOON.> FOR THE RADIANT, HE WILL KILL YOU <AND YOUR ENTIRE PLANET.>
WE WILL PREPARE. <IT IS MY DUTY.> HE WILL TRY TO SHATTER OUR CONNECTION. BUT OUR CONNECTION IS FINAL. <PERMANENT.> FOR THE DURATION OF YOUR LIFE <YOU ARE PART OF EXISTENCE.>
SO HE HAS TO KILL ME.
<AND YOUR ENTIRE SPECIES.>
WHAT'S HIS NAME?
<...>
OKAY, SO, YOU KNOW WHAT? AS COOL AS I'M SURE ALL THIS COSMIC STUFF IS? I GOTTA BE HONEST-- I REALLY DON'T GIVE A SHIT RIGHT NOW. WHAT *I* CARE ABOUT IS FINDING THE SON-OF-A-BITCH THAT PUT MY BEST FRIEND IN A COMA.
YOU HELP ME FIND THIS RED BASTARD, YOU USE WHATEVER COSMIC CONNECTIONS YOU HAVE ACROSS TIME, SPACE AND *MATTER ITSELF* TO GET ME A LOCATION?
THEN I'LL DO WHATEVER COSMIC SHIT YOU *WANT.* DEAL?

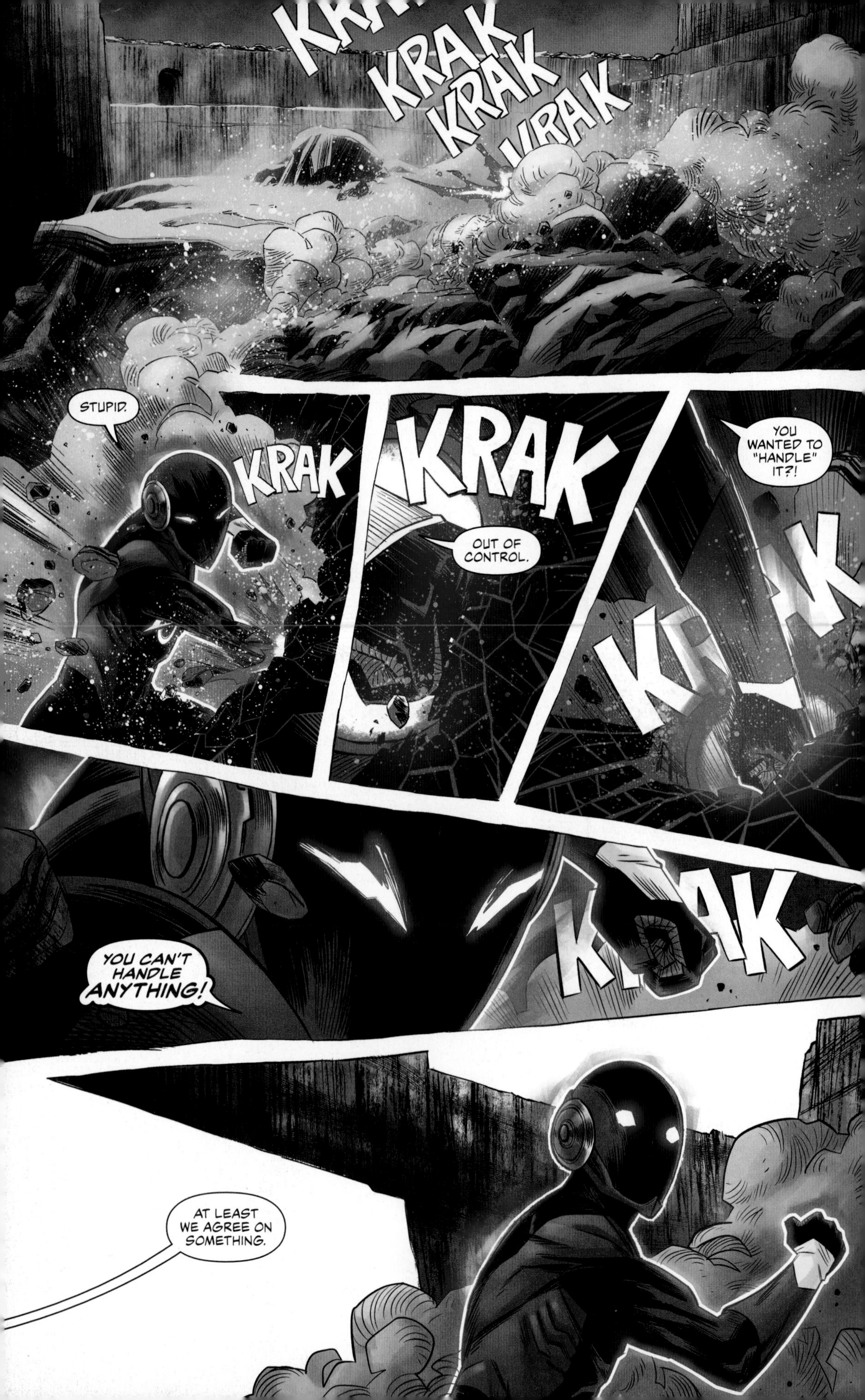
KRAK
KRAK
KRAK
KRAK
STUPID.
KRAK
KRAK
OUT OF CONTROL.
YOU WANTED TO "HANDLE" IT?!
YOU CAN'T HANDLE ANYTHING!
AT LEAST WE AGREE ON SOMETHING.

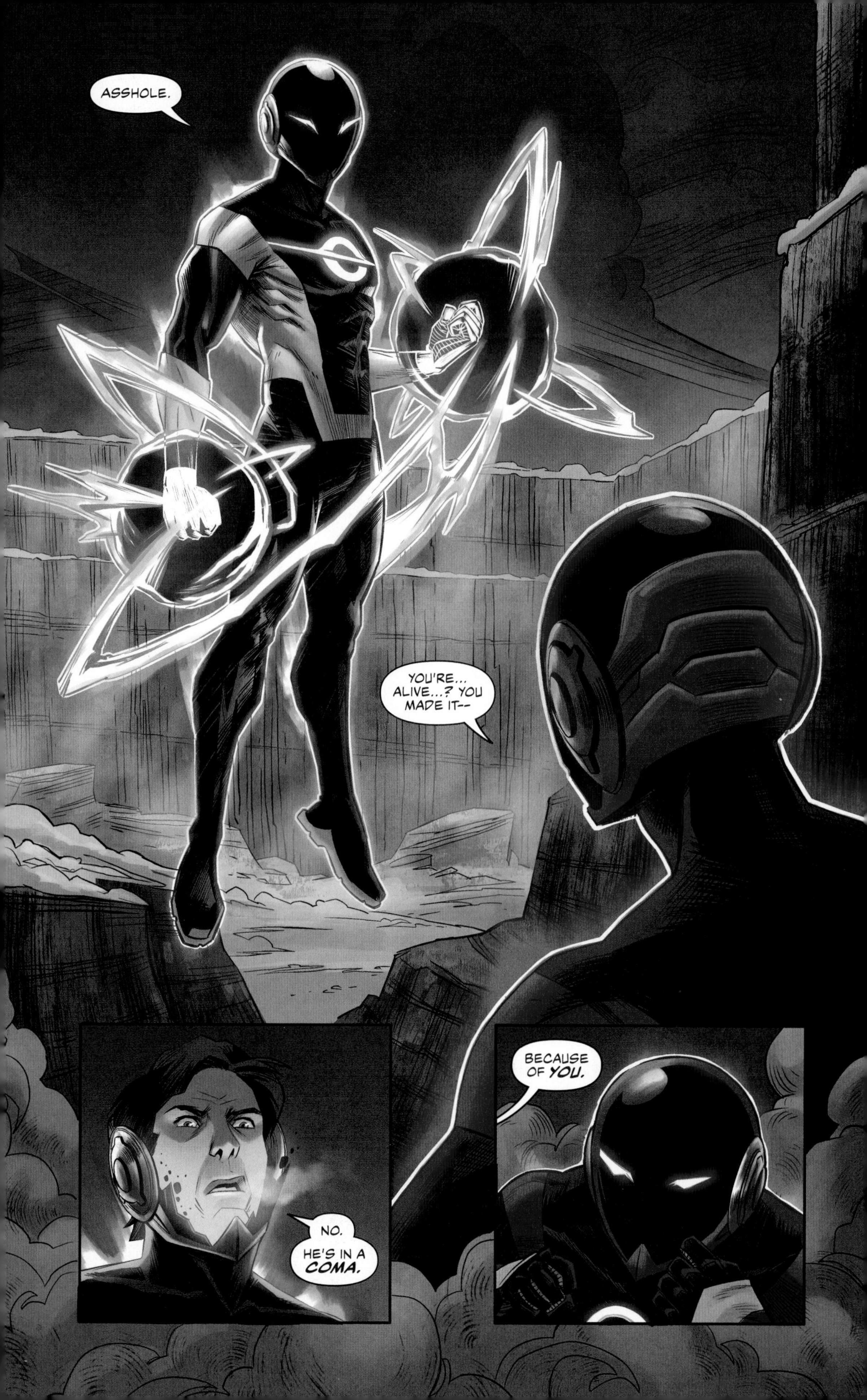
ASSHOLE.
YOU'RE... ALIVE...? YOU MADE IT--
NO. HE'S IN A COMA.
BECAUSE OF YOU.

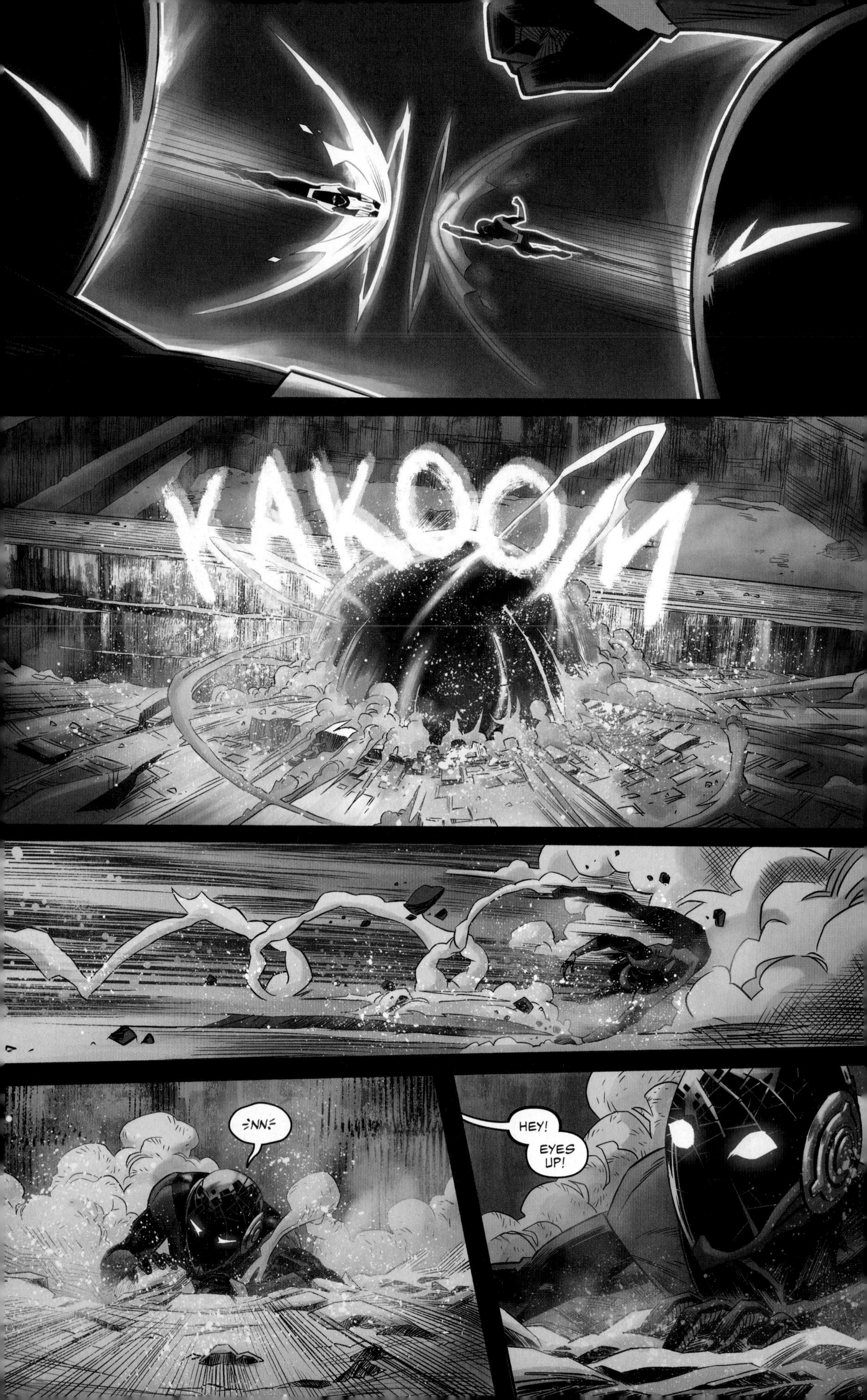
KAKOOM
NN
HEY!
EYES UP!

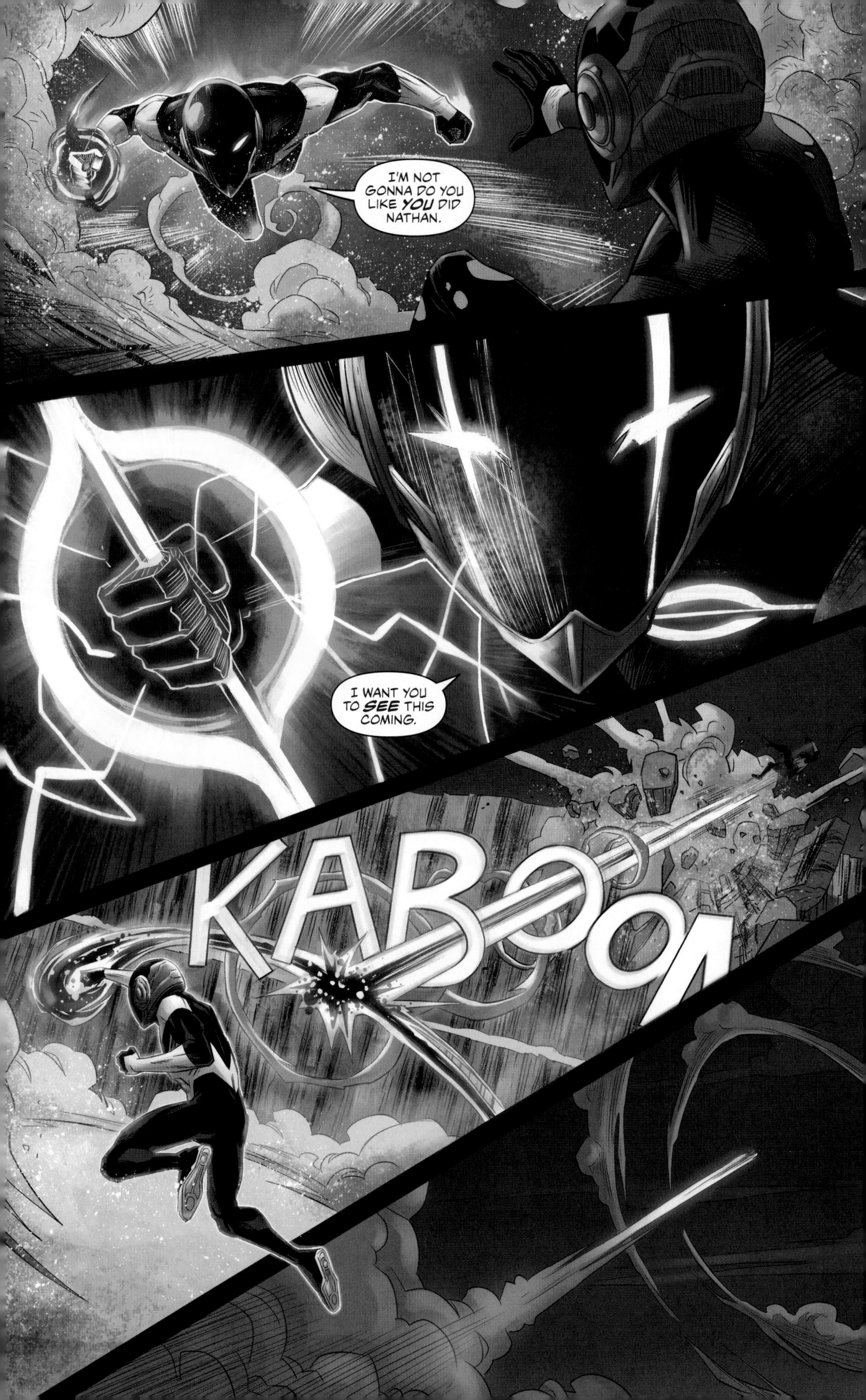
I'M NOT GONNA DO YOU LIKE *YOU* DID NATHAN.
I WANT YOU TO *SEE* THIS COMING.
KABOOOM

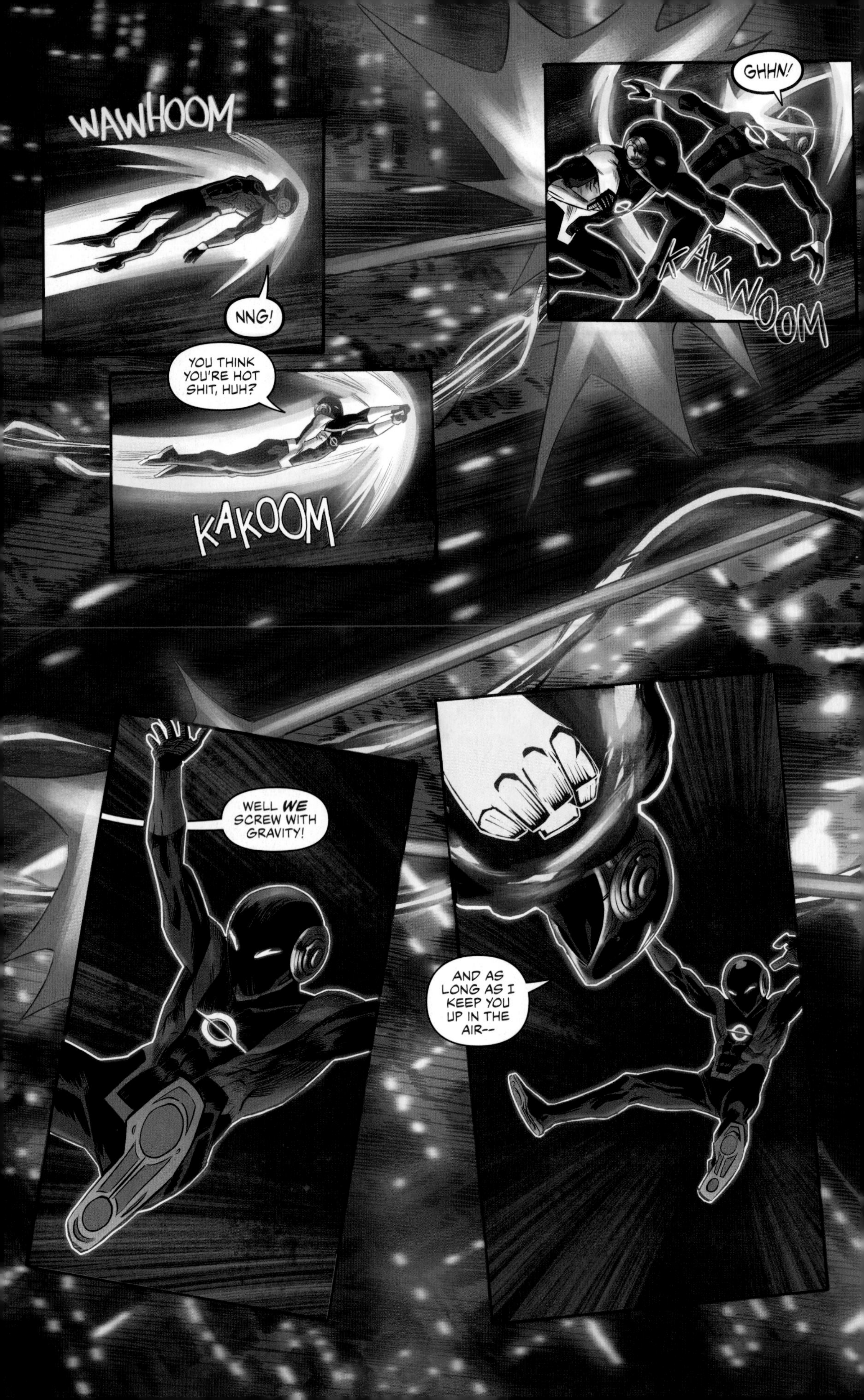
WAWHOOM
NNG!
GHHN!
KAKWOOM
YOU THINK YOU'RE HOT SHIT, HUH?
KAKOOM
WELL WE SCREW WITH GRAVITY!
AND AS LONG AS I KEEP YOU UP IN THE AIR--

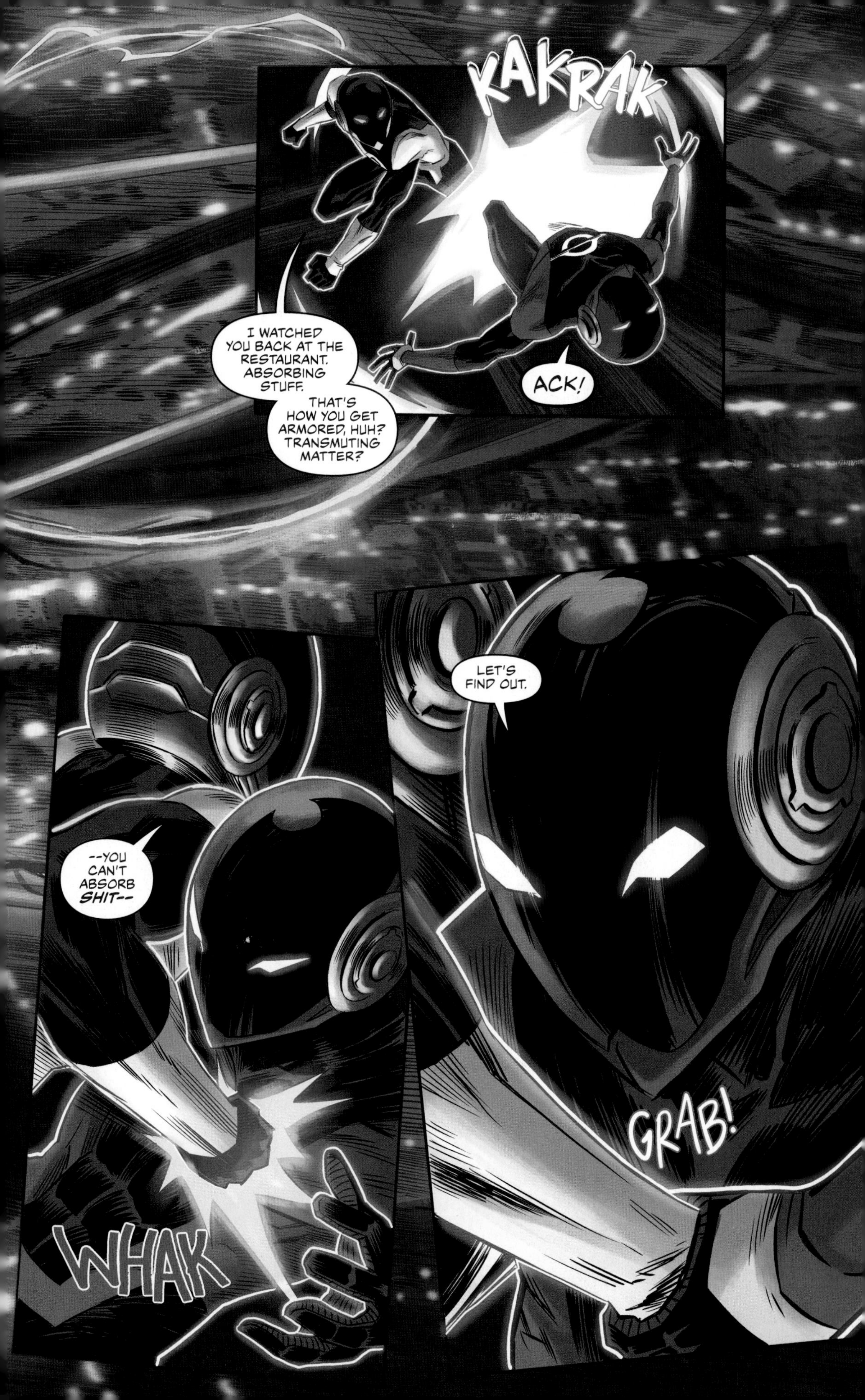
KAKRAK
I WATCHED YOU BACK AT THE RESTAURANT. ABSORBING STUFF.
THAT'S HOW YOU GET ARMORED, HUH? TRANSMUTING MATTER?
ACK!
--YOU CAN'T ABSORB SHIT--
WHAK
LET'S FIND OUT.
GRAB!

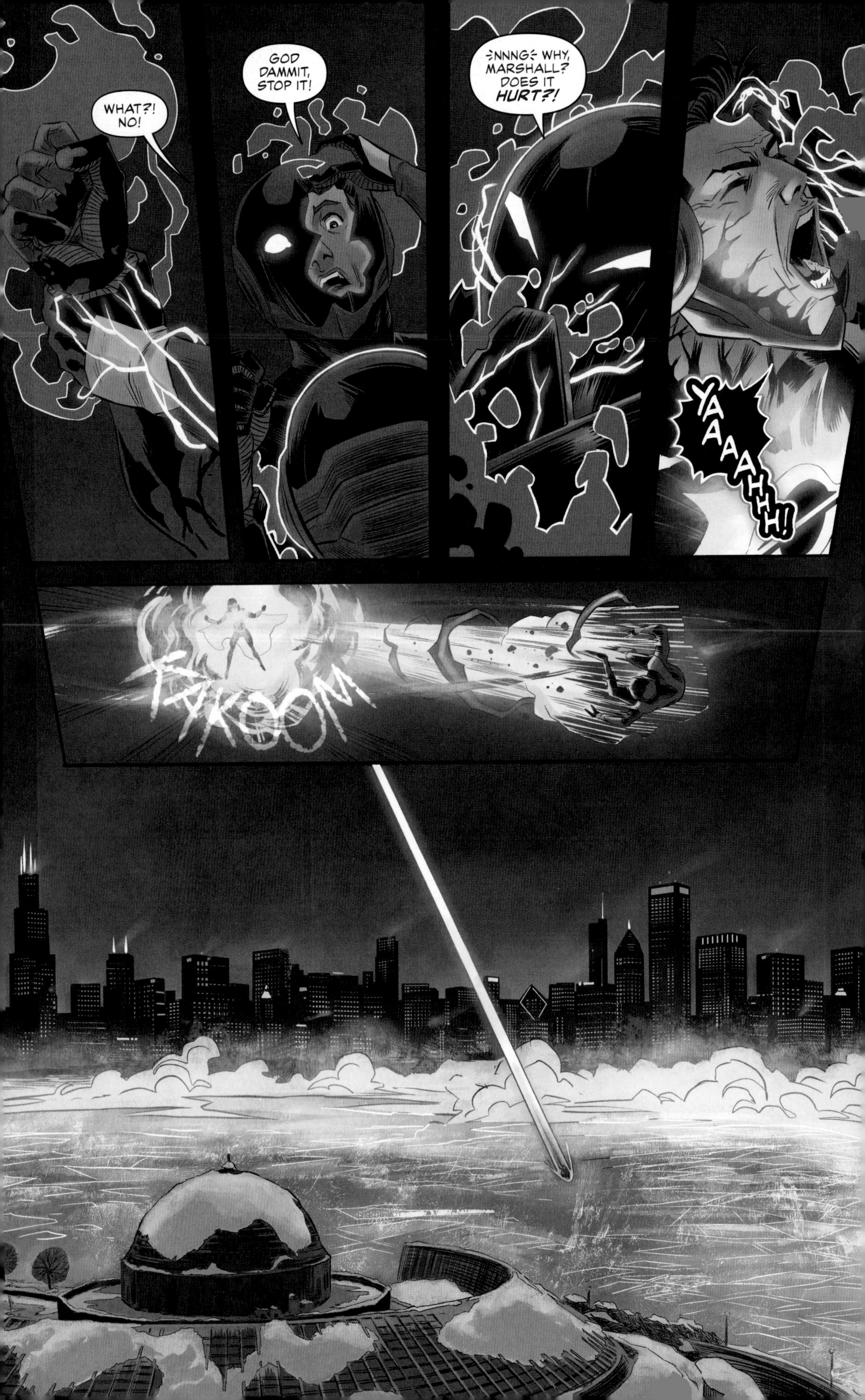
WHAT?! NO!
GOD DAMMIT, STOP IT!
NNNG WHY, MARSHALL? DOES IT HURT?!
YAAAAAHHH!
FFKOOM

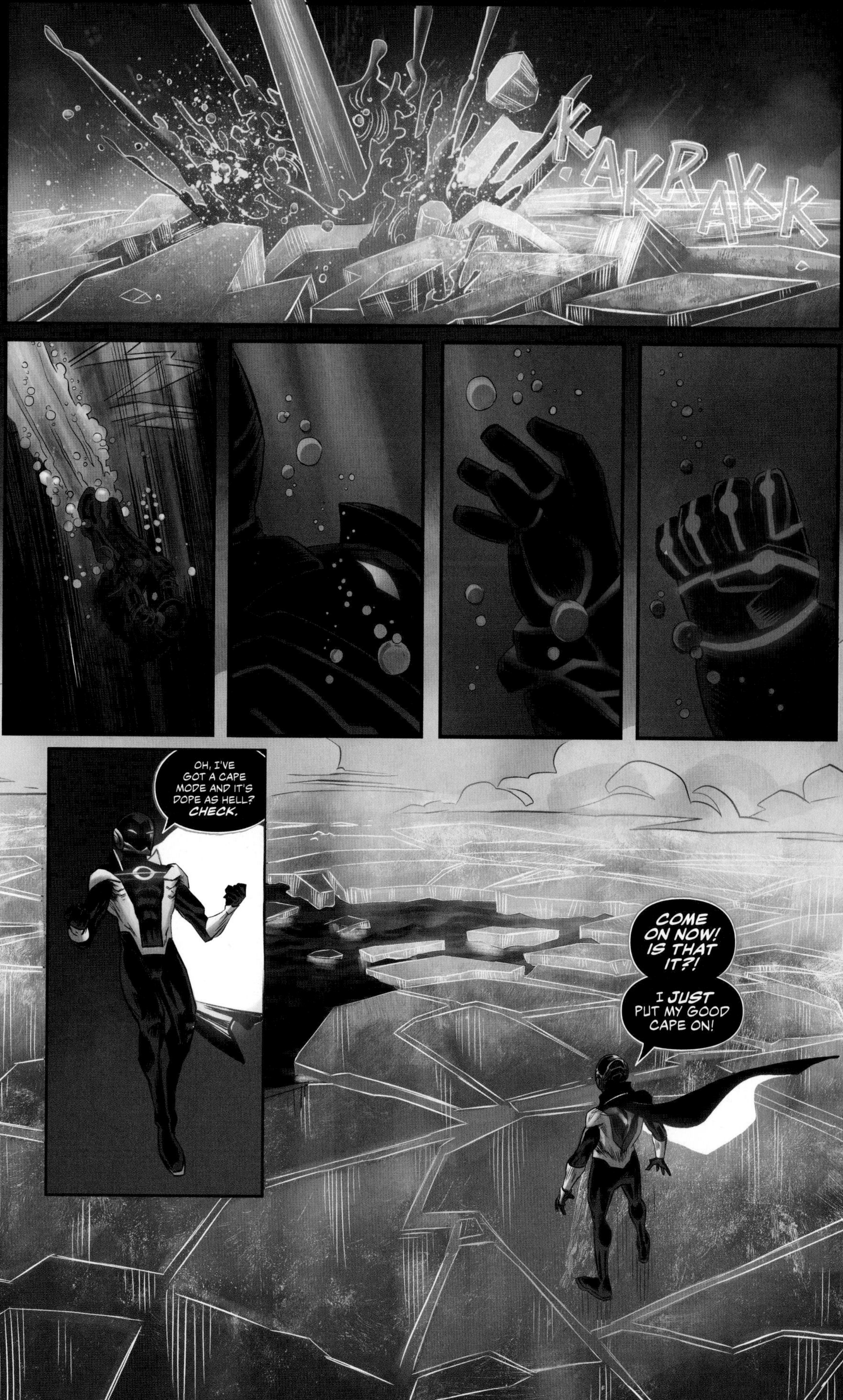

KAKRAKK
OH, I'VE GOT A CAPE MODE AND IT'S DOPE AS HELL? CHECK.
COME ON NOW! IS THAT IT?!
I JUST PUT MY GOOD CAPE ON!

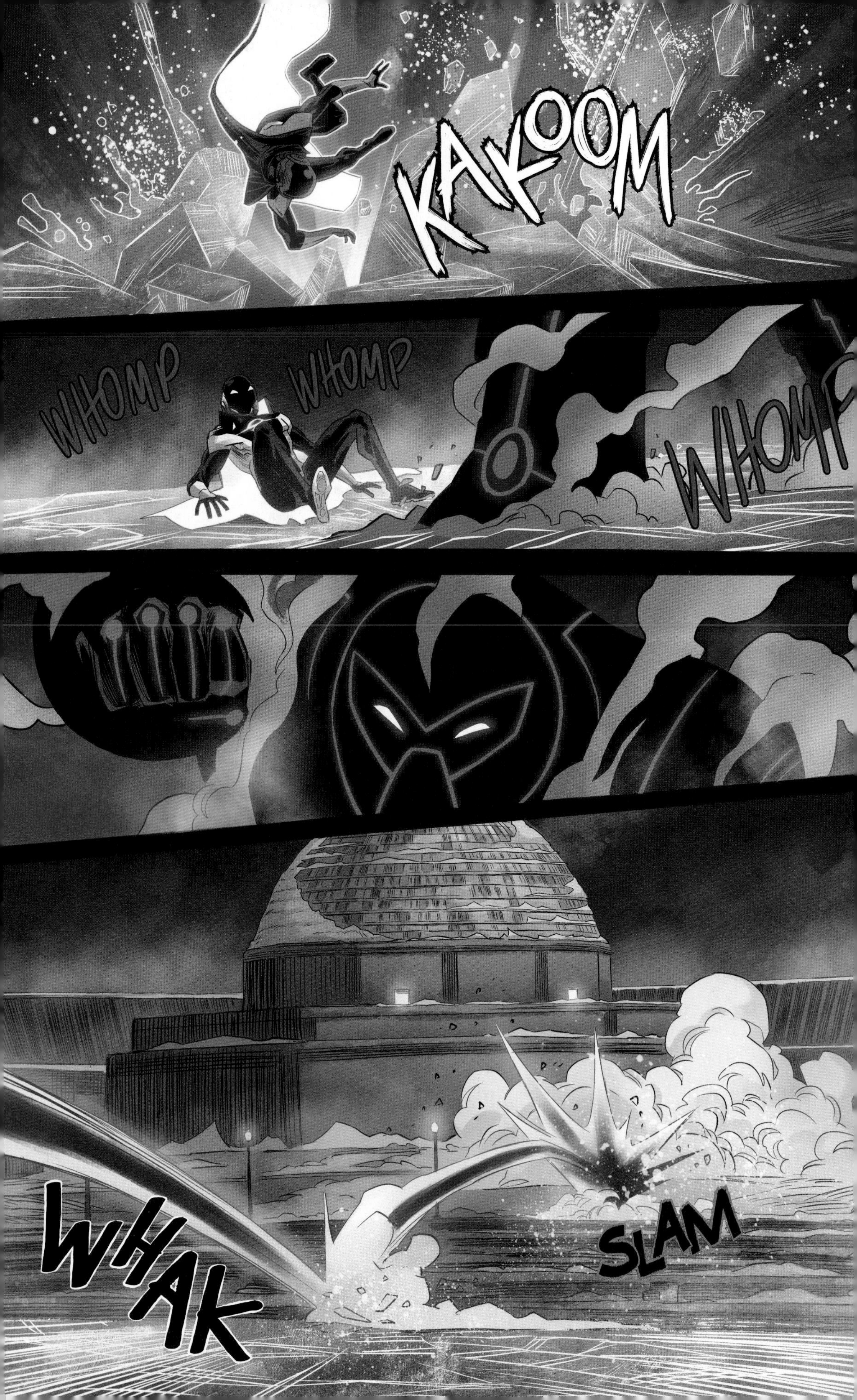
KAKOOM
WHOMP
WHOMP
WHOMP
WHAK
SLAM

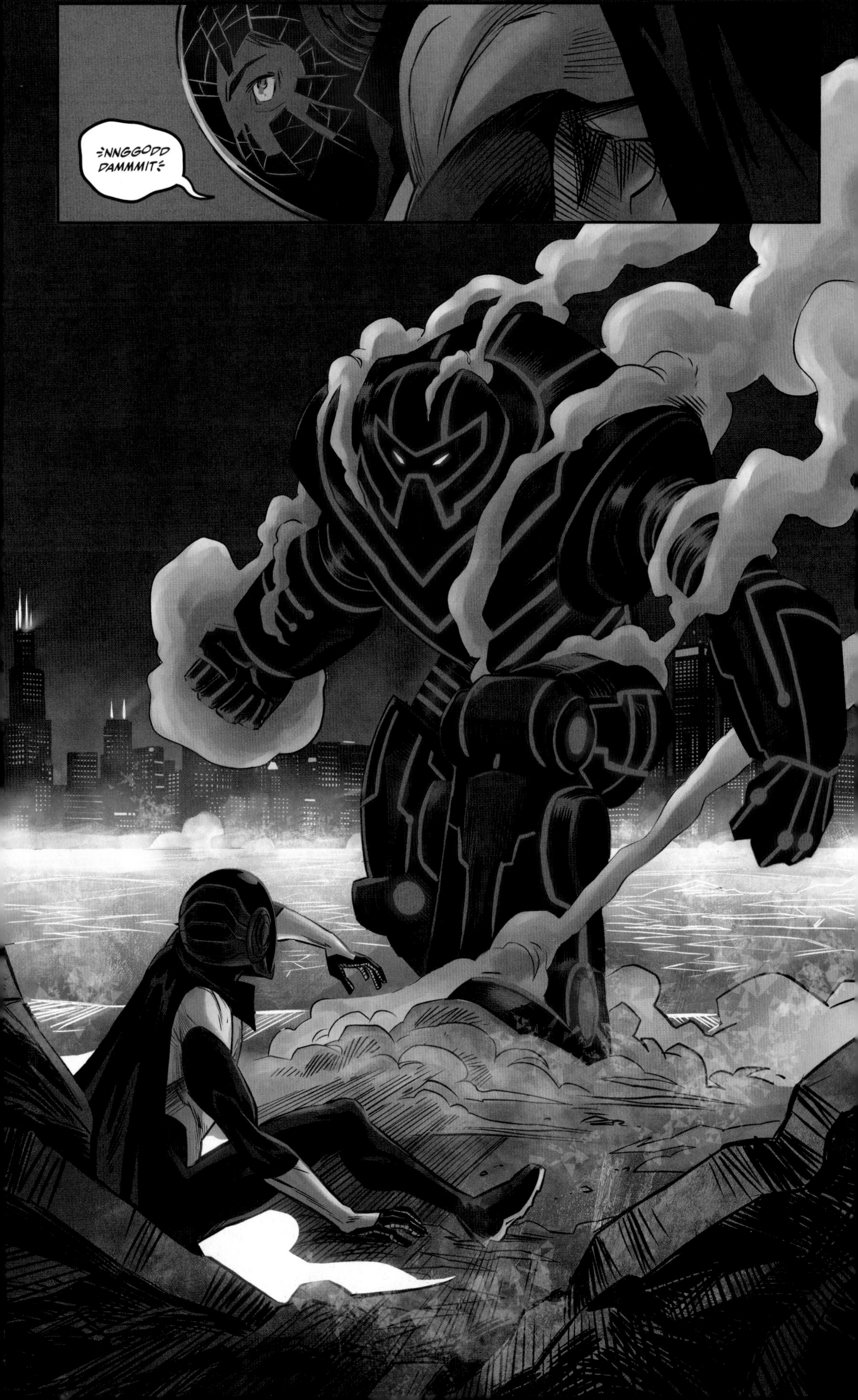
NNGGODD DAMMMIT

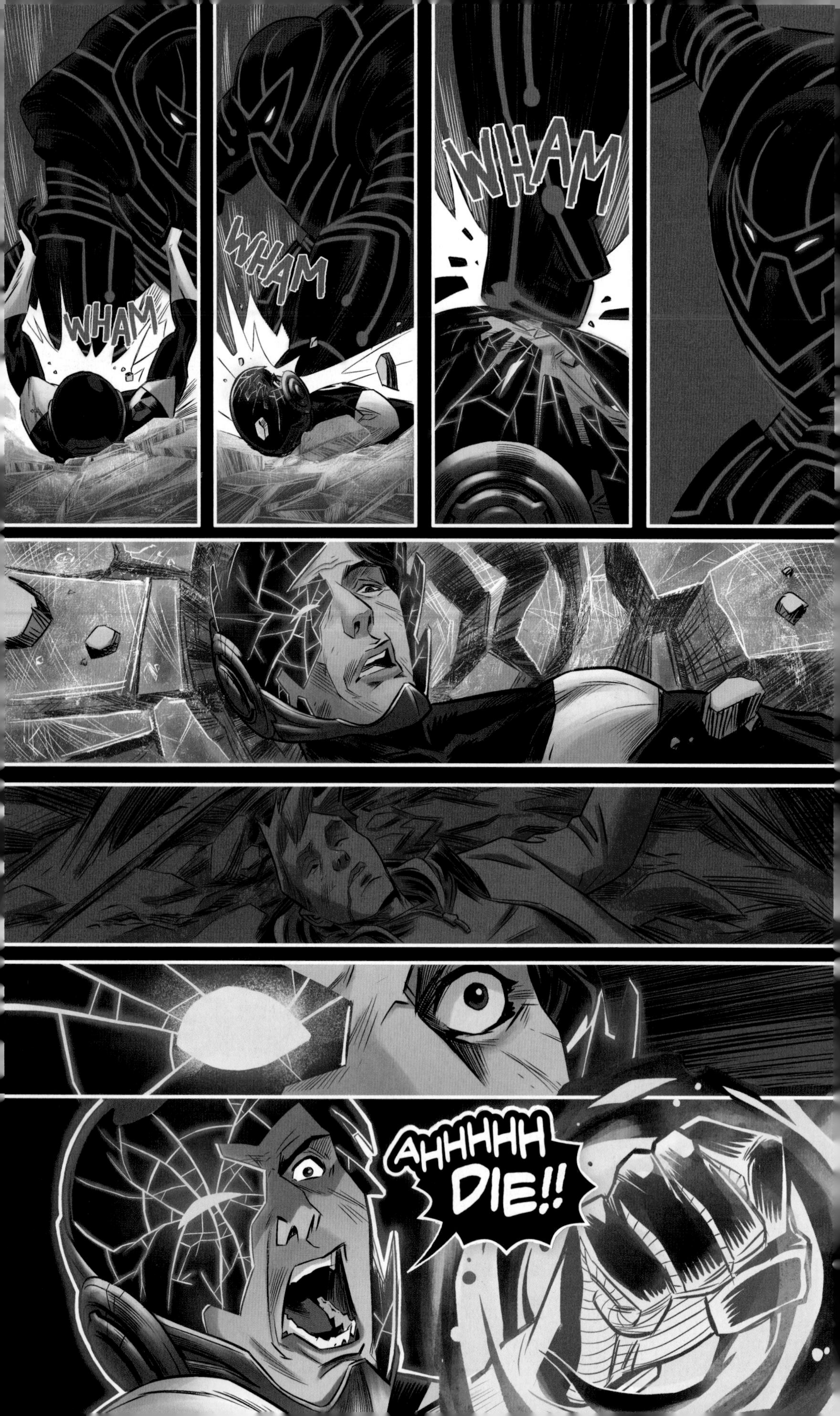
WHAM
WHAM
WHAM
AHHHHH DIE!!

GHHN!

KAKAMM

DIE DIE DIE!

YOU DROPPED A BUILDING ON MY BEST FRIEND! YOU TOOK AWAY THE *ONE* GOOD THING IN MY LIFE!

HE WAS A GOOD PERSON! *WAY* BETTER THAN ME, WHICH SUCKS FOR YOU, BECAUSE *THIS* IS ALL I HAVE NOW! AND I'M NOT STOPPING UNTIL YOU'RE *DEAD*--

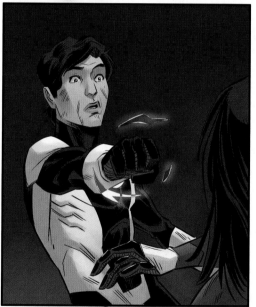

I JUST WANTED TO SCARE HIM. I DIDN'T MEAN... I DIDN'T...

HEY! SORRY! REALLY SERIOUSLY DON'T EVER SHOW UP *ANYWHERE* UNINVITED--

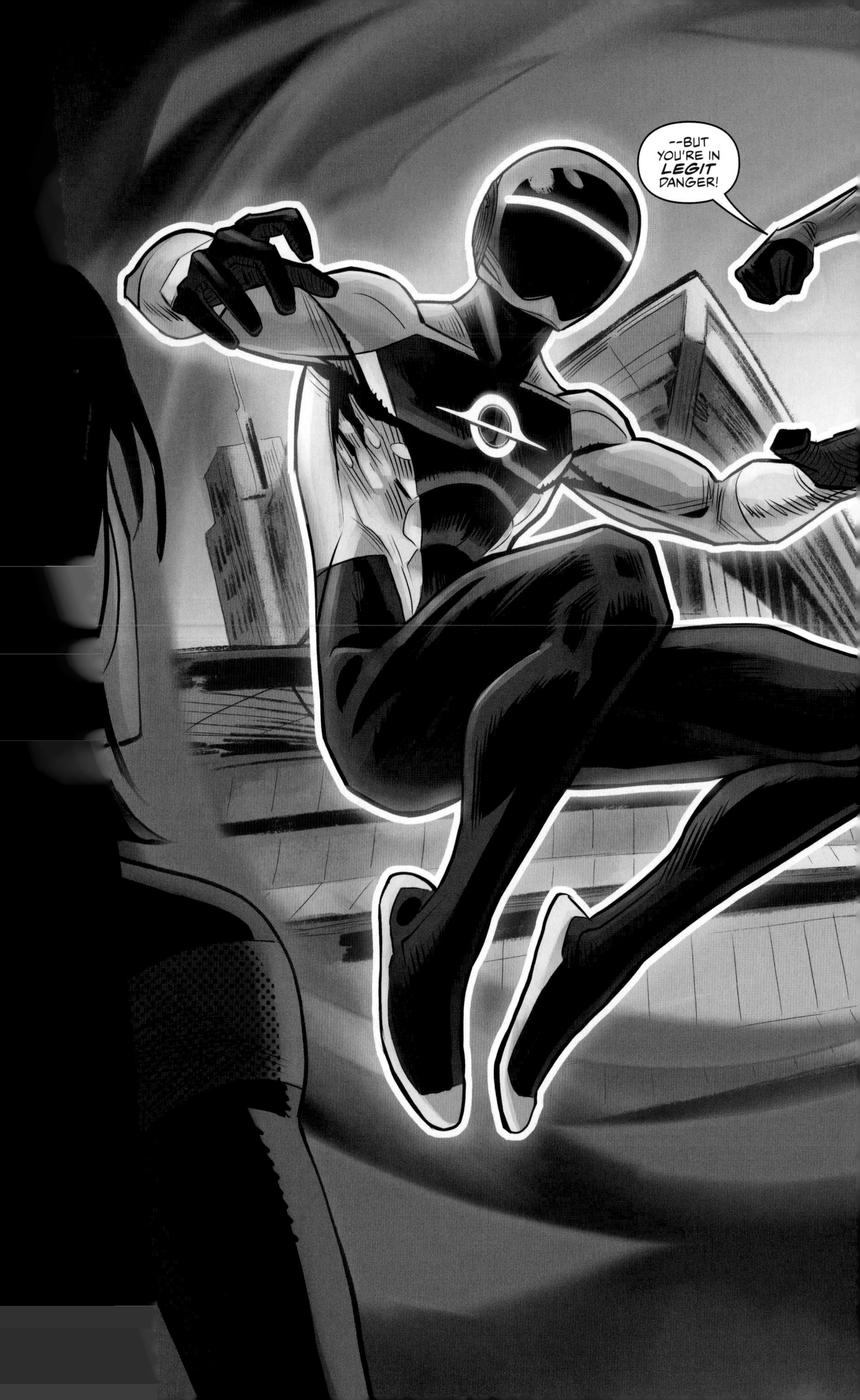
--BUT YOU'RE IN *LEGIT* DANGER!

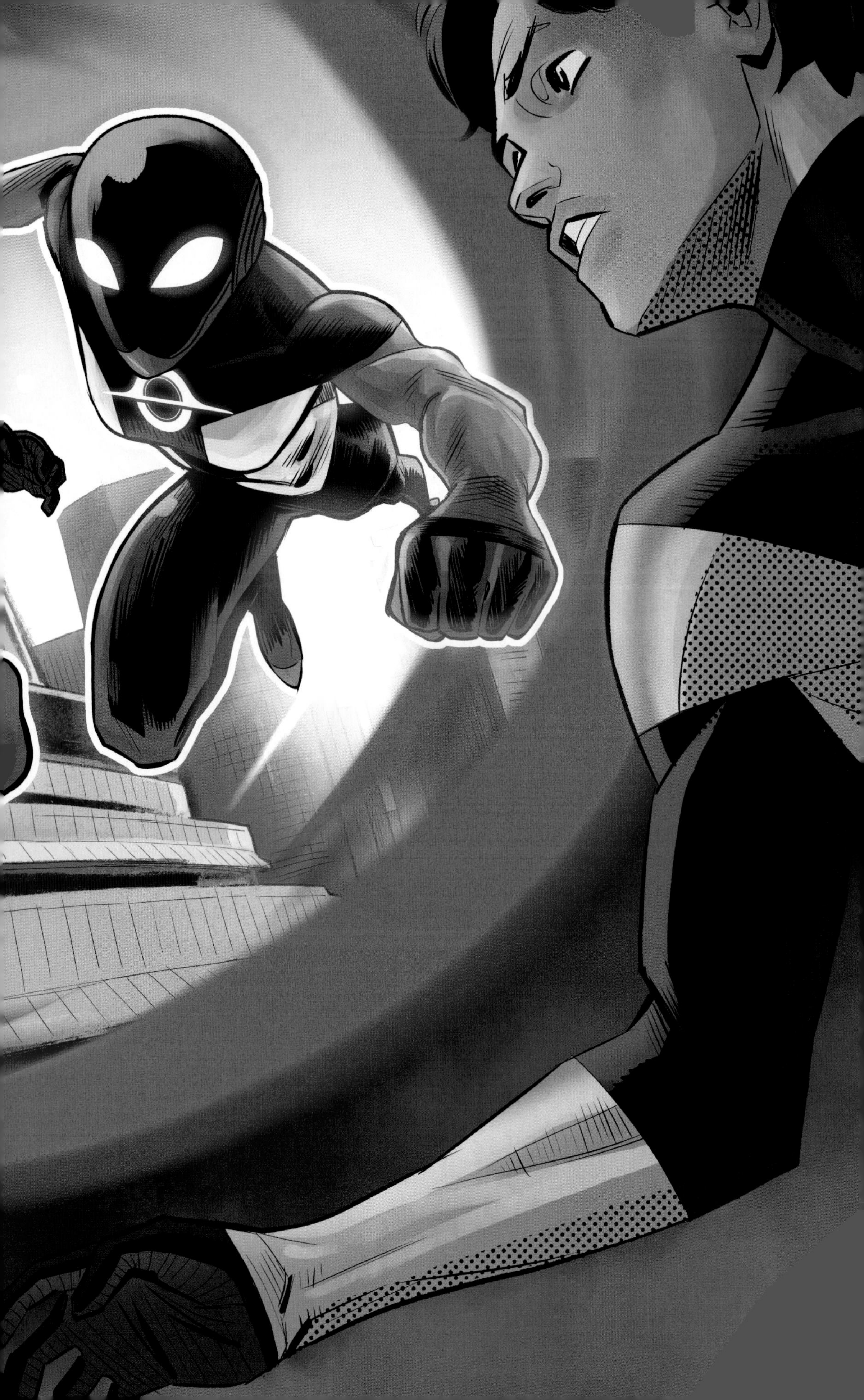

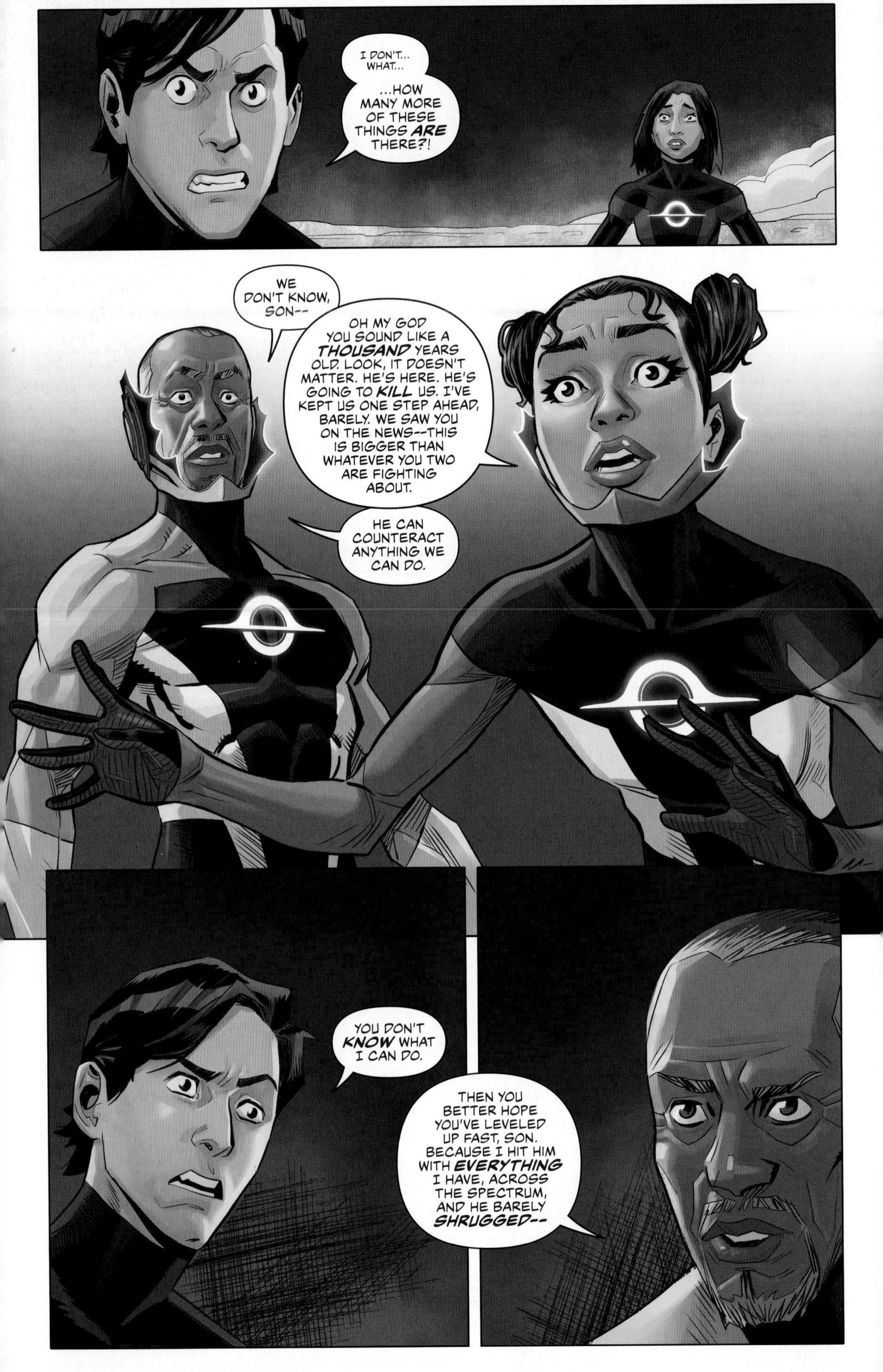
I DON'T... WHAT...
...HOW MANY MORE OF THESE THINGS ARE THERE?!
WE DON'T KNOW, SON--
OH MY GOD YOU SOUND LIKE A THOUSAND YEARS OLD. LOOK, IT DOESN'T MATTER. HE'S HERE. HE'S GOING TO KILL US. I'VE KEPT US ONE STEP AHEAD, BARELY. WE SAW YOU ON THE NEWS--THIS IS BIGGER THAN WHATEVER YOU TWO ARE FIGHTING ABOUT.
HE CAN COUNTERACT ANYTHING WE CAN DO.
YOU DON'T KNOW WHAT I CAN DO.
THEN YOU BETTER HOPE YOU'VE LEVELED UP FAST, SON. BECAUSE I HIT HIM WITH EVERYTHING I HAVE, ACROSS THE SPECTRUM, AND HE BARELY SHRUGGED--

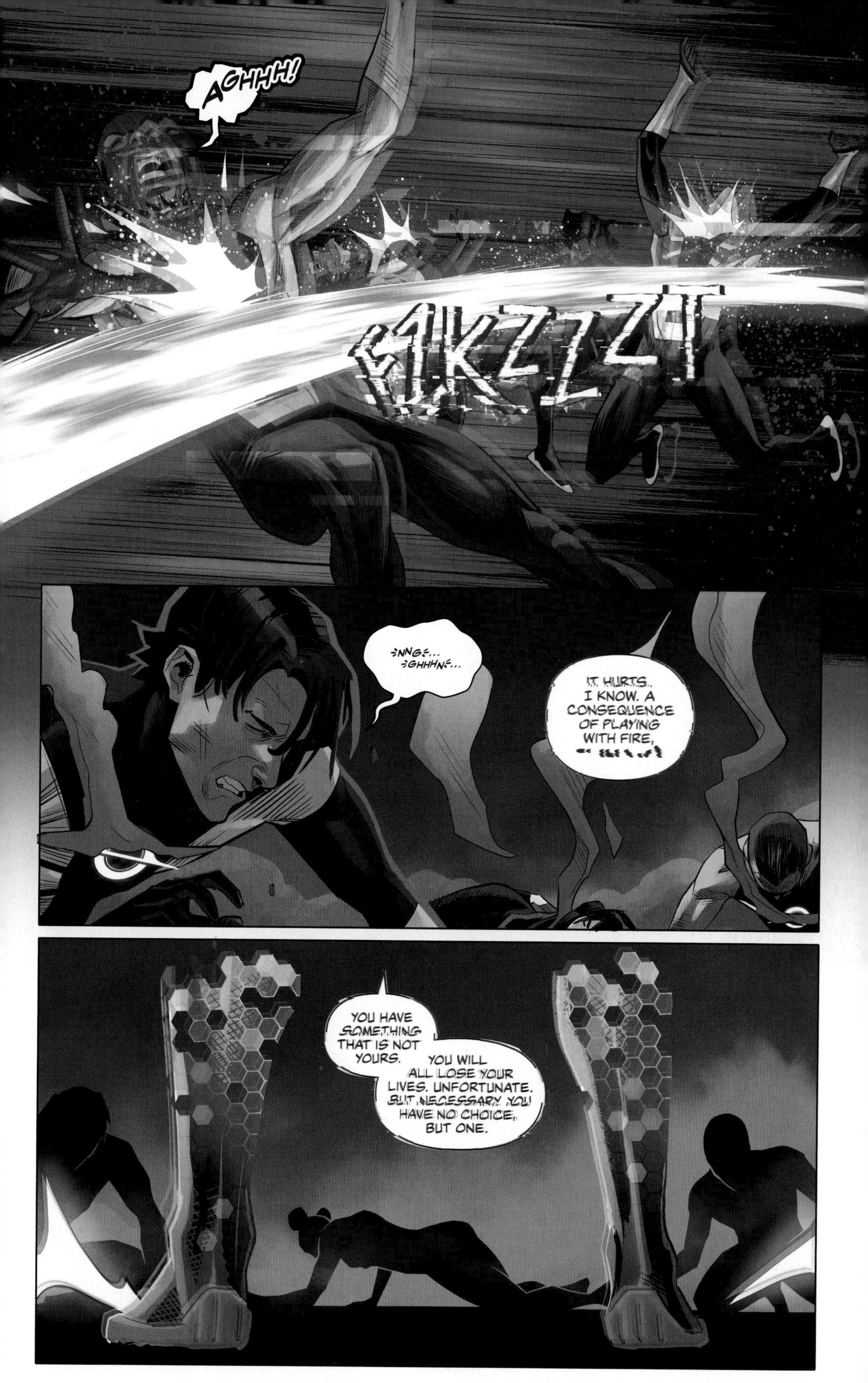
AGHHH!
SKZZZT
NNG... GHHHN...
IT HURTS. I KNOW. A CONSEQUENCE OF PLAYING WITH FIRE,
YOU HAVE SOMETHING THAT IS NOT YOURS.
YOU WILL ALL LOSE YOUR LIVES. UNFORTUNATE. BUT NECESSARY. YOU HAVE NO CHOICE, BUT ONE.

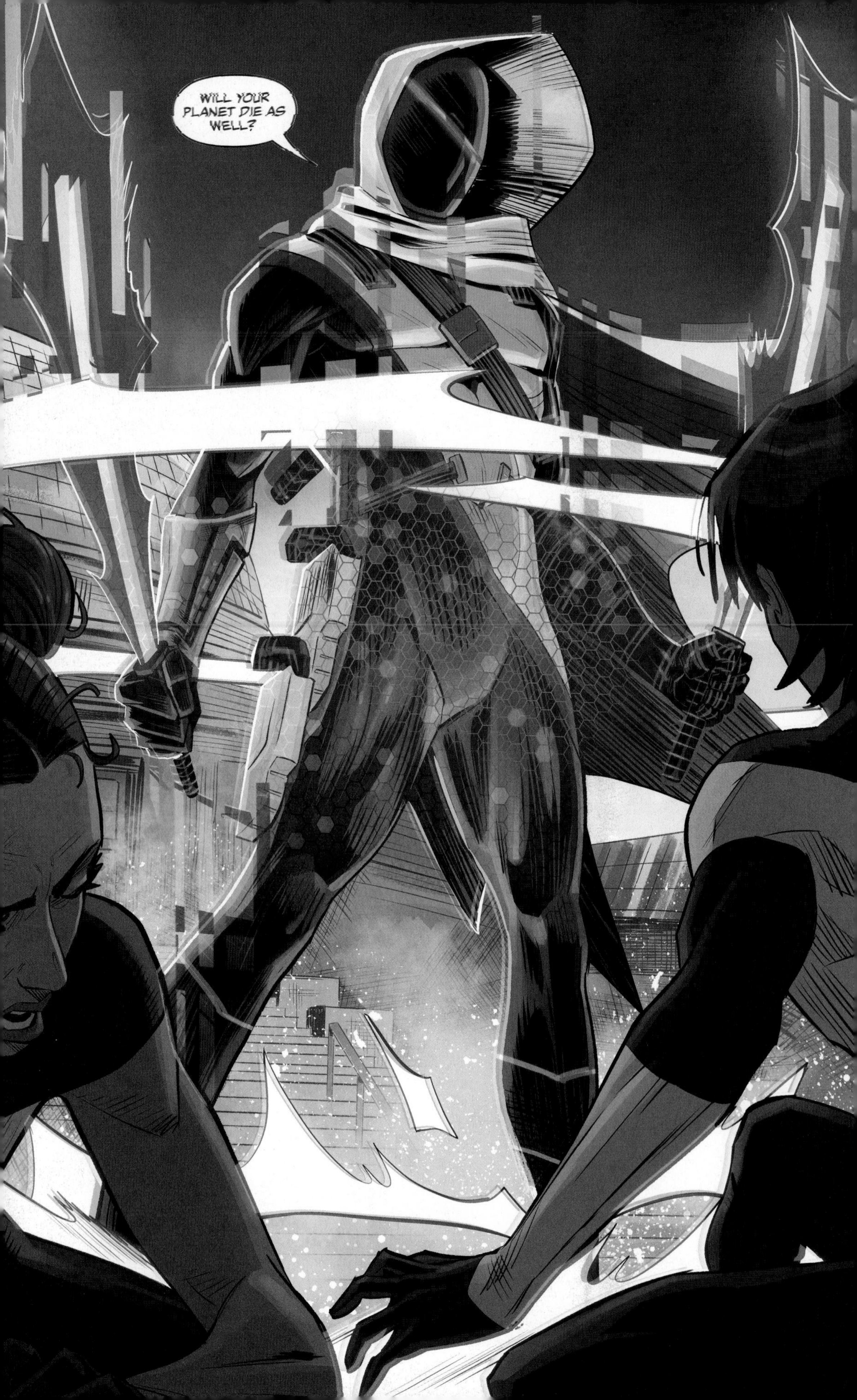
WILL YOUR PLANET DIE AS WELL?

CHAPTER SIX

TITLE   Red

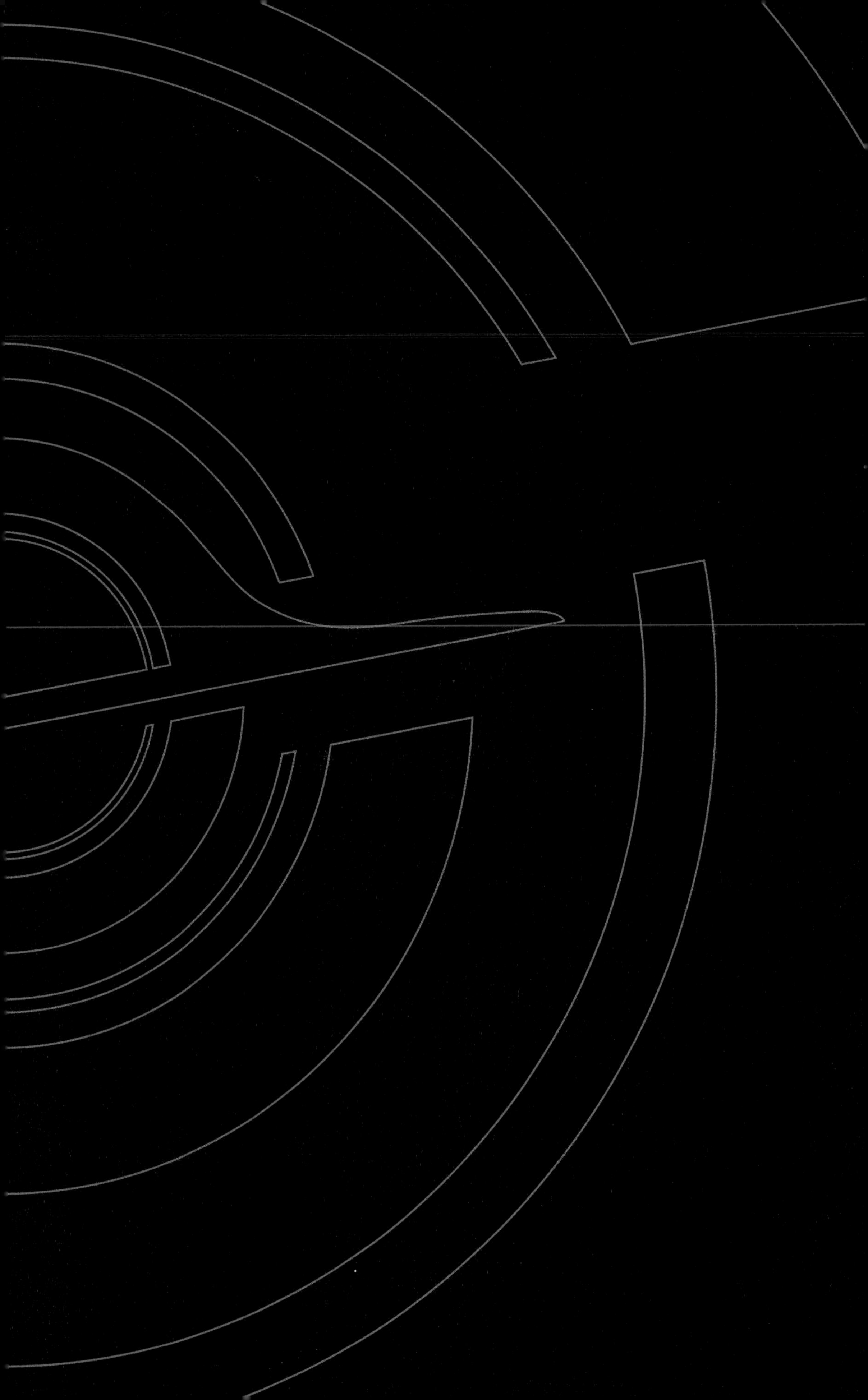

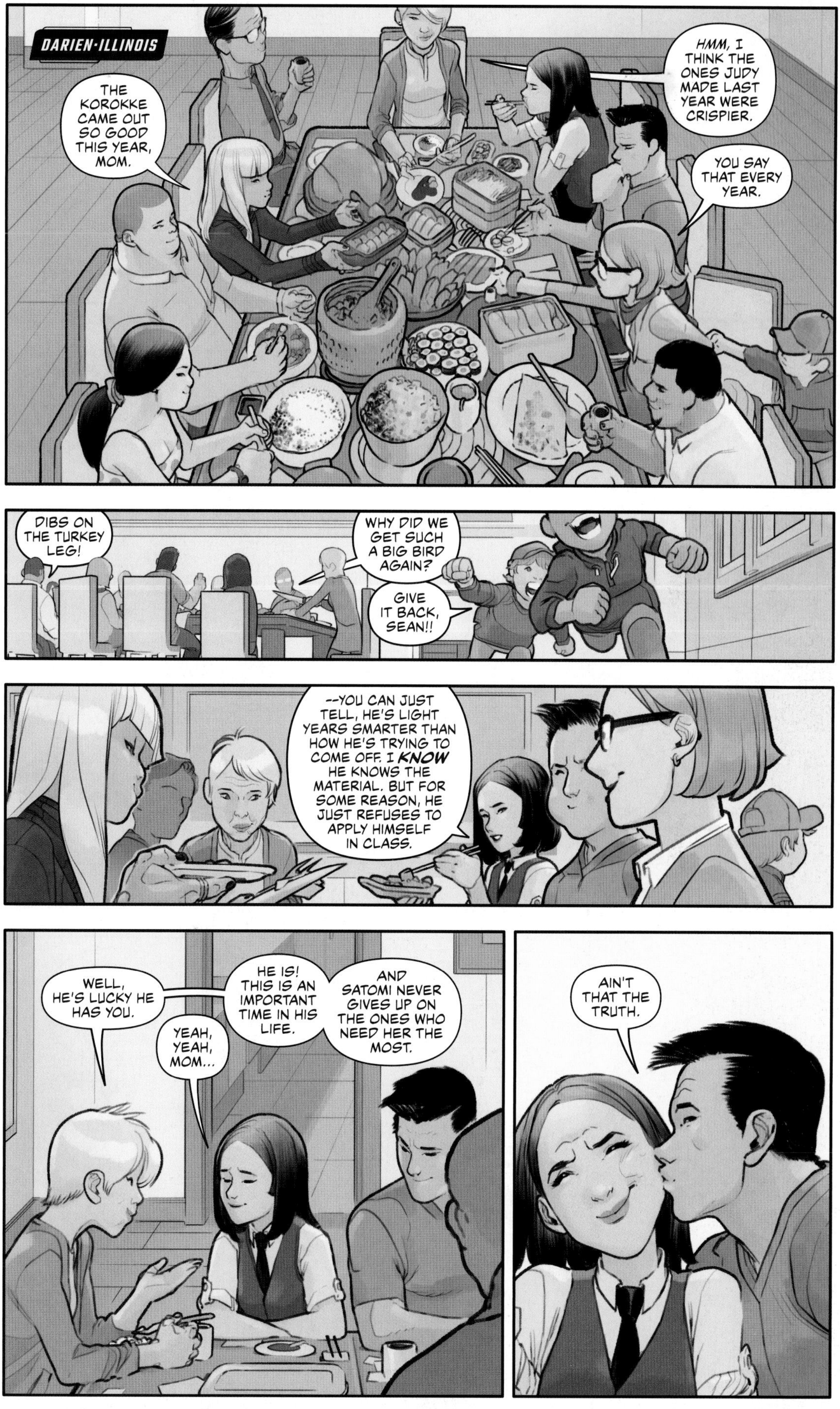
DARIEN·ILLINOIS
THE KOROKKE CAME OUT SO GOOD THIS YEAR, MOM.
HMM, I THINK THE ONES JUDY MADE LAST YEAR WERE CRISPIER.
YOU SAY THAT EVERY YEAR.
DIBS ON THE TURKEY LEG!
WHY DID WE GET SUCH A BIG BIRD AGAIN?
GIVE IT BACK, SEAN!!
--YOU CAN JUST TELL, HE'S LIGHT YEARS SMARTER THAN HOW HE'S TRYING TO COME OFF. I KNOW HE KNOWS THE MATERIAL. BUT FOR SOME REASON, HE JUST REFUSES TO APPLY HIMSELF IN CLASS.
WELL, HE'S LUCKY HE HAS YOU.
HE IS! THIS IS AN IMPORTANT TIME IN HIS LIFE.
YEAH, YEAH, MOM...
AND SATOMI NEVER GIVES UP ON THE ONES WHO NEED HER THE MOST.
AIN'T THAT THE TRUTH.

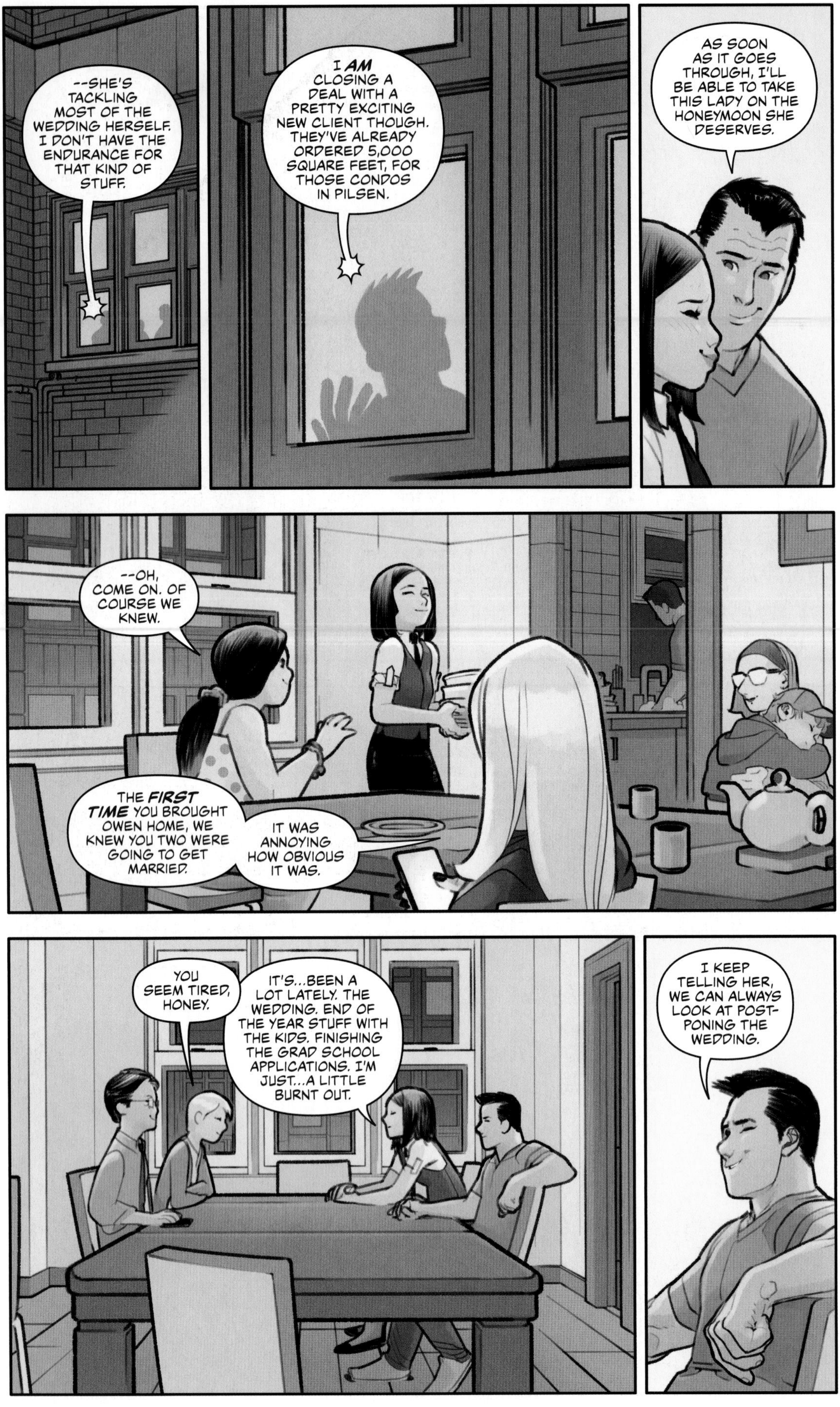
--SHE'S TACKLING MOST OF THE WEDDING HERSELF. I DON'T HAVE THE ENDURANCE FOR THAT KIND OF STUFF.
I *AM* CLOSING A DEAL WITH A PRETTY EXCITING NEW CLIENT THOUGH. THEY'VE ALREADY ORDERED 5,000 SQUARE FEET, FOR THOSE CONDOS IN PILSEN.
AS SOON AS IT GOES THROUGH, I'LL BE ABLE TO TAKE THIS LADY ON THE HONEYMOON SHE DESERVES.
--OH, COME ON. OF COURSE WE KNEW.
THE *FIRST TIME* YOU BROUGHT OWEN HOME, WE KNEW YOU TWO WERE GOING TO GET MARRIED.
IT WAS ANNOYING HOW OBVIOUS IT WAS.
YOU SEEM TIRED, HONEY.
IT'S...BEEN A LOT LATELY. THE WEDDING. END OF THE YEAR STUFF WITH THE KIDS. FINISHING THE GRAD SCHOOL APPLICATIONS. I'M JUST...A LITTLE BURNT OUT.
I KEEP TELLING HER, WE CAN ALWAYS LOOK AT POST-PONING THE WEDDING.

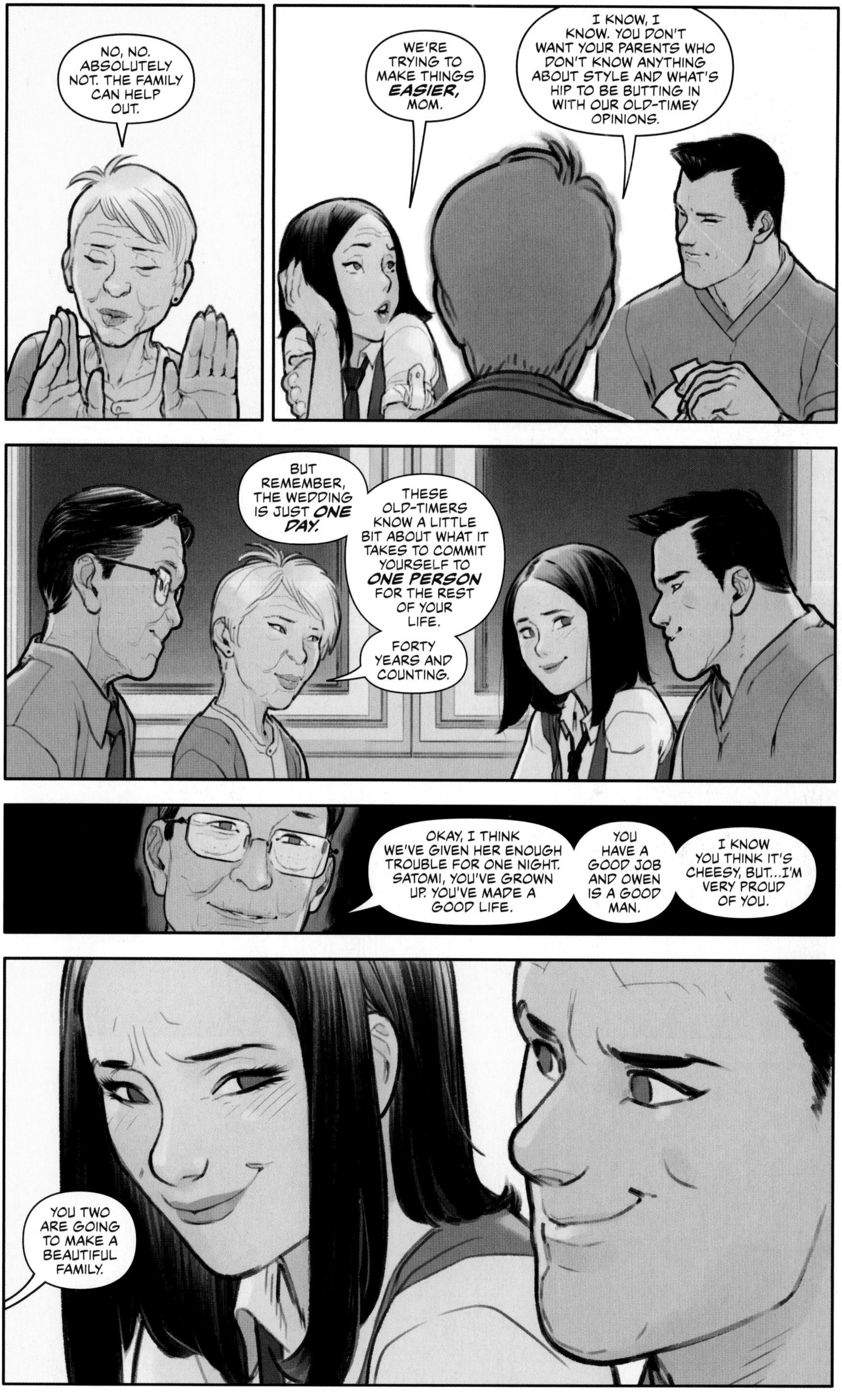
NO, NO. ABSOLUTELY NOT. THE FAMILY CAN HELP OUT.
WE'RE TRYING TO MAKE THINGS EASIER, MOM.
I KNOW, I KNOW. YOU DON'T WANT YOUR PARENTS WHO DON'T KNOW ANYTHING ABOUT STYLE AND WHAT'S HIP TO BE BUTTING IN WITH OUR OLD-TIMEY OPINIONS.
BUT REMEMBER, THE WEDDING IS JUST ONE DAY.
THESE OLD-TIMERS KNOW A LITTLE BIT ABOUT WHAT IT TAKES TO COMMIT YOURSELF TO ONE PERSON FOR THE REST OF YOUR LIFE.
FORTY YEARS AND COUNTING.
OKAY, I THINK WE'VE GIVEN HER ENOUGH TROUBLE FOR ONE NIGHT. SATOMI, YOU'VE GROWN UP. YOU'VE MADE A GOOD LIFE.
YOU HAVE A GOOD JOB AND OWEN IS A GOOD MAN.
I KNOW YOU THINK IT'S CHEESY, BUT...I'M VERY PROUD OF YOU.
YOU TWO ARE GOING TO MAKE A BEAUTIFUL FAMILY.

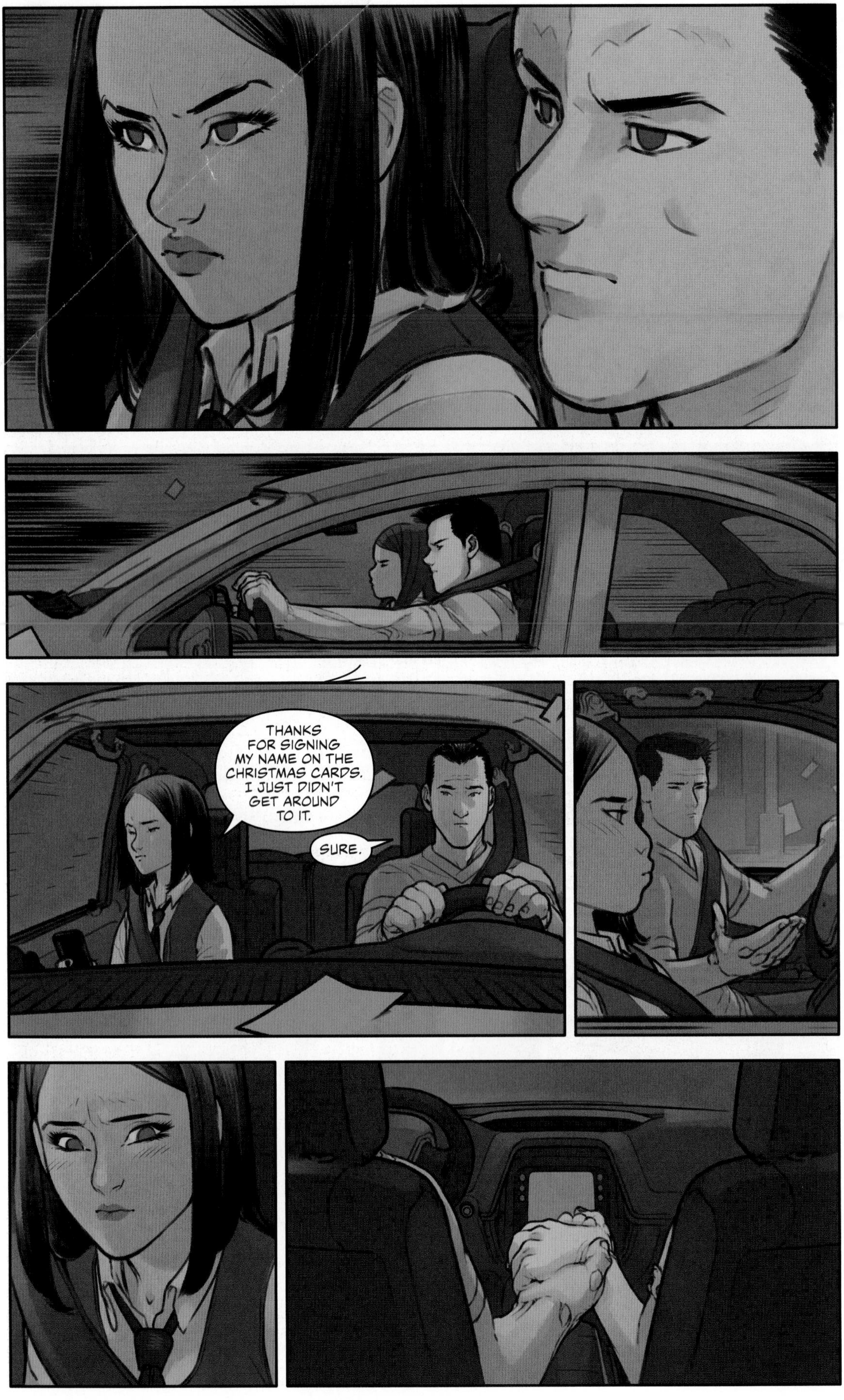
THANKS FOR SIGNING MY NAME ON THE CHRISTMAS CARDS. I JUST DIDN'T GET AROUND TO IT.
SURE.

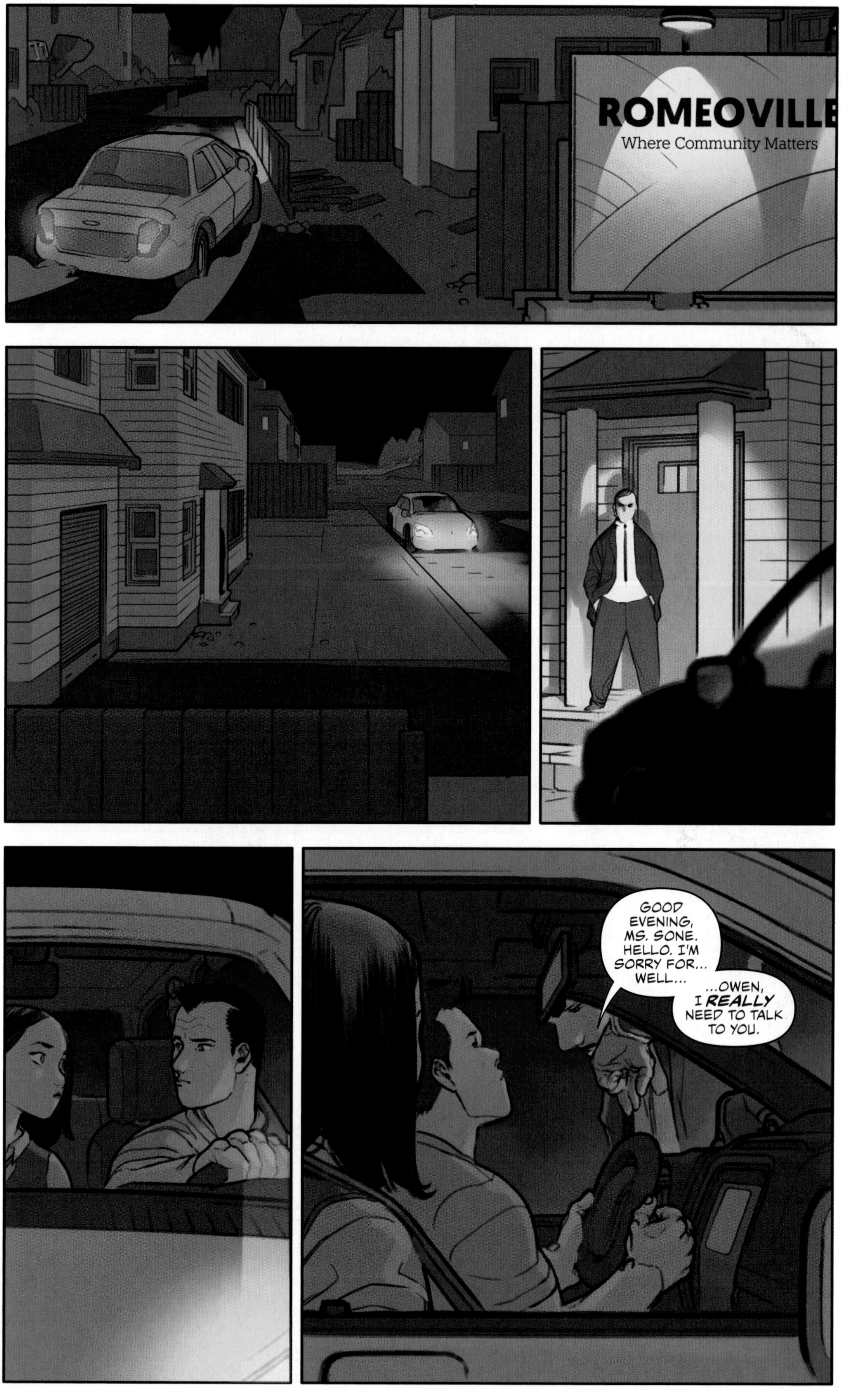
ROMEOVILLE
Where Community Matters
GOOD EVENING, MS. SONE. HELLO. I'M SORRY FOR... WELL...
...OWEN, I REALLY NEED TO TALK TO YOU.

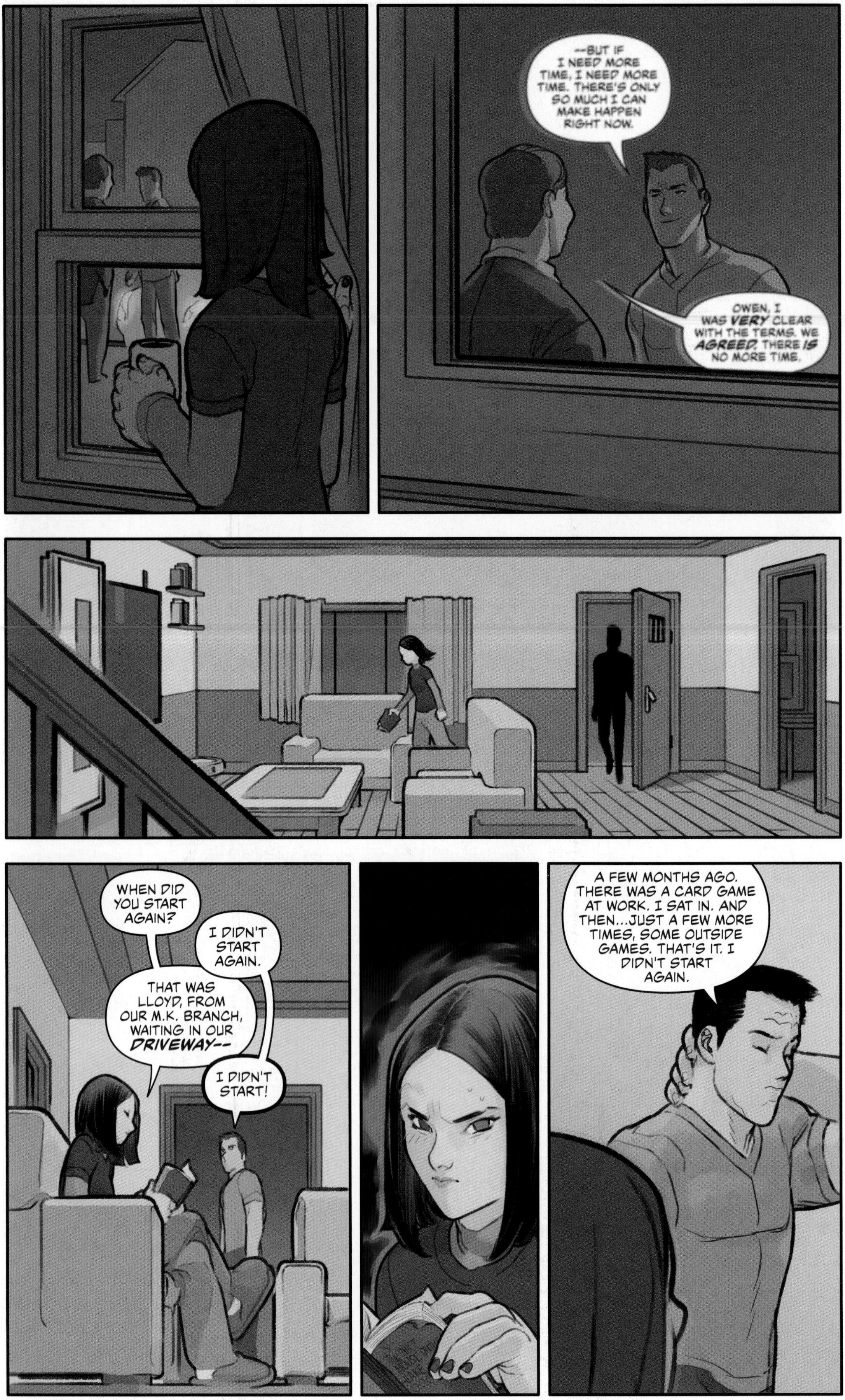
--BUT IF I NEED MORE TIME, I NEED MORE TIME. THERE'S ONLY SO MUCH I CAN MAKE HAPPEN RIGHT NOW.
OWEN, I WAS *VERY* CLEAR WITH THE TERMS. WE *AGREED.* THERE *IS* NO MORE TIME.
WHEN DID YOU START AGAIN?
I DIDN'T START AGAIN.
THAT WAS LLOYD, FROM OUR M.K. BRANCH, WAITING IN OUR *DRIVEWAY--*
I DIDN'T START!
A FEW MONTHS AGO. THERE WAS A CARD GAME AT WORK. I SAT IN. AND THEN...JUST A FEW MORE TIMES, SOME OUTSIDE GAMES. THAT'S IT. I DIDN'T START AGAIN.

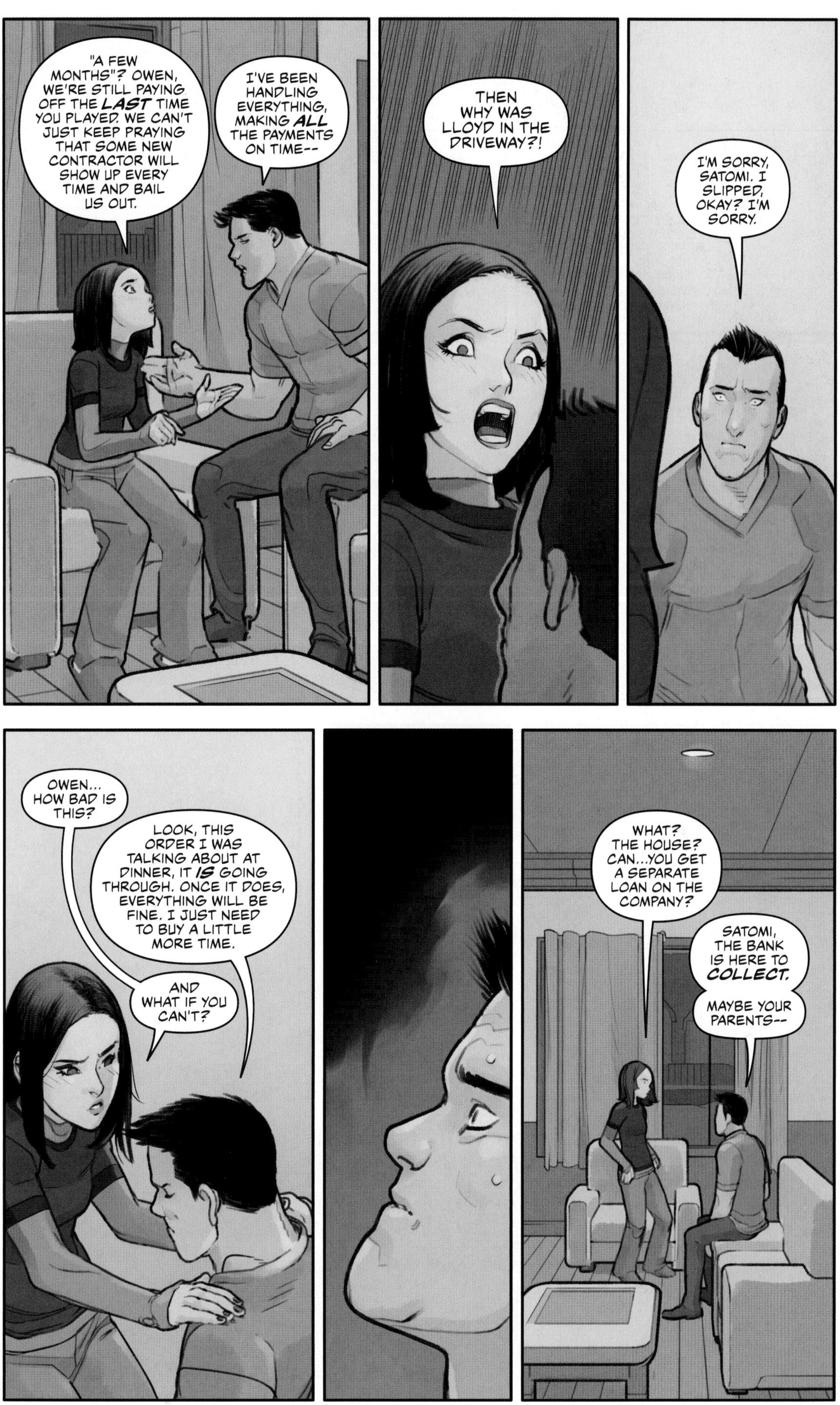
"A FEW MONTHS"? OWEN, WE'RE STILL PAYING OFF THE LAST TIME YOU PLAYED. WE CAN'T JUST KEEP PRAYING THAT SOME NEW CONTRACTOR WILL SHOW UP EVERY TIME AND BAIL US OUT.
I'VE BEEN HANDLING EVERYTHING, MAKING ALL THE PAYMENTS ON TIME--
THEN WHY WAS LLOYD IN THE DRIVEWAY?!
I'M SORRY, SATOMI. I SLIPPED, OKAY? I'M SORRY.
OWEN... HOW BAD IS THIS?
LOOK, THIS ORDER I WAS TALKING ABOUT AT DINNER, IT IS GOING THROUGH. ONCE IT DOES, EVERYTHING WILL BE FINE. I JUST NEED TO BUY A LITTLE MORE TIME.
AND WHAT IF YOU CAN'T?
WHAT? THE HOUSE? CAN...YOU GET A SEPARATE LOAN ON THE COMPANY?
SATOMI, THE BANK IS HERE TO COLLECT.
MAYBE YOUR PARENTS--

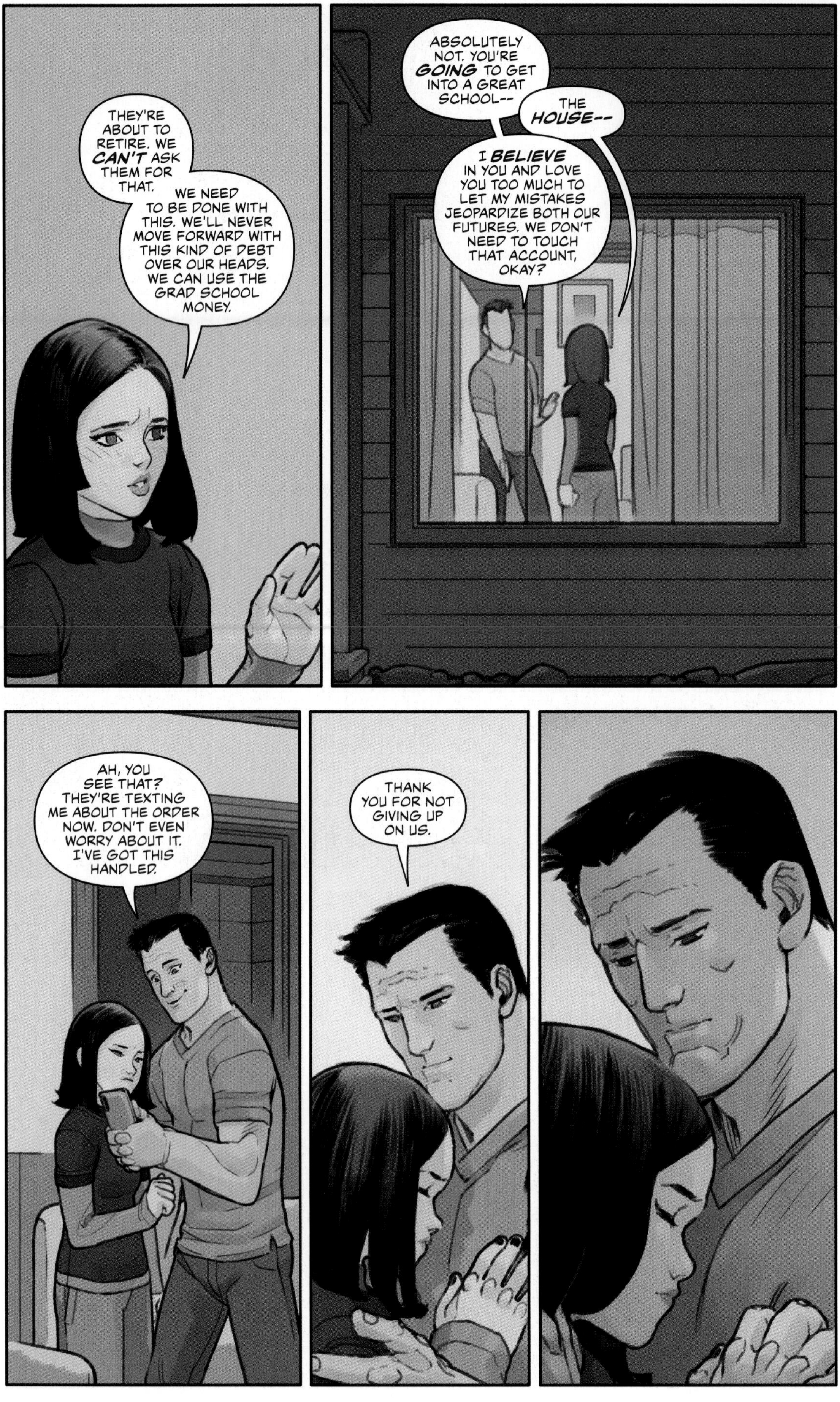
THEY'RE ABOUT TO RETIRE. WE CAN'T ASK THEM FOR THAT.
WE NEED TO BE DONE WITH THIS. WE'LL NEVER MOVE FORWARD WITH THIS KIND OF DEBT OVER OUR HEADS. WE CAN USE THE GRAD SCHOOL MONEY.
ABSOLUTELY NOT. YOU'RE GOING TO GET INTO A GREAT SCHOOL--
THE HOUSE--
I BELIEVE IN YOU AND LOVE YOU TOO MUCH TO LET MY MISTAKES JEOPARDIZE BOTH OUR FUTURES. WE DON'T NEED TO TOUCH THAT ACCOUNT, OKAY?
AH, YOU SEE THAT? THEY'RE TEXTING ME ABOUT THE ORDER NOW. DON'T EVEN WORRY ABOUT IT. I'VE GOT THIS HANDLED.
THANK YOU FOR NOT GIVING UP ON US.

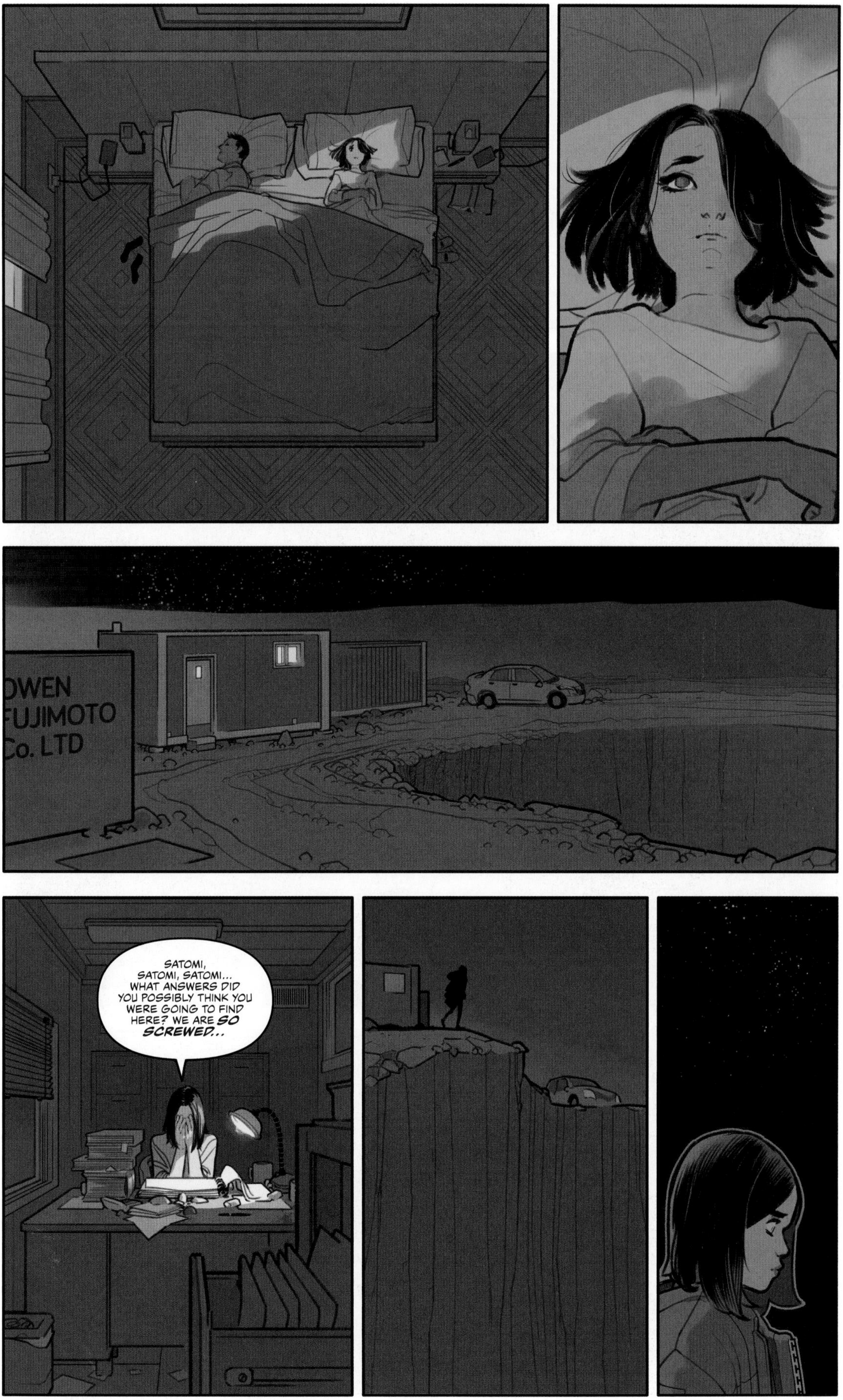
OWEN FUJIMOTO Co. LTD
SATOMI, SATOMI, SATOMI... WHAT ANSWERS DID YOU POSSIBLY THINK YOU WERE GOING TO FIND HERE? WE ARE SO SCREWED...

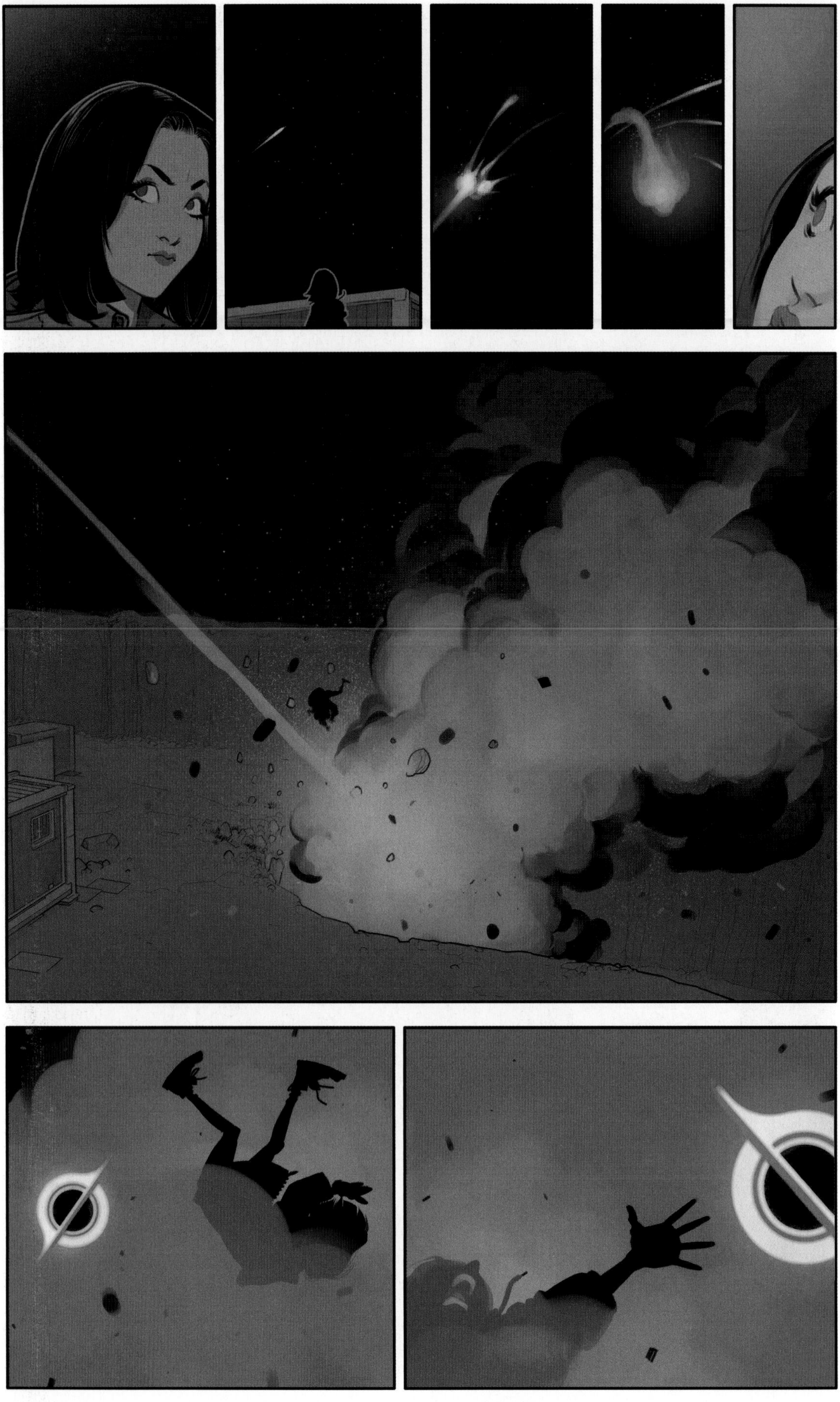

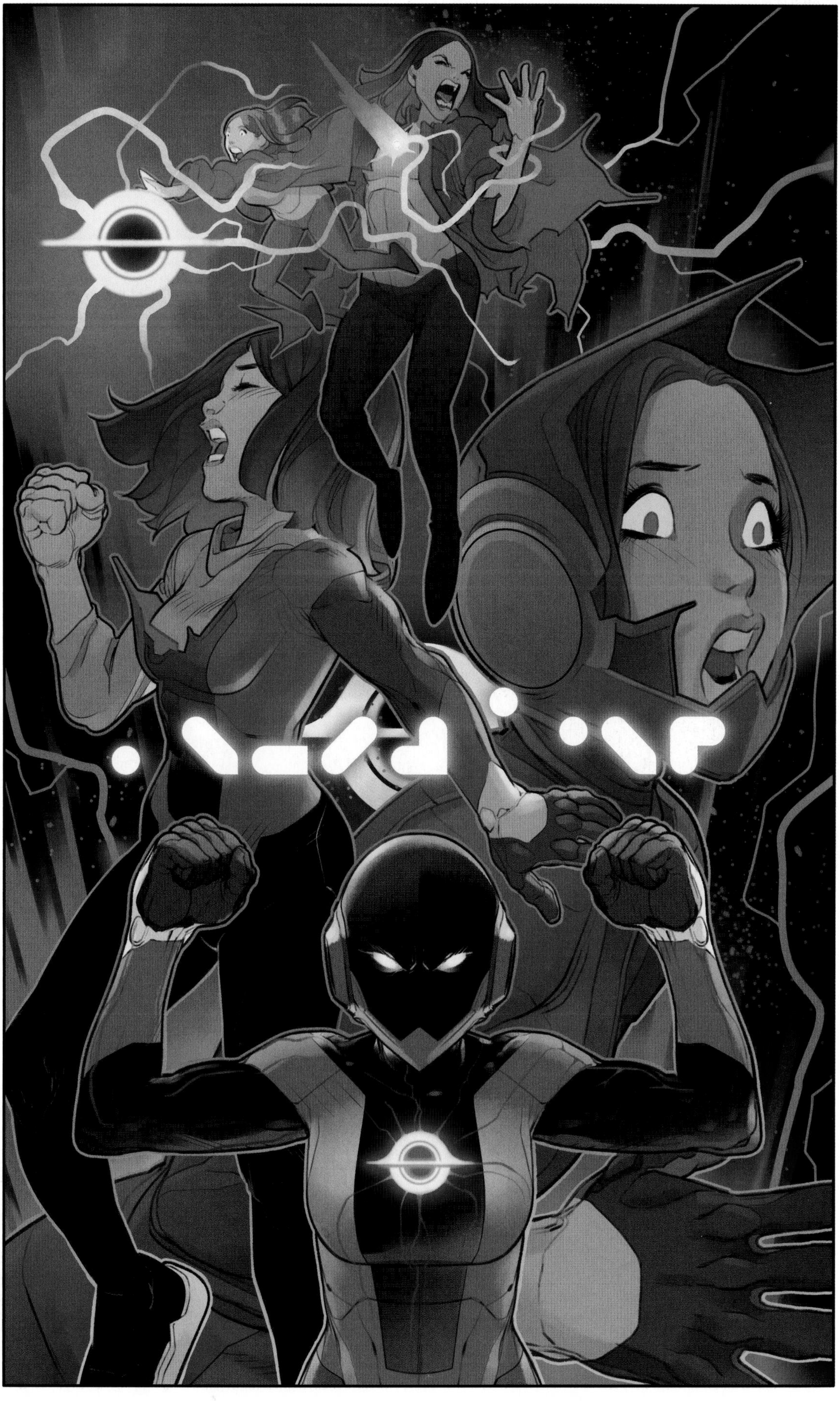

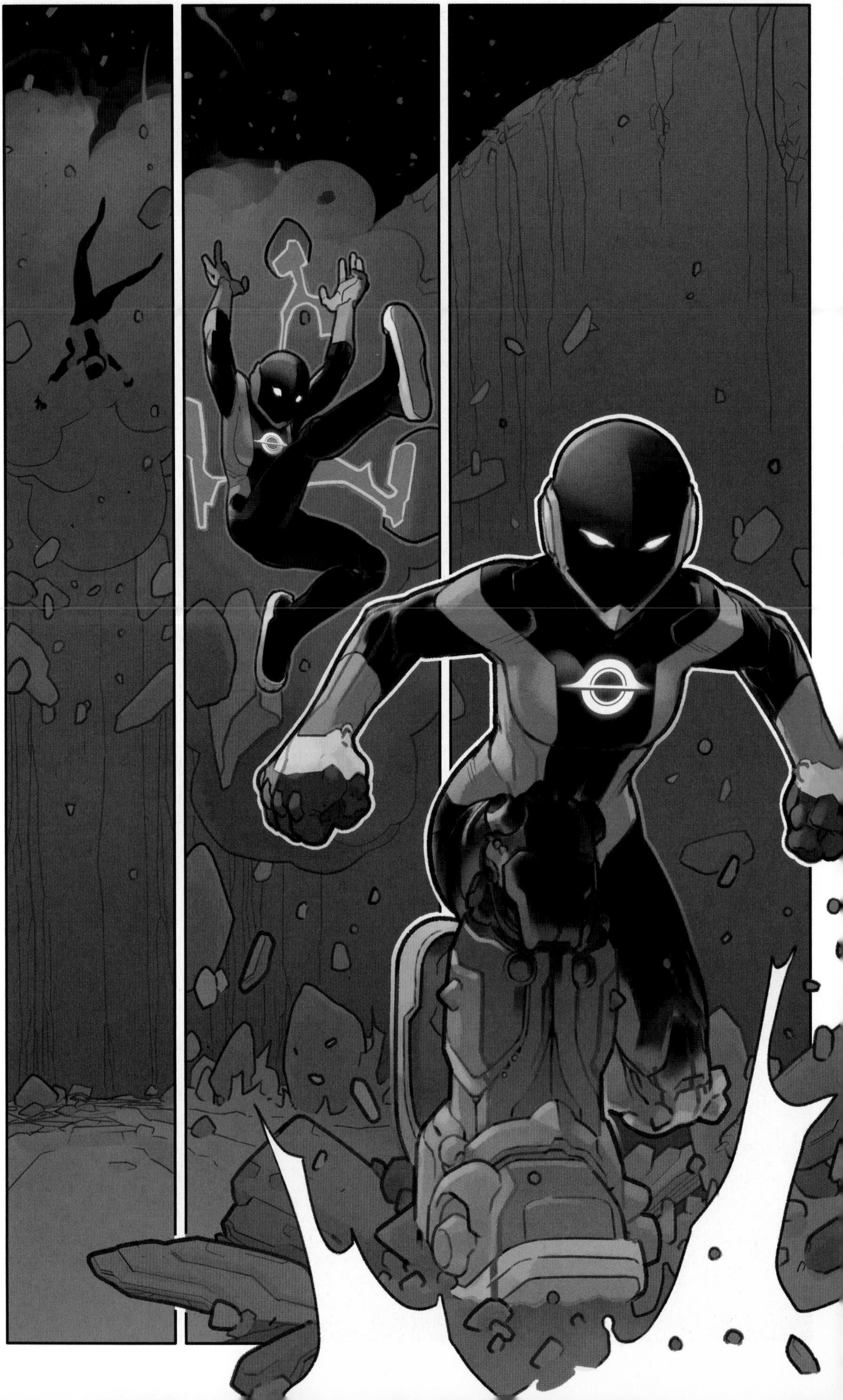

I--I'M OKAY? HOW AM I OKAY?!

DID...DID I JUST...

...ABSORB A BUNCH OF ROCKS?! I'M... ABSORBING THINGS?

HUH.

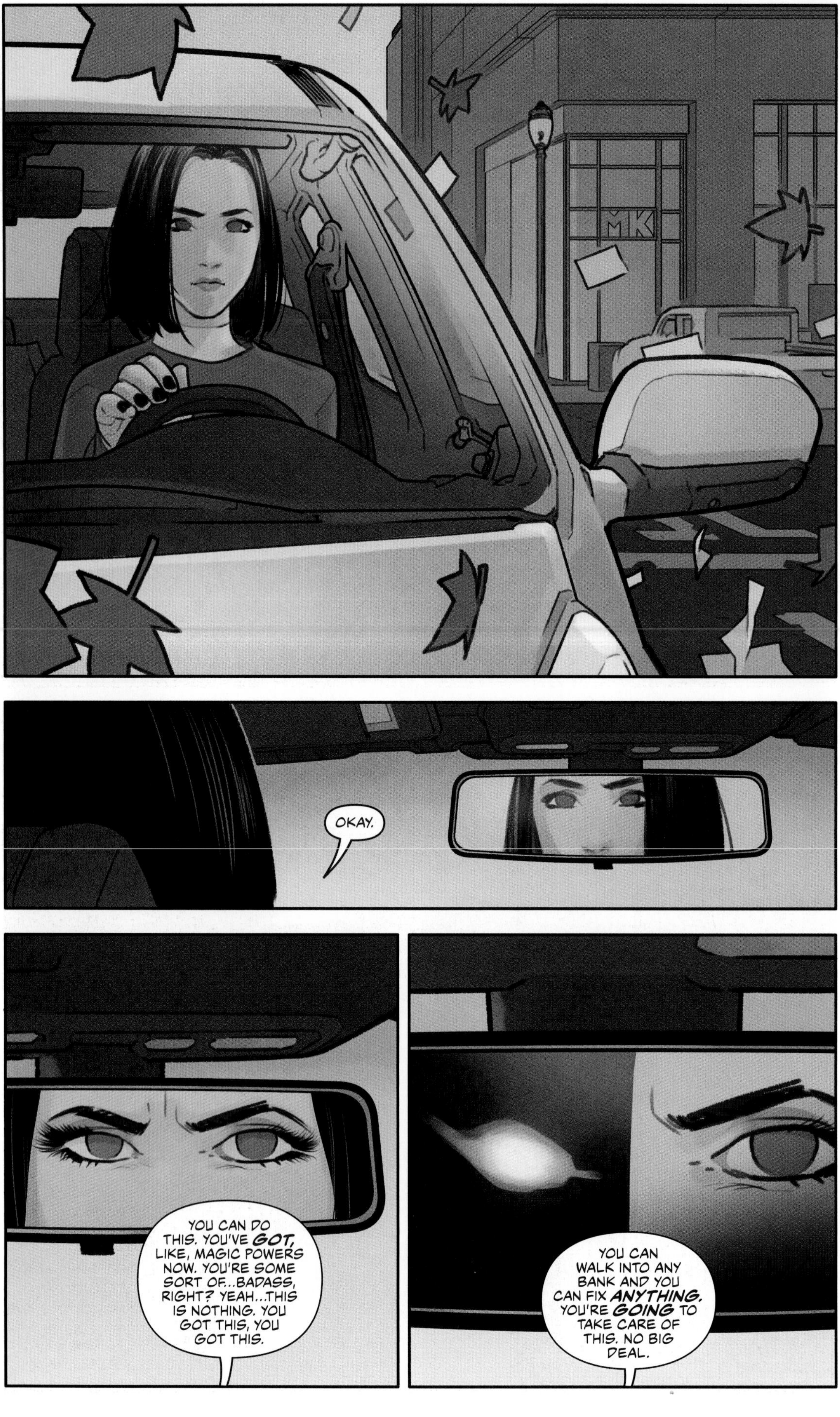
OKAY.
YOU CAN DO THIS. YOU'VE GOT, LIKE, MAGIC POWERS NOW. YOU'RE SOME SORT OF...BADASS, RIGHT? YEAH...THIS IS NOTHING. YOU GOT THIS, YOU GOT THIS.
YOU CAN WALK INTO ANY BANK AND YOU CAN FIX ANYTHING. YOU'RE GOING TO TAKE CARE OF THIS. NO BIG DEAL.

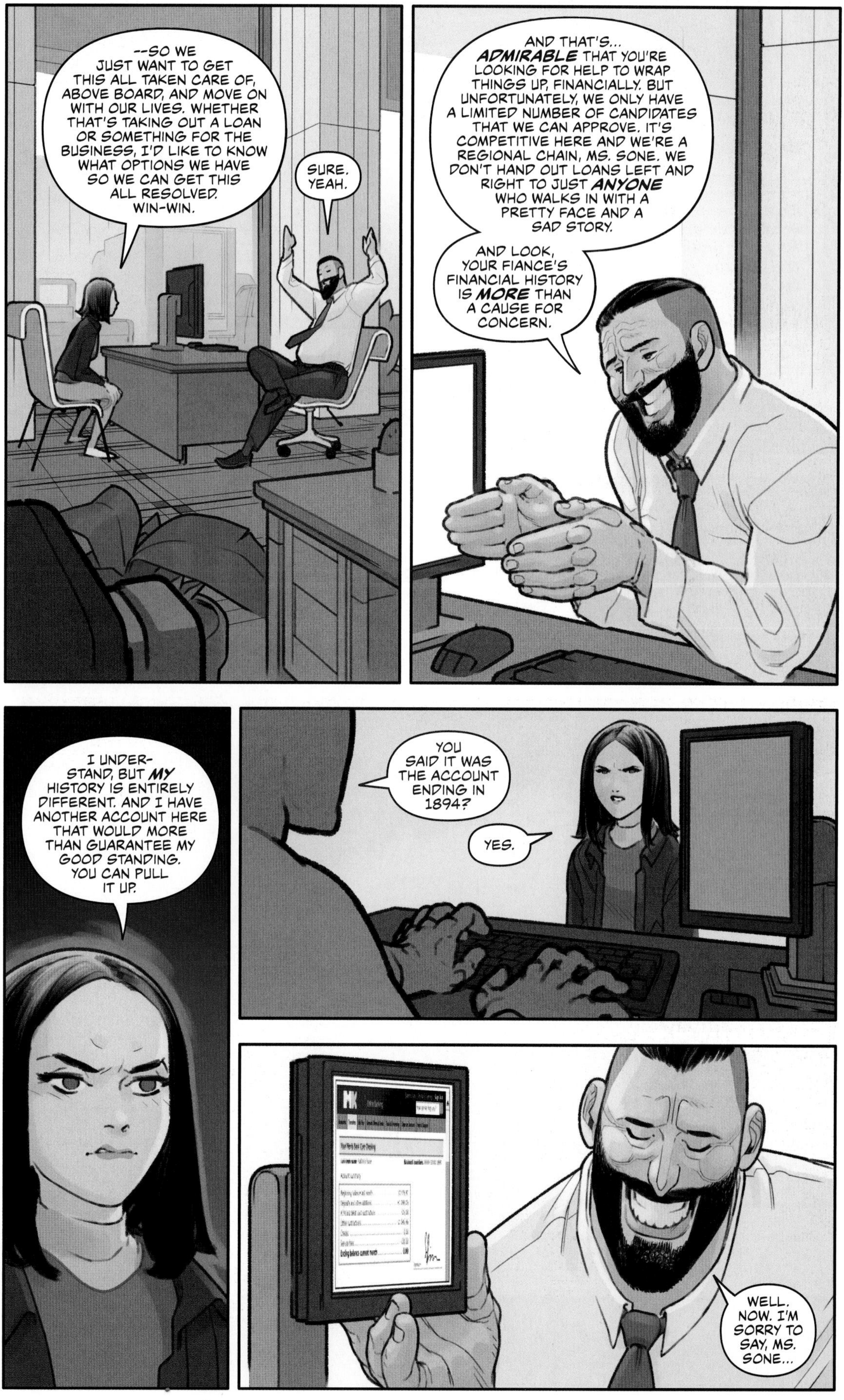
--SO WE JUST WANT TO GET THIS ALL TAKEN CARE OF, ABOVE BOARD, AND MOVE ON WITH OUR LIVES. WHETHER THAT'S TAKING OUT A LOAN OR SOMETHING FOR THE BUSINESS, I'D LIKE TO KNOW WHAT OPTIONS WE HAVE SO WE CAN GET THIS ALL RESOLVED. WIN-WIN.
SURE. YEAH.
AND THAT'S... ADMIRABLE THAT YOU'RE LOOKING FOR HELP TO WRAP THINGS UP, FINANCIALLY. BUT UNFORTUNATELY, WE ONLY HAVE A LIMITED NUMBER OF CANDIDATES THAT WE CAN APPROVE. IT'S COMPETITIVE HERE AND WE'RE A REGIONAL CHAIN, MS. SONE. WE DON'T HAND OUT LOANS LEFT AND RIGHT TO JUST ANYONE WHO WALKS IN WITH A PRETTY FACE AND A SAD STORY.
AND LOOK, YOUR FIANCE'S FINANCIAL HISTORY IS MORE THAN A CAUSE FOR CONCERN.
I UNDER-STAND, BUT MY HISTORY IS ENTIRELY DIFFERENT. AND I HAVE ANOTHER ACCOUNT HERE THAT WOULD MORE THAN GUARANTEE MY GOOD STANDING. YOU CAN PULL IT UP.
YOU SAID IT WAS THE ACCOUNT ENDING IN 1894?
YES.
WELL. NOW. I'M SORRY TO SAY, MS. SONE...

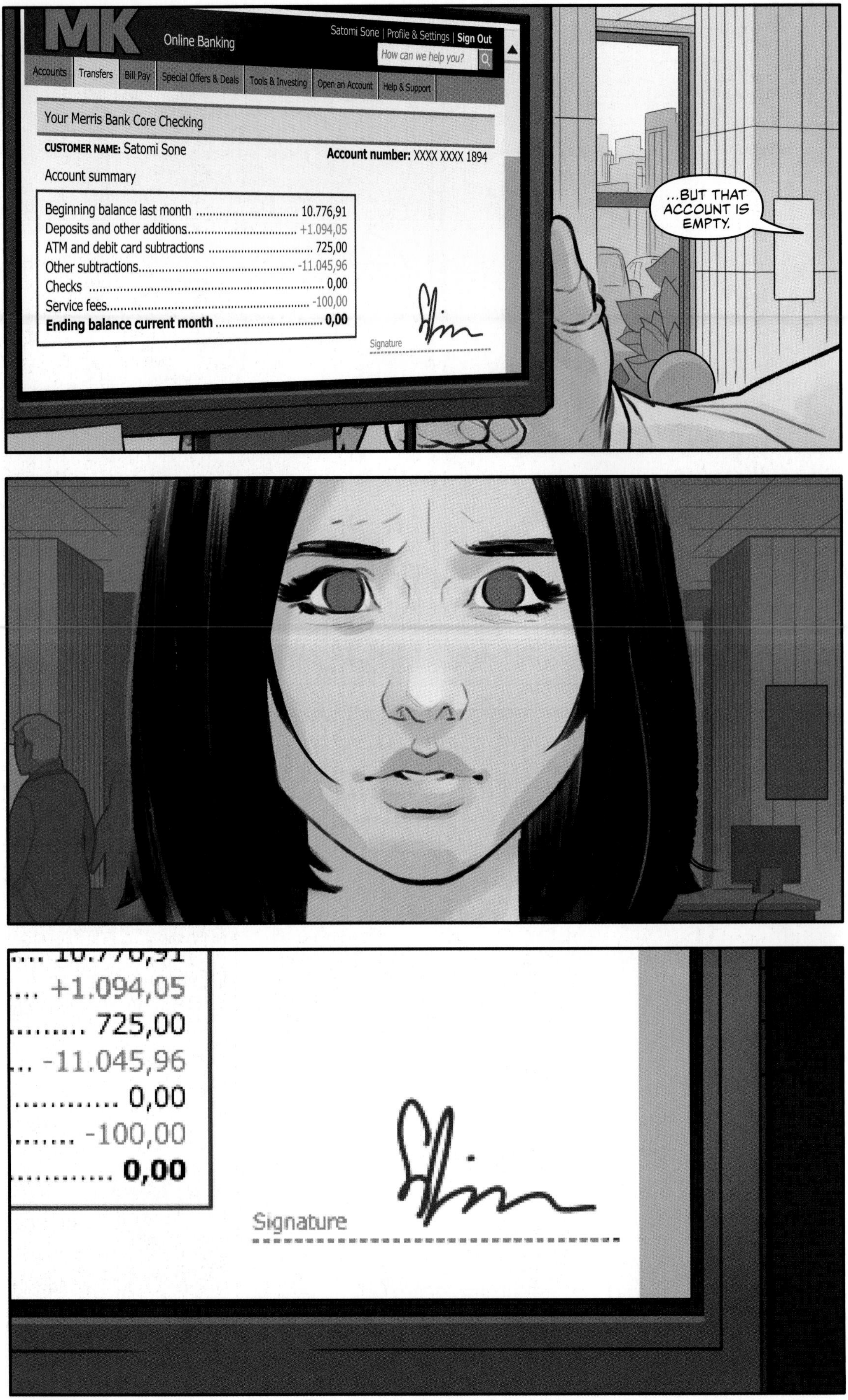
MK
Online Banking
Satomi Sone | Profile & Settings | Sign Out
How can we help you?
Accounts
Transfers
Bill Pay
Special Offers & Deals
Tools & Investing
Open an Account
Help & Support
Your Merris Bank Core Checking
CUSTOMER NAME: Satomi Sone
Account number: XXXX XXXX 1894
Account summary
Beginning balance last month 10.776,91
Deposits and other additions................................ +1.094,05
ATM and debit card subtractions 725,00
Other subtractions.. -11.045,96
Checks 0,00
Service fees.. -100,00
Ending balance current month 0,00
Signature
...BUT THAT ACCOUNT IS EMPTY.
... +1.094,05
.... 725,00
... -11.045,96
.... 0,00
.... -100,00
.... 0,00
Signature

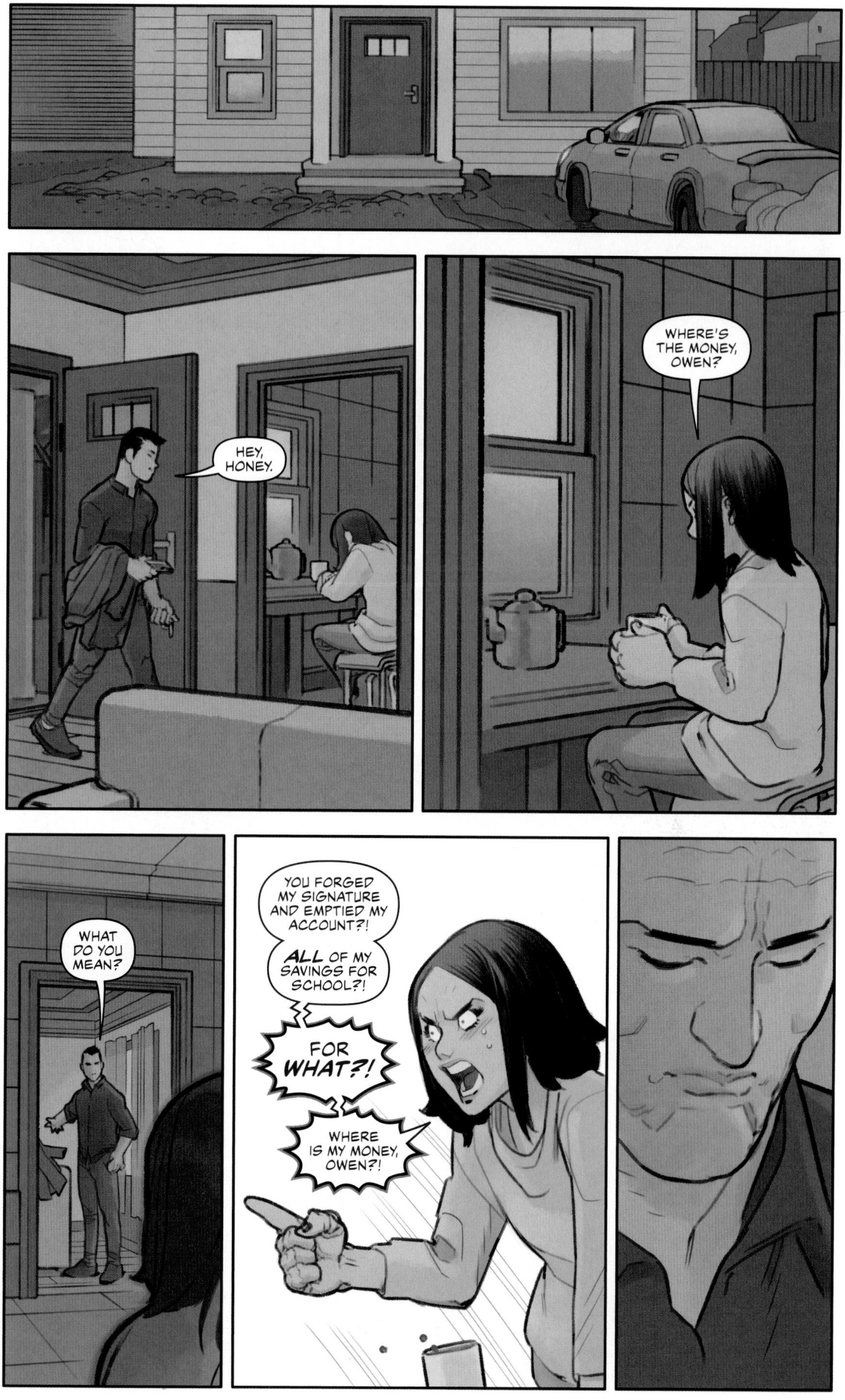
HEY, HONEY.
WHERE'S THE MONEY, OWEN?
WHAT DO YOU MEAN?
YOU FORGED MY SIGNATURE AND EMPTIED MY ACCOUNT?!
ALL OF MY SAVINGS FOR SCHOOL?!
FOR WHAT?!
WHERE IS MY MONEY, OWEN?!

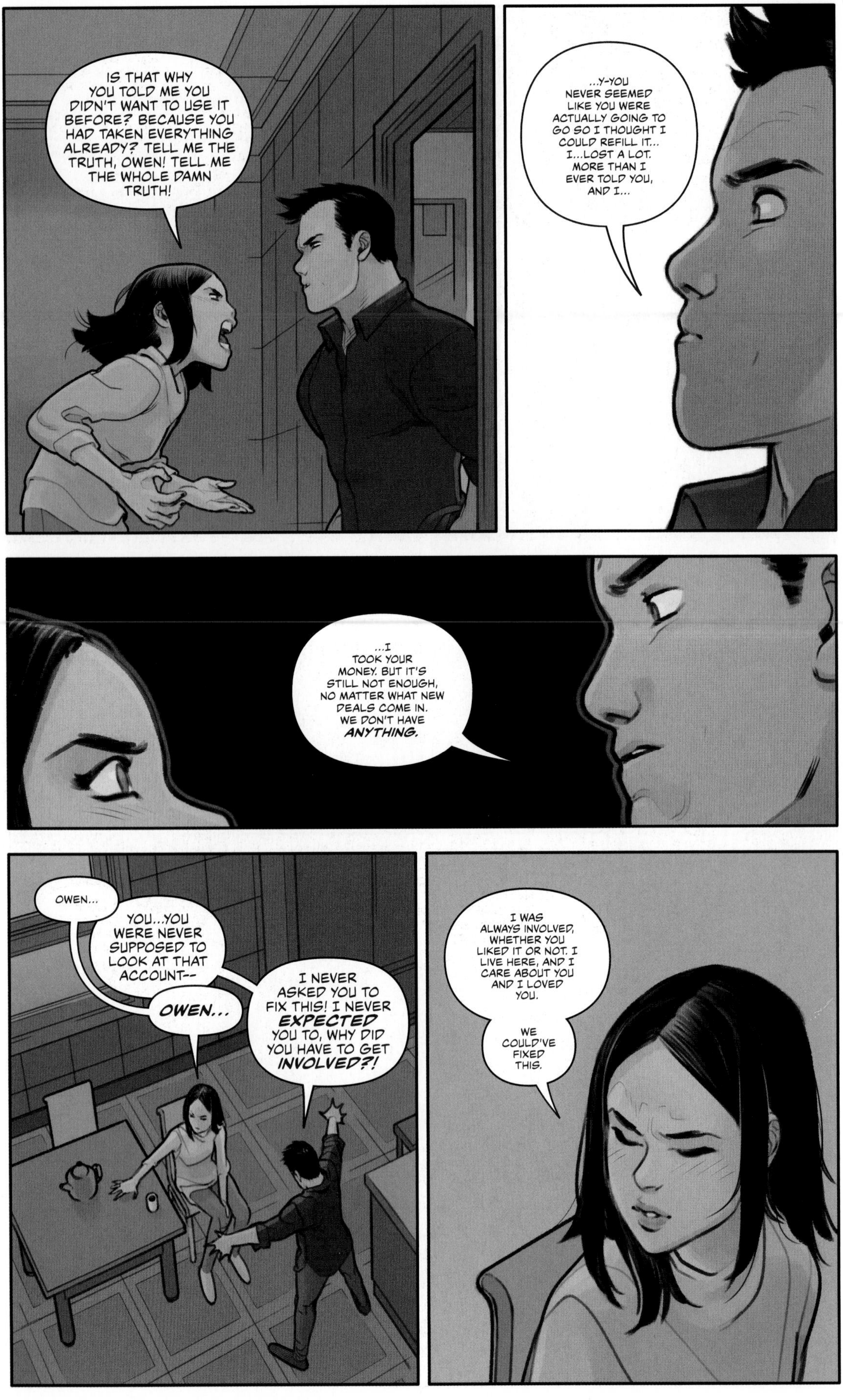
IS THAT WHY YOU TOLD ME YOU DIDN'T WANT TO USE IT BEFORE? BECAUSE YOU HAD TAKEN EVERYTHING ALREADY? TELL ME THE TRUTH, OWEN! TELL ME THE WHOLE DAMN TRUTH!
...Y-YOU NEVER SEEMED LIKE YOU WERE ACTUALLY GOING TO GO SO I THOUGHT I COULD REFILL IT... I...LOST A LOT. MORE THAN I EVER TOLD YOU, AND I...
...I TOOK YOUR MONEY. BUT IT'S STILL NOT ENOUGH, NO MATTER WHAT NEW DEALS COME IN. WE DON'T HAVE ANYTHING.
OWEN...
YOU...YOU WERE NEVER SUPPOSED TO LOOK AT THAT ACCOUNT--
OWEN...
I NEVER ASKED YOU TO FIX THIS! I NEVER EXPECTED YOU TO, WHY DID YOU HAVE TO GET INVOLVED?!
I WAS ALWAYS INVOLVED, WHETHER YOU LIKED IT OR NOT. I LIVE HERE, AND I CARE ABOUT YOU AND I LOVED YOU.
WE COULD'VE FIXED THIS.

YOU?! YOU DON'T HAVE A *CLUE* HOW ANY OF THIS WORKS. YOU'RE A TEACHER WHO'S NEVER DEALT WITH ANYTHING BIGGER THAN A KID WHO DOESN'T WANT TO READ.

YOU *SHOULD'VE* LET ME HANDLE IT. NOW YOU'VE WALKED INTO A BANK ASKING FOR ANOTHER LOAN?

DO YOU *KNOW* HOW EMBARRASS-ING THAT IS?

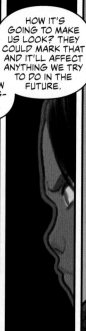

HOW IT'S GOING TO MAKE US LOOK? THEY COULD MARK THAT AND IT'LL AFFECT ANYTHING WE TRY TO DO IN THE FUTURE.

YOU *RUINED* THIS, SATOMI! OKAY?! DO YOU *GET* THAT NOW?! YOU DON'T KNOW THE *FIRST* THING ABOUT HANDLING *REAL* RESPONSIBILITY, MUCH LESS HANDLING A *BANK*--

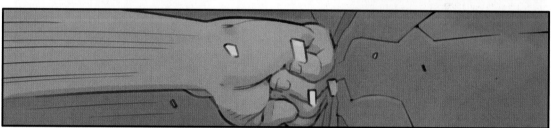

YOU'RE THE REASON WE'RE SITTING IN A HOUSE WE'RE ABOUT TO LOSE. *YOU'RE* THE REASON WE'VE BEEN IN A HOLE THE *ENTIRE TIME I'VE KNOWN YOU. YOU'RE* THE REASON WE'RE HERE.

I MAY BE A SMALL-TOWN TEACHER, BUT DON'T FOR A *SECOND* TRY TO CONVINCE ME THAT I'M RESPONSIBLE FOR HOW WE ENDED UP HERE.

I *CAN'T* DO THIS ANYMORE, OWEN.

SATOMI, WAIT. PLEASE.

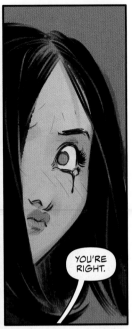

YOU'RE RIGHT.

THIS IS MY FAULT. I DID THIS. I LOST THE HOUSE. I FUCKED EVERYTHING UP. I'M SO SORRY. I'M SO, SO SORRY FOR WHAT I'VE DONE TO US. I JUST...I JUST NEEDED MORE TIME.

I'M... I'M SICK. OR SOMETHING. THERE'S SOMETHING WRONG WITH ME AND I... I NEED HELP, SATOMI.

AND I CAN'T...I CAN'T DO THIS WITHOUT YOU. I SHOULD HAVE NEVER SAID WHAT I SAID. I CAN'T FIX THIS.

I CAN'T FIX ANYTHING WITHOUT YOU.

PLEASE DON'T GIVE UP ON ME.

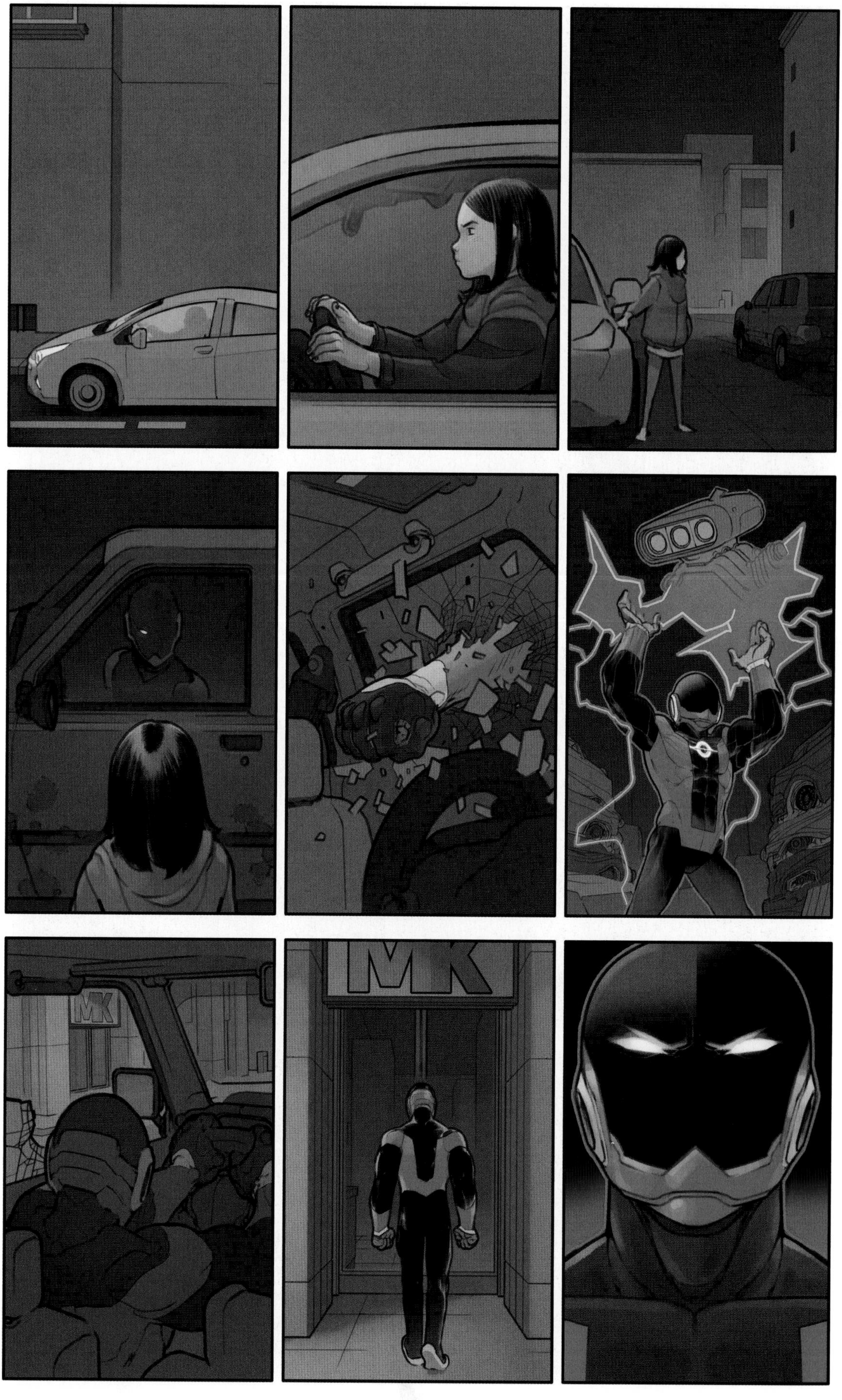
MK
MK

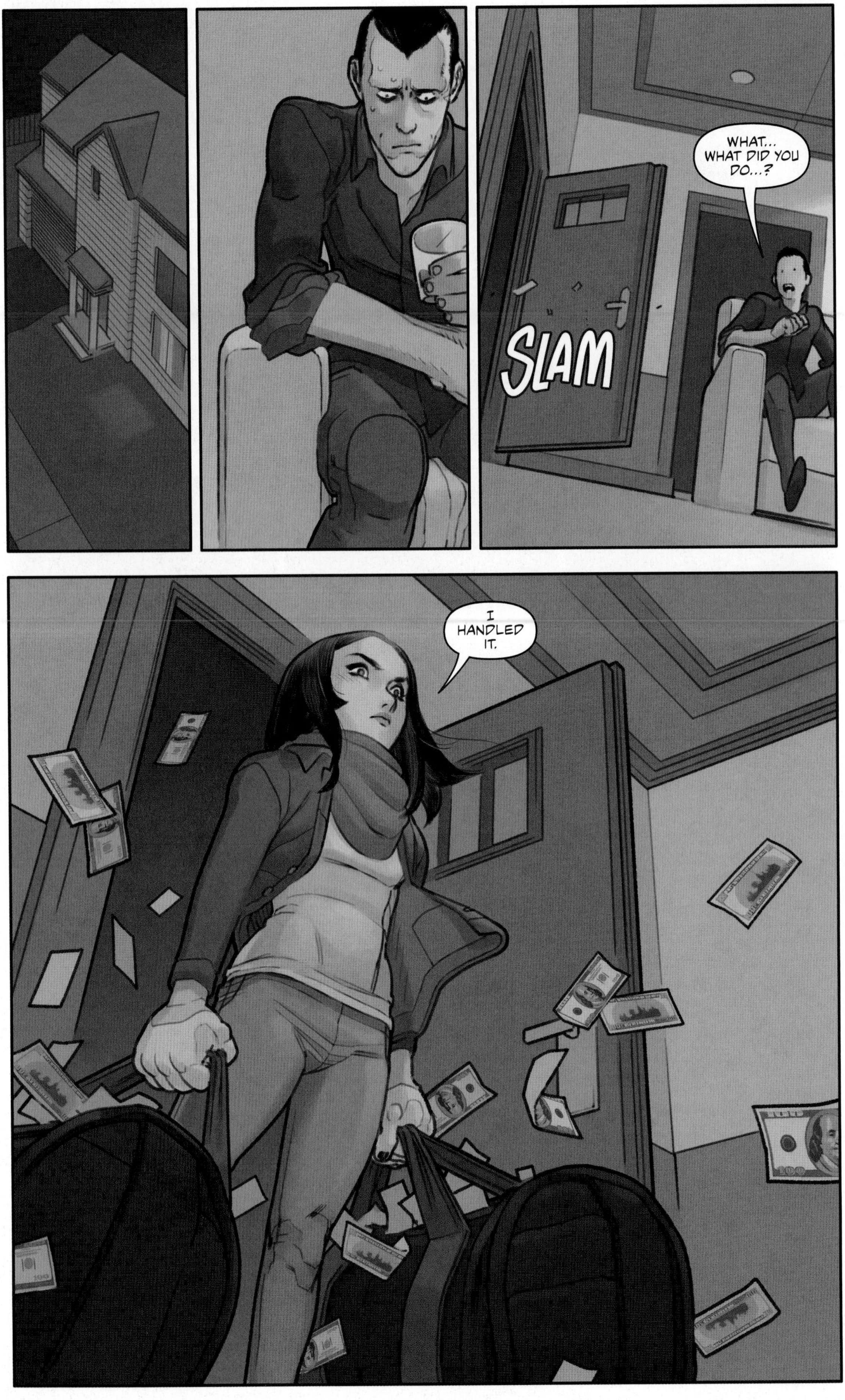
WHAT... WHAT DID YOU DO...?
SLAM
I HANDLED IT.

COVER
GALLERY

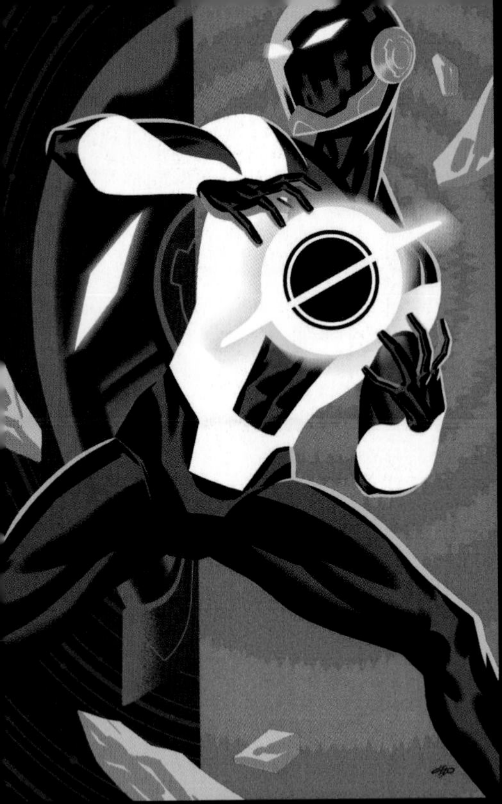

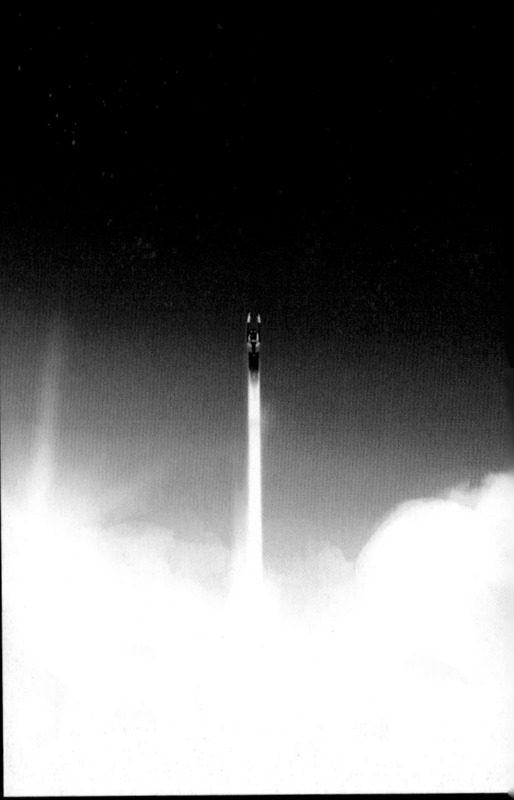

01 [A]
ichael Cho

#01 [B]
Marcelo Costa & Eduardo Ferigato

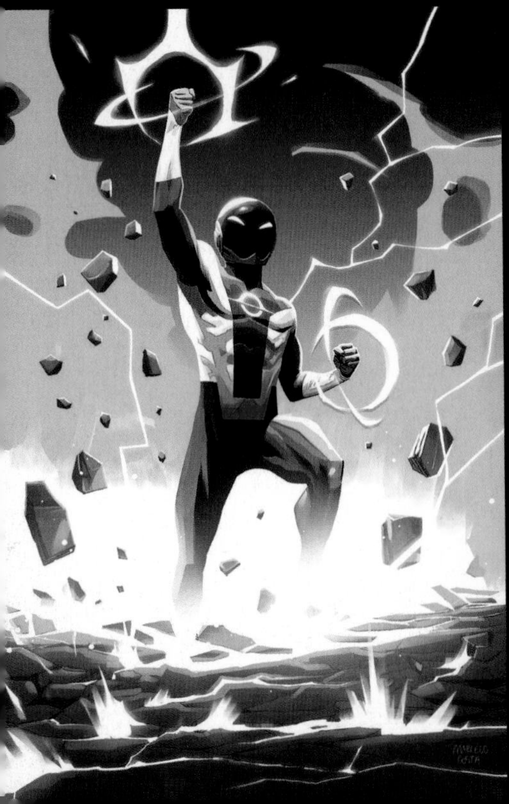

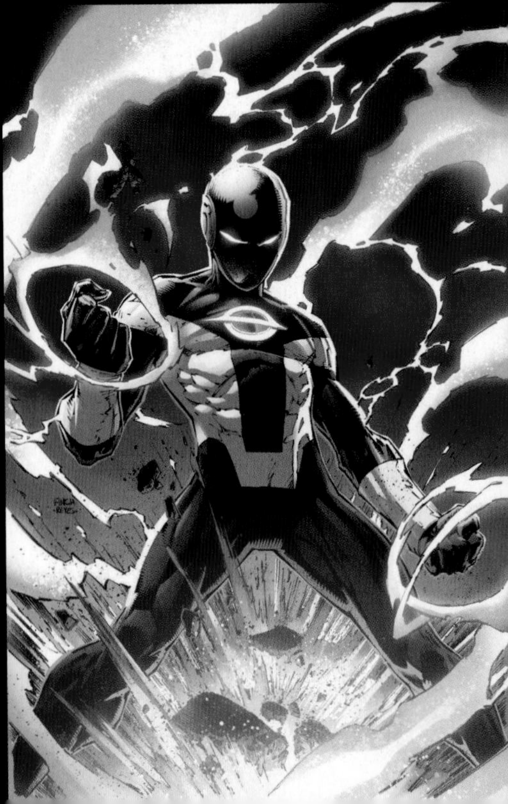

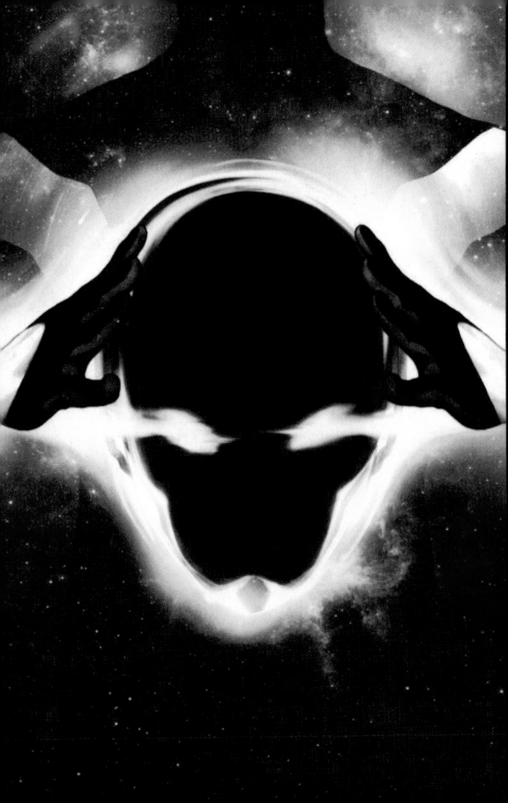

#01 [F]
Goñi Montes

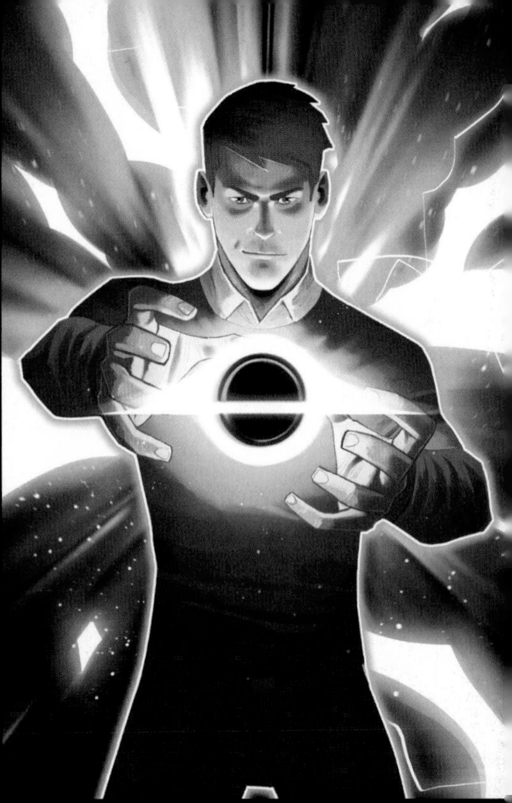

#01 [Ga] (unused)
Marcelo Costa

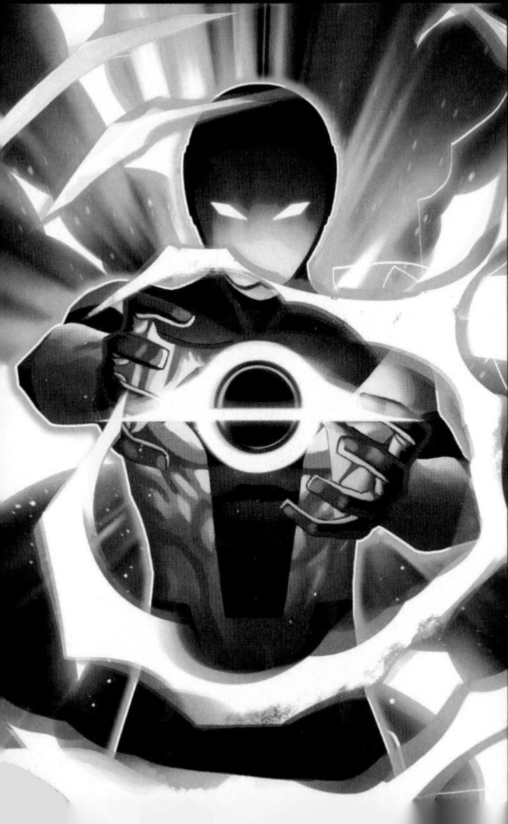

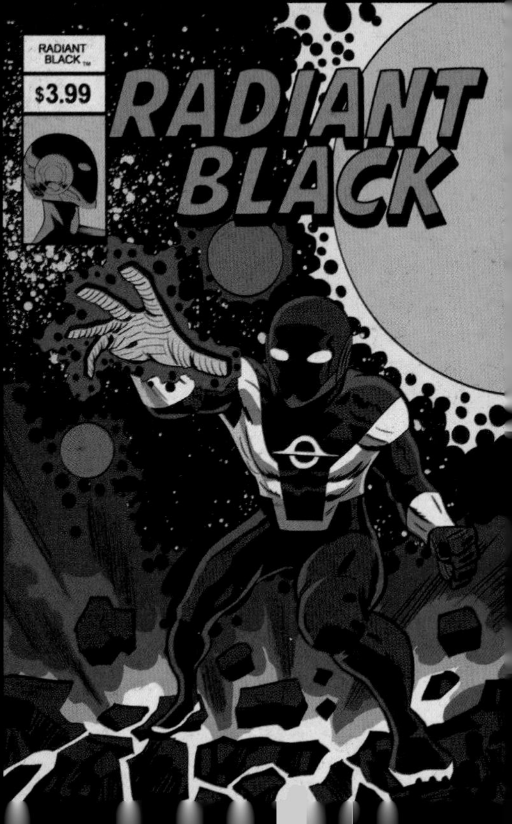
RADIANT BLACK ™
$3.99
RADIANT BLACK

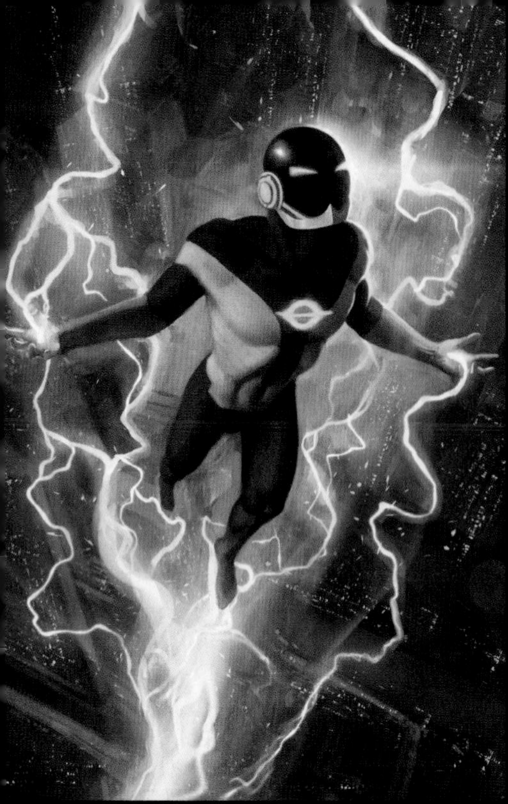

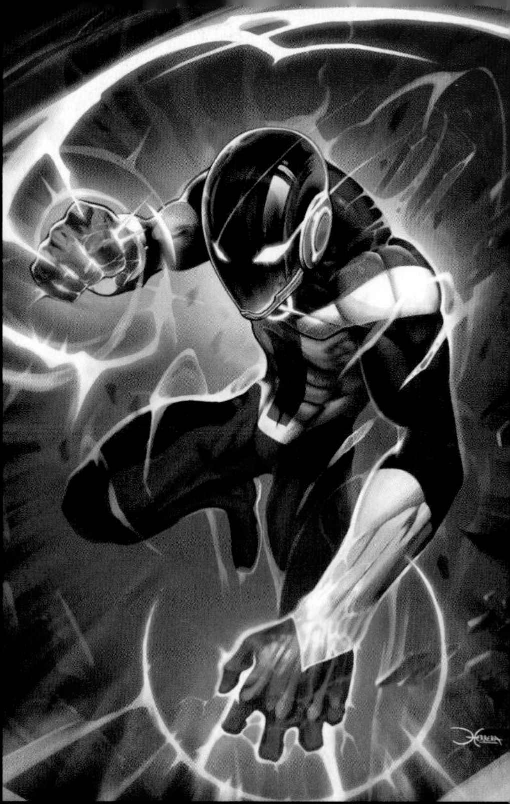

#01 [Out of the Vault]
Aaron Bartling

#01 [TFAW]
Mauricio Herrera

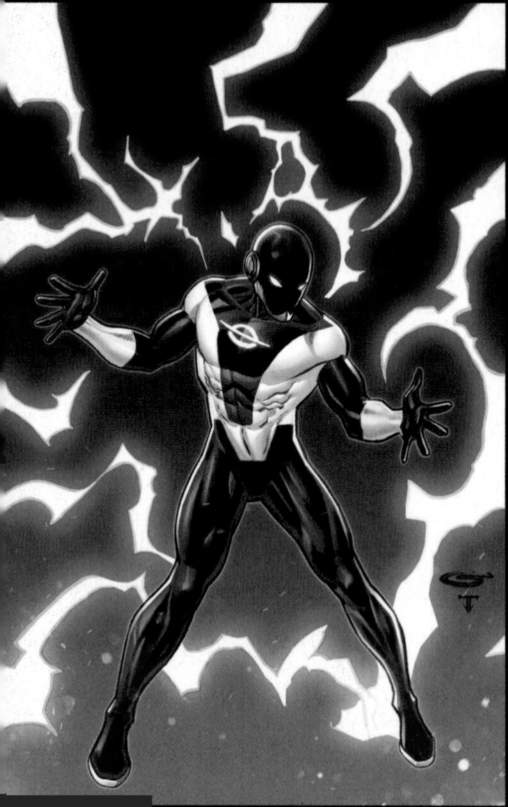

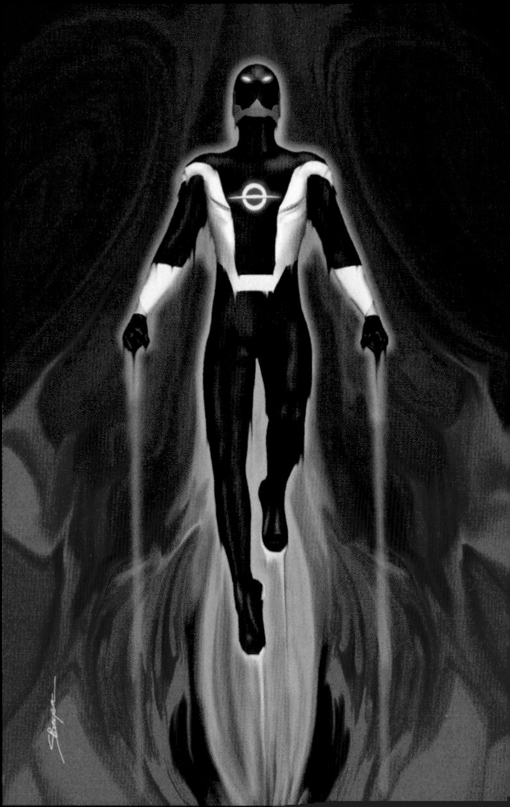

ingdom of Ca

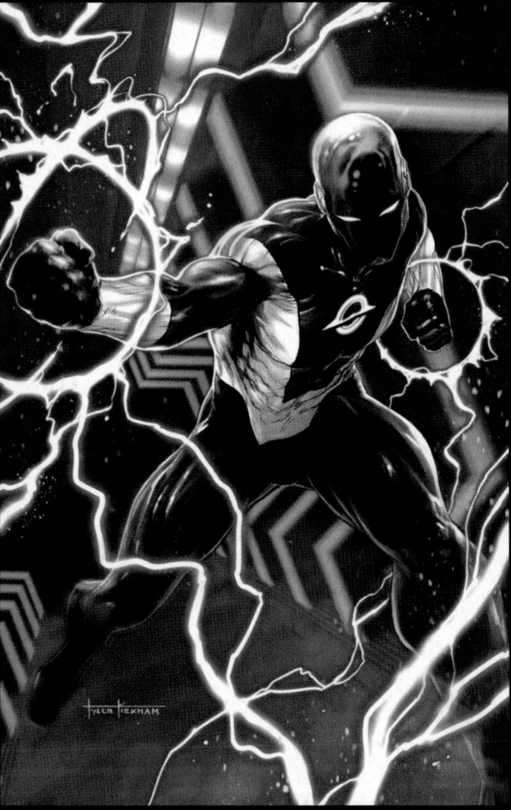

#01 [Comics Vault Live]
Tyler Kirkham

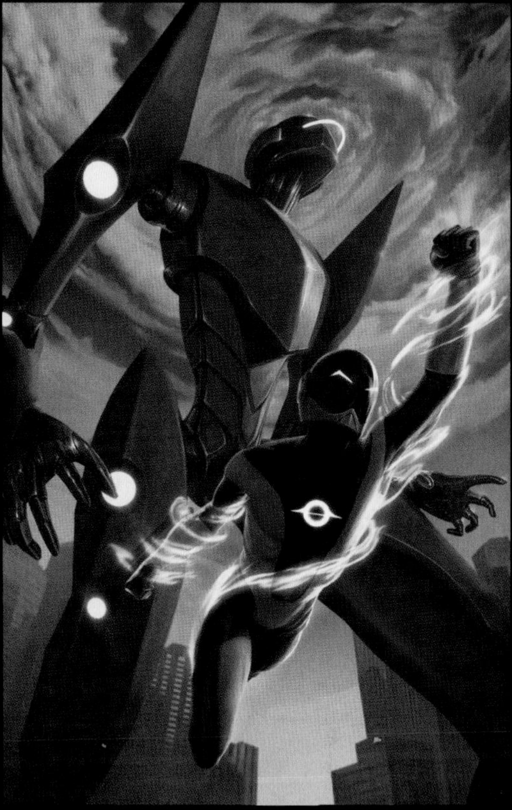

#01 [Second Printing]
Carlos Dattoli

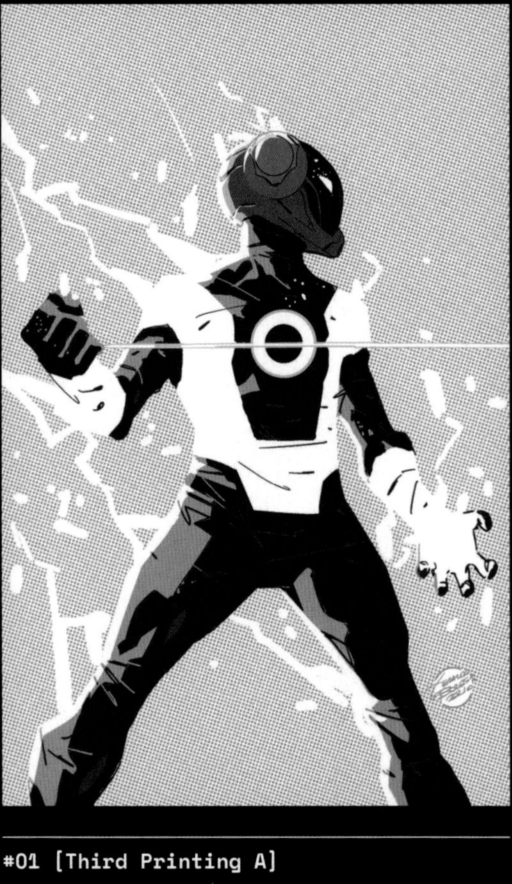

#01 [Third Printing A]
Geraldo Borges w/ Marcelo Costa

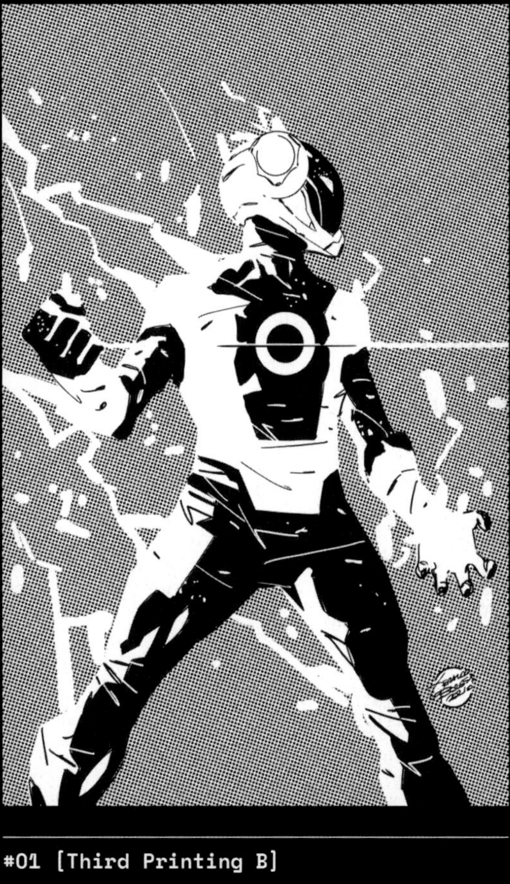

#01 [Third Printing B]
Geraldo Borges

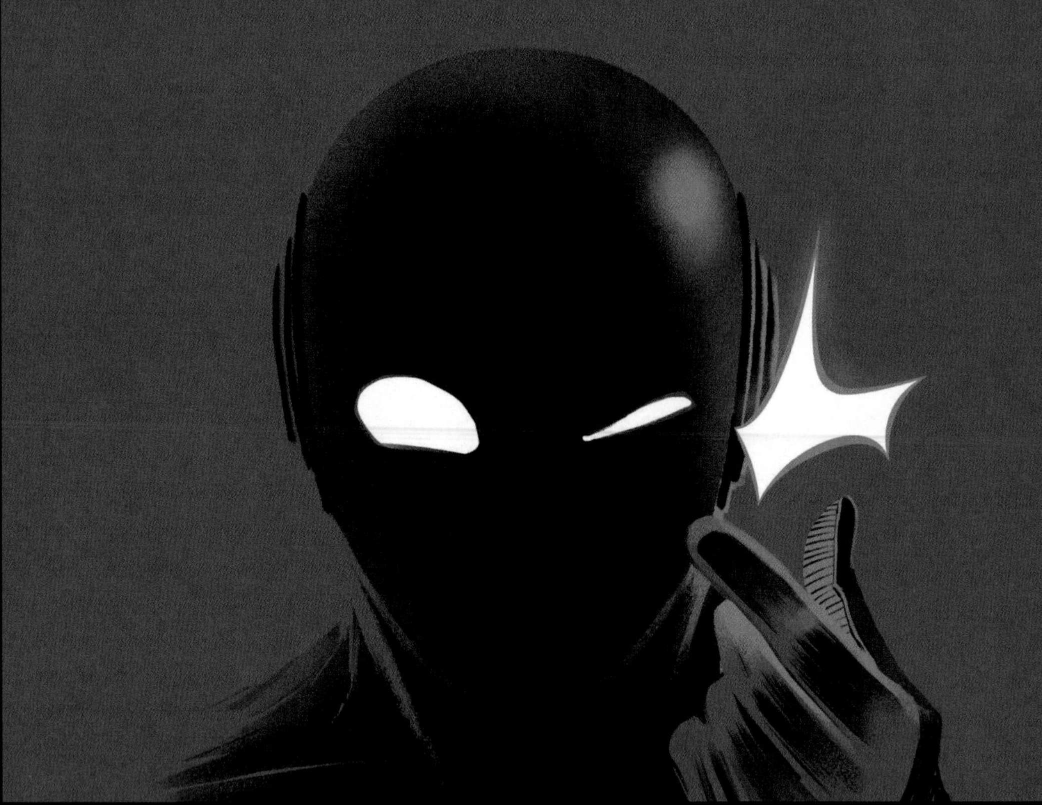

#02 [A]
Marcelo Costa

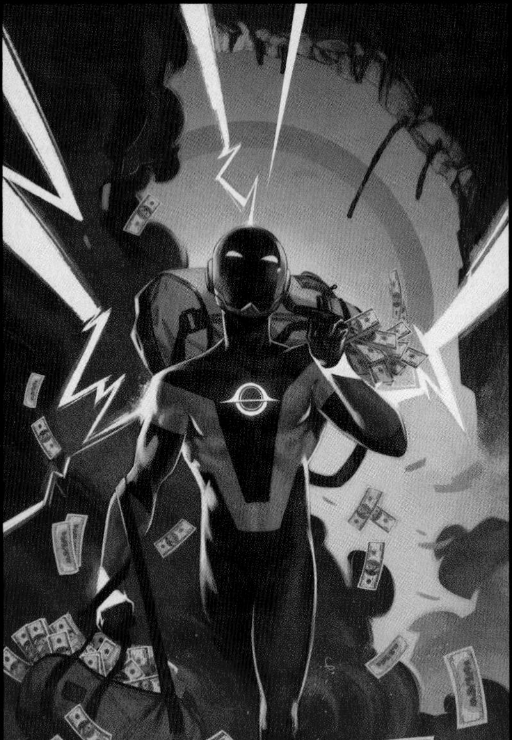

#02 [B]
Diego Greco

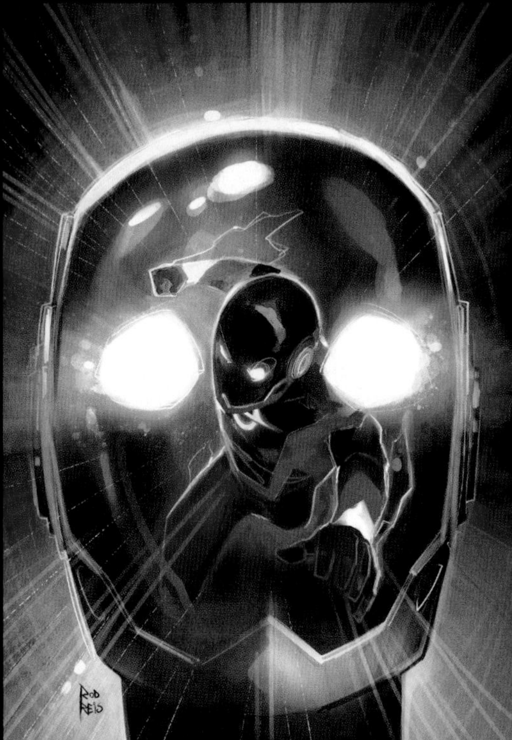
ROD REIS

#02 [C]
Rod Reis

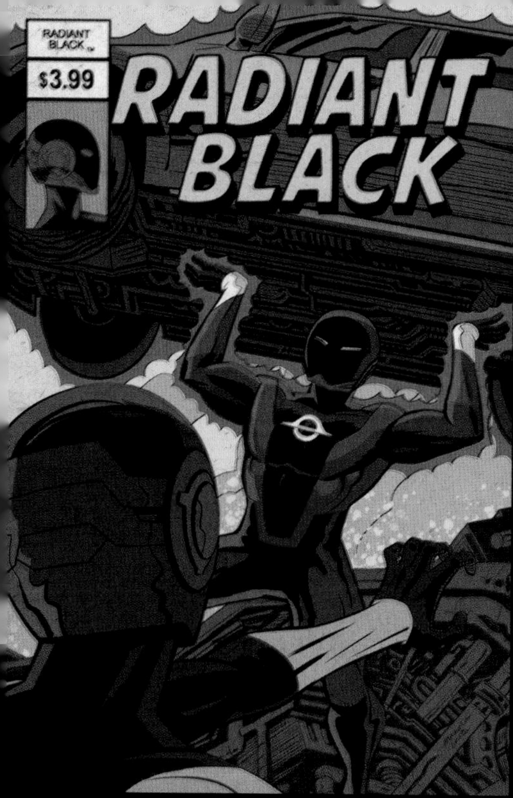
RADIANT BLACK
$3.99
RADIANT BLACK

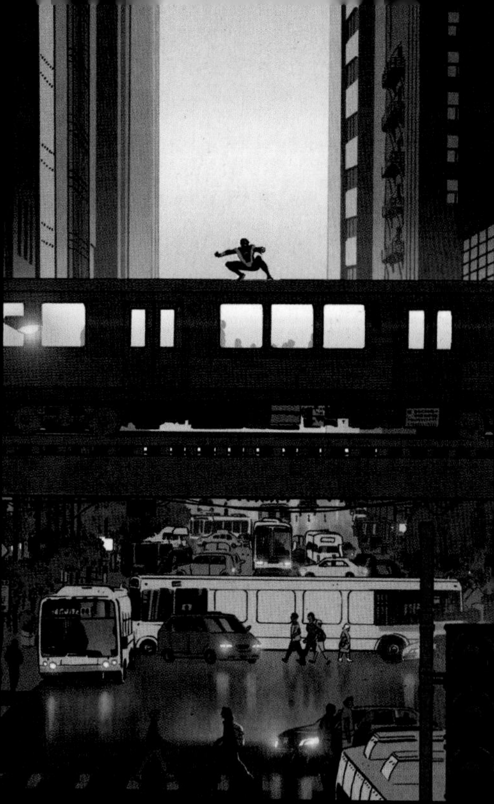

#02 [Stadium Comics]
Marcelo Costa

#02 [Second Printing]
Tom Reilly

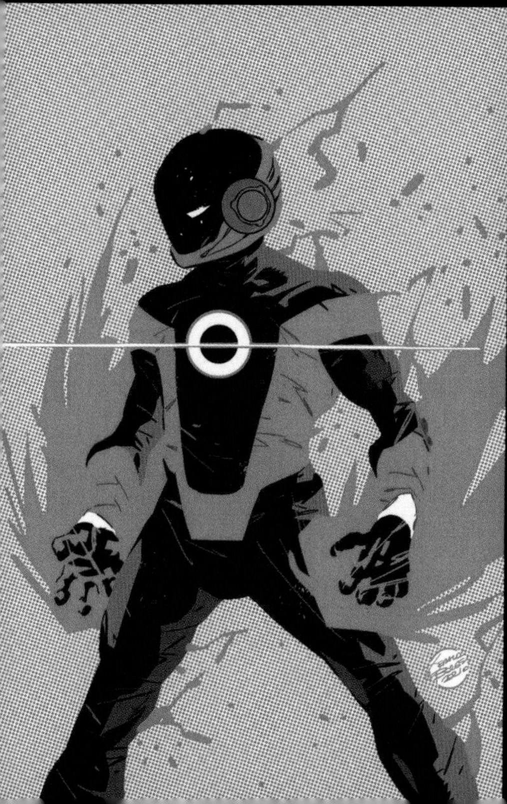

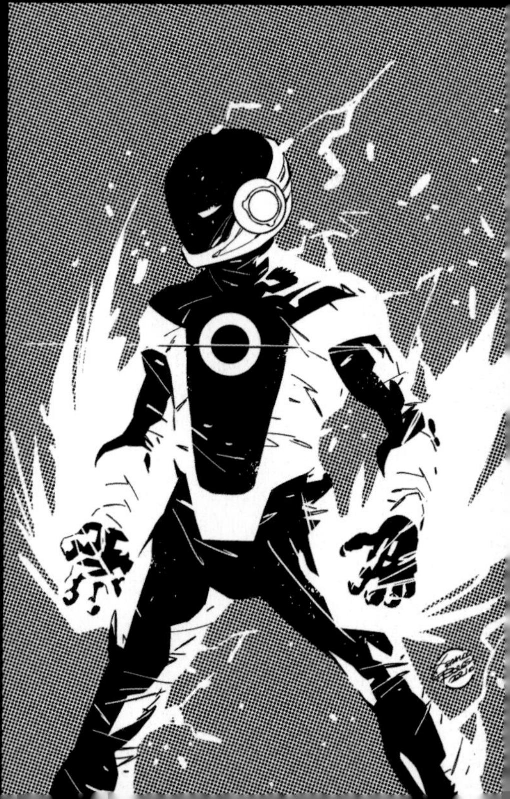

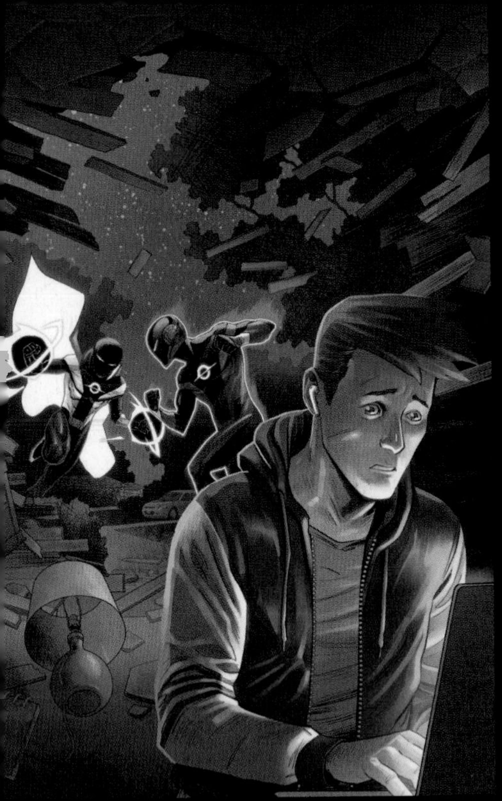

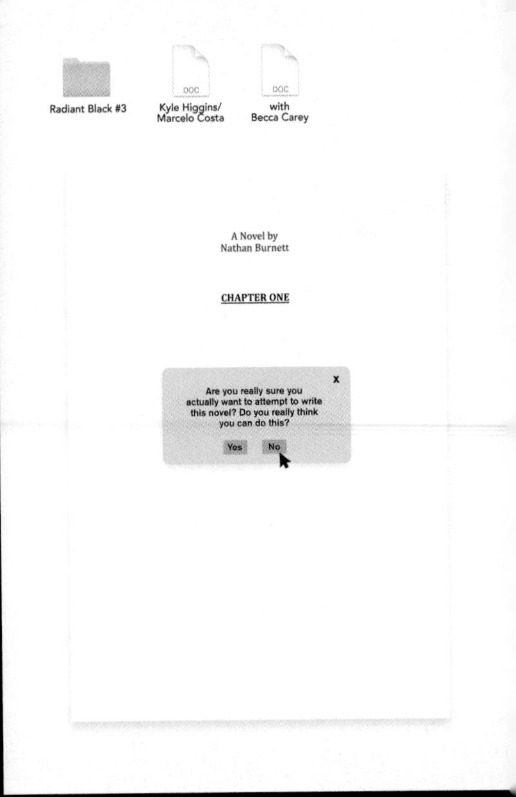
Radiant Black #3
Kyle Higgins/
Marcelo Costa
with
Becca Carey
A Novel by
Nathan Burnett
CHAPTER ONE
Are you really sure you actually want to attempt to write this novel? Do you really think you can do this?
Yes
No
x

03 [A]
arcelo Costa

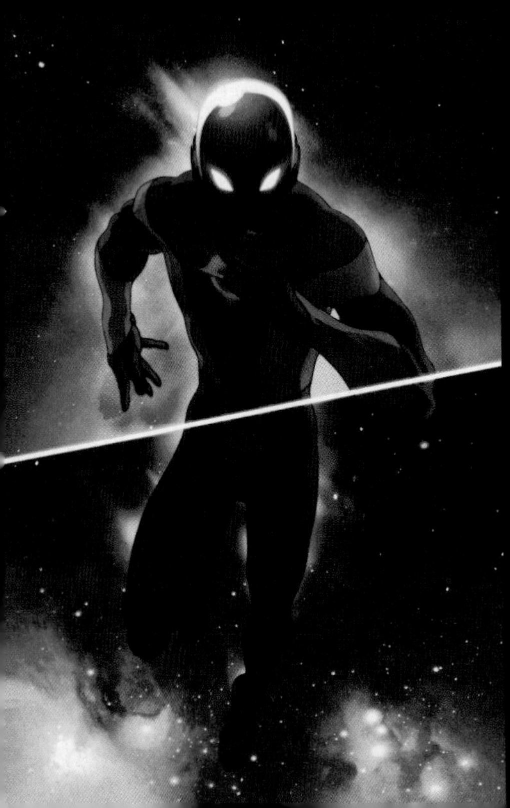

#03 [B]
Becca Carey

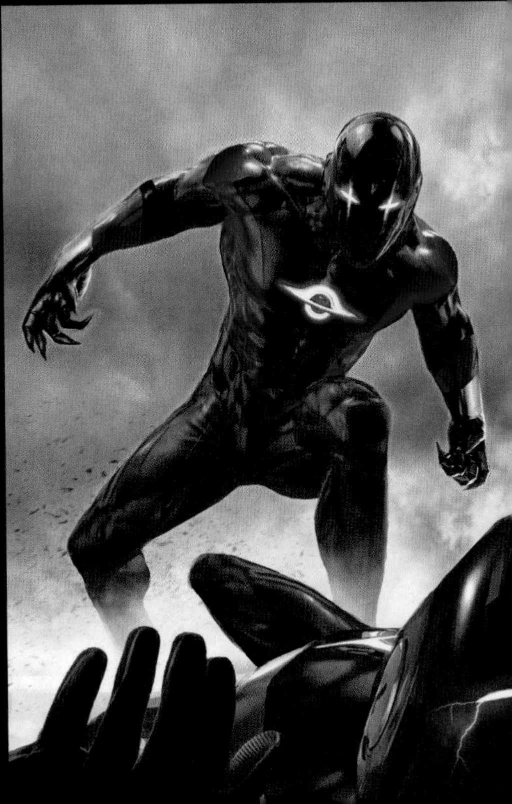

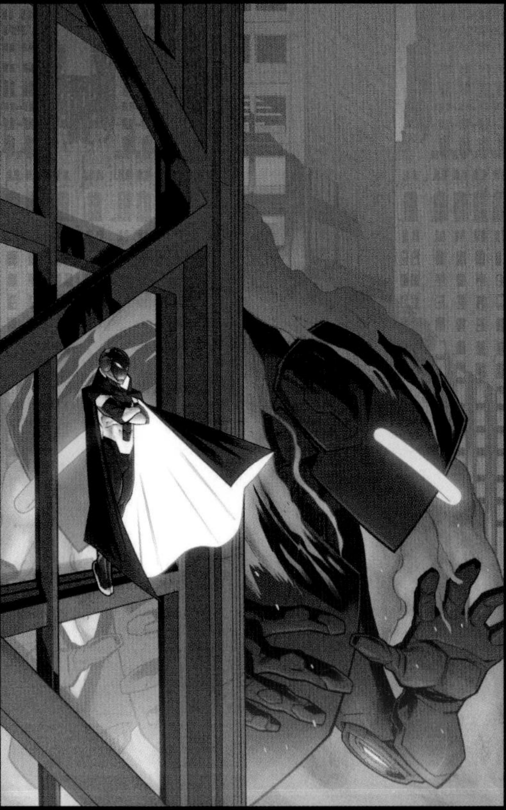

#03 [Second Printing]
Cian Tormey w/ Matt Wilson

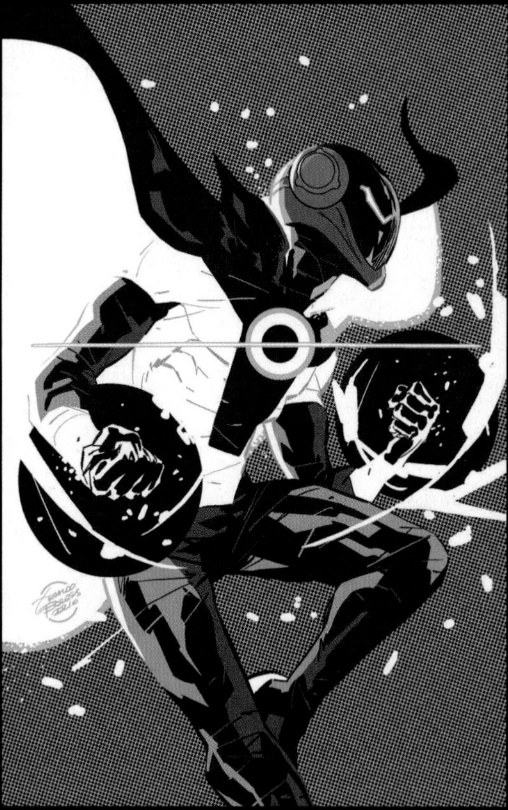

#03 [Third Printing A]
Geraldo Borges w/ Marcelo Costa

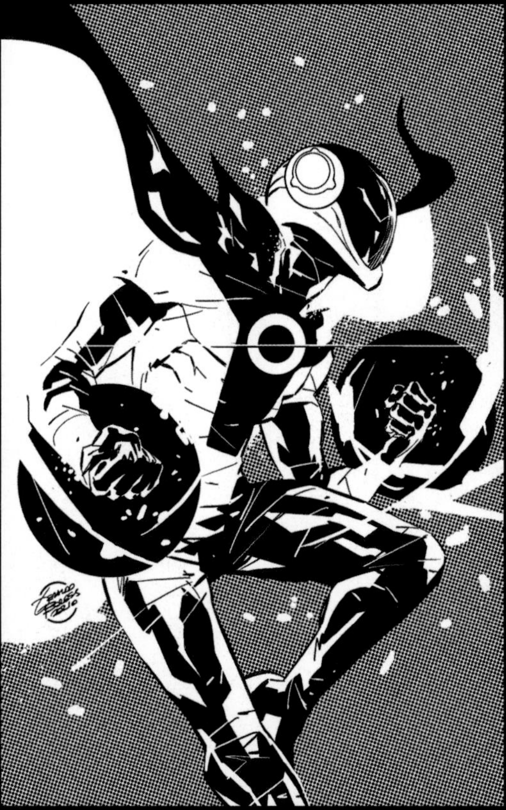

#03 [Third Printing B]
Geraldo Borges

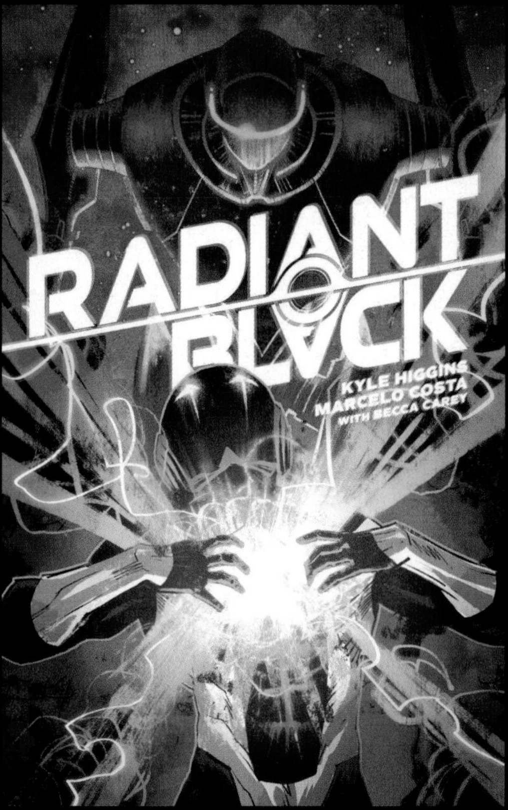
RADIANT BLACK
KYLE HIGGINS
MARCELO COSTA
WITH BECCA CAREY

#04 [A]
Eduardo Ferigato w/ Marcelo Costa

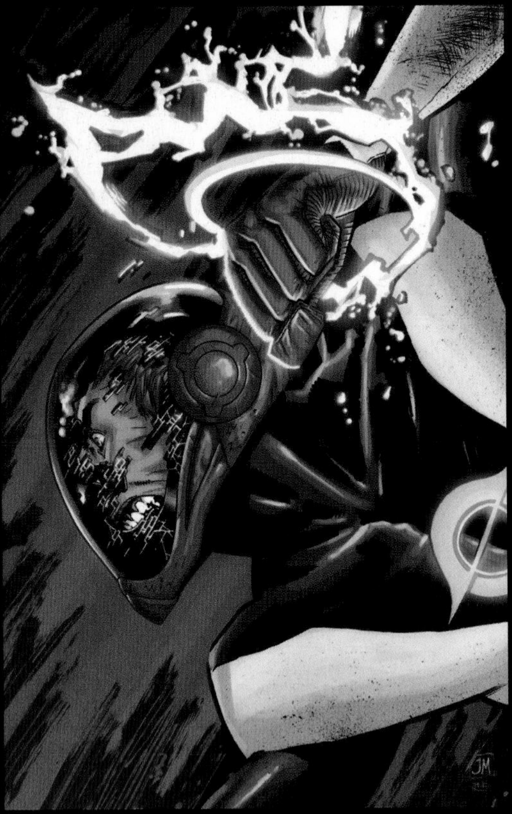

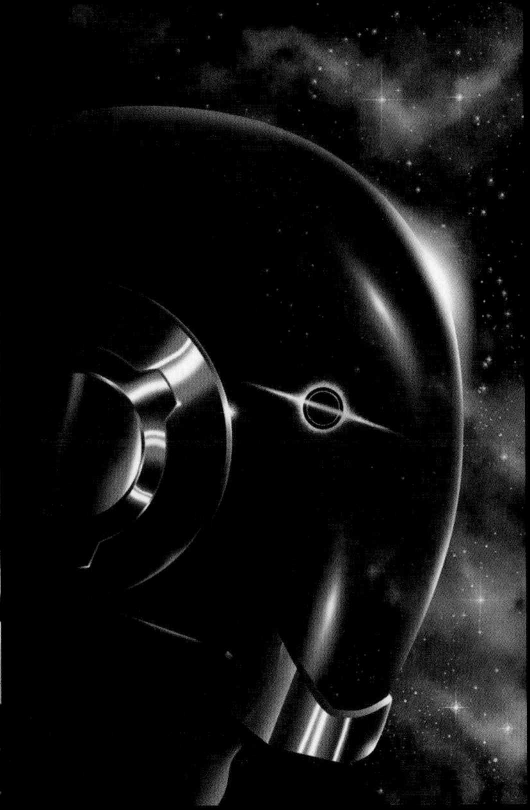

#04 [B]
Justin Mason w/ Pete Pantazis

#04 [C]
Doaly

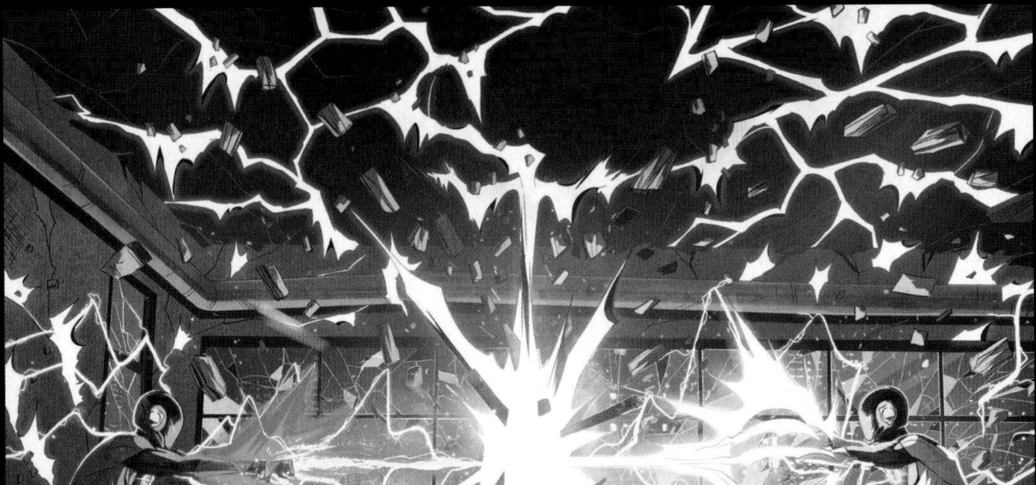

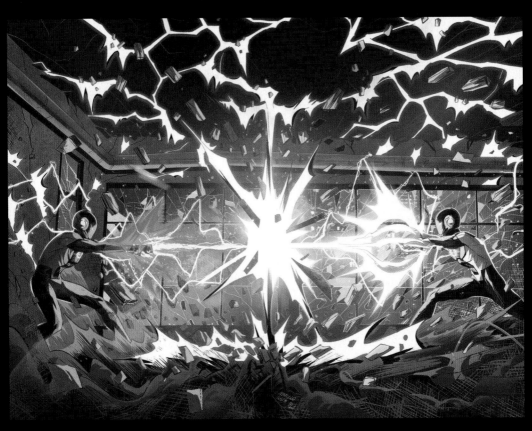

#04 [Second Printing]
Marcelo Costa w/ Igor Monti

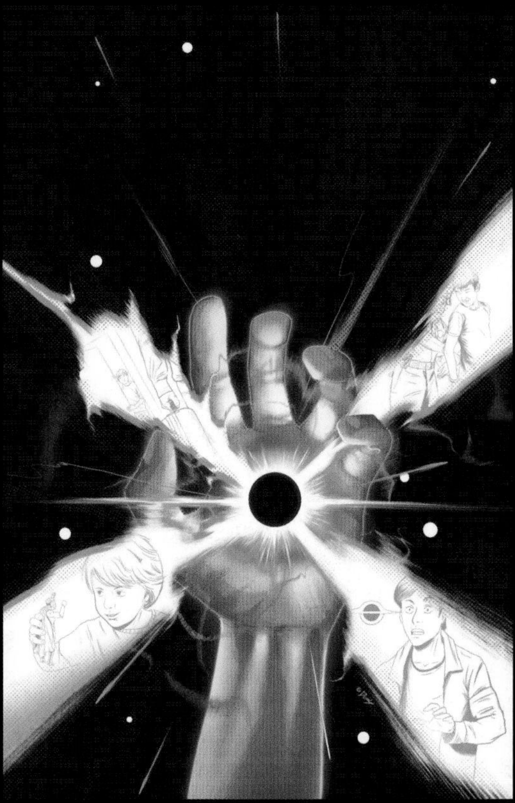

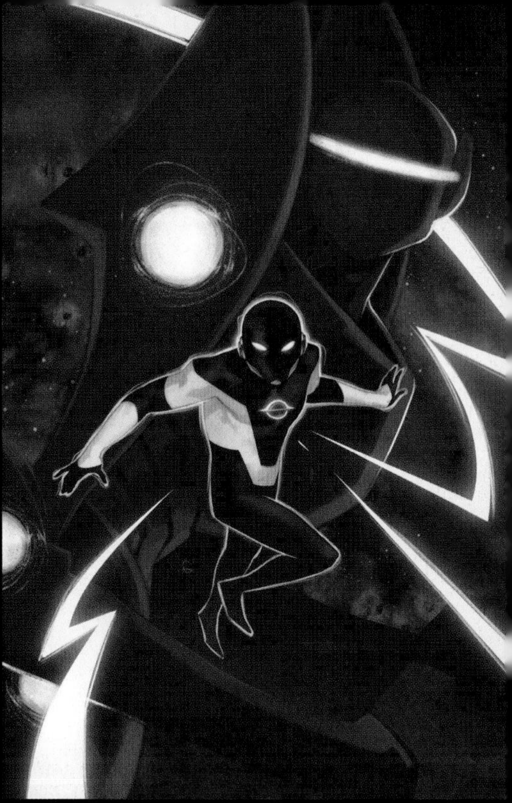

#05 [A]
Doaly

#05 [B]
Diego Greco

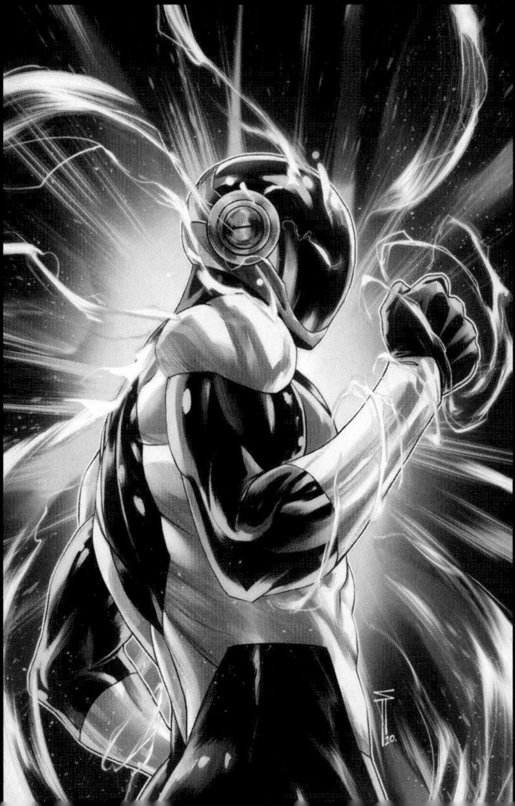

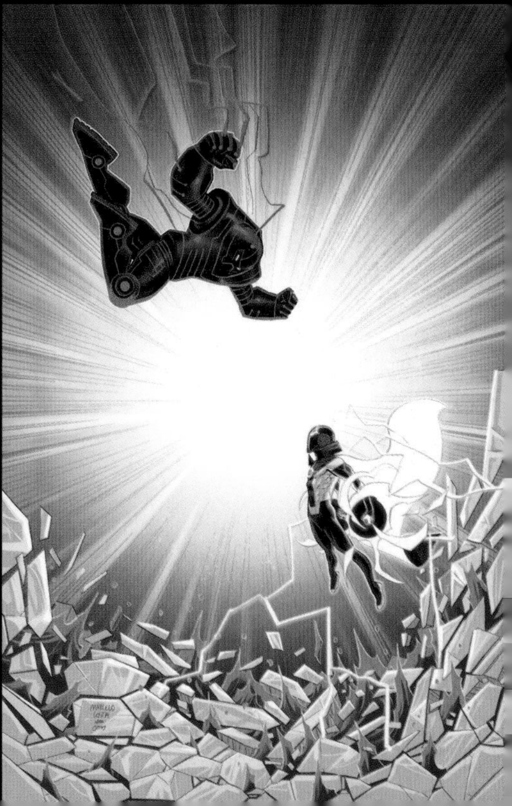

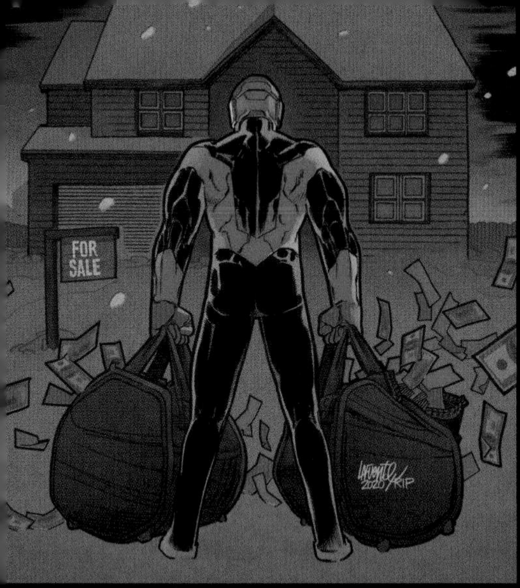
FOR SALE

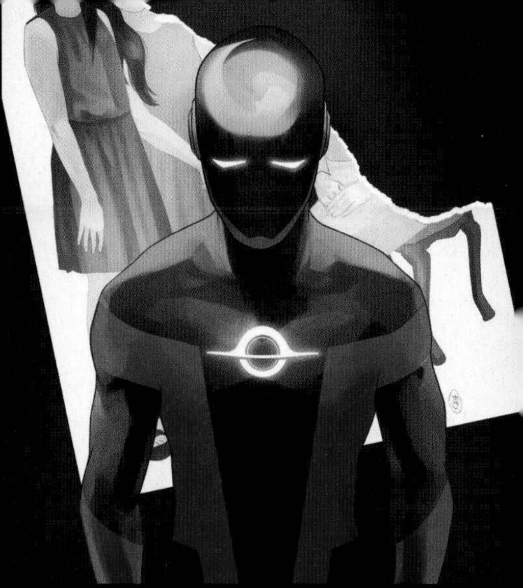

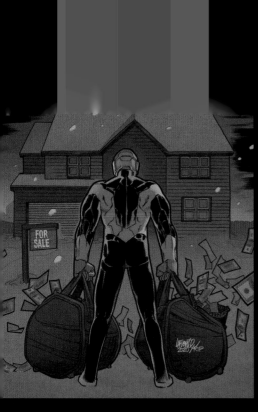

#06 [A]
Darko Lafuente w/ Miquel Muerto

#06 [B] (Spoiler-Free)
Kira Okamoto

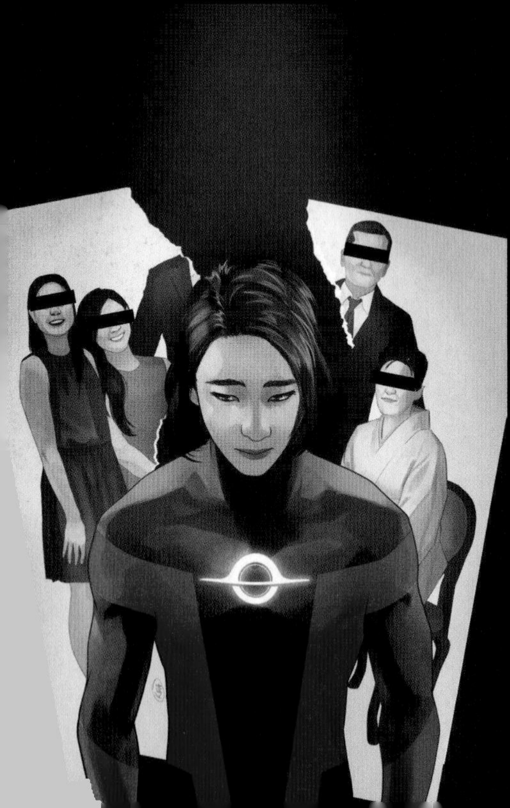

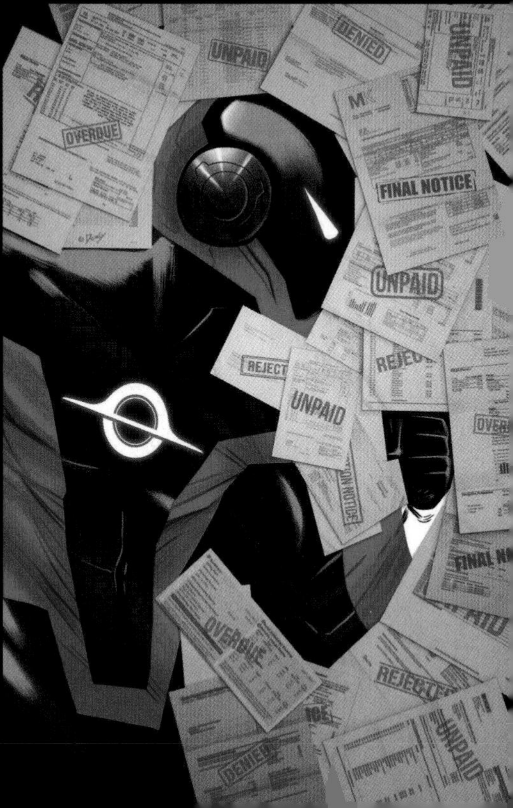
UNPAID
DENIED
UNPAID
OVERDUE
FINAL NOTICE
UNPAID
REJECT
UNPAID
OVERDUE

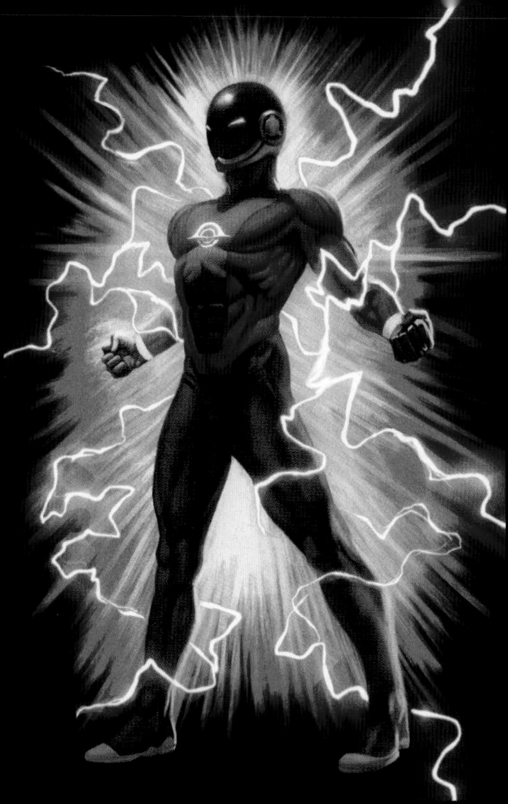

#06 [Out of the Vault]
Aaron Bartling

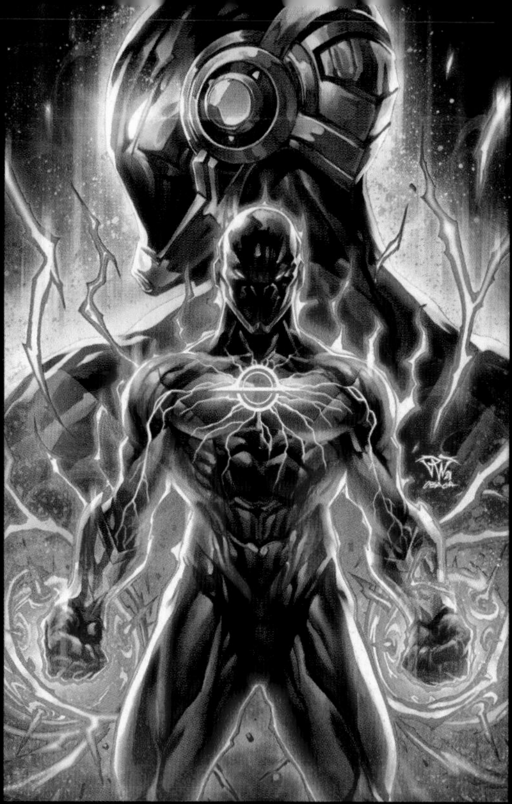

#06 [Two Twenty-One Comics]
Paolo Pantalena

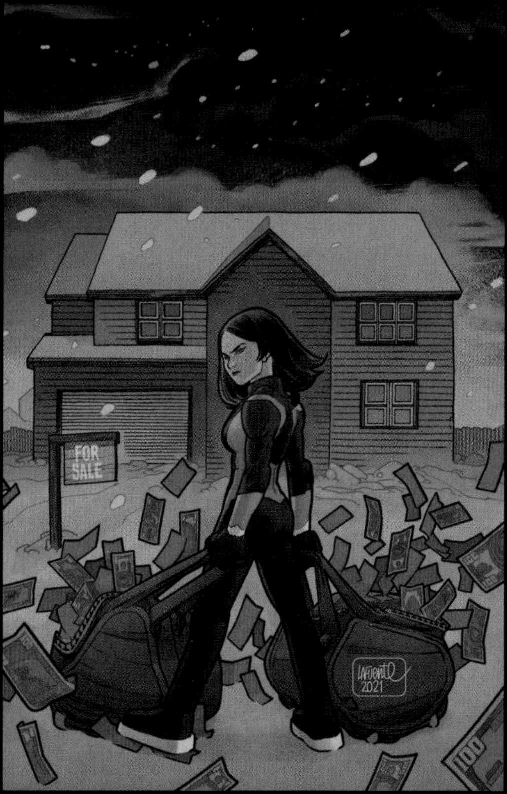
FOR SALE
2021

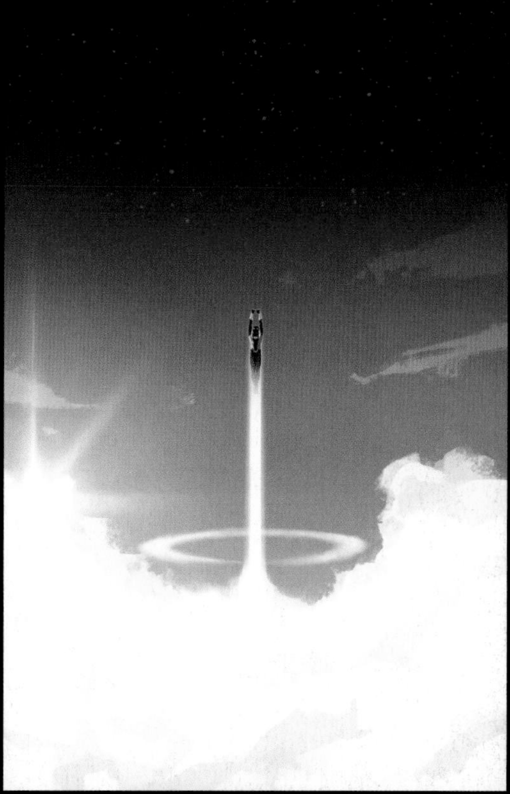

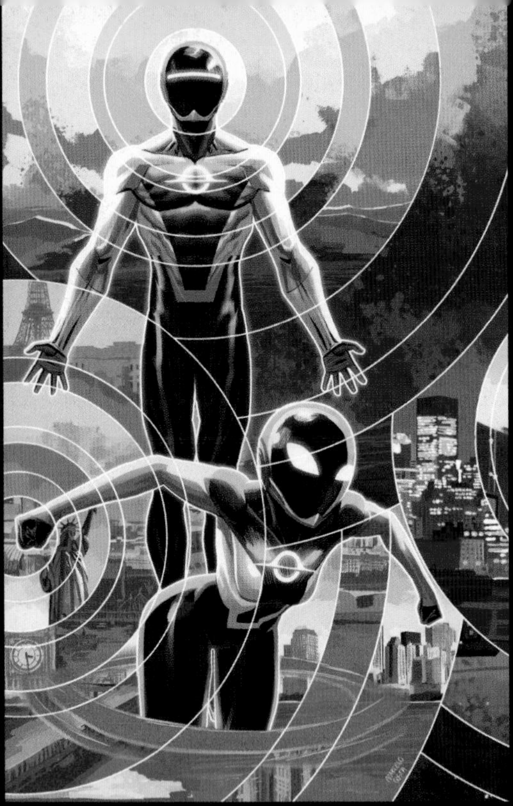

#06 [Coliseum of Comics]
Marcelo Costa

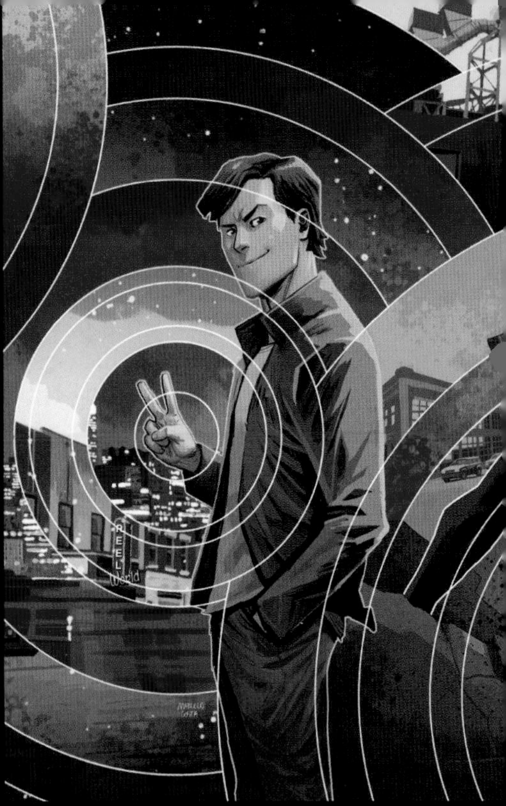

#05 [Coliseum of Comics]
Marcelo Costa

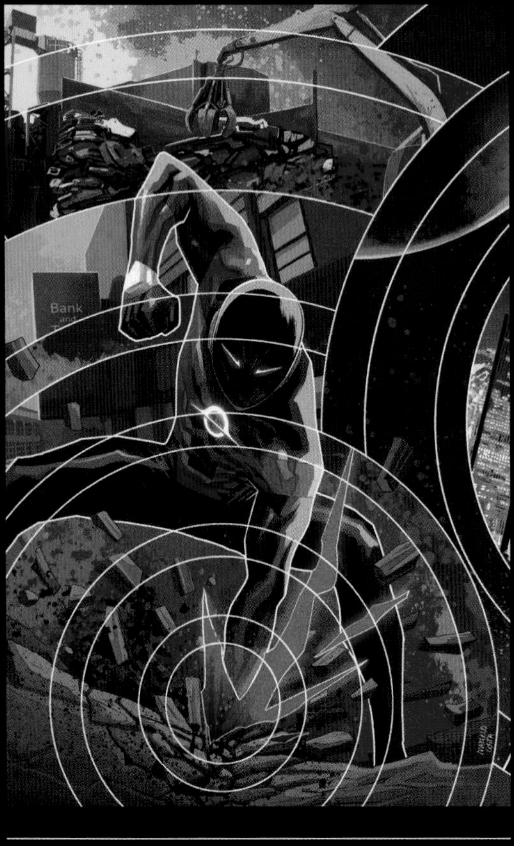
Bank

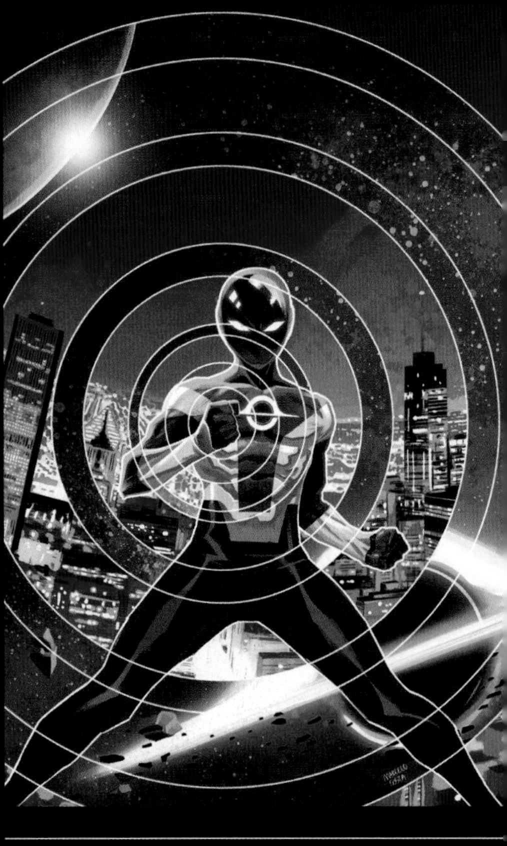

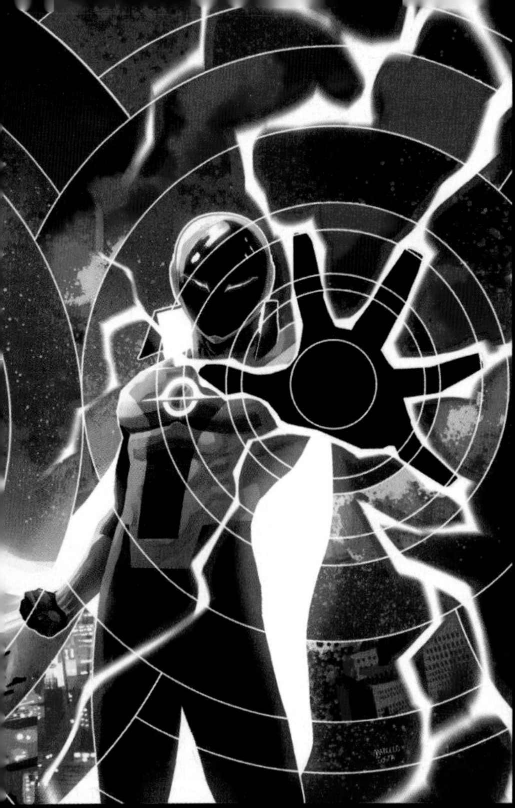

#03 [Coliseum of Comics]
Marcelo Costa

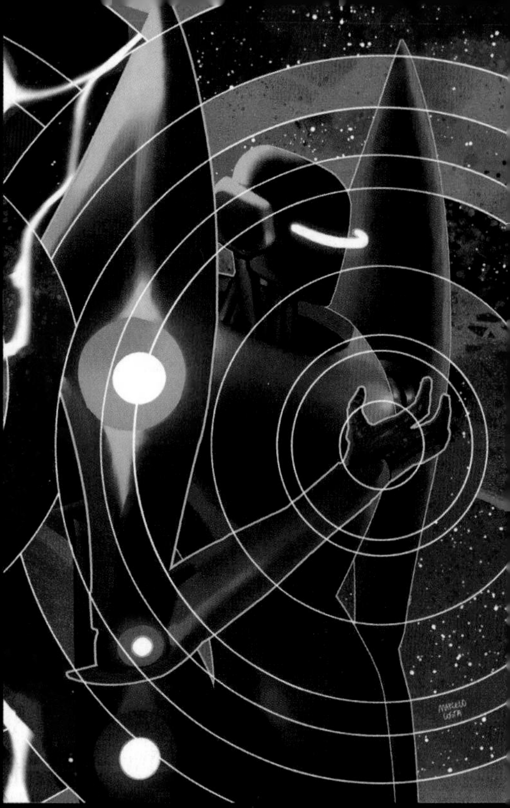

#04 [Coliseum of Comics]
Marcelo Costa

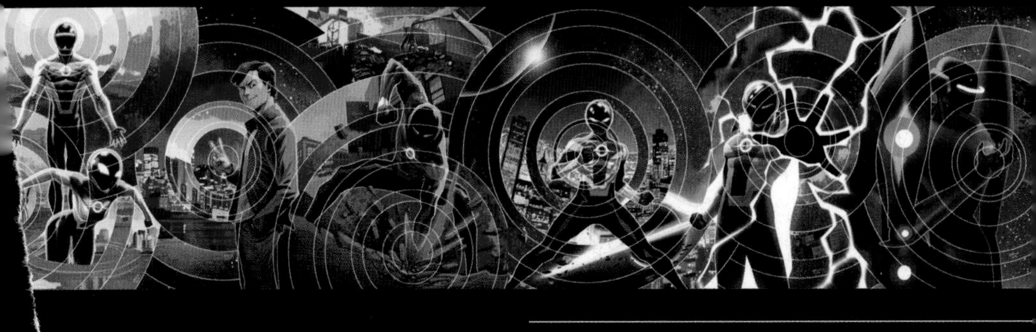

#01-#06 [Coliseum of Comics]

READ RADIANT

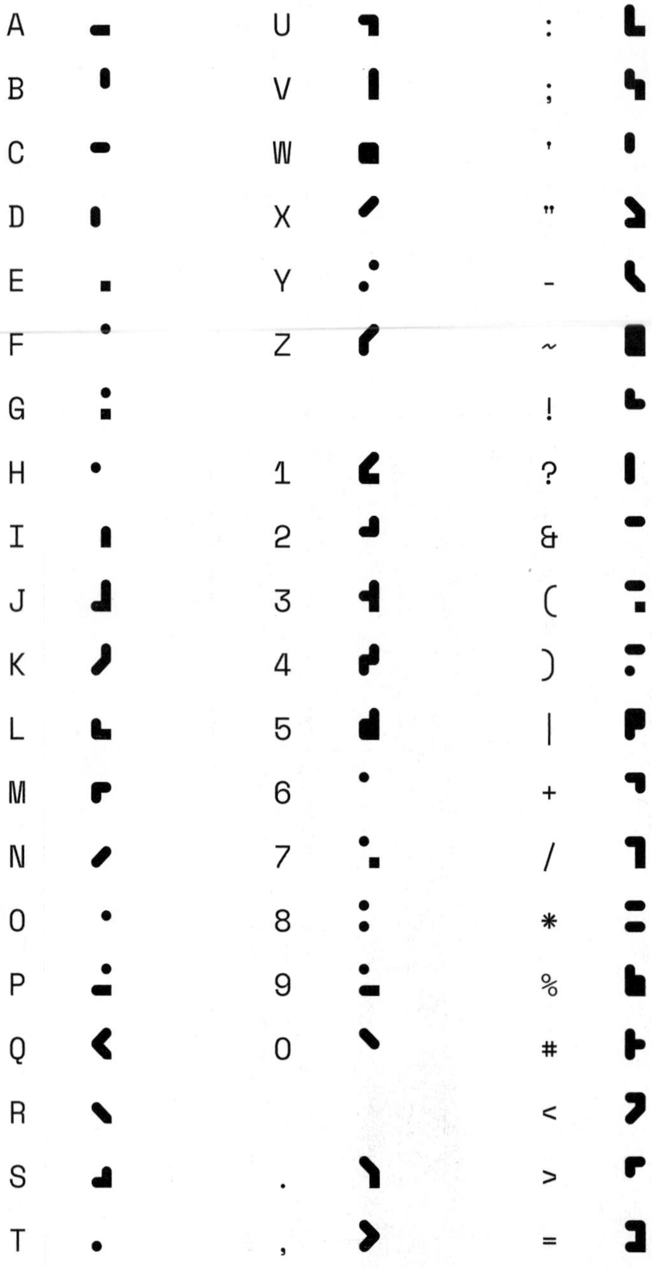
A
B
C
D
E
F
G
H
I
J
K
L
M
N
O
P
Q
R
S
T
U
V
W
X
Y
Z
1
2
3
4
5
6
7
8
9
0
.
,
:
;
'
"
-
~
!
?
&
(
)
|
+
/
*
%
#
<
>
=